1 MONTH OF
FREE
READING

at

www.ForgottenBooks.com

By purchasing this book you are eligible for one month membership to ForgottenBooks.com, giving you unlimited access to our entire collection of over 1,000,000 titles via our web site and mobile apps.

To claim your free month visit:
www.forgottenbooks.com/free875619

ISBN 978-0-265-61146-3
PIBN 10875619

ANNALS OF WYOMING

The ANNALS OF WYOMING is published biannually in the spring and fall and is received by all members of the Wyoming State Historical Society. Copies of previous and current issues also are available for sale to the public and a price list may be obtained by writing to the Editor.

Communications should be addressed to the Editor. The Editor does not assume responsibility for statements of fact or opinion made by the contributors.

ANNALS OF WYOMING articles are abstracted in
Historical Abstracts. America: History of Life

Annals of Wyoming

Volume 49   Spring, 1977   Number 1

KATHERINE A. HALVERSON
Editor   -

JOHN C. PAIGE
WILLIAM H. BARTON
ELLEN E. GLOVER
Editorial Assistants

Published biannually by the
WYOMING STATE ARCHIVES AND HISTORICAL
DEPARTMENT

Official Publication of the Wyoming State Historical Society

WYOMING STATE HISTORICAL SOCIETY

OFFICERS 1976-1977

The Wyoming State Historical Society was organized in October, 1953. Membership is open to anyone interested in history. County Historical Society Chapters have been organized in Albany, Big Horn, Campbell, Carbon, Crook, Fremont, Goshen, Hot Springs, Johnson, Laramie, Lincoln, Natrona, Niobrara, Park, Platte, Sheridan, Sweetwater, Teton, Uinta, Washakie and Weston Counties.

State Dues

Life Membership $100.00
Joint Life Membership (Husband and Wife).............................. 150.00
Annual Membership.. 5.00
Joint Annual Membership (Two persons of same family at
  same address)... 7.00
Institutional Membership 10.00

Send State Membership Dues To:
Wyoming State Historical Society
Executive Headquarters
Barrett Building
Cheyenne, Wyoming 82002

Table of Contents

COVER NOTES

The cover photograph of Elk Mountain was taken by Joseph E. Stimson in the early 1900s. Stimson was official photographer for the Union Pacific Railroad from 1903 to 1935. For the following ten years he conducted his own business in Cheyenne as artist-photographer. Stimson died in 1952. His superb collection of scenic views in Wyoming, on glass plate negatives, is now among the holdings of the Wyoming State Archives and Historical Department.

Elk Mountain has always been a landmark in south-central Wyoming and dominates the valley from which it rises to an elevation of 11,000 feet. Fort Halleck was built near the foot of the mountain to protect wagon trains on the Overland, or Cherokee Trail, and was an active military post from July 20, 1862, until July 4, 1866. A good part of the building materials from the fort, and all its supplies, were moved to a site just south of present-day Laramie for the construction of Fort Buford, later re-named Fort Sanders, a protective post for Union Pacific construction workers. The site of Fort Halleck is on the Norman Palm ranch, where today the ruins of the blacksmith shop are the only trace of the original fort buildings.

A legend handed down over the years is about a white stallion that wintered his large band of wild horses on Elk Mountain. One winter his band was snowed under and all the animals starved to death. The image of this stallion has ever since been visible in the snows on the mountain. In 1918, reportedly, his whole form was traced in the snow, and he could be seen running across the face of the mountain with his mane and tail flying in the wind.

The Lightning Creek Fight

By

BARTON R. VOIGT

The era of America's Sioux wars had long since passed by the turn of the twentieth century. Sitting Bull had been dead for nearly a decade. Red Cloud was a feeble old man, living out his years on South Dakota's Pine Ridge Reservation. Towns and ranches had replaced the isolated military posts that once stood guard over the Sioux. Indians and whites, however, had not yet learned to live with one another. The Indians held on to remnants of their old life-style, while the whites continued to despise them as barbarians. Indian hunting rights were a major source of irritation. Treaty provisions and new state game laws often conflicted, which resulted in Indians being fined or jailed for hunting as they had always hunted.

The state of Wyoming felt itself particularly plagued by out-of-state Indians ignoring game laws. Bannocks from Idaho often hunted in the Jackson Hole country, and the eastern part of the state attracted Sioux from South Dakota reservations. The issue was eventually brought before the Supreme Court of the United States, which held in the Race Horse case, that the Indians' hunting privileges had been repealed by Wyoming's admission to statehood.[1] This ruling gave Wyoming authority to enforce its game laws against the Indians.

Despite the Supreme Court decision, however, Wyoming counties along the South Dakota border continued to be the scene of lengthy fall excursions by Indian parties from Pine Ridge Reservation. As whites in the area became increasingly bitter about the situation, serious trouble was inevitable. Finally, in October, 1903, a posse's attempt to arrest a band of Sioux on Converse County's Lightning Creek brought on a fatal battle.

The events leading up to the fight on Lightning Creek began on September 30, 1903, when United States Indian Agent John R. Brennan authorized a party of Oglala Sioux Indian families to leave the Pine Ridge Reservation. Led by William Brown, the Indians journeyed south of the Black Hills into Wyoming. A second party of Sioux, under Charlie Smith, left Pine Ridge on October 20 with a pass similar to the one granted Brown's party.

---

[1]For a brief account of the Race Horse case, see T. A. Larson, *History of Wyoming* (Lincoln: University of Nebraska Press, 1965), p. 305.

About a week later, the two bands came together on Little Thunder Creek, in Weston County, Wyoming. Traveling together, they headed slowly back toward the reservation.

Meanwhile, reports were brought to Newcastle, county seat of Weston County, of Indians killing pronghorn antelope and livestock. A posse was organized by Sheriff William H. Miller, and on October 23 it left Newcastle in search of the Indians. Seven days later, the posse unsuccessfully tried to arrest the combined Brown and Smith parties. The following day another arrest attempt resulted in a pitched battle. In the brief exchange of gunfire, Sheriff Miller, a deputy and two Indians were killed outright. Three other Indians later died of wounds received in the fight.[2]

Nine men from the William Brown party were arrested after the fight and taken to Douglas for a preliminary hearing on the charge of murder. On Saturday, November 14, 1903, they were brought before Justice of the Peace H. R. Daniels.[3] Acting as prosecuting attorney for Converse County was W. F. Mecum. The Indians were defended by the United States Attorney for the District of Wyoming, Timothy F. Burke. Agent Brennan and an interpreter from Pine Ridge were also present.

Because of an accident, Attorney Burke did not arrive in Douglas until the morning of the hearing. Failing to find a suitable place where he could in secrecy take the Indians' statements, and not wishing to have the statements made public, he decided not to call any of the Indians to the stand in their own defense. Instead, he placed their hopes for acquittal on the weakness of the prosecutor's case.

County Attorney Mecum produced ten witnesses for the state— eight members of the posse and two sheepherders who had been in the vicinity of the fight. He methodically recreated the incident from the arrival in Newcastle of reports of Indians killing game to the posse's examination of abandoned Indian wagons after the battle. According to their testimony, the posse members had been deputized to go out and arrest Indians for killing antelope.[4] They left Newcastle on October 23, heading southwest toward Little Thunder Basin, where the Indians had been seen. The first day out they arrested nine Soux near the Cheyenne River and sent

---

[2]Details of both the Indian and white accounts of the fight, and the events leading up to it; can be found in U.S. Congress, Senate, Committee on Indian Affairs, *Encounter Between Sioux Indians of the Pine Ridge Agency, S. Dak., and a Sheriff's Posse of Wyoming,* 58th Cong., 2d sess., 1903, S. Doc. 128 (hereinafter referred to as S. Doc. 128).

[3]The defendants were He Crow, Fool Heart, Jesse Little War Bonnet, Charging Wolf, David Broken Nose, James White Elk, Red Paint, Jack High Dog and Iron Shield.

[4]The posse's testimony can be found in S. Doc. 128, pp. 56-95.

them with B. F. Hilton to Newcastle.[5] The remainder of the posse continued its search. Along Porcupine Creek they came upon the trail of what later proved to be the Smith and Brown parties.

The posse followed the Indians for several days, eventually crossing into Converse County. On the morning of October 30, they met a local cowboy, Frank Zerbes, who reported that the Indians had camped on the Dry Fork of the Cheyenne River the previous night. Zerbes offered to guide the posse to the Indians, and Miller agreed. At about 10:30 a.m. they rode into the Indian camp. They saw what they later estimated to be twenty to twenty-five male Indians, with their families. Few of the Indians could speak English, but Sheriff Miller succeeded in explaining that he had a warrant for their arrest. The Indians could not decide what to do, since both of their leaders, Charlie Smith and William Brown, were out of camp. Sheriff Miller offered to wait, and the posse was fed by Mrs. Brown.

Charlie Smith returned to camp early in the afternoon, with an antelope over his saddle.[6] Smith, who was a Carlisle Indian School graduate, understood English very well. When Sheriff Miller read him the warrant, he indicated that he did not intend to go to Newcastle, but that he would wait until he could get Brown's opinion when he came back. The sheriff then advised the Indians not to do anything rash, and once again agreed to wait.

Late in the afternoon, Brown rode into the camp. Miller read the warrant again, this time to both of the Indian leaders. Brown showed a willingness to accompany the posse, but Smith now adamantly refused to go. Members of the posse quoted Smith as saying, "I am no damn fool, and know more of the law than you do. I do not live in Newcastle, and I will not go there."[7]

The Indians then broke camp and proceeded down the Dry Fork. The posse was not certain whether or not the Indians intended to go to Newcastle. When the procession came to a fork in the road, one route leading to Newcastle and the other toward the reservation, the sheriff rode ahead and tried to turn the Indians in the direction of Newcastle. But Smith instructed them to turn toward Pine Ridge. In what seemed to the posse to be a threatening move, many of the Indian men then rode up and took a defiant

---

[5]On November 3, nearly two weeks later, Agent Brennan found these Indians still being held in jail, without having been charged with a crime. In later testimony, he contended that they "were not part of the Smith or Brown parties, nor connected with them in any way. They were on their return from a visit with some of their friends at the Crow Agency. Five of the party were between the ages of 65 and 80 years." Ibid., p. 31.

[6]In later statements, the Indians denied that Smith had an antelope on his horse.

[7]Posse members D. O. Johnston, James C. Davis and Ralph Hackney, for instance, said he used words to that effect. S. Doc. 128, pp. 57, 73, 77.

—Courtesy of author

Sheriff William H. Miller

stance near the whites. James C. Davis testified that Jesse Little
War Bonnet, one of the defendants, brazenly "kept riding with us,
all the time bucking his horse into us, trying to get a fight out of
us if he could."[8]

Seeing the futility of further attempts to arrest the Indians with
so small a posse, Miller retreated to seek reinforcements from area
ranches. The posse first rode to the Fiddleback ranch, about
twenty miles distant, where they spent the night. There they
enlisted the aid of two cowboys, Stephen Franklin and Charles
Harvey. Franklin and Harvey advised the sheriff that the Indians
would probably travel down the Lightning Creek road. At 7:30
in the morning Miller sent Frank Zerbes and Jack Moore south

---

[8]*Ibid.*, p. 74.

from the Fiddleback with instructions to find the direction the Indians had gone, and to meet the possee at Jake Mills' cow camp on Lightning Creek.

En route to Lightning Creek, Miller's forces were strengthened by the addition of four more men. John Owens, a veteran lawman and Indian fighter, reluctantly joined the posse when Sheriff Miller assured him that there was going to be trouble.[9] Wolf hunter Louis Falkenberg was picked up at the Oleson ranch. And two strangers from Wessington, South Dakota, Henry Coon and George Fountain, joined later in the day. Including Zerbes and Moore, who were trailing the Indians, the posse now numbered thirteen men.

Sheriff Miller's party reached the Mills cow camp in midafternoon. Half of the men had eaten dinner, and the others had just begun when Zerbes and Moore came racing in to report that the Indians were little more than a mile away. The horses were immediately brought up, and Sheriff Miller once more took his men out to confront the Indians.

The Smith and Brown parties were traveling north along the road parallel to Lightning Creek. As the posse rounded a sharp bend in the road, the Indians suddenly came into view. The head of the Indian procession had just passed through a gate in a wire fence. Several of the posse members estimated in their testimony that two or three wagons were through the gate, and that eight men were riding in the lead.[10] When the Indians saw the posse, they retreated back through the gate. Many of them dismounted and moved toward the creek. John Owens, who had practically taken over the leadership of the posse, warned Sheriff Miller to turn his men out of the road because the Indians intended to fight. The posse quickly rode down into the creek bed. They left their horses at the fence and ran upstream behind the protection of the bank. Miller and Owens, who were in the lead, ran nearly one hundred yards up the creek. The others spread out behind them.

While the posse remained behind the bank, Miller and Owens climbed to the top and walked toward the Indians. As they approached, they took turns shouting for the Indians to surrender. Owens testified that after they had gone about fifteen yards from the creek, an Indian fired at them from up near the corrals. At the sound of the shot, the rest of the posse jumped up on the bank, and a general firing ensued.

Spread out among the trees as they were, each white man could see only part of the field of battle. Owens and Miller directed their attention to their left, leaving the rest of the posse to deal

[9]*Lusk Herald,* December 30, 1948.
[10]John Owens' testimony was most precise on this part of the incident. S. Doc. 128, p. 89; *Tbid.*

SIOUX INDIANS HELD IN DOUGLAS, WYOMING, JAIL FOR MURDER OF SHERIFF MILLER OF WESTON COUNTY

1. Iron Shield.   2. Charlie Crow.   3. Red Pin.   4. High Bull.   5. Broken Nose.

6. High Dog.   7. James White Elk.   8. Charge Wolf.   9. Jesse Little War Bonnet.

with the Indians to their right. All of the posse except Zerbes, who was armed only with a pistol, fired upon the Indians. After a few volleys, the Indians broke and fled.

The battle was brief—it lasted no more than three or four minutes—but the results were disastrous. Louis Falkenberg was dead, shot through the neck. Sheriff Miller lay bleeding to death from a severed femoral artery in his left thigh. Two Indians were dead upon the field. Charlie Smith, his wife, and another Indian man were mortally wounded. One elderly Indian man, shot in the back, fled to the reservation, where he survived.

Sheriff Miller died in the Mills cabin thirty minutes after the battle. Fearing that the Indians might return, the posse kept guard in the cabin throughout the night. Early in the morning, James Davis and Ralph Hackney left for Newcastle with the bodies of Miller and Falkenberg. The rest of the posse went out to the scene of the fight to search the Indian wagons that had been left behind. Much to their surprise, they found several Indian women on the field, huddled around a fire they had built for Charlie Smith, who was still alive. The whites took Smith into the ranch house, and sent the Indian women to Lusk with Stephen Franklin for a doctor. Smith died that night.

When word of the fight reached Newcastle, a new posse was quickly formed to arrest the fleeing Indians. Crook County Deputy Sheriff Lee Mather organized the posse, reportedly from hundreds of area miners who volunteered for the duty.[11] The posse took the train to Edgemont, South Dakota, where they picked up horses and supplies. Near the Lampkins ranch on Hat Creek, they confronted a large group of Indian families. The Indians offered no resistance, and after being fed at the Lampkins ranch, they were taken to Edgemont. On November 5, Converse County Sheriff John McDermott released the women and children to the custody of Agent Brennan and transferred the nine men to a Douglas, Wyoming, jail.

The posse's testimony at the preliminary hearing clearly placed the blame for the Lightning Creek fight on the Indians, particularly Charlie Smith because of his attitude the day before the battle. The testimony, however, was useless to the prosecutor. Posse members identified six of the nine defendants as having been present during the confrontation on October 30, but they failed to identify any of them as having shot Sheriff Miller or Deputy Falkenberg the next day. The only defendant recognized as being at the scene of the fight was Jesse Little War Bonnet. Six of the posse members swore that they saw him that day, but only two,

[11]Lee Mather interview, n.d., W.P.A. Statewide Historical Project, Wyoming State Archives and Historical Department, Cheyenne.

Charles Harvey and Ralph Hackney, claimed that he fired any shots. And both men admitted that he fired only as he was fleeing up the creek, after Miller and Falkenberg were hit.

After listening to County Attorney Mecum present his case, defense attorney Burke entered a demurrer to the evidence and asked that the defendants be discharged. Burke's main argument was that, despite the posse's allegations, no proof existed that any of the defendants had committed the crime with which they were charged. Without comment, Justice Daniels sustained the demurrer and released the prisoners.

The preliminary hearing had resulted in the acquittal of the defendants, but it had not brought out the Indians' version of the incident. Consequently, U. S. Attorney Burke was instructed by the Justice Department to go to Pine Ridge and reconstruct the affair from the Indians' viewpoint. From November 28 to December 1, Burke took sworn statements from Agent Brennan and fourteen Indians who had been present during the fight. According to the Indian testimony, the William Brown party, consisting of twenty adults and their children, left the reservation on October 6.[12] Skirting the Black Hills, they traveled through the foothills, hunting and gathering berries, roots and herbs. Several of the men shot deer along Sage and Horse creeks in South Dakota, but they denied killing deer or antelope in Wyoming.

The Smith party, made up of about sixteen adults and their children, left Pine Ridge on October 20. About one week's journey found them in Weston County's Little Thunder Basin, where they accidentally met the Brown party. The two groups agreed to travel together. Combined, there were fifteen wagons and nearly fifty people. With horses, teepees, camp equipage, and other supplies, the assemblage formed a ponderous, slow-moving procession.

In no hurry to return home, the Indians traveled only a few miles a day, making several camps and taking time out to hunt rabbits and prairie chickens. They purchased venison, mutton and hides from sheepmen, who gladly traded for beadwork and moccasins.[13] On the evening of October 29, they camped near the Dry Fork of the Cheyenne River. The next morning several of the men went out to hunt. Late in the morning, seven white men rode into camp and asked to speak to a chief. Since both Charlie Smith and William Brown were absent, the whites were invited to eat with Mrs. Brown while they waited.

----

[12]The Indians' statements can be found in S. Doc. 128, pp. 32-54 and 112-34.

[13]At least one sheepherder later acknowledged just such a transaction with these Indians. Isaac Robbins interview, August, 1904, Eli S. Ricker Collection, Nebraska State Historical Society, Lincoln.

When the two Indian leaders returned to camp, they talked at length with Sheriff Miller. Brown at first agreed to let the sheriff arrest them because he assumed the permit from Agent Brennan would justify their absence from the reservation. But when Smith refused to go with the whites, Brown sided with Smith.[14]

All of the Indians who testified, with the exception of Brown, claimed that neither Smith nor Brown fully explained what the posse wanted on October 30. They further stated that because they did not understand the sheriff's purpose, they took no hostile actions when he tried to turn them toward Newcastle. Jesse Little War Bonnet asserted that he rode up among the whites only to find out what was happening, not to start a fight.[15]

Following Smith's orders, the Indians ignored the posse and proceeded down the road toward the reservation. They went about twenty-five miles before camping for the evening. Anxious to get out of Wyoming because of the confrontation with the white men, they set out early the following morning. By 4:00 p.m. they had pushed their cumbersome caravan nearly fifty miles. As they approached the Jake Mills cow camp on Lightning Creek, their column was spread out for almost a mile along the road. They did not know that the posse was still after them, and had taken no precautions to defend themselves. Most of the men were riding in the wagons with their families. Their weapons were packed away.

Hope Clear, an eighteen-year-old girl, was at the head of the procession and was first to see the posse as it rounded a bend in the road. She recognized the men as the ones who had come to their camp the day before. As she told Burke,

> I was ahead of the wagons and there were two little boys with me and we were driving some loose ponies. I got off my horse to open the gate and then I saw the white men aiming their guns at me, so I started back to the wagons as fast as I could go.[16]

The Indians testified that the white men fired at them without warning. Hope Clear said that the first shot knocked the horse out from under the eleven-year-old boy, Peter White Elk, who was with her, just as they fled back through the gate. The second shot hit him in the back of the head, killing him instantly. Hope Clear's horse was then shot out from under her, and several more shots passed through her clothing. By that time, the Indians had begun to react to the sudden attack. The three lead wagons fled west up the fence line. The twelve rear wagons turned and raced back

---

[14]Brown was a central figure that day, as he was one of the few Indians who could speak English. His statements can be found in S. Doc. 128, pp. 20-21, 45-48 and 126-28.

[15]*Ibid.*, p. 45.

[16]*Ibid.*, p. 49.

Charles Harvey and Ralph
shots. And both men admitte
up the creek, after Miller an

After listening to County
defense attorney Burke ente
asked that the defendants be
was that, despite the posse's
of the defendants had commi
charged. Without comment,
rer and released the prisoners

The preliminary hearing l
defendants, but it had not bri
incident. Consequently, t ‹
the Justice Department to g‹
affair from the Indians' viewp
ber 1, Burke took sworn st
fourteen Indians who had bee
ing to the Indian testimony,
of twenty adults and their chil
6.[12] Skirting the Black Hill
hunting and gathering berries,
shot deer along Sage and Ho
denied killing deer or antelo

The Smith party, made u
children, left Pine Ridge on C
ney found them in Weston C
they accidentally met the Bro
travel together. Combined, t
fifty people. With horses, tee
plies, the assemblage formed a

In no hurry to return '
miles a day, making so
rabbits and prairie ch
hides from sheepme
sins.[13] On the e
Fork of the C
men went ou‡   ‹ it
into camp a   ak
and Willi
with M

... the first few shots.
... heavy wagons on the
... creeks. Some of the
... in South Dakota,
... they encountered.[20]
... reservation. The one
... hungry and exhaust-
... Hope Clear, Mrs.
... where he had died,
... morning. There they
... wounded and covered
... white men came and

... after public controversy.
... differed in so many
... by one side or the
... defended their sheriff.
... posse account of the
... hero. Nebraska and
... many Wyoming citizens,
... the preliminary hearing
... that "public sentiment
... quite a demonstration
... were released."[22]

an eighteen-year-...
was first to see the ...
recognized the ...
day before. As the ...
... proceeding brought
... to be heard about the
... extremely dissatisfied
... Governor Fenimore Chat-
... Congressman Frank W.
... the posse. Chatterton
... of allowing the Sioux
... who was from New-
... Agent Brennan, and
... as the root cause of

... to being shot at near
... were allowed to camp at
... ZumBrunnen interview, n.d.,

... were ... inted in
... South
... ook of

No-
ate

down the Lightning Creek road. Black Kettle, who had been in the second wagon, ran toward the creek. Gray Bear, father of Hope Clear, and Charlie Smith rode up the line toward their families.

According to both Hope Clear and her mother, only two Indians fired any shots. Hope Clear stated that just as she got to her wagon, she saw Black Kettle and her father getting down ready to fire. All the other Indians, with the exception of Charlie Smith, had fled. She saw Smith coming up from behind when he was shot. He did not appear to have his gun with him. Mrs. Gray Bear (Takes the Rope) described the action in much the same way:

> Those who were on horses [Gray Bear and Charlie Smith] all rushed up and got killed. My husband and another fellow [Black Kettle] did some shooting and they both got killed . . . . I saw Charlie Smith coming up with his gun in his scabbard on his saddle, so I don't think Charlie did any shooting.[17]

Hope Clear, Mrs. Gray Bear and Mrs. Charlie Smith were in the wagons that fled west along the fence. Hope Clear's statement to Attorney Burke gave the harrowing details of their flight:

> We started to go up the side of a hill, and just as we were going over the top of the hill, Mrs. Smith was shot. When she was shot, the blood began to flow pretty freely, and we started for a bank . . . . When we got Mrs. Smith down under this bank, I started back up the fence again and I met my father coming back on his horse. I let him off to the creek. They were still shooting at him . . . . We kept on going up this creek until it must have been along in the middle of the night, then my father got out and went and sat with his back up against the bank, and he sat there till he died.[18]

Last Bear, a sixty-five-year-old man, was in the fifth wagon from the front when the shooting began. His son was ahead driving horses with Hope Clear and Peter White Elk. Upon hearing the first shot, Last Bear took his son's horse and told the boy to get into the wagon with his mother. Just as he mounted the horse, Last Bear was shot through the back, the bullet coming out in front. He then turned and fled west along the fence. In his testimony, Last Bear swore that the Indians had not started the fight:

> I hold up my hand to the Great Father and say that I did not see any Indian shoot. Our guns were packed away in the wagons. I did not have anything to shoot with.[19]

The surviving Indians testified that, thoroughly terrorized, they

---

[17]*Ibid.*, p. 51.
[18]*Ibid.*, p. 50. Mrs. Smith, who was shot in the back, died a few days later.
[19]*Ibid.*, p. 17. Last Bear recovered fully from his wound.

all scattered and fled immediately upon hearing the first few shots. In their panic, they abandoned most of their heavy wagons on the divide between Lightning and Twenty Mile creeks. Some of the fleeing Indians were fired upon near Hat Creek, in South Dakota, but others were treated well by the whites they encountered.[20] Most of them managed to straggle into the reservation. The one large group apprehended near Edgemont, too hungry and exhausted to resist, surrendered with no desire to fight. Hope Clear, Mrs. Gray Bear and Mrs. Smith buried Gray Bear where he had died, and returned to the scene of the fight in the morning. There they found Charlie Smith still alive, but badly wounded and covered with frost. They stayed with him until the white men came and took him to the ranch house where he died.

The fight at Lightning Creek caused a bitter public controversy. The Indian and white versions of the affair differed in so many important details as to suggest outright lying by one side or the other. Weston County residents vehemently defended their sheriff. The *Newcastle Times* published an "official" posse account of the fight, portraying Sheriff Miller as a martyred hero. Nebraska and South Dakota editors, however, as well as many Wyoming citizens, condemned the actions of the posse.[21] At the preliminary hearing in Douglas, one observer even reported that "public sentiment largely favored the Indians and there was quite a demonstration when the justice announced that the prisoners were released."[22]

The preliminary hearing was the only legal proceeding brought against the Indians, but it was not the last to be heard about the fight. Three important Wyoming men were extremely dissatisfied with the results of the hearing. Acting Governor Fenimore Chatterton, Senator Francis E. Warren and Congressman Frank W. Mondell combined their efforts to support the posse. Chatterton and Mondell had long opposed the practice of allowing the Sioux to travel freely across state lines. Mondell, who was from Newcastle, also had a particular animosity toward Agent Brennan, and singled out bad management at Pine Ridge as the root cause of the killings.[23]

---

[20]Chief Eagle and William Brown both testified to being shot at near Hat Creek, S. Doc. 128, pp. 43 and 48; others were allowed to camp at the ZumBrunnen ranch near Kirtley, Jacob J. ZumBrunnen interview, n.d., W.P.A. Project, Cheyenne.

[21]Numerous newspaper articles concerning the fight were reprinted in S. Doc. 128, pp. 10-30. Also, the John R. Brennan Papers, at the South Dakota State Historical Resource Center, in Pierre, contain a scrapbook of news clippings about the incident.

[22]S. Doc. 128, p. 15.

[23]Frank W. Mondell to E. A. Hitchcock, Secretary of the Interior, November 17, 1903, copy in Fenimore Chatterton Papers, ·Wyoming State

Chatterton first stated his position on November 5 in reply to Agent Brennan's request that the Indians being held in Edgemont be released. The acting governor cited the Race Horse case as specifically giving Wyoming the right to prosecute the Indians.[24] In a letter of the same date to Senator Warren, Chatterton further set out his views:

> It is quite necessary now, for the protection of the residents of eastern and northern Wyoming that these Indians should not be allowed to leave their reservations, especially that they should not be allowed for the purpose of hunting, to come into this State unless they comply with the game law. I believe, too, that this is necessary for the protection of the Indians, as after their recent action there might be serious trouble between the settlers and Indians should the Indians again come into Wyoming for any purpose whatsoever. For fear of such trouble and the consequent discredit which might come upon the State, especially with eastern Indian sympathizers, I trust that you will urge upon the Department [Indian Affairs] that the Indians not be allowed to further trespass upon our territory.[25]

Congressman Mondell feared that the failure to prosecute the nine Sioux would not only lead to continued "harrassment" by out-of-state Indians, but would be cited as proof that the Indians had not even violated game laws. Like Chatterton, Mondell was worried about Wyoming's image, and realized that the release of the Indians left the state's case "in an unfortunate position before [the federal authorities] and the country at large."[26]

Hoping that more publicity would emphasize Wyoming's rights, Mondell and Warren used their influence in Washington to push for a thorough investigation of the Lightning Creek fight. They need not have worried that the incident would go unnoticed by the federal government. U. S. Attorney Burke was already questioning the Indians for the Justice Department. The Office of Indian Affairs, to protect its own image as well as for the Indians' benefit, sent Special Agent Charles S. McNichols out to make an inquiry into the situation. Major B. H. Cheever of the Sixth U. S. Cavalry traveled to Douglas for the preliminary hearing on behalf of the War Department. And on November 5, presidential secretary William Loeb, Jr. requested Attorney General P. C. Knox to report on the conflict at the next cabinet meeting.[27]

Archives and Historical Department, Cheyenne; John R. Brennan to Eben W. Martin, November 21, 1903, S. Doc. 128, p. 24.

[24] Telegram from Fenimore Chatterton to John R. Brennan, November 5, 1903. Brennan Papers.

[25] Fenimore Chatterton to F. E. Warren, November 5, 1903. Chatterton Papers.

[26] Frank W. Mondell to Fenimore Chatterton, November 24, 1903. Chatterton Papers.

[27] William Loeb, Jr. to P. C. Knox, U.S. Attorney General, November 5, 1903, Record Group 60 "Records of the Attorney General," letter file 16790 (1903), National Archives, Washington, D.C.

The various investigators were faced with one major problem—the Indian and white versions of the incident could not both be true. Furthermore, both sides had pictured themselves as totally blameless, thus leaving them both open to suspicion of having amended the facts. And there was the possibility, indeed the probability, that there was truth and fabrication in both accounts. Attorney Burke and Special Agent McNichols, who conducted the most thorough investigations, recognized two questions as basic to the conflict—who fired the first shot on October 31, and who was ultimately responsible for causing such a deadly situation to develop in the first place. The posse members all testified that the first shot was fired by an Indian to the left of Sheriff Miller. They further alleged that this shot came after the posse had run up the creek bed and after Miller and Owens had shouted for the Indians to surrender. The Indians, on the other hand, testified that the whites fired the first shot at eleven-year-old Peter White Elk, who was herding horses at the head of the Indian column. All but one Indian claimed that the posse fired without warning.[28]

With no incontrovertible evidence about the first shot available, Burke and McNichols were forced to rely upon the conflicting testimonies, and their own common sense. Although they analyzed the battle testimony independently, the two investigators reached similar conclusions. On November 16, McNichols reported from Crawford, Nebraska, to the Commissioner of Indian Affairs:

> Certainly, from the position of the Indians—scattered along the highway—they were not expecting a battle and only a small part of their band were yet in the immediate scene of the conflict when it began . . . . It would seem very unlikely that one of their number would precipitate it, when their party was so scattered . . . . All reason and common sense is against the theory that the Indians began the firing.[29]

Burke, in his report of December 17 to the U. S. Attorney General, would not definitely state that the posse had fired first, but he left little doubt as to whom he suspected:

> At the time of the shooting, on the second day, the Indians' . . . attitude . . . was not threatening or menacing. The approach of the Sheriff and his posse, after they left the road and took up a dry gulch under the creek bank, was threatening and menacing . . . .[30]

This contention that the posse was responsible for precipitating the battle had support from a highly unlikely source. W. F. Mecum, who prosecuted the case for Converse County, prepared

---

[28]Last Bear told Burke that he thought the whites had cursed the Indians before they opened fire. S. Doc. 128, p. 53.

[29]Ibid., p. 14.

[30]Timothy F. Burke to The Attorney General, December 17, 1903, Record Group 60 "Records of the Attorney General," letter file 16694 (1903).

for the preliminary hearing by studying the posse members' accounts of the fight. With the Indians' version unavailable to him, and relying solely on the whites' statements, Mecum sent the following information to Acting Governor Chatterton on November 9:

> The Posse got ahead, at a point on lance creek [sic], 6 mi below the Bever [sic] dams, 50 mi from Douglas, secreted their horses, and hid behind the bank of the creek, until the Indians should come along, *thus ambushing the Indians . . . .* The way the posse were situated and ready, it does not seem possible that an Indian could have shot first, though he might have tried to. Thirteen men with 30-30's and 30-40's ready for action, at a second's notice, it is a wonder that any Indians within 100 yds got away.[31]

McNichols, Burke and Mecum all felt certain that the posse had fired the first shot, or at least had forced it by their threatening advance upon the Indians. Beyond the argument over the first shot, however, was the question of ultimate responsibility for the incident. Indians had been reported illegally hunting game and killing cattle, and it was Sheriff Miller's duty to see that the laws were upheld. If the fight resulted from resistance to a legal arrest attempt, the Indians were at fault. But if Sheriff Miller and the posse went beyond the law in pursuing the Smith and Brown parties, the Indians had the right to defend themselves.

Attorney Burke's analysis of the posse's actions convinced him that Sheriff Miller had broken several pertinent points of law in the confrontation with the Indians. Miller was sheriff of Weston County, and the warrant had been issued in Weston County, yet Miller tried to serve it in Converse County. The warrant named only two persons, John Doe and Richard Doe, but after arresting nine Indians with it, Miller attempted to arrest nearly fifty more. And at neither arrest attempt were the Indians engaged at the time in the violation of any law of the state of Wyoming.[32]   Burke concluded that the evidence clearly indicated that the Indians were legally justified in resisting arrest.

Special Agent McNichols emphasized in his report that the posse did not have a particular band of Indians in mind when it sent out from Newcastle. Miller had no proof that the Indians he tried to arrest on October 30-31 had been killing game in Weston County. To the contrary,

> the important fact that Smith and his party did not leave the agency in South Dakota until October 20 should be kept in mind. The posse had left Newcastle on the morning of October 23; being organized on information reaching Newcastle about October 20 that Indians were unlawfully killing game in Weston County. At the time that this

---

[31]W. F. Mecum to Fenimore Chatterton, November 9, 1903. Chatterton Papers. Emphasis added.
[32]Burke to The Attorney General, December 17, 1903.

party was organized the Smith party could not have yet reached any part of the State of Wyoming.[33]

The warrant carried by Miller, dated October 22, specified that Indians had killed ten antelope on or about October 19.[34] At that time the Smith party was still on the reservation. In other words, the band that suffered all five of the Indian deaths could not possibly have been the Indians covered by the sheriff's warrant.

In assessing responsibility for the Lightning Creek fight, McNichols was not satisfied with a recital of technical illegalities on the part of the posse. His report contained a damning accusation that condemned not only the white men's actions, but their motivation:

> I can not escape the conviction that this band of 13 whites, *urged on by a local sentiment of race hatred,* has stained a page in Wyoming's history that no amount of bluster will ever efface.[35]

What McNichols insinuated was that the white expedition was an act of racial aggression rather than of law enforcement. According to the posse account published in the *Newcastle Times,* "several Newcastle men, feeling very incensed over the actions of the Indians, decided to put a stop to it."[36] This intense reaction, however, was not a common response to the killing of game animals by whites. Converse County Attorney Mecum reported to Acting Governor Chatterton on November 9 that antelope had

> not been protected by the white men, or the law as to the killing of antelope inforced [sic] against white men, who kill them at all seasons of the year.[37]

The accusation that the Indians had been killing cattle as well as game animals was never substantiated. Weston County Clerk Arthur L. Putnam reported that "although *no complaints had been filed by the stockmen,* Sheriff Miller thought it his duty to look after the matter."[38] Isaac Robbins, a sheepherder in the Cheyenne River area, met the Smith and Brown parties and paid one young Indian to work for him. Robbins, who knew the stockmen in the area, did not hear any of them complain about the Indians killing livestock.[39] And County Attorney Mecum stated that he had "not heard of a case where the Indians stole, or killed cattle, or done any other unlawful act in this Co. since I am Prosecuting atty."[40]

---

[33]S. Doc. 128, p. 13.
[34]*Ibid.,* pp. 96-97.
[35]*Ibid.,* p. 12. Emphasis added.
[36]*Ibid.,* p. 17.
[37]Mecum to Chatterton, November 9, 1903.
[38]Arthur L. Putnam to Fenimore Chatterton, November 10, 1903. Chatterton Papers. Emphasis added.
[39]Robbins interview, August 1904.
[40]Mecum to Chatterton, November 9, 1903.

Although the evidence clearly suggested that Sheriff Miller and his posse went to extraordinary lengths to arrest the Indians, Attorney Burke did not feel that they were motivated by any particular malice:

> I think a mistaken action on the part of the Sheriff of Weston county should not be attributed to any wrongful motive or purpose on his part, for Mr. Miller was known to me to be a good officer, a brave man, and one who intended to be right in all his actions. What I say of Sheriff Miller of Weston county I can also say of several of his posse . . . .[41]

Special Agent McNichols agreed with Burke's exoneration of Miller, concluding that the sheriff had probably accompanied the posse against his better judgment and only to protect his reputation as a brave man. But McNichols did not share Burke's benevolent attitude toward the posse:

> The sheriff's posse was no Sunday-school class. Cowboys and bartenders predominated in the makeup of the white party. Several of them were entire strangers to the original party. Sheriff Miller did not know whether they were men of coolness, judgment, and steady character. Their recommendation was that they had guns and were willing to join the party.[42]

Historians have generally propagated this theory of Sheriff Miller's comparative innocence in the Lightning Creek fight.[43] His past suggests, however, that Burke and McNichols failed to assign the dead lawman his full share of the blame for the events leading up to the fight. Although Miller was well known as a brave and honest sheriff, his conviction to do his duty seemed to increase whenever Indians were involved. For several years he had gone out of his way to arrest South Dakota Sioux for various legal infractions. In 1901 he even received a letter of congratulations from Wyoming's Governor DeForest Richards for performing this task so thoroughly.[44] Had Miller, who was responsible for the posse, not been so enthusiastic about arresting Indians, he could have returned to Newcastle after capturing the nine Sioux on October 23. But disregarding the limits of his jurisdiction, and exceeding the powers granted in his warrant, he continued to scour the country, looking for more Indians.

As fate would have it, the next band that the posse encountered was led by Charlie Smith. Miller and Smith shared bad feelings

---

[41]Burke to The Attorney General, December 17, 1903.

[42]S. Doc. 128, p. 14.

[43]*See,* for example, Ernest M. Richardson, "Sullen Sioux From Pine Ridge Reservation Brought On the Last Indian-White Blood-Letting in Wyoming," *Montana, the Magazine of Western History* Vol. 10, No. 3, 42-52; Mabel E. Brown, "Billy Miller—Martyr Sheriff," *Bits and Pieces* Vol. 3, No. 3, 1-7.

[44]Richardson, "Sullen Sioux," p. 46.

toward each other from earlier confrontations.[45]   Indians and whites agreed that the Indians probably would have submitted to the posse on October 30 had it not been for Smith.   Smith knew, however, that Miller could not legally arrest them.   Undoubtedly, he also understood the racist connotations behind an arrest attempt that never would have been made against whites.

The unfortunate deaths of five Indians and two whites at Lightning Creek did, indeed, "stain a page in Wyoming's history." There may be some doubt that the posse fired the first shot of the fight, but there is no doubt that they fired indiscriminately into the Indian families, killing a small boy, an old man, and a woman fleeing hundreds of yards from the battle.   At the preliminary hearing and during the investigations there was much interest in trying to determine which Indians had shot Sheriff Miller and Deputy Falkenberg.   But no one asked, at least publicly, which posse members had killed the defenseless Indian victims.

This disregard for Indian life, undoubtedly part of the frontier heritage, was not a trait common only to "bartenders and cowboys."   Senator Warren penned one of the most callous assessments of the fight in a letter to Acting Governor Chatterton on November 19:

> I can say with feeling emphasis that I am very, very sorry for the death of the sheriff and one of his deputeis, and I presume I ought to say that I am sorry for the death of the Indians; but if the Indian legend is right, that they go from here to the Happier Hunting Ground, and if Smith was as wicked as described, and we are the gainer in their increased respect of our laws by the severe punishment, then I venture to feel glad of the casualties on their side.[46]

The fight at Lightning Creek was an historical anachronism. The Sioux posed absolutely no threat to the people of Wyoming in 1903.   Yet a band of Indian families traveling through the state was treated almost as if it had been a war party.   Sheriff Miller and his men ignored their own laws in pursuing the Indians, and then shot down men, women and children in the fight that followed.   Evidently the racial hatred engendered during the decades of warfare between the two peoples prevented many whites from viewing the Indian as anything other than a mortal enemy.   It is not difficult to conclude, in the context of such sentiments, that the Charlie Smith and William Brown parties were confronted by the posse not because they were hunting, but because they were Indians.

---

[45]Smith, well educated and somewhat bellicose, had reportedly been greatly angered by earlier arrests of High Dog and others, and he and Miller had previously argued. Mecum to Chatterton, November 9, 1903; Richardson, "Sullen Sioux," p. 46; and Brown, "Billy Miller," pp. 3-5.

[46]Francis E. Warren to Fenimore Chatterton, November 19, 1903. Chatterton Papers.

A Game Cock

Told to me by Abe Abraham

There was a brewery in Buffalo in 1885 that was run by a German by the name of Fisher. This Fisher was always bragging about his beer; declaring it was the finest beer in the world.

He owned a buggy horse and was always bragging about it; claiming it could out trot any horse in the state and that he had a rooster that could lick any rooster that came around. "He was a son-of-gun of a rooster," Fisher declared.

One day Fisher was bragging about his rooster in Joe Sharp's barber shop and Joe said, "Yeah? Well, I've got a banty rooster that I'll bet can lick your 'son-of-a-gun' of a rooster."

"I'll bet you," Fisher said.

"All right; I'll call that bet."

The time and place was agreed upon which was to be at 3:30 the following day at Fisher's home at the end of Main street in Buffalo.

At the appointed time half of Buffalo followed Joe Sharp, carrying his banty rooster under his arm. Just before they reached Fisher's home, Joe slipped steel spurs on his banty.

No one knew that Joe's rooster was wearing spurs, neither did many know that Joe's banty was a game cock but they bet on Joe's banty, just the same. They all knew Joe and they were willing to take a chance on the card he had up his sleeve.

When they arrived at Fisher's everything was set and the two roosters were put to fighting. I never saw anything prettier in my life for every time the Dungbill made a pass at the game cock the banty would duck, circle and duck and then fly clear over the Dungbill's head and then duck again.

This kept up for a dozen or more rounds when Fisher said, "See, what did I tell you? Your little runt of a rooster is scared to death of my fighting cock."

Joe did not answer and the roosters kept on sparring, then, suddenly, the banty made a rush at the Dungbill; socked both his spurs into the big rooster's head and Fisher's rooster fell over backward—dead.

Joe had to help his rooster get his spurs out of the Dungbill's head and when Fisher saw the spurs, for the first time, he said, "Look, that scoundrel ties nails on his rooster's feet."

But the banty was declared the winner.

—By Ida McPherren
W.P.A. Manuscripts Collection
Wyoming State Archives and Historical
Department

Blazing the Bridger and Bozeman Trails

By

JOHN S. GRAY

Rumors of rich diggings in the remote Salmon River region on the western slope of the Continental Divide in present Idaho drew eager miners in the spring of 1862 from the played-out placer gulches of Colorado.

Reaching Fort Bridger over well-traveled trails, these gold-seekers headed north into an unfamiliar wilderness, where they lost themselves in snow-clad ranges and spring-flooded valleys. Wandering in all directions, the inveterate prospectors soon struck promising leads along the eastern slope of the Divide in present Montana. They found the richest deposits that summer on Grasshopper Creek, where the boom town of Bannack promptly mushroomed.

The following gold rushers from the east traveled the old emigrant road up the Platte, North Platte, and Sweetwater Rivers to South Pass. From there one trail looped southwest through Fort Bridger before heading north, while the Lander cut-off led more directly toward the Idaho wilderness. Both trails, however, were not only rugged, but exasperatingly circuitous, twice crossing the Continental Divide. Everyone recognized that the pressing need was a shorter and easier route to the new Eldorado.

Before long, enterprising guides were pioneering two cut-off routes. Bridger's trail left the North Platte at Red Buttes, a few miles above present Casper, and headed for the north-draining Big Horn Basin, lying between the Wind River range on the west and the Big Horn Range on the east; it then circled west up the valley of the Yellowstone and over the low Bridger range into the Gallatin Valley. The Bozeman Trail, leaving the North Platte a few miles lower down, skirted the eastern base of the Big Horns before swinging west to merge with Bridger's trail. Both saved important mileage and made easier traveling, especially Bozeman's. But at the time, Bridger's was safer, for the Big Horns formed a rampart against the Sioux bands jealously defending their favorite hunting grounds on the plains.

The story of the blazing of these cut-off routes to Montana has been told before[1], but new sources support a fuller and more accurate account of these pioneering ventures.

Most unexpected is the finding that a tiny sporting party blazed the Bridger trail in 1862, thereby sparking the development of both cut-offs. This was while the first wave of gold-seekers were losing themselves in the Idaho wilderness, and two years before Jim Bridger conducted the first emigrant train over the route. The sporting Englishman who braved the unknown with a mere handful of retainers was Edward Shelley, the skirt-chasing nephew of the celebrated poet, Percy Bysshe Shelley!

Herbert O. Brayer, who discovered Edward Shelley's diary in England, has sketched the story of this hunting excursion, supplying scattered diary excerpts[2]. Leaving Kansas City on May 26, 1862, Shelley traveled with some British friends to Denver, where a local paper saluted their arrival on July 7[3]. Two days later the party started north along the front range, pausing to hunt and fish before rolling in to Fort Laramie on August 3. Other members of the party went no farther, but Shelley would push on to winter at Fort Benton, the American Fur Company post at the head of navigation of the Missouri.

Shelly's venture was bold, if not foolhardy, for the Indians had recently shut down the Overland Stage Line along the Sweetwater, prompting its new proprietor, Ben Holladay, to move it a hundred miles south to a shorter and safer trail across southern Wyoming. This was sometimes called the Bridger Trail, but to avoid confusion we shall retain its earlier and more common name, the Cherokee Trail. Heading north from Denver, it entered the mountains at Laporte, Colorado, turned west near present Laramie, Wyoming, crossed the North Platte (here flowing north), surmounted the Continental Divide by Bridger's Pass, and coursed across the arid Bitter Creek country to join the old trail shortly before reaching Fort Bridger. Moving the stage line confronted Lt. Col. William O. Collins, 11th Ohio Cavalry, with the burden of guarding the new as well as the old trail with his few companies.[4]

Despite the danger, Shelley started up the North Platte on August 11 with apparently three light wagons and four or five hired teamsters and guides. Only one of his men, probably picked up in Denver, can be named, but he is a key one—William Orcutt.

[1]See Grace R. Hebard and E. A. Brininstool, *The Bozeman Trail*, (Glendale: The Arthur H. Clark Co., 1960); Dorothy M. Johnson, *The Bloody Bozeman*, (New York: McGraw-Hill Book Company, 1971).

[2]Herbert O. Brayer, "Western Journal of Edward Shelley," *Chicago Westerners Brand Book*, Jan., 1957. All further information on Shelley's trip, not otherwise documented, is from this source.

[3]*Rocky Mountain News*, July 12, 1862. Hereafter cited as *RMN*.

[4]Agnes Wright Spring, *Casper Collins*, (New York: Columbia University Press, 1927).

None of the tiny party seemed dismayed to find the stage stations and trading posts largely deserted and some in ashes.

On reaching the Sweetwater, Shelley passed several camps of detachments of Ohio Cavalry guarding the route. Perhaps at one of them he met Col. Collins' guide and scout, old Jim Bridger, and thus learned of the Big Horn Basin access to Montana. In any case, on August 28, he left the upper Sweetwater and struck north over a fifteen-mile divide to the head of a stream, either the Little Popo Agie or Beaver Creek, and descended it to Wind River, near present Riverton, which he reached on September 3.

The scattered diary excerpts do not define Shelley's route in detail, but somehow he crossed the Owl Creek Mountains, running east and west to form the southern rim of the Big Horn Basin, and through which the Wind River has scoured an impassable canyon to emerge as the Big Horn River. Somewhere he forded this name-changing stream, for he crossed a major western affluent, Greybull River, on September 19. Brayer implies that he then re-crossed the Big Horn and struggled east over the formidable Big Horn range to reach the open plains. This is scarcely credible, for he was already in an open basin that led north to "a south fork of the Yellowstone," probably Clarks Fork, which he reached on October 5.

The scouting party soon fell in with a village of Blackfeet Indians, who proved so surprisingly friendly that Shelley wandered with them for the next month. Together they forded the Yellowstone and roamed north across the Musselshell. On the approach of winter, Shelley's party struck for Fort Benton, arriving there on November 1. There they first learned of the exciting new gold strike at Bannack, some 250 miles to the southwest. Two of the discharged hired hands, including William Orcutt, immediately left for these diggings, going by way of Deer Lodge.

Even the sketchy diary excerpts reveal that Shelley had traversed the key segment of the future Bridger Trail—the Big Horn Basin, west of the rampart of the Big Horns. To be sure, the knowledgeable Bridger would later modify the initial segment to make a shorter and easier entry into the basin and the final segment so as to travel more directly to the gold mines.

Word of Shelley's achievement soon reached Colorado. The first hint appeared an an editorial in the *Rocky Mountain News* of March 26, 1863, which recommended as "a shorter and better route" one that crossed from the Sweetwater to Wind River and on to the Yellowstone. Conclusive proof appeared in the same paper in the form of a letter written by J. B. ("Buzz") Caven at Bannack on February 8, 1863. The relevant part reads:

> It is now ascertained to a certainty that the most practicable route to this country lies east of the Wind River range . . . . Shelley, an English gentleman, came across this summer from Denver by that route and says that he never saw a better mountain road . . . . Mr.

(Orcutt, who came through with him, says it is not over 400 miles from Fort Laramie to the Three Forks [the junction of the Gallatin, Madison, and Jefferson to form the Missouri], and no elevation higher than between here and Deer Lodge. You must endeavor to make this public, for it is reliable. I am personally acquainted with Orcutt and know him to be a reliable man.[5])

One ellipsis in the above included the significant sentence: "John Jacobs may possibly go through to that point [Denver] for the purpose of guiding the emigration through, though it is not certain." John M. Jacobs, with John M. Bozeman, did indeed return that spring to guide emigrants back to the mines, but we must pause to identify these two pioneers.

Jacobs, later described as "a red-bearded Italian," was a mature veteran of the mountains. One source implies that he came west in 1842, but a better one dates it in 1849[6], the time of the California gold rush. If he reached those mines, he did not long remain, for he had been trading on the emigrant road when in 1850-1851 he settled a debt at Fort Owen, in Montana's Bitter Root Valley, by bringing in emigrant cattle. There are references to his trading on the road in summer and running cattle in Montana in the winter every year from 1857 through 1861[7]. In July 1862 he conducted an emigrant train of forty wagons from Soda Springs through Deer Lodge to Walla Walla[8]. By that fall, when the new strike at Bannack was draining miners from the lesser diggings at Deer Lodge, Jacobs joined the hegira.

Bozeman, a native of Georgia, was in his vigorous twenty-sixth year, large of stature and commanding in presence. In 1860 he had left his family in Georgia to join the Colorado gold rush[9]. Finding no fortune there, he left Denver on April 1, 1862, with the first party drawn to the Idaho mines. Following the Cherokee Trail to the North Platte crossing and then turning north to the lower Sweetwater, the party was so delayed by snow and poor grass that it did not reach Fort Bridger until May 28[10]. Later-starting trains overtook it there and together they headed north to lose themselves in the maze of mountains. Bozeman's splinter

---

[5]*RMN*, April 9, 1863.

[6]*Denver Commonwealth and Republican*, Sept. 17, 1863. Hereafter cited as *DC&R*.

[7]George W. Weisel, *Men and Trade on the Northwest Frontier*, (Missoula: Montana State University Press, 1955).

[8]Granville Stuart, *Forty Years on the Frontier*, (Glendale: The Arthur H. Clarke Co., 1957). See index.

[9]Merrill G. Burlingame, "John M. Bozeman, Montana Trailmaker," *Mississippi Valley Historical Review*, March, 1941. Hereafter cited as Burlingame, "Bozeman."

[10]Letter, Ham's Fork, May 30, 1862, in *RMN*, June 28, 1862.

group rolled into Deer Lodge on June 24[11], where he mined for a while before joining the fall exodus to Bannack.

Idled by winter, Bannackites escaped boredom by promoting town sites and short cuts. (Buzz Caven's letter, quoted above in part, reveals that he and "Major" William Graham were among the promoters of hopeful Gallatin City, located at the three forks of the Missouri. According to Joseph A. Emery, who reached Omaha from the mines by mackinaw boat on April 22, 1863, Graham was then exploring a 400-mile (!) cut-off from Gallatin City to Fort Laramie[12]. He apparently never carried out this project, but Emery reveals that rumors were circulating of an alternate short cut along the eastern skirts of the Big Horns, a trail familiar only to old fur traders plying between Fort Laramie and the Yellowstone.)

(It is more significant that Jacobs, Bozeman, and Orcutt all spent the winter in Bannack[13], where the latter was extolling Shelley's route. The idea of exploring it in reverse and then guiding pilgrims back at so much per wagon appealed more to the veteran Jacobs and fledgling Bozeman than the long-shot, back-breaking labor of mining. Before spring of 1863, they, together with Jacobs' half-breed daughter of seven winters, headed for a take-off base at over-promoted Gallatin City.

Jacob's departure from Gallatin City and his intention of exploring Shelley's route was recorded in a letter written by L. B. Duke on May 24, 1863 at that city: ". . . I would advise emigrants to take the route east of the Wind [River] range. Mr. Jacobs, an old and experienced mountaineer, left here on March 20th. He went through on that route to [Fort] Laramie, and may now be guiding emigrants back by this route . . . ."[14])

(Having left unseasonably early on March 20, the exploring trio plunged into the unknown, not to be heard of again until fifty-two days later, when they were only about 260 miles out and far east of Shelley's route.)(Besides weather, such slow progress suggests searching for a pass over the Bridger range into the Yellowstone Valley and fords across the Yellowstone and its southern affluents. In addition, we speculate that they first explored the Big Horn Basin and became disenchanted with its arid stretches and rugged southern rim. Either this disappointment, or the rumors of the old trader's trail, prompted them to seek a better passage around the northern extremity of the Big Horns and south along its eastern skirts.)

---

[11]Stuart, *Forty Years,* p. 211.
[12]*Nebraska Republican* (Omaha), April 24, 1863.
[13]"Persons in Montana During the Winter of 1862-3," *Montana Historical Society Contributions,* Vol. 1, p. 334.
[14]*RMN,* July 2, 1863.

On the morning of May 11, they were on the east bank of the Big Horn River near the mouth of Rotten Grass Creek, some twelve miles below the mouth of the impassable Big Horn Canyon. There they spotted an Indian war party and fled furiously up Rotten Grass Creek to vanish among its brush-lined breaks. They had actually glimpsed, not Indians, but James Stuart's large prospecting party, which had left Gallatin City a month after the exploring trio. Merely hoping to pass the time of day, the disgusted prospectors gave up the pursuit of the skittish explorers.[15]

Two days later Jacob's party encountered a less imaginary scare, when they found themselves in the near presence of a real war party of braves, apparently Crows. Knowing they would be plundered at the very least, Jacobs tossed his rifle and bullet-pouch into a clump of sagebrush. The warriors stripped them of every possession, but then relented sufficiently to turn them loose on three broken-down ponies without grub. Jacobs recovered his rifle, but found only five balls in his bullet pouch. It made little difference, however, for they could find no game on their 250 mile flight southward to the emigrant road on the North Platte.[16]

(This flight on empty stomachs and crippled ponies undoubtedly took them along the eastern base of the Big Horns, providing the opportunity of recognizing its superiority as an emigrant road. Yet for fear of Indians and starvation, they could scarcely have tarried to locate emigrant campsites with the necessary wood, water, and grass. They limped into safety on the North Platte at the mouth of Deer Creek in a destitute and famished state, probably two weeks later, say about May 27.)

At this time Deer Creek, some twenty-five miles below present Casper, boasted a thriving trading post, a squad of Ohio Cavalry, and a telegraph station with Oscar Collister as resident operator. The latter's reminiscences[17] mention the arrival there in the summer (?) of 1863 of Bozeman and Jacobs from Montana, they having staked out (?) a new cut-off along the east slope of the Rockies. Although the explorers had originally intended to reach Fort Laramie, 105 miles farther down the Platte, they apparently remained at Deer Creek to recuperate.

Jacobs probably knew the proprietor of the trading post, Joseph Bissonette, a forty-five year old Frenchman[18]. He served not only

---

15James Stuart, "Journal of Yellowstone Expedition of 1863," *Montana Historical Society Contributions*, Vol. 1, p. 148.
16Idem.
17Oscar Collister, "Life of . . . as told by Himself to Mrs. Chas. Ellis of Difficulty, Wyo.," *Annals of Wyoming*, July and October, 1930. Hereafter cited *in the text* by the name Collister.
18John D. McDermott, "Joseph Bissonette," in LeRoy R. Hafen, *Mountain Men and the Fur Trade*, (Glendale: The Arthur H. Clark Co., 1965), Vol. 1, p. 49. The latter hereafter cited as *Mountain Men*.

emigrants, but the nearby Sioux, and sent seasonal trading parties out to the Yellowstone by the old trader's trail. One of his employees was another old Frenchman, John Baptiste Boyer, who had traded for years on the upper Missouri before moving out to the Platte; with him was his twenty-six year old, half-Sioux son, Michel (Michael, or "Mitch") Boyer, destined to win fame as a scout and guide before his Indian relatives snuffed out his life with General George A. Custer on the Little Big Horn.[19] Another of Bissonette's employees was the twenty-nine-year-old Rafael Gallegos, of New Mexican origins[20].

While the spent explorers were recuperating at Deer Creek, the spring migration was already on the road. Samuel Word[21], diarist, and George W. Irvin II[22], a reminiscence recorder, having left St. Joseph for the Idaho mines, pulled into Fort Laramie on June 22. Although Irvin recalled that they met Jacobs and Bozeman there, he is contradicted by Sam Word's copious diary. It mentions neither them or any cut-off at this point, but does record on June 30, when they reached Deer Creek, that both guides were there and had been gathering wagons to take their new cut-off for two weeks, i.e., since about June 16. In view of the heavy traffic, the further implication is that Jacobs and Bozeman were capturing few of the passing wagons. Nevertheless, Word and Irvin, deciding to join the venture, tarried for some days while a stronger train gathered.

While waiting, Word struck up a friendship with trader John Boyer (whom he called Bovier, and others called "Old Bouillion") and thereby gathered useful information about the cut-off and gold mining. "He seems to have taken quite a fancy to me, while he talks little with others," he recorded, "and presented me with a cradle and rocker and and shovel and pick worth $15-20—a handsome present. I shall ever remember old man Bovier for his kindness. He is an honest old backwoodsman and mountaineer."

Among the slowly gathering wagons appeared that of Robert and James Kirkpatrick, who would also leave reminiscences of their experience[23]. Crossing to the north bank of the Platte, the

---

[19]"Ft. Pierre Journals . . . ," *South Dakota Historical Collections,* 1918, index; "Father C. Hoecken's Baptismal Journal," idem, Vol. 23, p. 230; John Boyé affidavit, Fort Laramie, June 27, 1866, in *Joseph Bissonette Claim,* Hse. Ex. Doc. No. 80, 41st Cong., 3rd Sess., Ser. No. 1454. The latter hereafter cited as *Bissonette Claim.*

[20]Ra hae Gallegos Affidavit, Fort Laramie, June 27, 1866, in *Bissonette Claim.* p 1

[21]Sam Word, "Diary, 1863," *Montana Historical Society Contributions,* Vol. 8, p. 37. This and all subsequent trail diaries, etc. will be used to construct the text; each will be referenced on its initial appearance, but further citations will be keyed *in the text* by using the source's name.

[22]George W. Irvin II, "Overland to Montana," *Butte Miner,* Holiday Edition, Jan. 1, 1888.

[23]Michael Gene McLatchy, "From Wisconsin to Montana, the Reminis-

train celebrated July 4 by appointing a committee to draft rules and by electing as captain one of their own number, James Brady from Missouri.

On the morning of July 6, 1863, the assembled train, still numbering only forty-six wagons and eighty-nine men, with additional women and children, pulled out to become the first to pioneer what would become famous as the Bozeman Trail. Since Jacobs and Bozeman had been unable to lay out the route and campsites over the first half of the coming journey, they took Rafael Gallegos, undoubtedly familiar with the old trader's trail, to guide the train as far as the crossing of the Big Horn River. Train accounts refer to him only as "Rafeil" or "the Mexican."

After winding slowly for some 125 miles over dry, sagebrush country, the train nooned on July 20 to enjoy the sweet mountain water of a branch of Clear Creek, near present Buffalo. The sudden appearance of 150 mounted Sioux and Cheyenne braves prompted hasty defense measures, but instead of attacking, the chiefs merely asked for a parley. Against Bozeman's advice, the emigrant ladies spread a feast for the visitors, during which sundry loose articles vanished and one belligerent brave threatened Gallegos. At the ensuing council, the chiefs bluntly forbade any trespass of their cherished hunting grounds, and threatened reprisals unless the train turned back to the Platte road. The emigrants asked for time to consider the matter.

That evening the train held a meeting which initiated a debate that would bring endless repercussions. Word recorded that "many of our men are timid and cowardly and immediately determined to go back . . . . Some are in favor of going on anyway, others are not." Within days he acknowledged his own preference for retreat. Robert Kirkpatrick recalled that all the train voted to return except five families, while his brother James remembered that all but four wagons favored this course. The conclusive proof that the majority opposed bearding the Indians lies in the fact that the entire train retreated four miles the next afternoon and twelve the day after in an atmosphere of apprehension and acrimony.

We can not so easily establish the attitudes of the leaders, however. Word recorded that at this initial meeting "our guides tell us it is dangerous and have ordered a retreat until we can get reinforcements. That is the conclusion this evening." Robert Kirkpatrick recalled that Bozeman pronounced it madness to proceed, but his brother contradicted this by claiming that Bozeman, Jacobs, Captain Brady, and apparently Gallegos advised going on.

---

cences of Robert Kirkpatrick," M.A. Thesis, 1961, Montana State University, Bozeman; James Kirkpatrick, "A Reminiscence of John Bozeman," in John W. Hakola, ed., *Frontier* Omnibus, (Missoula: Montana State University Press and Historical Society of Montana, 1962).

Our best resolution of these contradictions, prompted by subsequent events, is that all four leaders agreed that because of the women and children they should seek reinforcements, but disagreed on the course to pursue should reinforcements prove unobtainable. But even this degree of discord among leaders soon triggered bitter arguments among their followers.

As a sullen compromise that satisfied no one, it was finally decided to send couriers back to Deer Creek to ask for a military escort, and to induce James Creighton's large Bannack-bound merchant train, which some knew to be following on the Platte road, to come out and swell their ranks. George W. Irvin and some nameless emigrant volunteered to join Gallegos on this mission. After dark of July 22, the trio stole out of camp to speed to Deer Creek. For the next week debate and apprehension shook the train as it retreated on alternate days back to the North Fork of Powder River, near present Kaycee, only about seventy-five miles from Deer Creek.

The couriers covered the 110 miles back to the telegraph station in good time, for they arrived there on July 25, as shown by the emigrant diary of Joseph A. Emery[24], who recorded on that day at Deer Creek that an emigrant train on a new cut-off had been turned back by Indians. The messengers transacted their business within three days, for they must have left on the 27th to reach the anxious train on the 29th, as Word's diary reveals.

Courier Irvin recalled that promptly on reaching the telegraph station they wired Fort Laramie for a troop escort and that the wire was relayed to the Omaha headquarters of Gen. Thomas J. McKean, commanding the military District of Nebraska. "The answer soon came that no aid could be rendered to the party by the military," Irvin wrote, because "all the country north to the Yellowstone . . . was Indian country, upon which emigrants had no right to enter." This answer came by July 26, for on that day emigrant Lucia Park Darling[25], then camped at the Horseshoe Creek telegraph station, recorded in her diary that "the command at Fort Laramie has forbidden the troops to help a train surrounded by Indians on the new route."

Since Lt. Col. Collins had gone to Ohio to recruit more companies to bolster his original four in guarding the two overland trails, Major Thomas L. Mackey, 11th Ohio Cavalry, was commanding Fort Laramie[26]. When his wire to Omaha yielded no

---

[24]Joseph A. Emery, "Omaha to Virginia City, May 31-Sept. 25, 1863," microfilm of typescript, Montana Historical Society Library.

[25]Lucia Park Darling, "Diary, 1863," microfilm, Montana Historical Society Library.

[26]Robert A. Murray, *Fort Laramie*, (Fort Collins: The Old Army Press, 1974), p. 86.

authority, one way or the other, for reasons shortly to be disclosed, he could only follow his own judgement.   He obviously felt that in the face of a troop shortage he could not afford to divert a detachment for several months, especially on a mission that by violating treaty rights could easily trigger an Indian war.   He therefore not only refused the escort, but in effect outlawed the cut-off.   Furthermore, he wired the Deer Creek post, through operator Collister, to send out a guide as an agent of the military to bring the train immediately back to the Platte road.   This latter is inferred from subsequent events and the confused recollections of Collister.

At this rebuff, the couriers may have tried to induce the Creighton train to take the cut-off.   According to several diarists who traveled off and on with this merchant train[27], it reached Deer Creek about July 26, but none mentions such a request.   In any case it made no move toward the cut-off, presumably because of the army ban.   Having thus failed in their mission, the couriers left to rejoin their stranded outfit.   Gallegos apparently remained at Deer Creek, since no one mentions him again, but all accounts agree that John Boyer accompanied the other two to bring the train back.   The fact that no new guide was needed for this purpose reinforces our inference that Boyer had been selected as the agent of the military to insure the train's return.

The couriers reached the stalled train on July 29, reporting the failure of their mission and that Boyer was sent to guide them back. At this proof that indecision and compromise had brought nothing but delay, dissension in the train reached new heights.   "My old friend Bovier . . . ," Word recorded, "thinks it a shame that we did not go on; says Rafeil is a coward and ought to be shot.   Says we could go through yet, but he cannot go with us.   Could only get leave [permission?] to guide us to the Platte.   He is in the employ of the government [paid agent to insure return?] and cannot do as he wishes."

A stampede of oxen the next day damaged some wagons and limited the retreat to one mile.   As Irvin recalled, the majority had accepted the decision to abandon the expedition—but not John Bozeman and nine other bold men.   As midnight flipped the calendar to July 31, this resolute group set out on horseback, with one pack horse laden with provisions, determined to press on to Bannack despite the army ban and Indian threats.   Only two of Bozeman's companions have been identified—George W. Irvin, who has left the only account, and Mike J. Knoch[28].

To avoid the Indian-infested plains, Bozeman wisely abandoned

---

[27]Joseph A. Emery (see fn. 24); Lucia Park Darling (see fn. 25); R. D. Ross, "Journal of a Trip Across the Plains in 1863," *North Dakota Historical Society Collections,* Vol. 2, p. 219.
[28]Burlingame, "Bozeman."

his proposed cut-off to lead the party up the North Fork of Powder River into the concealing Big Horns.   While crossing the range on the second night out, they lost all their grub in an accident to their pack horse.   Pushing on down Ten Sleep Canyon they reached the Big Horn Basin and picked up Shelley's trail.   After four nights of fast travel on empty stomachs, but without meeting Indians, they reached Clark's Fork of the Yellowstone.)

On this journey Bozeman proved himself a born leader.   He inspired the famished men to their best and most cheerful effort, and guided them so true in the darkness that either he and Jacobs had indeed explored the area, or he possessed a keen instinct for country.   Irwin was sufficiently impressed to write:

> Bozeman was six feet two inches high, weighing two hundred pounds, supple, active, tireless, and of handsome, stalwart presence. He was genial, kindly, and as innocent as a child in the ways of the world. He had no conception of fear, and no matter how sudden a call was made on him day or night, he would come up with a rifle in his hand.   He never knew what fatigue was, and was a good judge of all distances and when you saw his rifle level, you knew that you were not to go supperless to bed.

After veering west up the Yellowstone Valley, Bozeman led his party over the Bridger range into the Gallatin valley by a low pass that I-90 approximates today—Bozeman Pass.   As they approached the three forks, the appetizing aroma of frying bacon drew them to the lonely camp of two miners.   The latter watched in awe as their entire larder vanished down ten bottomless gullets, but they were game enough to serve an electrifying dessert—word of a recent hot placer strike at Alder Gulch, which had nearly depopulated Bannack in favor of booming Virginia City.   Bozeman's party rode in to these diggings on August 22[29], well satisfied that their cross-country exploit had beaten most of the emigrants there.

Meanwhile, John Boyer was shepherding the thwarted wagon train over a time-losing back-trail that proved dry and alkaline. The previous friction, and now second thought about their hasty retreat, were eroding even old friendships.   As evidence of demoralization, Word wrote that "the train is going helter-skelter, pell-mell, every man for himself, kind of busted up, and only part corraling together."   As their hired leader, it was up to Jacobs to maintain cohesion, but some emigrant was plying both guides with whiskey.   Perhaps Bozeman could have held their allegiance, but lacking such impressive leadership qualities, Jacobs failed.   By the time they reached the Platte road at Red Buttes on August 9th, the train members were on the way to make Jacobs the scapegoat for their miseries.

---

[29]*Society of Montana Pioneers Register* (Helena, 1899), indexed.

Since guides became superfluous on the crowded road, the resentful train ignored Jacobs and promptly broke up. Some paused to rest at inviting camps, while others sought out other trains willing to adopt them. The crowning mortification came when they began to hear that a military escort had come out to their aid after all, only to find them gone! Sam Word heard the rumor in garbled form on August 9, the very day they reached the Platte road. The Kirkpatrick brothers got it in more accurate form a week or two later when halfway up the Sweetwater.

The newly-amplified truth is that on July 25, when Major Mackey relayed to Omaha the Deer Creek request for an escort, he first learned that departmental orders of July 19th had just transferred all the posts in present Wyoming from General McKean's District of Nebraska to Col. John M. Chivington's District of Colorado[30]. Although McKean relayed the wire to Chivington in Denver, it had to proceed by stage coach from Julesburg. This was the reason Mackey had to make his own temporary decision, which denied the escort, as we have described.

A Denver newspaper picked up the story, as follows:

A telegram received yesterday [July 29] at headquarters in this city from a party of emigrants at or near Clear Creek, about 100 miles out from Omaha [an error taken from the Omaha relay wire instead of the original Deer Creek wire], requesting protection from a band of Indians, who had assumed so threatening an attitude that the train dare not proceed further. It consists of about 100 [sic] wagons en route to Bannack City. It had also sent an application to Fort Laramie for assistance, but without effect. The dispatch was forwarded to Col. Chivington, who was at Fort Halleck, preparing to go into the mountains [after Indians], when last heard from.[31]

The dispatch, forwarded by stage coach, met the returning Chivington, who promptly issued orders for Major Mackey to send an escort to aid the stalled train. These orders could not have reached Fort Laramie before John Boyer was guiding the train back to the Platte, but Mackey did send out Lt. William H. Brown with a detachment of his Company A, 11th Ohio Cavalry, as documented by the Denver paper:

Lt. Brown of the 11th Ohio Cavalry called on us yesterday [September 16] to confirm the statements of Mr. Jacobs [to be quoted later] .... Lt. Brown was in command of the escort sent out to the train. He took three months' rations and had orders to escort the train to Bannack. When he arrived at Powder River, to his great chagrin the train had broken up and returned by different routs to the old road.

The Sioux and Cheyennes are constantly crowding back the Crows

---

[30]*Official Records, War of the Rebellion,* Vol. 22, Part II, p. 764.
[31]*DC&R,* July 30, 1863.

in that country. The Indians are a miserable set, very poorly armed, and with no real hostile intentions . . .[32]

The remnants of Jacobs' shattered train plodded on toward the Idaho mines. Some hurried on to take the Lander trail at South Pass and reach Bannack in the first week of September. Sam Word, taking the roundabout route through Fort Bridger and Salt Lake City, did not arrive until September 29. The Kirkpatricks lagged slowly to the middle reaches of the Sweetwater, where they met a trader to the emigrants who was about to leave for Denver. They decided to throw in the sponge and return with him. Backtracking to the lower Sweetwater, they turned south toward the Cherokee Trail. Traveling slowly to hunt, they covered some sixty-five miles to intercept it west of the North Platte crossing. There they met a heavy migration from Denver to Montana, and promptly changed their minds again. Turning west, they proceeded to Fort Bridger and then north to reach Bannack on October 16.

But what of the disgusted Jacobs? He abandoned his alienated charges no later than on the lower Sweetwater and headed for the Cherokee Trail and Denver ahead of the Kirkpatricks. On reaching Big Laramie Station, near present Laramie, on September 1, he had a conversation with a Bannack-bound traveler from Denver. This was N. H. Webster, whose diary at this date and place reads: "Had a long talk with John Jacobs this evening. He is from Bannack; before he left [obviously his train, not the city] there was a report of new diggings being found a hundred miles east of Bannack [at Virginia City]; it was, he said, only reported; he did not know how true it was."[33] Jacobs reached Denver about September 10.

This aborted attempt of 1863 to conduct the first emigrant train over a short cut east of the Big Horns delivered Bozeman, mostly via Shelley's route, to Virginia City, but Jacobs only to Denver. Both would guide trains to Montana next year, but by different trails, and the pair apparently never again associated together. From the moment of parting at the base of the Big Horns on July 31, 1863, Bozeman's career soared into full flight, while Jacobs' career ground looped.

Jacobs had no more than reached Denver when he called a public meeting to promote another emigrant train that he proposed to guide over his short cut to the new mines. The *Denver Commonwealth* carried an enthusiastic account of this meeting held on September 14 at the Old Criterion Saloon, saying, "Mr. Jacobs has the project in tow. He is an old mountaineer, having spent four-

---

[32]*DC&R*, Sept. 24, 1863.
[33]N. H. Webster, "Journal to Montana, 1863," *Montana Historical Society Contributions,* Vol. III, p. 300.

teen years in this country and visited all the new diggings." The pilot painted a glowing picture of his cut-off, claiming it to be 400 miles shorter, well-wooded, well-watered, and strewn with promising placer deposits the whole distance from Deer Creek to Gallatin City. The article noted that "Mr. Jacobs offered to pilot a party of 150 or 200 through this fall on the new route, if such a party can be made up to go." Another item indicated that he had applied to Col. Chivington for another escort, with results as yet unknown.[34]

The rival *Rocky Mountain News* ignored Jacobs and his public meeting, but confirmed that an application had just come to Chivington to furnish an emigrant escort. It expressed the opinion that it should be refused, since the route unjustly violated treaty rights of the Indians to the country east of the Big Horns. This atypical observation of the Indian-baiting *News* can only be explained by its other pages, then filled with opposition to any trail that bypassed Denver. It could hardly have been ignorance that prompted it to give an account; from no acknowledged source, of the aborted train, leaving the impression that it was still besieged by Indians, starving, and awaiting the recently requested escort![35]

It was undoubtedly misleading stories of this genre that brought Jacobs to the editor of the *Commonwealth*:

> Mr. Jacobs called on us yesterday [September 16] to correct a wrong impression concerning the route advocated to the Beaverhead mines. The train that was stopped on it some time since was under his charge and consisted of 47 wagons, containing 88 men, besides their families. They were at the eastern base of the Big Horn mountains and were getting along well, when about 140 Indians, men, women and children, came to talk, beg and bluff, as is their custom. They were Sioux, and he was in Crow country, and he told them he had no quarrel wtih them, nor had they any business to stop him. They went away, and that was the last he saw of them. But the people composing the train became very scared and wanted to go back. To pacify them he sent for an escort, and when it arrived the most of the train had gone back and taken the old route. Had they been less chickenhearted, there would have been no trouble. Mr. Jacobs says there is no more real danger on this route than there is on the other.[36]

That Jacobs' emigrants were apprehensive for their families and voted to return is true. That their leaders were unanimously bold and resolute we have been unable to establish. But to make a public charge that the emigrants had been "chicken-hearted" does establish one thing—that diplomacy was not Jacobs' forte. This incautious charge launched a fatal boomerang. But at the moment, Chivington apparently took a dim view of furnishing another

[34]*DC&R*, Sept. 17, 1863.
[35]*RMN*, Sept. 17, 1863.
[36]*DC&R*, Sept. 17, 1863.

escort after the summer's fiasco. For this and perhaps other reasons, Jacobs' promotional splash died aborning within a week. Hundreds of Coloradoans did leave for the mines that fall, but not with Jacobs nor by his proposed cut-off.

After lying low for a couple of months, the still-hopeful promoter tried again. Both Denver papers accepted a paid notice, dated December 16, that Mr. Jacobs was at old Jim Baker's ranch on Clear Creek, just outside of town, where he could be consulted by anyone interested in joining a company to take his cut-off the next spring[37]. Then on January 8 the Rev. L. B. Stateler presided at a public meeting of this company, at which they appointed officers and drew up articles of agreement specifying the conditions under which Jacobs would lead them through. The guide described "his new route . . . with the aid of his map . . . . He stated that he had spent 15 or 20 years in that section of the country and was familiar with every locality."[38]

This second promotional push seems to have been progressing favorably, but the lapse of time enabled the boomerang to strike back in February. The *News* spread on its front page a letter just received from thirty-nine of Jacobs' irate customers of the preceding summer, including Sam Word and Captain James Brady. This devastating missive, or missile, was dated at Virginia City, Idaho Territory, December 23, 1863, and read:

> The undersigned, who were members of a train of near fifty wagons that attempted to come to this country last summer by a new route leading from the Platte R. above Fort Laramie directly north along the east base of the Big Horn Mts., desire to make a statement through your paper in their own behalf and for the benefit of the public at large.
>
> Having learned recently from several sources not to be questioned, that Mr. John Jacobs, who is in your city engaged in trying to get a train of wagons to come through by the above route, is constantly representing that if it had not been for the cowardice of the members of the train referred to, he would have safely conducted it through, we have this to say—that Mr. Jacobs was in charge of our train; had full and entire control over it by the unanimous consent of all in it; that he represented that he had come through on the said route from this country at the instance of people here for the sole purpose of conducting immigration through, and we felt, from the professions he had made as to his knowledge of the country and acquaintance with Indian customs, that he was a fit person to take charge of the train. We were, however, disappointed in him. On the first appearance of danger he "weakened." A hundred or so Indians visited us and warned us not to go farther, and notwithstanding a marked majority of the train were emphatically in favor of going on [sic], he argued against it, and taking the responsibility on himself, he turned us back, representing that we would likely all be destroyed if we went farther.

---

[37]*RMN* and *DC&R*, Dec. 23, 1863.
[38]*RMN*, Jan. 20, 1864.

We take the responsibility of saying that Mr. Jacobs, as we believe, is a coward and unfit to take charge of a train. He may be a very good guide, and probably is; at least he ought to be well acquainted with the route referred to; but he is wholly unfit to command, owing to his consummate cowardice, to which all in our train will bear testimony. We have not a word to say against the route; we believe it to be a practicable one and think a train could come safely through on it with a firm man to command it. Mr. Jacobs, in that case, would answer for a guide, but he is unfit to act outside his place as such. We have deemed it due ourselves to say this much, having no interest whatsoever in the route.

We all here remark that Mr. John Bozeman, who is a firm and determined man and well acquainted with said route, having been over it several times, has just left here for the Missouri River at Omaha for the purpose of piloting immigration through by said route. He will leave the Platte River not far from Fort Laramie early in the season. We can recommend him to the public.

You will oblige us by giving this a place in your columns.[39]

Of course Jacobs, who had himself provoked this overdrawn letter, protested its publication, but the *News* merely challenged him to deny its authenticity and refused to give his project any further publicity. Jacobs watched in dismay as his second effort collapsed like a punctured balloon. The Rev. L. B. Stateler did proceed to the mines that spring, but not with Jacobs.

The closing paragraph of the letter, it should be noted, warmly recommended Bozeman as a competent leader and announced his recent departure for Omaha to pilot emigrants out early the next spring. He had indeed left Virginia City early in December with Milton S. Moody's outfit bound for Salt Lake City with a tempting cargo of gold dust. Since two of the notorious Henry Plummer's gang of road agents botched the job of robbing this party, the chroniclers of the Montana vigilantes have told of it and Bozeman's connection with it.[40]

Presumably Bozeman continued on to Omaha, though we have had no opportunity to scour its local papers. If so, he was late in starting back in the spring. He may have revealed the reason in a letter he wrote his mother two years later: "I have never been sick a minute in this country," he told her, "except when I had the measles two years ago."[41] If the crowds and contagion in Omaha laid the giant low, it would explain his delayed start in the spring of 1864.

Still other promoters were vying for the honor of taking the first successful train over the Bozeman trail. In the fall of 1863 an Omaha paper announced that a Mr. Comstock had already organ-

[39]*RMN,* Feb. 3, 1864.

[40]Thomas J. Dimsdale, *The Vigilantes of Montana,* (Norman: University of Oklahoma Press, 1953), Chap. 10; N. P. Langford, *Vigilante Days and Ways,* (New York: A. L. Burt Company, 1912), Chap. 28.

[41]Burlingame, "Bozeman."

ized a company to leave there the next April 15 by this new route to Bannack[42]. Nothing more is known of this outfit, but was its pilot William A. ("Buffalo Bill") Comstock, who had for some years traded and worked for the Overland Stage Line on the Platte and whose brother-in-law was Eleazer Wakeley, a supreme court judge in Omaha?[43]

Sioux City and Yankton also entered the lists by promoting the rival Niobrara trail, which ascended the Missouri to the mouth of the Niobrara and then turned westward up the latter, parallel to the Platte, to intercept the old trader's trail to the Yellowstone. To publicize it, C. M. Davis, president of the Gallatin Townsite Co., returned to Yankton to hold a public meeting there on February 20, 1864. He read a letter from George L. Tackett, a veteran trader on the Platte, which sketched the old trader's trail in detail. As a lure for emigrants, the Yankton paper flaunted a table of distances from Sioux City via Yankton to Virginia City that totalled 849 miles[44] Not until 1865, however, did Col. James A. Sawyer make the first exploratory traverse of the Niobrara route with a government-financed wagon road expedition.

The flood of emigrant traffic that headed for eastern Idaho in the spring of 1864 found itself on arrival in the newly-proclaimed Territory of Montana. (Although several trains would for the first time successfully negotiate the Bozeman trail, a good many more would choose the alternate route that Jim Bridger inaugurated that spring.)

Since both were cut-offs from the long-used Platte road, the frequent claim that they started from the Missouri, or Forts Kearny or Laramie, is hardly tenable. (Throughout 1864 the Bridger Trail left the North Platte at Red Buttes, while the Bozeman trail left it about fifteen miles lower down near the eastern edge of present Casper at the lower Platte bridge, built and operated by John Richard, Sr., an old-time Indian and emigrant trader[45].) This should not be confused with the better known upper Platte bridge five or six miles farther upstream and originally built by Louis Guinard, but by this date also owned by Richard[46] It should be noted that in later years the departure for Bozeman's trail would move a good many miles farther downstream.

The course of Bridger's little-studied trail appears, with some

---

[42]See *DC&R*, Nov. 11, 1863.
[43]John S. Gray, "Will Comstock, the Natty Bumppo of Kansas," *Montana. The Magazine of Western History,* Summer, 1970, p. 2.
[44]Yankton *Dakotaian,* March 1 and Feb. 18, 1864.
[45]John D. McDermott, "John Baptiste Richard," in *Mountain Men,* Vol. II, p. 289.
[46]Robert A. Murray, "Trading Posts, Forts and Bridges of the Casper Area," *Annals of Wyoming,* Spring, 1975, p. 5. Hereafter cited as Murray, "Trading Posts."

minor errors, on the road map issued by the Wyoming Highway Department. On the basis of trail diaries, checked against modern topographical maps, we calculate the distance from Red Buttes to Virginia City at about 510 miles; this is via Bridger's detour over the Bridger range, about thirteen miles longer than the more direct Bozeman Pass. On a similar basis, we calculate the distance from the lower Platte bridge to Virginia City by the better-studied Bozeman trail at about 535 miles; this is via Bozeman's Pass, but includes a detour of twenty-five miles that all the trains of 1864 made by first striking the Yellowstone near present Billings. It should be noted also that Bozeman's trail merged with, and thereafter followed on, Bridger's trail at the Rock Creek branch of Clarks Fork, near present Boyd, Montana.

For a large train, which inevitably included ox-powered wagons, fifteen to eighteen miles represented the maximum consistent day's drive. Since layovers for rest, washing, and repairs averaged one day a week, whether on Sunday or not, fifteen miles a day represented a good standard rate of progress. A slower rate signalled extra trouble, deliberate leisure, or planned halts, usually for prospecting. This standard rate yields an expected transit time of thirty-four days over Bridger's and thirty-six days over Bozeman's route.

Foreseeing the swollen migration of 1864, Col. Collins wrote from Fort Laramie on April 25 that an emigrant train coming from Denver was expecting to pick up an escort at his post, and asked for instructions on diverting troops for such purposes[47]. The next day John S. Collins[48], Idaho bound by the Lander trail, met Jim Bridger at Fort Laramie assembling his first train. Col. Collins released Bridger from his employment as post scout on April 30 to allow him to pilot these wagons through[49]. With the Colonel's grateful blessing, he was intent on opening the safer route through the Big Horn Basin, which would require no military escort.

Within a few days the expected train hauled in from Denver, some 200 miles and two weeks distant. It probably included the disgruntled John Jacobs, still hoping to pick up some followers. It certainly included the Rev. L. B. Stateler, who has left the only account of this train, skimpy and reminiscent though it is[50]. Additional clues to this and other trains, however, may be gleaned from the register of the Society of Montana Pioneers; the latter can-

[47]Official Records of the War of the Rebellion, Vol. 34, Part III, p. 304.
[48]John S. Collins, My Experiences in the West, (Chicago: The Lakeside Press, 1970), p. 21.
[49]Cecil J. Alter, Jim Bridger, (Norman: University of Oklahoma Press, 1962), p. 304. Hereafter cited as Alter, Bridger.
[50]E. J. Stanley, Life of L. B. Stateler, (Nashville: The Methodist Publishers, 1907), p. 175 ff.

vassed Montana for residents who had come before the close of 1864, recording their points of departure, routes, and places and dates of arrival, albeit with some errors. Only B. F. Bisel and A. M. Morgan specified that they had come with Bridger's first train[51]

With the wagons already recruited, Bridger soon started for Red Buttes, some 140 miles and ten days distant. Jacobs, having abandoned the idea of risking the Bozeman route again, probably tagged along to organize late-comers to follow in Bridger's footsteps. Bridger tarried a few days at Red Buttes until his outfit totaled sixty-two wagons, according to Howard S. Stanfield, who came along some days after they had left. There are several references to Bridger's departure in May, but only the recently-published diary of Stanfield[52] fixes the date as May 20.

In order to avoid the impassable Wind River canyon, Bridger ascended the east-flowing Poison Spider Creek for only a few days before winding northwest over sagebrush plains to present Lysite on a forks of Bad Water Creek, a west-running branch of Wind River. This was about seventy-five miles out, where James Roberts[53], a diarist of a following train, recorded that Bridger had met a band of Indians, whose hostility turned to an effusive welcome on recognizing their old friend Bridger. Statleer tells the same story, identifying the band as chief Washakie's Shoshones.

At this point Bridger turned north up present Bridger Creek, crossing the rugged Owl Creek Mountains to a header of Kirby Creek, which he descended, circling west to its mouth on the Big Horn River just below the impassable canyon at present Lucerne. In this rough passage the Statelers' wagon overturned down a steep declivity, but without serious injury to any of the party. On this sixty-mile stretch Bridger traveled slowly, scouting out the trail and pausing for road work on the rough places for the benefit of following trains.

As trail diaries make quite clear, Bridger immediately crossed to the open west bank of the Big Horn. All hands turned to felling trees, whipsawing the logs into crude lumber and constructing a fairly substantial ferryboat to cross the spring-swollen stream. Once across, they buried the boat for following trains to use, and headed forty-five miles down the west bank, as diaries reveal, to camp opposite the mouth of No Wood Creek at present Manderson.

---

[51]*Society of Montana Pioneers Register,* (Helena, 1899), indexed. Hereafter cited *in the text* by the key word register.

[52]Jack J. Detzler, ed., *Diary of Howard Stillwell Stanfield,* (Bloomington: Indiana University Press, 1969).

[53]James Roberts, "Notes of Travel, Wisconsin to Idaho, 1864," typescript in Wisconsin Historical Society Library.

(They soon turned west so as to strike in one day's drive the necessary water in Greybull River, a western affluent of the Big Horn. Ascending the Greybull to a suitable ford south of present Burlington, they then made a dry march of twenty-five miles north to present Garland, where they forded the Stinking Water, another western tributary now more euphoniously called Shoshone River. After this fording, about 230 miles out, the train laid over for a few days to rest and recruit the stock. Here we leave them temporarily to pick up the story of three other trains destined to overtake and join them at this halt.)

(The first of these following trains was a small trader's outfit of ten wagons, according to Stanfield, and dubbed "the independents," apparently because they needed no hired guides. It included Baptiste ("Big Bat") Pourier[54], marked for a long and distinguished career as an army scout. His reminiscences reveal that he went as a hired teamster with John Richard, Jr., the half-Sioux son of the trader and owner of the Platte Bridges[55]. The group probably also included Amede Bessette, another French-Canadian Indian trader who had been in charge of one of the bridges for two years[56], and Jose Miraval and family, another old trader of New Mexican origins[57]. They had left Red Buttes only a few days behind Bridger himself.)

(The second train was an emigrant company that Jacobs had succeeded in recruiting at Red Buttes. Howard Stanfield found this group gathering there on May 25 and decided to join it by paying Jacob's fee of $5 per wagon. Not until May 30 did Jacobs assemble sixty-seven wagons and start out in Bridger's wake. In short order Stanfield was complaining bitterly that Jacobs as a guide was superfluous, and as a leader was dictatorial, cowardly, and a liar. On June 7 they reached the Big Horn, where they found the independents searching for the buried ferryboat. On finding it, the latter crossed that afternoon and Jacob's train the next day.)

(The third train was another emigrant outfit under Captain Allensworth, which left Red Buttes on June 2 to be quickly overtaken by others to swell the company to over one hundred wagons.)

---

[54]"Baptiste Pourier," *Eli Ricker Interviews*, Nebraska Historical Society Library, microfilm from Micro Photo Div., Bell & Howell.

[55]Brian Jones. "Those Wild Reshaw Boys," *Sidelights of the Sioux Wars*, English Westerners' Special Publication No. 2, (London: 1967).

[56]Amede Bessette obituary, *Dillon* (Montana) *Examiner*, March 1, 1918; Amede Bessette, "A Story of Joseph A. Slade," typescript in Montana Historical Society Library.

[57]Pourier Interview, see fn. 54; 1860 Census, Miraval City, unorganized Nebraska Territory, Family #326; 1870 Census, Fort Fetterman, Albany County, Wyoming, Family #362.

Diarist Cornelius Hedges[58] recorded that they hired as pilot a local Frenchman named Rouleau at $5 per wagon. This was Hubert Rouleau[59], another employee of John Richard, Sr. Despite some dissension, they reached the Big Horn and ferried across on June 12.

All three of these trains had forded the Stinking Water to camp with Bridger's resting outfit by June 18. The next day Bridger pulled out in the lead, ascending Sage Creek northward into Montana to reach and cross Clarks Fork near present Bridger. Another twenty miles northwest took him to the crossing of Rock Creek near present Boyd, where Bozeman would later pick up the same trail. The route then led west to present Absarokee on Stillwater River, then west up the latter and across to and down Bridger Creek to its mouth on the Yellowstone. Halts had been made to allow prospecting in the mountains, but now Bridger hastened up the Yellowstone, crossing Boulder River at present Big Timber, and continuing twelve more miles to the crossing of the Yellowstone, about 368 miles out. Here they halted again to build another ferryboat.

The following companies paused even longer for prospecting, but some wagons hurried on, and this, together with complaints, especially in Jacobs' outfit, brought shifts in allegiance that destroyed the composition of the original companies. Nevertheless, nearly all gathered again at the Yellowstone ferry to celebrate the Fourth of July with Bridger. After ascending the north bank of the big river to the mouth of Shield's River, a grand division took place. Only twenty wagons stayed with Jacobs to take the shorter Bozeman Pass into the Gallatin valley. The rest followed Bridger on his detour that led north up Shield's River, west up Brackett's Creek and over the Divide, then southwest down Bridger Creek, where they spotted Jacobs a little ahead at the future site of Bozeman.

Now on well-rutted roads, the wagons spread out as they headed west across the Gallatin and Madison Rivers, south up the latter, and then west again to mountain-girt Virginia City. They rolled in over a period of days with the peak centering on July 10. Bridger is said to have reached the Gallatin on July 6[60], still some twenty miles from Virginia City. Based mostly on the pioneer register, A. M. Morgan and B. F. Bisel of his company arrived there on July 6 and July 8; Amede Bessette of the independents arrived on

---

[58]Cornelius Hedges, "Diary of Overland Trip to Montana from Iowa, 1864," mss., Montana Historical Society Library.

[59]Charles E. Hanson, "Hubert Rouleau," *Mountain Men*, Vol. 9, p. 347; Hubert Ruleau affidavit, Fort Laramie, June 27, 1866, in *Bissonette Claim*.

[60]Mrs. E. Lina Houston, *Early History of Gallatin Co. Montana*, (Bozeman, 1933), p. 11.

the latter date, with Stanfield and J. L. Perkins of Jacobs' train made it on the 10th and 11th; Thomas Wilcox and Cornelius Hedges of Allensworth's company pulled in on the 9th and 10th.

Taking July 8 as an endpoint, Bridger pioneered his 510-mile route in fifty days, a substandard rate because of road-working, ferry-building, and prospecting halts. The other trains that benefited by his work in the van made it in as little as thirty-eight days, including layovers. As Bridger had foreseen, it was a completely safe passage, for none had encountered Indian trouble.

It was no triumph, however, for Jacobs. He had not only forsaken his own route, but had once again alienated his charges. He faded into complete obscurity, for we have found no further record of him.

Six more identifiable companies safely traversed Bridger's route later in the season. James Roberts, the partial diarist already mentioned, left Red Buttes on June 10 in a train of 129 wagons piloted by Joseph Knight[61], another Indian trader from the Platte bridges; Robert Vaughn[62], who misnamed this guide as McKnight, reached Virginia City on July 13 to complete the thirty-four-day passage. Diarist William W. Alderson[63] started on June 15 with Captain Joe Todd's company of 12 horse-wagons that traveled off and on with sixteen ox- and eighteen mule-wagons, but stopped to settle thirty days later at the about-to-be-born town of Bozeman on July 13th.

Diarist William E. Atchison[64] left on June 22 with over one hundred wagons that had hired for $300 a guide he called Rocky Mountain Bob, who remains unidentified unless he was either Robert Dempsey or Robert Hereford, who had long shuttled between summer trading on the road near Green River and winter cattle-herding in Montana[65]. Atchison rolled into Virginia City on July 27 for a thirty-six day passage; Ethel A. Maynard[66], whose reminiscent letters place him in this same train, registered his arrival on July 28.

The incomplete trail letters of Franklin L. Kirkaldie[67] reveal that he left the Platte on July 13 with a company of seventy wagons captained by Joseph V. Stafford, a veteran of the California gold

---

[61]Murray, "Trading Posts."

[62]Robert Vaughn, *Then and Now*, (Minneapolis, Tribune Printing Company, 1900), p. 22 ff.

[63]William W. Alderson, "Across the Great Plains to Montana, 1864," typescript, Special Collections, Montana State University Library, Bozeman.

[64]William E. Atchison, "Diary of 1864," typescript, Montana State University Library, Bozeman.

[65]Stuart, *Forty Years*. See index.

[66]Letters of E. A. Maynard, Bozeman, March 20 and April 7, 1936, typescript, Wyoming State Archives and Historical Department.

[67]Franklin L. Kirkaldie, "Letters of May 1, 1864-March 30, 1869," typescript, Montana State University Library, Bozeman.

rush, who registered his arrival on August 24 at the Yellowstone after a forty-three day passage. A Bozeman Trail company found this outfit camped at present Livingston on August 25, and Stafford's obituary[68] reveals that he remained to help establish the new diggings at Emigrant Gulch, a few miles south up the Yellowstone. Still another train included the family of young Tom LeForge[69], destined to live among the Crows and win fame as an army scout; he disclosed that he came by the Bridger route late in the season with a trader's outfit from St. Joseph under Molette and Gus Beauvais, the latter presumably Francis Augustus Beauvais, the brother of Geminien P. Beauvais[70], a well-known Indian trader on the Platte.

In the meantime, Jim Bridger was piloting a few disillusioned gold-seekers back over his trail. William E. Atchison met him on the Bridger detour on July 21, and Franklin Kirkaldie did the same at Greybull River on August 1. On reaching Fort Laramie he was promptly re-hired as post scout, with his contract apparently pre-dated to August 3[71]. This employment was brief, however, for he left Red Buttes again on September 18 to make his second trip of the season to Montana. The diary of John Owen[72], a proprietor of Fort Owen in the Bitterroot valley a little south of Missoula, Montana, reveals that this party traveled very slowly, shortening the trail and doing considerable road work before reaching the Big Horn crossing. Sickness and straying oxen delayed their arrival at the Stinking Water until November 1, when Owen's diary terminated. Another member of the hapless party, Samuel Anderson, registered his arrival in Virginia City on December 18, having left the wagons snowbound on the Yellowstone. When Bridger returned is not of record, but all his work went for naught, as his trail carried no traffic in ensuing years.

Only three major trains are known to have ventured over the rival Bozeman Trail in 1864. Although Bozeman himself successfully piloted the lead outfit, it did not leave the lower Platte bridge until after half a dozen trains had departed on Bridger's route. Dr. Burlingame's analysis[73] has long since puntured the once-popular myth that Bridger and Bozeman raced neck-and-neck

[68]Joseph Stafford obituary, *Helena Independent*, March 21, 1915.
[69]Thomas B. Marquis, *Memoirs of a White Crow Indian*, (New York: The Century Company, 1928), p. 4 ff.
[70]Charles E. Hanson, "Geminien P. Beauvais," *Mountain Men*, Vol. 7, p. 35.
[71]Alter, *Bridger*, p. 309.
[72]Seymour Dunbar and Paul C. Phillips, *Journal and Letters of Major John Owen, 1850-71*, (New York: Edward Eberstadt, 1927), Vol. 1, p. 309ff.
[73]Burlingame, "Bozeman."

across the wilderness, and the present findings scotch it entirely by furnishing refined dates for the passages of both.

If Bozeman had indeed wintered in Omaha, he did not leave before late April, and whether alone or with recruited followers is unknown. Unfortunately, no known diarists accompanied his outfit. The best we have are the reminiscences of John T. Smith[74], a veteran of the California gold rush, who overtook Bozeman on the cut-off, and three pioneers who registered their arrivals with Bozeman's own train.

The first mention of Bozeman while he was still on the Platte road appears in the reminiscences of Robert Vaughn, who traveled the Bridger trail with diarist James Roberts in Joe Knight's company. Neither at Fort Laramie on May 30, nor at the lower bridge on June 7, does Roberts mention Bozeman or his cut-off, but Vaughn recalled that he met the guide assembling a train for his route. He located this at Fort Laramie and adds that he also met Joe Knight there and chose his train; but Robert's record proves that the latter occurred at the lower bridge. The fact that Vaughn had a choice of cut-offs implies that by June 7 Bozeman was at the lower bridge recruiting wagons.

The next mention of Bozeman appears in the diary of William Atchison, who reached the lower bridge on June 20. Having noted that the Bozeman cut-off began there, he recorded: "Had quite a discussion whether this or the Bridger cut-off should be taken. The Bridger men prevailed and we drove five miles further to upper Platte bridge." This wording suggests that at least some wagons were there, committed to the Bozeman trail, but not Bozeman himself who had already left. Further evidence will be presented to support this inference.

This preliminary evidence indicates that Bozeman's train left the Platte road between July 7 and July 20, an interval covered by no other available diaries, but we must pause to reject the previous best-guess date of July 1. It stems from a single, second-hand source, a son's uncritical editing of skimpy notes left by father Albert J. Dickson[75], who took the Lander route. Easily recognizable events recounted in this speculative expansion, when dated at all, are sometimes off by weeks! It cites July 1 as the date on a note, left on the trail by friends ahead, advising that they were leaving on Bozeman's trail, the editor implying with Bozeman himself. Unfortunately, this departure date applies to a late component of the Townsend train, which *followed* Bozeman, as we shall see.

---

[74]John T. Smith, "The Bozeman Trail, 1864," *Bozeman Chronicle*, Dec. 30, 1891.

[75]Arthur J. Dickson, *Covered Wagon Days*, (Cleveland: The Arthur H. Clark Co., 1929).

We can fix the date of Bozeman's departure as on or about June 18, by reasoning from information in the reminiscences of John T. Smith. He reached the lower bridge the day before Bozeman left, and after resting his stock, he followed on the third day after Bozeman left. Mitch Boyer, speeding alone on horseback, overtook Smith, who gave him a message asking Bozeman to wait two days. Smith then joined the waiting Bozeman at the Powder River crossing, the site of future Fort Reno about ninety-six miles out. Smith agreed to help Bozeman, but by following immediately behind so as to avoid Bozeman's fee of five dollars. They then proceeded in tandem for another 154 miles, passing the site of future Fort Phil Kearny and on to the Big Horn crossing at the site of future Fort C. F. Smith. There they celebrated the Fourth of July, the only date Smith gives, before tackling the difficult ford the next day.

Assuming the tandem trains traveled a standard fifteen miles a day, their arrival at the Big Horn on July 4 implies a departure from Powder River on June 27. If the overtaking Smith made sixteen miles day from the lower bridge, he had arrived there June 17, left on the 21, and Bozeman preceded him on the 18th. And if Bozeman left on the 18th, he made fourteen miles a day and waited two days at Powder River for Smith to overtake him.

This now suggests that when Atchison reached the bridge on June 20, he found Smith there on the eve of departure, and this prompted the debate, in which the Bridger men prevailed, probably because Smith's outfit was too small for safety. If we assume either faster or slower rates of travel, it jeopardizes this whole framework of close timing. We therefore adopt June 18 as Bozeman's departure date, at least until some direct diary entry calls for revision.

On leaving the Big Horn, the tandem trains headed northwest to strike the Yellowstone about two miles below present Billings, as Smith recalled. They then turned southwest, ascending the river to the mouth of Clarks Fork, then up the latter and its Rock Creek branch to present Boyd. This was the detour that added twenty-five extra miles. Jim Bridger in 1866 would eliminate this hog-leg by taking a rougher passage straight west from the Big Horn to present Pryor on Pryor's Fork and present Edgar on Clarks Fork. Picking up the tracks of Bridger's earlier trains, Bozeman followed them to and beyond the Yellowstone ferry. Smith recalled also that part of the company took Bozeman's Pass, while he himself diverged over Bridger's detour.

By this time terminal scattering was spreading the arrivals at Virginia City. Only John L. Sweeney's arrival there on August 3 has been previously noted in the pioneer register, but both Isaac Dean and H. A. McAllister, who also specified traveling in Bozeman's own train, registered their arrivals on July 29. Bozeman and Smith must also have arrived at this earlier date, for Smith says that after a few days in the city the pair trekked back to the Gallatin Valley, arriving in time to figure in the first formal meeting of the Bozeman Townsite Association on August 9[76].

It was thus Bozeman, with no contribution from Jacobs, but with some trail-prospecting assistance from John T. Smith, who successfully piloted the first emigrants over the trail that deservedly bears his name. He made the passage safely, without Indian interference, in forty-two days, including prospecting layovers. This transit time affords further assurance that our calculated departure date is not likely to be far wrong. (Clearly, Bozeman and Bridger ran no race. Both traveled leisurely, with Bozeman starting a month later and arriving three weeks later than Bridger.)

The ill-fated Townsend train, also of emigrant composition, was the second to venture over the Bozeman trail. Its components had passed the scenes of several Indian raids along the Platte road above Fort Laramie, and would itself suffer a severe attack on the cut-off. How early it began to assemble is not clear, but when diarist Kate Dunlap[77], heading for the Lander route, reached the lower bridge on June 27, she found "a number of wagons preparing to leave" by the new cut-off.

Several groups that left the Platte over a period of five days finally consolidated themselves out on the trail. Diarist T. J. Brundage[78] left with the first group, as noted by Kate Dunlap, on June 29. Diarist Benjamin W. Ryan[79] followed with another section the next day. "E. W.,"[80] who wrote a letter about their Indian battle to the *Montana Post*, just established at Virginia City, left with the last group on July 1st. By July 3, all had reached the rendezvous some thirty-four miles out.

While waiting for the late groups, Brundage and Ryan recorded that on July 1 they held an election of officers that chose A. A. Townsend of Wisconsin as captain. Brundage said they hired two French guides for $600 to pilot them as far as the Big Horn crossing. Ryan gave the pay as $4 per wagon and named them as "John Boyer and Raphael Gogeor." while Zera French[81], another battle chronicler for the *Montana Post*, referred to "our old guide, Boyer." There can be no doubt that these were the Deer Creek traders of the previous year's aborted train, the French John Boyer and New Mexican Rafael Gallegos. We take these pains in

[76]Burlingame, "Bozeman."

[77]S. Lyman Tyler, ed., *Montana Gold Rush Diary of Kate Dunlap*, (Denver: Old West Publishing Co., 1969).

[78]Elsa Spear, ed., "Diary of T. J. Brundage, 1864," typescript, Montana State Historical Society Library.

[79]Benjamin W. Ryan, "Bozeman Trail Diary to Virginia City in 1864," *Annals of Wyoming*, July, 1947, p. 77.

[80]Letter of "E. W.," *Montana Post*, Aug. 27, 1864.

[81]Letter of Zera French, Sept. 5, 1864, *Montana Post*, Sept. 17, 1864.

order to correct the widely accepted, but much later and second-hand statements that these guides were young Mitch Boyer and John Richard, Jr.[82]

When the consolidated train resumed the trail on July 4, it was a large one. Our four sources agree that it totaled 150 wagons, 369 (one says 375) men, 36 women, 56 children, and arms representing 1641 shots without reloading. One source adds that they boasted 636 oxen, 79 horses, 10 mules, and 194 cows, with a total evaluation of $130,000! It was July 7 when the company halted for breakfast, eighty-six miles out according to Ryan, on the Dry Fork of Powder River some ten miles short of the site of future Fort Reno.

While preparing to resume the trek that fateful morning, a party of Indian warriors approached. John Boyer went out to parley and returned to report that they were Cheyennes under Spotted Cow, who had turned back Bozeman's train the year before, and therefore not to be trusted, although they pretended only to want grub. After the nervous company furnished some provisions, Boyer shooed the warriors from the wagons. Fearing for the safety of a Mr. Mills, who had gone back in search of a stray ox, a party of mounted men went to his aid. T. J. Brundage, a member of this party, named the five others as his brother George Brundage, Asher Newby, E. Butterfield, Mr. Noton, and Dr. Crepin, a Frenchman.

After this party had ridden back about two miles, the Indians swarmed to attack them. The six managed to fight their way back to the corraled train with some aid from a rescue party, bringing Asher Newby with an arrow through his back. When Dr. Crepin's efforts to extract the arrow failed, Dr. Hall, an English surgeon with some military experience, took over and succeeded, with eventual recovery of the patient.

The trainmen, well-armed with long-range weapons, countered Indian efforts to burn them out and held them off in a battle that raged for several hours. As the sole casualty in this phase, A. Warren fell with a severe abdominal wound that proved fatal during the night. But three other fatalities occurred outside the corral. Mr. Mills, in search of his strayed cattle, was missing; his scalp was found by a following train. Frank Huddlemeyer, out hunting, was riddled with arrows and butchered, while an unnamed man out prospecting never returned and was considered killed.

The shaken train buried the bodies of Warren and Huddle-meyer, and the next day resolutely resumed its progress. On reaching the Big Horn, July 20, Boyer and Gallegos turned back,

---

[82]David B. Weaver, "Capt. Townsend's Battle on Powder River," *Montana Historical Society Contributions,* Vol. 8, p. 283.

as planned, carrying the train's mail. The company then followed Bozeman's detour to the Yellowstone and turned to pick up Bridger's trail. They made several halts for prospecting, one such party being run in by a horde of Crow Indians but without casualties. They did not reach the Yellowstone ferry until August 15. The passage took fifty-eight days, for Brundage did not roll in to Virginia City until August 25th, nor Ryan until two days later.

The third and final train on the Bozeman cut-off was composed of avid prospectors, many of whom diverged to the new gold strike at Emigrant Gulch. Diarists Richard Owens[83] and John Hackney[84] and reminiscence-recorder David B. Weaver[85] all reached the lower bridge on July, where they waited for more wagons to gather. On the 12th they moved a short distance out on the trail and waited some more. When sixty-seven wagons had assembled, they organized into four sections, each under its own captain, but all under Major Cyrus C. Coffinbury. On July 16 they started the journey in earnest.

It was this train that discovered the scalp of Mr. Mills and the ravaged graves from the Townsend train. They also followed Bozeman's detour to the Yellowstone, but halted longer for prospecting. After crossing at the Yellowstone ferry, they camped near present Livingston on August 25. There they found Captain Stafford's company, which had come by Bridger's trail, awaiting the return of emissaries they had sent upstream to Emigrant Gulch. The Coffinbury train followed suit, waiting several days. A good many from both trains decided to try their luck there, arriving on August 27, as told by David Weaver. Hackney and Owens soon proceeded on to reach Virginia City on September 8 to complete the slow passage of fifty-nine days.

Canny Jim Bridger had solved the problem of a safe cut-off to Montana in 1864, but his route was promptly abandoned for reasons that remain obscure. The trail Bozeman pioneered that same season was easier to travel, but proved increasingly perilous. Emigrants dared not risk this route in 1865, because of the outbreak of Indian hostilities and General Patrick E. Connor's Powder River Campaign against the hostiles later that summer.

To protect the heavy emigrant and merchant travel over Bozeman's trail in 1866, General Henry B. Carrington brought out a sizeable force of troops to establish and garrison new Forts Reno, Phil Kearny, and C. F. Smith. But their arrival before the consent

[83]Richard Owen, "Diary, Omaha to Idaho, 1864," typescript, Montana Historical Society Library.

[84]John S. Hackney, "Over the Plains to the Idaho-Montana Gold Fields in 1864," typescript, Montana Historical Society Library.

[85]David B. Weaver, "Early Days in Emigrant Gulch," *Montana Historical Society Contributions,* Vol. 7, p. 73.

of the Indians had been obtained merely provoked what has come to be known as Red Cloud's War, which christened the road, "the bloody Bozeman trail." Bloody it was indeed, for in the spring of 1867 John Bozeman started from Bozeman for Fort C. F. Smith, only to meet death at the hands of some raiding Blackfeet Indians on the "safest" segment of the trail. The war ended with the Sioux treaty of 1868, which called for the abandonment of the Bozeman trail and its "protective" forts—until re-conquered in the Sioux War of 1876.[86]

In the meantime, however, the completion of the Union Pacific Railroad in 1869 had furnished Montana with improved overland communications with both the east and west.

---

[86]John S. Gray, *Centennial Campaign, The Sioux War of 1876*, (Fort Collins: The Old Army Press, 1976).

In Wyoming

Did you ever see the sunrise
    And the high and rolling plains?
Did you ever smell wet sagebrush
    After sudden springtime rain?
Have you ever felt the smart
    And sting of gravel in your face?
Then you've never known the
    Glamour of that God-forsaken place—Wyoming.

Have you seen the clear cut sky line
    When the evening shadows fall?
When the mountains look like cardboard
    and you hear the coyote's call?
Have you seen the painted badlands
    In their yellow, red and blue?
Then you'll never know how lonesome
    Life can be until you do—in Wyoming.

Have you seen the sand and sagebrush
    Stretch for miles and miles away?
While down the hills along the draws
    The cooling shadows lay?
It's lonesome and it's desolate—
    It's off the beaten track
But once you've caught the lure of it
    You're homesick till you're back—in Wyoming.

—By Mrs. Cecil Howrey
W.P.A. Manuscripts Collection, No. 760
Wyoming State Archives and Historical
Department

Asa S. Mercer and "The Banditti of the Plains": A Reappraisal

By

CHARLES HALL

Charles "Pat" Hall, executive director of the Wyoming Bicentennial Commission, became interested in Asa Mercer and his book, *Banditti of the Plains,* long before he moved to Wyoming. Hall had been a part-time dealer in books about the American West, so he knew the accepted version of the story about the cattlemen's suppression of Mercer's book.

When he moved to Cheyenne Hall began his own investigation into the book's history. Over a period of three or four years he found much to add to the story at the Historical Research and Publications Division of the Wyoming State Archives and Historical Department and at the Western History Research Center at the University of Wyoming. He also visited with the Mercer family at Hyattville, and was allowed to borrow documents, including Mercer's own business journal, for microfilming. He has also talked extensively with Anita Webb Deininger, Buffalo, Mercer's granddaughter.

His biggest find was at a garage sale in Cheyenne. The family of John Charles Thompson, long-time editor of the Wyoming State Tribune, was selling items that had been stored in the family garage. Hall bought an orange crate filled with documents relating to the Johnson County War. Included was the only known extant copy of the October 16, 1892, edition of *The Northwestern Live Stock Journal,* the Mercer publication the cattlemen actually did attempt to suppress.

From this find and others Hall has attempted to piece together the story, based somewhat upon logical supposition, about what really happened when Mercer's book, *The Banditti of the Plains,* was published in 1894.—Editor.

Once upon a time, there was a book printed in Cheyenne which told the true story of Wyoming state officials' complicity in the arson and murder of the Johnson County Cattle War.

The "cattle barons" couldn't afford to have the truth known, so they secured a court injunction against the book's publication and illegally confiscated all remaining copies. Then they raided the author's printing shop; beat him up; destroyed the plates of the book; broke up his press and burned the building to the ground.[1]

Later, these same cattlemen burned almost all known copies of

---

[1] N. Orwin Rush, *Mercer's Banditti of the Plains,* (Tallahassee: Florida State University Library, 1961), p. 13.

the book, but a few were saved and spirited out of the state during a wild, midnight ride across the Colorado state line.[2]

The book's publication and the cattlemen's suppression of it were completely ignored by the contemporary press, indicating that a conspiracy of silence existed among local newspaper editors.[3]

During the ensuing years since the book first came out in 1894, copies of it have been stolen from Wyoming public libraries or mutilated, thereby destroying the incriminating evidence. Even the copies in the Library of Congress were stolen.[4]

The newspaper published by the book's author was also suppressed. Very few copies of it survive today and the cattlemen have even stolen district court records of law suits involving the author of the book.[5]

Today, this book, *The Banditti of the Plains,* is one of the choicest items in the field of Western Americana. Even a copy in poor condition of the 1894 edition will bring $200 or more at auction or private sale.

With the exception of the facts about the book's value, every bit of the foregoing is just a fairy tale. How this wild legend was ever started is unknown, but it continues to be foisted off on the public today. Such scholarly institutions as the University of Oklahoma Press, for example, have been duped by the tale.

The evidence to disprove the suppression story was always there. Why it wasn't found by other writers is puzzling. Perhaps, it was "too good a story" to ruin—too much a part of the Western mystique.

That mystique actually began with the Johnson County Cattle War and has grown in volume and importance to this very day. All our contemporary preoccupation with the romance of the cowboy can be traced right back to this one conflict between "cattle barons" and "rustlers". Even the very meaning of the word "rustler" was changed by the Johnson County War. So, it is difficult to overstate the importance of this incident in the development of the west. The Johnson County War "signified an accomplishment social and political revolution."[6]

Likewise, the suppression of a book is important, if it really happened. In the history of printing in this country, there have been very few attempts at suppression. This writer knows of only

---

[2]Letter, Phillip A. Rollins to James T. Gerould, Oct. 12, 1923, reproduced in the University of Oklahoma Press reprint of *The Banditti of the Plains,* Norman, 1954, p. xiv.

[3]Rush, *Mercer's Banditti,* p. 43.

[5]*Ibid,* p. 45.

[4]Asa S. Mercer, *The Banditti of the Plains,* (Norman: University of Oklahoma Press, 1954), xxxv.

[5]*Ibid,* p. 45.

[6]Phillip A. Rollins, *The Cowboy,* (New York: Scribners, 1936), p. 344.

three such attempts — all, interestingly, in the field of Western Americana. *The Banditti of the Plains* is supposed to have been one. The other two were *A Cowboy Detective,* by Charles Siringo, and *The XIT Ranch and the Early Days of the Llano Estacado,* by J. Evetts Haley. The Siringo and Haley books also contained material that defamed certain well-known characters. Court injunctions against the publications of both books resulted in changes in the offensive material.

Only *Banditti* is thought to have been suppressed by illegal means, hence the importance of proving or disproving the suppression story once and for all.

The Banditti of the Plains was written by Asa Shinn Mercer and was published in 1894. It told, for the first time in book form, of the complicity of Wyoming's elected officials in the so-called Invasion of Johnson County by members of the Wyoming Stockgrowers Association and their hired Texas gunmen in April of 1892.

Since the cattlemen had committed premeditated murder and arson and suborned state officials, including the governor, it was easy to believe that the later suppression of Mercer's book would have been the least of their crimes.

Mercer was a western publicist and newspaperman. He had been first president of the University of Washington. Were it not for his later links with the Johnson County War, Mercer had assured himself of a permanent niche in the history of the West in 1866, when he took a shipload of single women to the bachelor settlers of Washington Territory.[7]

Since Mercer left no known memoirs, and almost no documentary evidence exists to prove or disprove the suppression story, it is necessary to know something of Mercer's background and business dealings in order to render some judgement about his reasons for writing the book and its alleged suppression. If we can disprove some salient parts of the suppression story, then it is logical to assume that all of it is probably false.

Mercer left Washington Territory in 1876 and moved to Texas where he edited and/or published, in rapid succession, four newspapers: the Bowie *Cross Timbers,* the Vernon *Guard,* the Wichita Falls *Herald,* and the Mobeettie *Panhandle.* In April, 1883, Mercer was attending a livestock meeting in Dodge City, Kansas, when he met S. A. Marney, the "roving commissioner" for the *Texas Live Stock Journal* of Fort Worth. It was Marney who suggested they form a partnership to publish a livestock-oriented paper in Cheyenne, Wyoming, where the cattle trade was then booming.

---

[7]Delphine Henderson, "Asa Shinn Mercer, Northwest Publicity Agent", *Reed College Bulletin,* January, 1945, pp. 21-32.

Mercer thought it was a good idea and advanced Marney the money necessary for a two-month canvass "among the cattlemen and business firms of the city and territory."[8]   Then Mercer went to St. Louis where he purchased a press, type and the necessary office fixtures.   The St. Louis Type Foundry had done business with Mercer when he was proprietor of the papers in Texas.   That firm sold him the material he needed on credit.   The total cost of the Country Campbell press, type and fixtures was something in excess of $3000.

Meanwhile, Marney had secured an office in Cheyenne in the old Wyoming Block, on the south side of 17th Street between Thomes and O'Neil Avenues, near the present downtown area.

The first issue of the *Northwestern Live Stock Journal* came out on Friday, November 23, 1883.   It was an ambitious eight-page effort.   J. B. Morrow, editor of the *Cheyenne Daily Leader,* gave the new publication a paragraph in his issue of November 25, noting: "The first number of the *Northwestern Live Stock Journal* came out yesterday.(sic)˙ It is bright and newsy and presents a very neat appearance.   There seems to be no reason why it should not succeed."

And succeed it did.   During the first few months, the success of the paper seemed to be phenomenal.   The *Stock Journal* soon increased from eight to sixteen pages on alternate issues and rival Cheyenne editors were appalled at the new publication's ability to solicit advertising.[9]

In the spring of 1884, Mercer gave Marney a full half-interest in the firm, but the solicitor soon began to be a liability.   The original agreement between the two men specified that Mercer was to be in charge of all editorial and office decisions and that Marney was to spend all his time on the road, soliciting business and advertising for the paper. ˙

Marney suddenly developed a dislike for travel and began to meddle in office affairs.   He had previously installed his brother-in-law, Frank J. Burton, in the office as bookkeeper.   Matters came to a head˙on July 21, 1884, when Marney returned from a week on the road to find that Mercer had fired Burton and hired a man named Trimble to take his place.   Marney demanded that Mercer reinstate Burton and in the ensuing argument Marney called Mercer "a damned liar."   Mercer hit Marney in the˙face and the two partners fell over the office railing in the ensuing struggle.[10] ˙

At this point, Editor John F. Carroll of the *Cheyenne Demo-*

---

[8]*Cheyenne Daily Leader,* July 22, 1884.
[9]*Cheyenne Daily Sun,* July 23, 1884.
[10]*Cheyenne Democratic Leader,* July 22, 1884.

cratic Leader takes over the story. Carroll tells it with much relish, getting in his first digs at the seemingly successful Mercer and Marney. The *Democratic Leader* devoted two full columns to the fight in the July 22 edition titling the story "A Woman's Weapon—She Smashes a Spittoon on a Man's Head."

> "Mrs. Annie F. Mercer, the wife of A. S. Mercer, then appeared in the arena. Incensed and violent, she caught up a large majolica spittoon which was close at hand and made an attempt to go to the rescue of her struggling husband. This time Burton caught her and disarmed her while Moore (another employee) made vigorous attempts to pull Marney off and separate the two men.
>
> "Just at this point a new element of belligerency made its appearance in the persons of two children, a girl about ten years of age and a boy somewhat older, both children of Mercer, who came to the rescue, each with a rock in hand ready to strike a blow for their father.
>
> "In order to head off this new danger, Burton let go of Mrs. Mercer and blocked the way so as to prevent these children from interfering. Released now and with opportunity, Mrs. Mercer again snatched up the spittoon and rushing around to where she could get the proper opening she dealt Marney a terrible blow on the back of the head, lacerating it in a dreadful manner and breaking the spittoon into a dozen fragments."[11]

That ended the fracas. A doctor was summoned to treat Marney's wounds—fortunately they proved to be superficial—and brother-in-law Frank Burton dashed away to file charges of aggravated assault against Mr. and Mrs. Mercer. Later in the day, Laramie County Prosecuting Attorney Frank Baird and Dr. Hunt, who had dressed Marney's wounds, appeared before a judge and requested that the charge against Mrs. Mercer be changed to assault with a deadly weapon (majolica spittoon) with intent to kill.[11]

Mercer paid a fine of $10 and costs, but his spirited wife had to post bond of $1000 pending her later appearance in district court. The charges, however, were later dropped.

Needless to say, this spelled the end of the Mercer-Marney partnership in the *Northwestern Live Stock Journal*. Mercer scraped up $2000 somewhere to buy out Marney's interest and sent his former partner packing.

During the next few days a lot of unanswered questions about the *Stock Journal's* success were going to be asked again and answers would be forthcoming. The first answer came the next day when the sheriff served a writ of attachment on the newspaper office to satisfy a claim of $457.90 filed against Marney by Francis E. Warren. It seems Marney had purchased furniture on credit from the Warren Mercantile Co., and then neglected to pay.

---

[11]The doughty Mrs. Mercer was one of the "belles" he had transported to Washington Territory.

Before the day was out, other Cheyenne business firms had served their own papers on the down-but-not-yet-out newspaper. Craig, Davis & Company held a bill against Mercer to the amount of $347 for furniture the editor had ordered for his new home. A painter named J. E. Tuttle served notice that Mercer owed him $60 for decorating costs on the same house.

During the next few days, Mercer and his attorneys did their best to scrape up enough to pay off the debts. First a mortgage of $1,064 was given to the Warren Mercantile Co. Mercer gave a similar mortgage on his furniture and carriage to Craig, Davis & Co.[12]

Then Mercer began hounding Thomas Sturgis, secretary of the Wyoming Stock Growers Association, to pay the money that group owed him for printing the WSGA's 1884 Brand Book. Sturgis came through on July 29 with an odd amount, $499.24, which was evidently just the sum needed by Mercer at the time, no more, no less.

Mercer paid $143.30 to the Stockgrower's National Bank "in satisfaction of the promissory note of Mercer & Marney" and a payment of $305.04 went to the St. Louis Type Foundry.[13] The *Stock Journal* was finally back in business again—mortgaged to the hilt, but back in business.

In the years to follow between 1884 and 1892, Mercer was involved in a series of problems with the newspaper's creditors. Only the fanciest of financial footwork kept the publication out of receivership and records indicate that some of the creditors never did get their money. The records of these lawsuits are still filed in the Laramie County District Court Clerk's office and there are no indications that any records have been tampered with or stolen.[14]

Mercer continued to publish the *Stock Journal* without interruption. In September of 1887 he relinquished total control over the newspaper in favor of a "partnership" of sorts with Thomas B. Adams, then secretary of the Wyoming Stock Growers Association. An entry in one of Mercer's business journals, found by the author, shows that "Asa S. Mercer has this day by bill of sale transferred all the material presses, cases, imposing stones, etc used in printing the *Northwestern Live Stock Journal* to the Northwestern Live Stock Journal Publishing Company. Officers, A. S. Mercer, President and Thomas B. Adams, Secretary."[15]

---

[12]*Cheyenne Democrati Leader,* July 24, 1884.

[13]Manuscript receipt, Wyoming Stock Growers Association collection, Western History Research Center, Laramie.

[14]See State Journal Company vs. A. S. Mercer, Civil Appearance Docket 5-196; A. S. Mercer vs. St. Louis Type Foundry, 5-130, and Annie Mercer vs. St. Louis Type Foundry, 5-329, Laramie County District Court records.

[15]"Scrapbook of Asa Mercer," p. 242, loaned by the Don Mercer family,

A check of WSGA records for the same period fails to reveal any official sanction of Adams' part in this rather odd publishing arrangement, but the inference is obvious.   Thomas Adams, full time apologist for the WSGA, would surely use his good offices in the publishing company to make sure "the voice of the cattleman was heard in the land."

In the fall of 1892 the cattlemen and the Republican party did make an attempt to suppress one particular issue of the paper. That issue—of October 14, 1892—contained the famous "Confession of George Dunning", who was one of the hired gunmen on the invasion of Johnson County.   Dunning's story of how he was hired by H. B. Ijams, then secretary of the Wyoming Stock Growers Association, "for $5 a day wages . . . and $50 bounty for every man that was killed by the mob in the raid on Johnson County" set Wyoming right on its ear.

Coming less than three weeks before Election Day, the "Dunning Confession", though undoubtedly true, was well calculated to turn the tide of victory over to the Democrats.   The Republicans were the party in office in April of that year when the Johnson County War had taken place.   A Republican governor, Amos Barber, did everything in his power to help the invaders on their mission.   The Democratic party knew the damning effect Dunning's confession would have upon Republican chances for an election victory and ordered 24,000 extra copies printed to distribute throughout the state.[16]

The regular issue of the *Stock Journal* had been printed and gone out through the mails to some 1400 subscribers on Friday, October 14.   While Mercer's printers labored through Saturday to produce a sufficient number of copies for the Democratic party, the Republicans and cattlemen labored to think of a way to stop them.

They finally dragged out an old judgement of $1439.80, first secured against Mercer in 1891.   The sheriff had already served papers on this judgement a couple of times and "no property could be found."   The judgement in favor of the St. Louis Type Foundry was against Mercer and he had put everything into his wife's name.

The sheriff was ordered to serve the papers again by none other than Wyoming's Attorney General Potter, who was also implicated by the Dunning Confession and who just happened to be representing the St. Louis Type Foundry in the matter!

So, the Republicans succeeded in closing down the *Stock Journal* office for two weeks and confiscated the 24,000 "hand-

Hyattville, for microfilming, Roll H-193a, Historical Research and Publications Division, Wyoming State Archives and Historical Department, Cheyenne.
16*Cheyenne Daily Sun,* October 18, 1892.

bills" printed for the Democrats but they could do nothing about the copies already mailed out or sold on the streets. Editor John Carroll of the *Democratic Leader* said: ". . . one thing is certain, the paper was in enormous demand and would have sold like hotcakes on a frosty morning if copies could be anywhere purchased. During yesterday a dollar and even more was freely offered for a single copy of the paper. Those in town were worn threadbare with assiduous reading."[17]

It was probably from this incident alone that the legend of suppression sprang. It has all the important parts—court injunction against the paper, closing down the printing office, confiscation of remaining issues—and undoubtedly, the Republicans and cattlemen burned those 24,000 copies of "Dunning's Confession" that were so illegally confiscated. But this had been the newspaper, not the book. The incident took place in 1892, not 1894. And no one destroyed the press and type or burned down the building.

One other similarity should be mentioned. The "Dunning Confession" was also an important part of *The Banditti of the Plains.* It was reprinted verbatim in that book. So true stories about a raid on Mercer's print shop and confiscation of the "Dunning Confession" could easily have come down to us as an attempt to suppress the book two years later.

Until recently, there were no known copies of the *Northwestern Live Stock Journal* in existence after 1887, leading some students of the period to speculate that the cattlemen must have done a much more comprehensive job of suppression than just one issue.[18]

The simple, unromantic facts are that many such newspapers did not survive because there was no reason to save them at the time. As we live through history day by day in our own periodicals, few of us have the foresight to save any of them or the descrimination to know which ones to save.

Thus it becomes extremely difficult to place in proper perspective Asa S. Mercer's part in the Johnson County War. All we have today to go on are brief mentions in other contemporary newspapers, often biased politically, and a few scattered clippings in the Francis E. Warren scrapbooks at the Western History Research Center at the University of Wyoming.

It is interesting to speculate that the Johnson County Cattle War might never have taken place had it not been for an editorial that appeared in the *Stock Journal* in June of 1889. It is just as interesting—and even less a speculation—to theorize that the true story of what happened in that conflict would never have been told had

[17]*Cheyenne Democratic Leader,* October 17, 1892.
[18]The writer had the good fortune to discover a copy of the *Stock Journal* of October 14, 1892, the same copy which contains the "Dunning Confession." It is believed to be unique.

it not been for Mercer's decision to print the "Confession" of George Dunning.

If the foregoing sounds like the editor did a bit of jumping from one side of the fence to the other, such was certainly the case.

The extent of Mercer's loyalty to the cattlemen who patronized his paper was shown in June of 1889 following the tragic lynching of James Averell and "Cattle Kate" Watson, alleged "rustlers". Mercer applauded the murders in print and advocated more:

> "There is but one remedy and that is a freer use of the hanging noose. Cattle owners should organize and not disband until a hundred rustlers were left ornamenting the trees and telegraph poles of the territory. The hanging of the two culprits merely acts as a stimulus to the thieves. Hang a hundred and the balance will reform or quit the country. Let the good work go on and lose no time about it."[19]

Could this editorial have been the framework of an idea that led to the eventual planning of the Johnson County "Invasion?" Mercer was certainly privy to most of the stockmen's plans and, according to the later story of one cattleman, actually helped plan the "Invasion."

Thus, if Mercer had been the paid hireling of the cattlemen through the good years, then turned against them following their incredible attempt at wholesale murder in 1892, it is easy to understand why they held him in such contempt.

The picture of the courageous editor who printed the truth in the face of economic coercion and legal and physical harassment begins to pale before such evidence. Mercer had had ample time and innumerable opportunities to become "the courageous editor" before. It was only when he knew that the cattle business was in a terrible slump and felt quite sure the cattlemen were in a fix they'd never get out of that he suddenly acquired his "courage."

Mercer acted out of expediency. He had long-range plans to turn the *Stock Journal* into a Democratically aligned general circulation newspaper.[20] If his publication of the "Dunning Confession" turned the tide at the polls in November of 1892—and it did—he expected political patronage from the new administration to help save his failing newspaper. He could not know that problems within the Democratic administration and the financial crash of 1893 would alter these plans.

Mercer's motives for writing *The Banditti of the Plains* have also been set forth as altruistic. This is scarcely the case. He only

---

[19]*Northwestern Live Stock Journal,* quoted in the Laramie *Boomerang,* August 31, 1889.

[20]The first issue of the *Wyoming Democrat* came out in early February of 1893. Evidence indicates that Mercer continued to publish the *Stock Journal* for a few weeks after that. He sold his press, type and equipment to J. D. Hurd on July 19, 1893.

began to write the book after the *Stock Journal* and its sucessor, the *Wyoming Democrat,* had failed. As the new, and somewhat self-appointed apologist for Democratic-Populist principles in Wyoming, Mercer hoped that his book would influence the election of 1894 in the same way that the "Dunning Confession" had influenced the election of 1892.

Besides the word-of-mouth folklore that is still bandied about by those in Cheyenne old enough to recall the first faint stirrings of the Mercer-*Banditti* legend, a significant amount of false information has been put into public print.

Prime examples are two of the popular reprints of *Banditti,* one by the Grabhorn Press and another by the University of Oklahoma Press. The forewords to both of these books have given far too much credence to the legend of the suppression of the first edition.

The foreword to the Grabhorn Press edition was written by James Mitchell Clarke, son of A. B. Clarke, one of the "Invaders." Clarke wrote:

> "The book had scarcely appeared when a court order was handed down commanding that all the plates and all copies remaining in the publisher's hands be destroyed."

In the foreword to the later reprint by the University of Oklahoma Press, William H. Kittrell wrote:

> "For his boldness in publishing this provocative book, Mercer paid dearly. Copies of the books were seized and burned. He was jailed. The plates were destroyed . . . his publication was closed down, and he never completely recouped his fortunes."

These are the standard litanies of Mercer's difficulties, but there is absolutely no proof to justify the book-suppression stories when a researcher tries to run them down.

Only two men "who were there" have left any documentary evidence to prove or disprove the suppression of the book. One was Phillip Ashton Rollins who was, among other things, the author of a book entitled, *The Cowboy,* published by Scribners in 1922.

Rollins was the owner of a copy of the first edition of *Banditti.* He presented it to Princeton University librarian James T. Gerould in 1923 with a covering letter that said in part:

> "The book was printed in 1894, was advertised, and was immediately suppressed by a court injunction in the course of a law suit instituted in Wyoming. All of the books printed were impounded and placed in the basement of a building in Cheyenne, to await the day when they would be destroyed by burning. There being ways and ways of procuring desirable things, several hundred of the books found themselves one night in a wagon drawn by galloping horses and headed for the Colorado line. The copy handed you herewith was one of those which began that night ride on the wagon. The marks on the back flyleaf represent in part, I am told, the doings of the fire hose that was called into play for a few moments. You will recognize some of the other

marks as indicating the course of bullets. I saw these bullets started on their way."

And from this, too, sprang the legend. It is interesting to note that Rollins wrote 390 pages about the cattle industry and the romance of *The Cowboy* and never once mentioned the alleged "midnight ride" to Colorado. If he "was there"—if he "saw these bullets started on their way"—why didn't he record the details of this unique incident in his book? This writer believes that Rollins was probably in the vicinity of Cheyenne in 1892 and "heard" from someone about the raid on the newspaper and the confiscation of the "Dunning Confession" handbills. After acquiring a copy of *Banditti*, he concocted the story of the "midnight ride" to Colorado and his participation in it to explain the rumors he might have heard about the book.

Another man who "was there" was Ralph Mercer, son of *Banditti's* author. In answer to a written query from Lola Homsher, Wyoming State Historian, in 1954, Ralph Mercer wrote:

This is fiction. Father's book was never suppressed by court injunction nor was he ever jailed.[21]

There is a preponderance of secondary evidence to dispute the suppression story. For instance, a thorough search of the Laramie County District Court records shows there was never a court action of any kind brought against the book. Dockets and files agree in numerical order and there are no missing records of any kind.

N. Orwin Rush claims he searched Cheyenne newspapers and there was absolutely no mention of the publication of the book, nor its suppression. He implies a "conspiracy of silence" existed among other editors. This implication is ridiculous, given the volatile political and editorial climate of the times.

The book was printed in Denver at the job plant of *The Rocky Mountain News* under the supervision of Tom Patterson, editor of that paper, who was attempting to exert control over Democratic politics in Wyoming.

There was ample notice of the publication of the book in both Cheyenne newspapers, *The Cheyenne Daily Leader* and *The Cheyenne Daily Sun*. As a matter of fact, *The Cheyenne Daily Sun* published a lengthy review of the book in its August 22, 1894, edition.

When Mercer and son, Ralph, went on the road promoting the sale of the book, mention was made of their visits in the Lusk, Buffalo, Sheridan and Douglas newspapers.

---

[21]Ralph Mercer to Lola Homsher, June 9, 1954, Wyoming State Archives and Historical Department.

It is understandable that Mr. Rush could easily have missed paragraphs in the out-of-state papers, but how he avoided finding a full-column review in *The Cheyenne Daily Sun* is puzzling.

But the integral point of the suppression story concerns the "raid" of the cattlemen on Mercer's print shop and the destruction of his press and type and the burning of the building.

Assuming the incident—or any part of it—really happened, it is inconceivable that the contemporary press would have ignored it. Yet a painstaking search of all the available newspapers reveals no mention whatever of the alleged raid. A similar search of the records of the Cheyenne Fire Department shows that no call was made to 1713 Ferguson Avenue—where the *Stock Journal* was published—during the year 1894.

Yet the above paragraph is poor proof when compared with the fact that, in August of 1894 when *Banditti* was published, the *Northwestern Live Stock Journal* had been out of business for thirteen months!

How could the cattlemen have raided Mercer's office and destroyed his equipment in the fall of 1894 when he had sold that same equipment to J. D. Hurd in July of the previous year?

This evidence is irrefutable and proves that the raid on the print shop could not have taken place.[22]

There was a raid on the newspaper office and there was a "court injunction" and there was confiscation of printed material, but all these ingredients of the legend took place in 1892 and involved copies of the newspaper, not the book, which was published two years later when Mercer no longer had any printing facilities of his own.

Thus, in the light of research, the legend of the suppression of *Banditti of the Plains* and the motives of its author in writing the book do not hold water.

And it's a pity, too. Perhaps it was "too good a story" to ruin.

---

[22]*Cheyenne Daily Leader*, July 20, 1893. The item reads: "A few weeks ago, without any preliminary convulsions, the *Live Stock Journal* passed quietly out of existence. Yesterday, J. D. Hurd, late of the *Evanston Register*, leased the plant and will conduct a weekly as was issued in the past."

Black Hills Sooners:
The Davy Expedition of 1868

By

GRANT K. ANDERSON

"Great Overland Expedition to the Black Hills," boomed Yankton's *Union and Dakotaian* of December 14, 1867. The front page article announced plans for a caravan to depart from Yankton, Dakota Territory, the following spring under the leadership of Captain Peter B. Davy. It would, according to the *Union and Dakotaian,* "open up that beautiful and fertile region to settlement and cultivation and establish in her beautiful valleys a thriving and energetic people . . . who will prospect and bring to light the weight of her slumbering wealth and prospect her undeveloped and comparatively unknown mines." The coveted Black Hills gold fields would be opened at last to impatient miners.[1]

The immeasureable ore deposits of western Dakota Territory were rumored to exist in the early 1800s. Plains Indians undoubtedly knew gold existed in their sacred Papa Sapa. However, they were not eager to share this information with the fur traders and explorers moving onto the Great Plains. Despite this attempt at secrecy, tales of gold appeared as early as 1804. In that year a Frenchman, writing to the lieutenant governor of Louisiana, made reference to the presence of nuggets in the Black Hills.[2] Similar rumors appeared periodically during the next half century. Although the gold was located deep in hostile territory, adventurous men set out for the Black Hills from time to time. Few returned, but those who did strengthened the belief that gold did exist in paying quantities.[3]

This presumption gained credence as the Army began exploring western Dakota Territory. In 1857, Lt. G. K. Warren led the first

---

[1]"Great Overland Expedition to the Black Hills," *Yankton Union and Dakotaian,* Dec. 14, 1867, p. 1.

[2]Watson Parker, *Gold in the Black Hills,* (Norman: University of Oklahoma Press, 1906, p. 6.

[3]*Ibid.;* Donald Jackson, *Custer's Gold. The United State Cavalary* Expedition of 1874, (Lincoln: University of Nebraska Press, 1972), Harold E. Briggs, "The Black Hills Gold Rush," *North Dakota Historical Quarterly,* Jan., 1931; Harold E. Briggs, *Frontiers of the Northwest,* (New York: Appleton-Century Co., 1940).

scientific expedition to the Black Hills. The detachment left Sioux City, Iowa, in July, bound for Fort Laramie. In the party was Dr. Ferdinand V. Hayden, a geologist, who had first observed the area in 1855 with General William S. Harney. Lt. Warren explored only the southern Hills region but he found traces of gold. Dr. Hayden spent time making observations and Lt. Warren noted the region's mineral wealth in his report. The report was not made public at the time, however, for fear it would create an Indian uprising.[4]

In 1859 Dr. Hayden continued his studies of the Black Hills. Captain W. F. Raynolds, Topographical Corps, was to assess the natural resources of the Yellowstone tributaries. Raynolds, accompanied by Hayden, moved westward from Fort Pierre in June 1859. Mid-July found them near Bear Butte in the northern Black Hills. While encamped there small amounts of gold were discovered. Raynolds suppressed news of this exciting find for fear his men would desert. The party left the Black Hills several days later, remaining in the field for another year. Raynolds' report, published almost a decade later, concurred with Warren's—there was gold in the Black Hills.[5]

Military exploration west of the Missouri River ended abruptly with the outbreak of the Civil War. The region was left to the Sioux as U. S. troops rushed south to battle the Confederacy. Nonetheless, civilian interest to open the Black Hills was beginning to gather momentum.

This civilian interest manifested itself from the very beginning of white settlement. The treaty of 1859 placed the Yankton Sioux on reservations and opened southeastern Dakota Territory to white settlers. Frontier communities sprang up along the Missouri River. From frontiersmen and reservation Indians early residents heard rumors of riches to the west. In particular, the city of Yankton possessed a keen interest in the mineral wealth of its territory. Dakota Territory was hardly organized when citizens planned to explore its mineral wealth.

Bryon M. Smith formed the Black Hills Exploring and Mining Association in January, 1861. With headquarters in Yankton, this was the first civilian organization devoted to opening the Black Hills to white settlers. Smith, an insurance man and promoter, held several public meetings in the territorial capital early in 1861. His message was warmly received as over half of

[4]Jackson, p. 4; Parker, pp. 15-16; James D. McLaird and Lesta V. Turchen, "The Dakota Explorations of Lieutenant Gouverneur Kemble Warren, 1855-1856-1857," *South Dakota History*, Fall, 1973.

[5]Jackson, pp. 4-5; Parker, p. 16; James D. McLaird and Lesta D. Turchen, "The Explorations of Captain William Franklin Raynolds, 1859-1860," *South Dakota History*, Winter, 1973.

Yankton's adult males became members. Prominent among these were Moses K. Armstrong, Wilmont W. Brookings, and Newton Edmunds, all of whom would play important roles in Dakota's history. Although enthusiasm abounded, the Civil War and Indian problems forced a postponement in opening the Black Hills.[6]

In ensuing years civilian interest continued to grow. Dakota's territorial legislature frequently memorialized Congress for a geological survey of western Dakota. The discovery of gold in Montana in 1862 spurred Yankton's residents to increase their efforts. Requests were made for wagon roads across Dakota's plains to this newest El Dorado. A military installation to protect emigrants was also proposed for the northern Black Hills.[7]

This renewal of activity also saw the rebirth of the Black Hills Exploring and Mining Association. Several well attended meetings were held in and around Yankton during January, 1865. To generate wider enthusiasm, a sixteen-page pamphlet was prepared for distribution throughout the East. George W. Kingsbury, of Yankton's *Union and Dakotaian* published the boomer literature which announced:

> The Black Hills Exploring and Mining Association desires to call the attention of miners and emigrants to the new and short route to the gold fields which passes through Sioux Sity, Iowa and Yankton, D. T., thence in a nearly direct line to the Black Hills and the mines of Montana and Idaho . . . An expedition under the patronage of the government is now organizing for the purpose of opening the road with which the party of miners sent out by this association will unite.

If this governmental assistance could be secured, the Yankton organization was confident its goal would be attained.[8]

On March 3, 1865, Congress approved the survey and construction of a road westward from the mouth of the Big Cheyenne River, through the Black Hills, to join the Powder River Road. W. W. Brookings, a member of the Exploring and Mining Association's correspondence committee, was appointed superintendent of the project. Most of the surveying work was completed the following summer. Brookings optimistically foresaw an expedition of several hundred miners accompanying the road builders into the Black Hills. As gold seekers began arriving in Yankton, he requested federal troops to escort the expedition.[9]

---

[6]Briggs, *Frontiers of the Northwest,* p. 28; Briggs, *The Black Hills Gold Rush,"* p. 74.

[7]Herbert S. Schell, *Dakota Territory During the 1860's,* (Vermillion: Government Research Bureau, University of South Dakota, August, 1954), pp. 37-38.

[8]Albert H. Allen, *Dakota Imprints,* pp. 7-8.

[9]W. Turrentine Jackson, *Wagon Roads West: A Study of Federal Road Surveys and Construction in the Trans Mississippi West 1846-1869,* (Berkeley: University of California Press, 1952), pp. 297-311.

No such escort was furnished, however, as governmental policy underwent a change. Newton Edmunds, Dakota's governor, had successfully negotiated a treaty with the Teton Sioux in 1865. In view of these treaty commitments the governor decided to abandon all road projects in western Dakota Territory. Rather than provide an escort, the Army notified Brookings, in February, 1866, it would not permit the expedition to proceed. Without army support, efforts to send an expedition to the Black Hills were suspended.[10]

Despite this setback, interest in the region did not diminish. Yankton residents were encouraged when they gained Dr. Hayden, of the Smithsonian Institution, as an ally. Hayden, who had visited the Hills with the Warren and Raynolds parties, planned to visit the region again during the summer of 1866.

In early October, 1866, Dr. Hayden returned to Yankton after successfully probing the Black Hills. He persuaded newly-appointed Governor Andrew J. Faulk to allow him to speak before a public meeting of the Dakota Historical Society. In a rousing presentation, Dr. Hayden spoke of the area's timber wealth, concluding his remarks by assuring his audience gold would be found in the Black Hills.[11]

Such a glittering account breathed new life into the Black Hills Exploring and Mining Association. Under the continued leadership of Byron Smith, the winter of 1866-67 was filled with activity. More public meetings were held, speeches given, and resolutions passed. Plans were formulated for an overland expedition the following summer. A broadside, printed by the Association, proclaimed, "Very many of the scientific institutions of the country will be represented and expect to accompany the expedition which will make the enterprise not only profitable, but an interesting one to all who desire to join it . . . the field is ample and all classes are invited to join . . ."[12]

In response to such advertisements, gold seekers made their way to Dakota's capital. By the spring of 1867, 100 to 150 eager men were in Yankton ready to invade the Black Hills. In early June the Army stepped in once again. Generals William T. Sherman and Alfred Terry issued orders prohibiting the march westward. Despite a great public outcry there would be no opening of the Black Hills for another season.[13]

---

[10]Schell, *Dakota Territory*, pp. 39-40.

[11]Max E. Gerber, "The Custer Expedition of 1874: A New Look," *North Dakota History*, Winter, 1973, pp. 5-6; Parker, pp. 19-21; James D. McLaird and Lesta V. Turchen, "The Scientist in Western Exploration: Ferdinand Vandiveer Hayden," *South Dakota History*, Spring, 1974.

[12]Briggs, *Frontiers of the Northwest*, p. 28; Allen, *Dakota Imprints*, p. 14.

[13]Robert F. Karolevitz, *Yankton: A Pioneer Past*, (Aberdeen, S. D.:

Late in November, 1867, Captain Peter B. Davy arrived in Yankton. A resident of Blue Earth City, Minnesota, Davy was a well-known guide and explorer. During the 1866 season he had led an expedition of 400 from south central Minnesota to the gold fields of Montana. From Fort Abercrombie the caravan had moved westward across northern Dakota Territory by way of Forts Berthold and Union, thence to the Montana diggings. On the return trip, Davy had explored a more southern route, through the Black Hills, which he felt would be shorter and better suited in his needs.[14]

In Yankton he discussed a possible expedition to the Black Hills during the 1868 season. A meeting of citizens and territorial delegates was held December 7, 1867, in the home of Solomon L. Spink, territorial secretary. Governor Faulk, chairman of the proceedings, introduced Captain Davy who spoke at length on opening the region to settlement. Eight prominent orators, including Secretary Spink, Gudion C. Moody, and Brookings, also addressed the gathering. A resolution was passed to appoint a committee to confer with Davy. When Armstrong, F. J. DeWitt and Edmunds had been appointed to such a committee, the meeting was adjourned.[15]

The committee met with Davy the next morning. It was pointed out that Smith, founder of the Exploring and Mining Association, opposed any expedition without a promise of military assistance. Despite this, the committee decided to cooperate fully with Captain Davy. The four promoters then canvassed the business district for financial assistance. In a matter of hours, $1500 was raised to defray organizational and advertising expenses.[16]

In a letter to Kingsbury, editor of Yankton's *Union and Dakotaian,* Captain Davy publically acknowledged his gratitude:

> Permit me through your valuable paper to return my sincere thanks to the citizens of Yankton and the Territory of Dakota for the very liberal encouragement they have rendered in aiding my efforts to open and establish a permanent route from the city of Yankton to that region of country known as the Black Hills.
> And in consideration thereof, I would respectfully state they may rest assured that no effort should be lacking on my part toward making the matter a success . . .

Northern Plains Press, 1972), p. 50; Parker, p. 20; Briggs, The Black Hills Gold Rush," pp. 74-75.

[14]Helen White, *Ho! For the Gold Fields: Northern Overland Wagon Trains of the 1860's,* (St. Paul: Minnesota Historical Society, 1966), Jacob Armel Kiester, *The History of Faribault County,* (Minneapolis, Minn.: Harrison & Smith, printers, 1896), pp. 256-257, 282-283; Briggs, *Frontiers of the Northwest,* p. 29.

[15]"Black Hills Meeting," *Yankton Union and Dakotaian,* Dec. 7, 1867, p. 3.

[16]*Ibid.,* p. 3.

I feel confident that my effort in opening a thoroughfare from
Minnesota, through Dakota, the Black Hills, and Montana (so essen-
tial to the interests of the public) will be crowned with success.[17]

The next days were filled with activity. Yankton was designated as the expedition's terminal with June 1, 1868, as the departure date. Armstrong, a member of the Exploring and Mining
Association since its inception, was appointed secretary and general agent. It was decided that he would handle affairs in Dakota
while Captain Davy would spend the winter of 1867-68 lecturing
about the expedition throughout Minnesota.

An informational article was prepared for publication in the
Yankton Union and Dakotaian. Entitled "Great Overland Expedition to the Black Hills," the article quoted Dr. Hayden's report
discussing the region's geography and wealth of timber and gold.
The advertisement proclaimed optimistically:

> Already large numbers have signified their intention to accompany
> the expedition and it is confidently predicted before spring there will
> be congregated together at the City of Yankton, D. T. thousands of
> determined prospectors and miners bound for the pine clad tops of
> the Black Hills, seeking and finding sufficient of the precious ores to
> overflow their buckskin bags and make their hearts rejoice in the
> contemplation of better days.

Those interested in accompanying the expedition were advised to
assemble in Yankton by May 20, 1868. It was determined to
print the article weekly beginning with the December 14, 1867,
issue through April, 1868.[18]

By early December preparations were moving smoothly in
Yankton. Captain Davy turned the operation over to his general
agent, Armstrong, and returned to Minnesota. After stopping
briefly at his Blue Earth City home, Davy began organizing the
eastern branch of the expedition.

Monday, December 16, 1867, found the frontiersman in Winona. He called on David Sinclair, editor of the *Weekly Republican.* and explained his idea. The same strategy used in Dakota
was employed, as they agreed to call a public meeting to inform
residents of the venture. The *Weekly Republican* discussed Captain Davy's proposal pointing out benefits to be reaped by the
state of Minnesota:

> By opening this route the greater portion of trade and treasure
> which for years has been passing over the southern route will find the
> way through Minnesota to Chicago and eastern markets. In view of
> this fact it is a subject that should deeply interest the people of
> Minnesota as we deem it an ialiotory [*sic*] step toward opening a lead-

---

[17]*Ibid.*
[18]"Great Overland Expedition to the Black Hills," *Yankton Union and
Dakotaian,* Dec. 14, 1867, p. 1.

ing thoroughfare to the rich settlements of Dakotah, Idaho and Montana by giving encouragement to Captain Davy in this enterprise.[19]

The following Wednesday, December 18, Mayor R. D. Cone presided over a hastily called meeting in Winona's council room. A large turnout reportedly gathered to hear the soldier of fortune. Captain Davy assumed the floor and quoted at length from Dr. Hayden's report. He informed the audience of his plans to depart from Yankton the following spring. Other speakers followed Davy, all talking about the timber and mineral wealth of the Black Hills. No firm action was taken; however, a committee was appointed to confer with local businessmen.[20]

The preliminary actions completed, Captain Davy returned to his Blue Earth City home for the Christmas holidays. On December 27, 1867, residents of that Minnesota community paid tribute to their voyager for his successful Montana expedition. Once again the good Captain spoke at length about the Black Hills and his plans for the 1868 season. The reception passed a series of resolutions which concluded:

> RESOLVED: That the citizens of Blue Earth City do most cordially and heavily endorse the project of Capt. Davy and cheerfully recommend him and his plans to the citizens of this state and especially to the cities east of us which must ultimately bear immeasureable benefits by his success.[21]

In response to this, Davy designated Blue Earth City as a Minnesota depot. The weekly *Minnesota South West* was enlisted to print accounts of the expedition. The Captain issued the same optimistic prediction of large numbers of recruits he had written for the *Union and Dakotaian*. As in the Yankton paper, this article would be printed on page one for the next several months.[22]

Davy next turned his attention back to Winona. He returned to the southeastern Minnesota city to determine what aid, if any, he would receive. A second meeting was called for January 3, 1868, at the courthouse. Mayor Cone again presided with Captain J. D. Wood appointed secretary. The usual round of speeches was delivered. In the words of an observer, "The meeting throughout was orderly and attentive and an evident disposition was manifested to give the movement a push ahead." The gathering adopted the resolutions passed by the Blue Earth City meeting of December 27. In addition, a local provision was included:

> RESOLVED: that a committee of two be appointed to receive subscriptions from the citizens of Winona to aid Captain Davy in or-

---

[19]"New Gold Region—The Black Hills of Dakotah," *Winona Weekly Republican*, Dec. 18, 1867, p. 3.
[20]*Weekly Republican*, Dec. 25, 1867, p. 3.
[21]*Yankton Union and Dakotaian*, Jan. 11, 1868, p. 2.
[22]*Minnesota South, West*, Dec. 28, 1867, p. 1.

ganizing his Black Hills expedition and advertising the city of Winona as his starting and outfitting point from the State of Minnesota. One half to be paid down—balance the first of March.[23]

In the next day's Winona's press the *Weekly Republican* and *Daily Democrat* bombarded their readers with details of the upcoming adventure. An account of Davy's 1866 expedition to Montana was presented and numerous columns were devoted to the wealth of the Black Hills. Benefits Winona would receive as a terminal point were also discussed. It appeared that these benefits formed the real basis of interest in opening the Black Hills. As an editor noted, "What we desire to especially impress upon the people of this city now is the importance of some early and concentrated action to carry out with the best results the objects discussed in the first meeting of businessmen in the Council Chamber. In remarking upon this subject we shall not attempt to conceal a somewhat selfish motive which we design appealing to. Its vastly beneficial results are too apparent to intelligent men to require much urging."[24]

As the media was arousing interest in Winona, Captain Davy left to check preparations in Dakota Territory. In Yankton he reported conditions in Minnesota as "extremely favorable as far as the public sentiment is concerned." Subscribers of the *Union and Dakotaian* were assured that large numbers of Minnesotans would be arriving in the territorial capital the following spring to help open the Black Hills.[25]

Mid-January 1868 found Davy and Brookings barnstorming southeastern Dakota Territory. Another round of public meetings was held with the now familiar orations delivered and resolutions passed. A favorable atmosphere prevailed and a newspaper account reported the promoters were "well received and their important enterprise encouraged in a substantial manner by the people."[26]

Back in Yankton, Davy conferred with Armstrong. They reviewed progress to date and recent developments. Armstrong commented on a letter Governor Faulk had received from Morris E. Ward of Cincinnati. Ward informed the Governor he was also planning an excursion to the Black Hills, via Omaha, during the 1868 season. When he learned of Davy's plans, Morris suggested a merger. His query went unheeded, however, as the Yankton

[23]*Weekly Republican*, Jan. 4, 1868, p. 1.

[24]"The Black Hills Gold Fields—Immigration" *Daily Democrat*, Jan. 9, 1868, p. 1; Jan. 8, 1868, pp. 1, 3; Jan. 10, 1868, pp. 1, 2.

[25]*Union and Dakotaian*, January 25, 1868, p. 2.

[26]*Ibid.*

based group decided to continue with their present plans.[27]   Much of the meeting was devoted to the possibility of federal intervention.   Another peace commission was in the field attempting to pacify the Sioux, thereby ending hostilities along the Powder River. Rumor had it a treaty was being negotiated which would place the Black Hills permanently in the hands of the Sioux.   Such an agreement would be disastrous to their plans.   Davy decided he would go to Washington to lobby against efforts to exclude white settlers from the Black Hills.   In the meantime, Armstrong was to tour several midwestern states.   It was hoped he would be able to gain new emigrants for the following spring as well as opposition to any new reservation.   In their absence, Brookings was placed in charge of affairs at Yankton.[28]

Both promoters visited in Sioux City on their way east.   Davy immediately called on the editor of the weekly *Register*.   He discussed the expedition at length and submitted several articles.[29] Armstrong, well known to Sioux City residents, arrived a couple of days behind Davy.   He spent a few days with friends discussing the opening of the Black Hills.   Disregard past failures, Armstrong told acquaintances, everything points to a successful journey come spring.   "There is no better man for a trip than our friend M. K.," heralded the *Sioux City Journal*.   Both newspapers filled future columns with glittering accounts of the upcoming invasion of the Black Hills.   As the nearest railroad terminus, Sioux City also expected to reap benefits from Davy's adventure.[30]

From Sioux City, Armstrong traveled by rail to Chicago.   He set up headquarters at the Briggs House and spent the next several days booming the expedition.   Armstrong's presence in Chicago generated numerous articles among the metropolitan press.   The potential wealth of the region was described as again Dr. Hayden's report was quoted verbatim.   The opening of an overland route to the Black Hills would, according to the *Times,* mean "Chicago will reap the whole trade, not only of this new mineral field, but of all northern Montana."   As in Winona, the possibility of economic gain was the cornerstone of support for the Davy expedition.[31]

His mission completed in Chicago, Armstrong next sought the support of the legislatures of Wisconsin and Minnesota.   He urged lawmakers to petition Congress against setting aside the Black

---

[27]Morris E. Ward to Andrew J. Faulk, Faulk papers, Dakota Territorial Records.

[28]*Union and Dakotaian,* Jan. 25, 1868, p. 2.

[29]"Black Hills Expedition" *Sioux City Register,* Jan. 25, 1868, p. 2.

[30]*Sioux City Journal,* reprinted in Union and Dakotaian, Feb. 1, 1868, p. 3.

[31]*Chicago Times,* Jan. 27, 1868, p. 4.

Hills for an Indian reserve. The *Chicago Times* had already suggested such action to the Illinois assembly:

> It would be well if the legislature of our own state would petition Congress against the policy recommended by the Indian Peace Commission which would result in locking up one of the richest and most accessible mineral fields in the northwest against the energy and enterprise of the whiteman for the purpose of furnishing but a temporary hunting ground for the indolent and wandering Indian.
> The matter is one in which the whole west is deeply interested.[32]

Journalistic comments of a like nature were found regularly in both the Minnesota and Dakota press. Persistent editorials attacked the peace commission for its attempt to reserve the Black Hills for the Sioux. Such an act would retard the development of the entire frontier, they contended. The upcoming expedition furnished frontier editors with considerable copy in attacking such proposed treaty provisions. As one weekly put it ". . . let us hope that the bold adventerous are not to be tomahawked and scalped by these worst of Minnesota's foes." It was hoped the peace commission would find any area, other than the Black Hills, where the Indians could be deposited.[33]

This support for Davy's expedition was also voiced in the halls of Congress. In February, 1868, Senator J. B. Wakefield of Minnesota introduced legislation to reopen road building in western Dakota Territory. He proposed construction of a federal road from the western border of Minnesota to the Missouri River, and on to the Black Hills. Instead of closing the region to settlers, Wakefield maintained the government should assist the forthcoming colonization in every way.[34]

Amid increasing public support, P. B. Davy returned to Winona in early February. He designated the city as eastern terminal of his expedition. From here the caravan would proceed through Rochester, Owatonna, Mankato, Jackson and Sioux Falls before joining with the Iowa and Nebraska contingents at Yankton around May 20, 1868. Peter Bauder, hotel operator and real estate promoter, was appointed agent for the Winona area. "Black Hills" headquarters in Winona was established in Bauder's office at Washington and Second Street. Emigrants were continually urged to accompany the expedition hailed as "the largest that ever sought the gold fields to the West of us by way of Minnesota."[35]

Activity remained brisk throughout February. Davy traveled to

---

[32]*Ibid.*

[33]*The South West* (Blue Earth, Minn.), Jan. 25, 1868, p. 4; *Mankato Weekly Record*, Jan. 25, 1868, p. 2; Union and Dakotaian, Jan. 18, 1868, p. 2.

[34]*St. Paul Pioneer Press*, Feb. 12, 1868, p. 1.

[35]*Daily Democrat*, Feb. 4, 1868, p. 4; "Headquarters," Feb. 7, 1868, p. 4.

St. Paul, spending a week at the Merchants Hotel advertising his adventure. Bauder remained in Winona handling the inquiries that arrived daily. The *Democrat* of February 21, 1868, reported an emigrant had purchased two wagons and supplies for the journey to the Black Hills.[36] The next week another five teams reportedly were outfitted in Winona.[37] Gold seekers in need of transportation were informed ". . . The Winona Wagon and Plow Manufactorary, Curtis and Mason, are getting up a number of wagons on contract for Captain Davy's expedition to be constructed in part with Flavey's Patent Thimble Skein with the antifriction Box Babbet Metal Linings." As the *Democrat* saw it "our businessmen are now receiving some of the many benefits to be reaped through the selection of Winona as a starting and outfitting point."[38]

In the meantime, P. B. Davy was constantly on the move. From St. Paul the Captain conducted a whirlwind tour of Iowa before returning to his home state. March, 1868, found the wanderer canvassing south central Minnesota to establish additional depots. Almost a week was spent at Rushford in Fillmore County. No public meeting was called, but an informational pamphlet was prepared and B. W. Benson appointed agent for the area. The local press, the *Southern Minnesotian,* wholeheartedly endorsed the scheme and admonished prospective fortune hunters, "Now is your time, boys, you will have to go to Alaska for adventure, if you let this opportunity pass unimposed."[39]

Waseca, terminus of the Winona and St. Peter Railroad, was also designated as a depot following a March 12 rally. James E. Child, editor of the weekly *Waseca News,* regarded it "the duty of every Minnesotian to to render encouragement to this great enterprise."[40] As so often happened, after Davy left town the local media was employed to generate enthusiasm. Follow up stories recounted suspected wealth of the Black Hills as well as Davy's preparations. The proposed line of march was laid out and Waseca residents advised "we are credibly informed that large parties are now ready in Montana and are only waiting until spring to start from the other direction to meet Captain Davy's expedition in the Black Hills."[41]

Child also viewed the expedition as a boon to Waseca's economy. "Being located in a rich agricultural country," the journalist

---

[36]*Daily Democrat,* Feb. 21, 1868, p. 4.
[37]*Daily Democrat,* Feb. 28, 1868, p. 4.
[38]*Daily Democrat,* March 11, 1868, p. 4.
[39]"Captain Davy's Overland Expedition to the Black Hills," *Southern Minnesotian* (Rushford, Minnesota), March 5, 1868, pp. 1, 4.
[40]"Capt. P. B. Davy's Expedition to the Black Hills of Dakota," *Waseca News,* March 20, 1868, p. 1.
[41]*Ibid.;* News, March 13, 1868, p. 4.

suggested, "its advantages for those desiring to purchase and outfit for the Black Hills are unsurpassed by any other locality." Editor Child made his point by advertising local enterprises such as wagon makers, livery stables, dry goods and grocery stores. The *News* apparently reasoned if the Davy expedition would stimulate the economy it should be promoted. In addition to opening the Black Hills, the venture was also bringing prosperity to local merchants.[42]

His work completed at Waseca, Davy returned to his home at Blue Earth City. The Captain spent a few days resting and drafting a news letter for distribution to the regional press. He explained his recent travels and informed readers the news from the East and other quarters made him confident the Black Hills would be opened by his legions. Emigrant groups supposedly were forming as far away as Chicago and Milwaukee. Interested gold seekers were encouraged to contact the agent in their area at once as the June 1 departure date was growing near. To further publicize his adventure, the pathfinder was embarking on another trip through Dakota Territory, southern Iowa and Missouri.[43]

On the eve of his departure, Captain Davy delivered a lecture at the Blue Earth City school on March 23, 1868. He predicted the expedition would be a complete success, noting the thousands who had indicated their plans to participate. Accounts stating the Black Hills would become an Indian reservation were unfounded, listeners were assured. In closing, Davy revealed the publication of a pamphlet outling the expedition. Carr Huntington, editor of the local *Minnesota Southwest* had prepared the twenty-eight page guide which was to be distributed to prospective members throughout the country.[44]

"A FORTUNE FOR THE MILLIONS. GRAND OVER-LAND EXPEDITION TO the Gold Fields and Pine Forests of the Black Hills of Dakota" broadcast the pamphlet which advertised "WANTED 10,000 able bodies, energetic, hardy and industrious pioneers to join Capt. Davy's grand overland expedition." The avowed goal of the campaign was the mineral wealth of the region. Several pages were devoted to describing the region and documenting the existence of gold. Listed as references who could attest to the region's wealth were frontiersmen, congressmen, and the governors of Minnesota, Dakota and Montana.[45]

---

[42]*News,* March 20, 1868, p. 4.
[43]*South West,* March 14, 1868, p. 1; March 21, 1868, p. 1; *St. Charles Herald,* March 20, 1868, p. 3; *Weekly Republican,* March 8, 1868, p. 3; March 18, 1868, p. 2; *Daily Democrat,* March 10, 1868, p. 4; March 17, 1868, p. 2.
[44]*South West,* March 21, 1868, p. 1; March 28, 1868, p. 1.
[45]Peter B. Davy, and Carr Huntington, *Capt. P. B. Davy's Expedition,* (The South West: Blue Earth City, Minnesota, April 1868) p. 20, 24.

But Huntington was quick to point out secondary benefits to be reaped by opening a permanent route from southern Minnesota to western Dakota. A settlement in the Black Hills would provide a link to connect the midwest with both the East and Pacific Coast. With this goal in mind, the circular invited:

> . . . the attention of Farmers, mechanics, and other businessmen who have the pluck to emigrate and better their fortunes . . . secure a home, establish a business, and obtain a foothold in advance of thousands of the timid, who when they find the way is open, will pounce down upon the country.

Also "to consumptives and other invalids we would say, if you would wish to prolong your life and be restored to health make arrangements to accompany this expedition." Obviously, the promoters felt the Black Hills had something to offer anyone interested in going.[46]

For those planning on making the journey, the guide contained the following instructions:

> Everyone accompanying the Expedition should provide themselves with six months supplies, gun and ammunition, pick, pan and shovel. Those who can provide themselves with a horse to ride, it is desirable to do so. Oxen and a light thimble skein wagon are the best mode of transportation. A fee of ten dollars is required from each adult to defray the expenses of organizing the Expedition.

Emigrants were also told to "pay no attention to rumors (Indian or otherwise) the Expedition is certain to go through."[47]

As the departure date neared, Captain Davy hurried to Winona in early April, 1868. He spent several days at the eastern terminus finalizing plans for the first leg of the journey. The mild spring weather prompted the conductor to announce the caravan would depart Winona as soon as the prairie grasses were sufficient for grazing the work stock. He was hopeful the weather would cooperate, allowing him to arrive in Yankton by the May 20 meeting date.[48] This is borne out in a letter Davy sent to James Moloney, manager of the North Western Hotel in Sioux City, Iowa. He informed his agent he positively would be in Iowa by May 15, adding "everything looks favorable for a large party which will number thousands." Plans called for spending a day or two in Iowa before moving on to Yankton, the central collecting point. A week or so would be spent in Yankton, coordinating the various detachments and organizing for the final leg of the journey to the

---

[46]*Ibid.*, pp. 18-19.

[47]*Ibid.*, p. 19.

[48]*Wabasha Herald*, April 2, 1868, p. 4; *Daily Democrat*, April 8, 1868, p. 1.

Black Hills. June 1 was still the anticipated departure date, the Captain assured his agent.[49]

By the end of April, gold seekers were anxiously awaiting the signal to begin. One detachment of Blue Earth City residents had already been dispatched to Yankton. Others remained, waiting, as the *Winona Daily Democrat*'s April 30 issue indicates "there are ten or twelve teams already equipped at Wabashaw roady [sic] for a start as soon as the order is given by the gallent Captain: and so it is all over the State, in every community there are more or less getting ready to go." While last minute preparations were being made, Davy rested at his Blue Earth City home in an attempt to recover from an attack of lung fever.[50]

Yankton, Dakota Territory, was also bustling with activity. Hills bound emigrants were arriving daily to join the Captain. A carnival-like atmosphere prevailed. Past failures were forgotten as confident prospectors prepared to settle the Black Hills.

Unknown to these emigrants, a message was received at Fort Sully, Dakota Territory, late in April, 1868, which would prohibit the expedition from departing. The Communique, issued to Brevet Major General D. S. Stanley, explained governmental opposition thus:

> The country to which it [the Davy expedition] is proposed to explore is unceded Indian territory and such an expedition therefore, if made, will be made in violation of the law. It is especially important at this time that this territory be preserved inviolate, as it is the region selected by the Indian Peace Commission for a reservation for the Sioux and other northern tribes. The Brevet Major General commanding therefore directs that you prevent the proposed expedition, using force if necessary. Should you find that troops will be needed you will take them from any of the posts in your district at your discression. It is desirable to notify at once the organizer of the expedition that they will not be permitted to carry their design into execution.

To this end, Stanley contacted Dakota's Governor Faulk, who ordered the directive published in Yankton's *Union and Dakotaian*.[51]

The government's action produced strong opposition in the territorial capital. Once again the Army was threatening to exclude white settlers from the Black Hills. Some of the emigrants suggested an armed invasion of the Black Hills while others optimistically argued the government could be persuaded to rescind the order. Editor Kingsbury, vocal Davy supporter, urged mod-

---

[49]*Sioux City Register*, April 11, 1868, p. 2, April 18, p. 2.

[50]Daily Democrat, April 30, 1868, p. 1, April 24, 1868, p. 1; *Union and Dakotaian*, April 4, 1868, p. 2; April 11, 1868, p. 3.

[51]*Union and Dakotaian*, May 2, 1868, p. 2.

eration while at the same time editorially requesting the Army reverse its position.[52]

Captain Davy was in Winona when informed the Army intended to terminate his expedition. He immediately sent a telegram to the Secretary of Interior requesting him to countermand the orders issued by the military. The soldier of fortune refused to abandon his scheme without a fight. Telegrams were also dispatched to congressmen and political leaders of several states asking their support in his struggle. The Captain also announced the fortune seekers assembled in and around Winona would depart for Yankton as scheduled. If and when governmental opposition could be removed, the caravan could still reach the Black Hills during the 1868 season. With this idea in mind, Davy left for Yankton to personally continue the battle.[53]

During the interval, Minnesota and Dakota editors speculated on the expedition's fate. Most voiced disappointment at the sudden turn of events. Affairs were proceeding smoothly, and everything pointed to success, before the Army stepped in as it had in 1867. A majority of journalists still predicted success for Davy "in spite of the shortsighted policy which appears to have assumed a temporary ascendance among our authorities," as one publication termed it.[54] Editorial blasts were leveled at the peace commission's action which meant ". . . the richest sections of Dakota Territory are closed to the civilized world—its useful and valuable minerals, its millions of pine, its wonderful and inexhaustible fields for scientific research are given over to the control of savages and uncivilized Indians who neither know the worth or can derive from them the remotest benefit."[55] To such editors, the governmental action amounted to nothing short of a complete surrender to the Sioux nation. They argued the reservation scheme would not bring peace to the frontier. Instead, the Army should assist in opening the Black Hills, garrison troops there, and place the Indians elsewhere. Other columns told of the preparations Davy and the men who planned to follow him had made. For any number of reasons, such frontier editors hoped "it may be found not inconsistent with the obligations of the Government to the Indians to allow the expedition to proceed."[56] Much the same sentiments appeared regularly as journalists waited for a final decision regarding the Davy expedition.[57]

---

[52]Ibid., May 2, 1868, pp. 2-3.
[53]Weekly Republican, May 6, 1868, p. 3; Daily Democrat, May 7, 1868, p. 4.
[54]Union and Dakotaian, May 16, 1868, p. 2.
[55]Ibid., May 30, 1868, p. 3.
[56]Mankato Union, May 8, 1868, p. 4.
[57]Cheyenne Daily Leader, May 15, 1868, p. 1; South West, May 16, 1868, p. 1.

The enterprising Captain arrived in Yankton late on the evening of May 29, 1868. From local leaders he learned all appeals had been turned down and the expedition was doomed to failure. Governor Faulk, a Davy supporter from the beginning, had issued a directive stating he could not sanction an armed invasion of the Black Hills in defiance of military orders.[58] Davy remained a few days in the territorial capital. He considered calling a public meeting but decided against it. Instead, the Captain met with several groups of supporters and explained what had gone wrong with his scheme. He also informed them it was senseless to continue in their efforts to open the Black Hills. The area was reserved for the Sioux by the Laramie Treaty and the Army would use force if necessary to keep white men out of the region.

Before leaving Yankton in early June, Davy wrote the following letter to the editor of the *Union and Dakotaian*:

> I do not desire to leave Yankton without first having expressed my unqualified thanks to Hon. M. K. Armstrong, Gov. Edmunds, Sec. Spink, Hon. W. W. Brookings, C. H. McIntyre, F. H. DeWitt, yourself and others for the interest manifested in my behalf in the endeavor to promulgate and carry to a successful conclusion the Black Hills expedition.
>
> These men have proven by their acts in the encouragement of the enterprise their devotions to the interest of the people of Dakota and deserve to be remembered with gratitude by every true Dakotan.
>
> The development of the richest portion of Dakota would have resulted largely to its benefit, but for the present our enterprise has failed. All we can do is await our time when the futility of this Grand Reservation scheme will be made apparent to the Government at which time I hope I shall be able to control in some feeble degree the interest of the Nobleman of the West—the Pioneer of America.[59]

Davy accepted the failure of his expedition philosophically. Upon settling affairs in Dakota's capital, he retired to his Minnesota home and became active in local politics. He had known the risks involved when he gambled his time and money to open the Black Hills. What bothered him the most was the fate of those who answered the call to join him. Over 300 soldiers of fortune had assembled in Yankton by June, 1868. Most were young men who had given up good positions to accompany Davy westward. Disappointed at the sudden turn of events, a few returned to their homes. Most, however, booked passage on steamboats bound for the Montana mines. It would be another seven years before adventurers would be allowed to penetrate the Black Hills.[60]

The Davy Expedition of 1868, although a failure, has earned its place in the history of Dakota Territory. True, there was nothing

---

[58]*Union and Dakotaian*, May 30, 1868, p. 3.
[59]*Union and Dakotaian*, June 6, 1868, p. 2.
[60]George W. Kingsbury, *History of Dakota Territory*, (Chicago: S. J. Clarke Publishing Company, 1915), pp. 870-871.

novel about Davy's planned overland route from Yankton to the Black Hills. Throughout the 1860s visionary citizens had cast their eyes upon the region. Several attempts had been made to open the Black Hills before P. B. Davy arrived in the territorial capital. The same cast of characters—M. K. Armstrong, W. W. Brookings and Newton Edmunds among others—were found in every previous effort. The Captain was merely a new leader of an old group with an old idea. They hoped Davy, being a well-known guide and promoter, would be able to accomplish their goal where lesser men before him had failed.

Support for Davy's proposal came from a number of sources. Residents of Dakota wanted to develop the western portion of their territory to hasten statehood. What better way of attracting settlers, they reasoned, than opening the gold fields they were sure existed in the Black Hills. The lure of sudden riches had already attracted settlers to California, Idaho and Montana. Why not Dakota? For his part Governor Faulk felt the Hills area had to be settled before it was taken over by the newly created Wyoming Territory. In addition, a strong population in the Black Hills would go a long way toward ending hostilities in the region.

The effort to develop western Dakota Territory also found encouragement in neighboring Minnesota. Some residents viewed the scheme as a chance for adventure. The possibility of economic gain, however, was the real basis for support by most Minnesotans. Towns such as Winona, Waseca, and Blue Earth City foresaw profits as shipping and outfitting points for a permanent settlement in the Black Hills. Such benefits were far more important to the people of Minnesota than the mineral and timber wealth of the Black Hills.

In spite of widespread encouragement, Davy knew the success of his mission rested on governmental support. Yankton residents had been trying for almost a decade to open the Black Hills. Thus far the Army had thwarted every attempt. The Captain had been let to believe the military would allow him to proceed in 1868. But once again federal authorities stepped in at the last moment to stop this largest and best organized of the Hills bound, filibustering expeditions. The Laramie Treaty of 1868 had placed the Black Hills in the hands of the Sioux for the time being. There would be no further Yankton based attempts to open the Black Hills until after the 1874 Custer Expedition.

Unusual Nicknames

Nicknames prevalent throughout the West in early days have always intrigued those interested in Western lore. They were given to cowboys, gamblers and other Western characters, usually because of some peculiarity of speech or manner, locality from which the person was said to have originally come, from some humorous incident in which the person named had a leading part, and even ironically, to bestow characteristics in which he was lacking.

Of these names, Hartville, both as mining camp and cow-town, had its full quota, and some of the most unusual are as follows:

Snake River Jack, Montana Bill and The Ogallala Kid, were names borne by men who "hailed from" these localities. Red, Blackie, The White Swede and Cotton (short for Cotton-top) were descriptive of coloring and complexion. Three-fingered Charlie needs no explanation, but he was a fiddler of no mean ability and was in great demand for playing at dances. Step-and-a-half John had been injured by a fall from a horse, and walked with one long and one short step. Sister Mary was so called from his softness of speech and his effeminate bearing.

Vinegar Bill was not sour of face as might have been supposed upon hearing him so addressed, but he had made the mistake of attempting to take a mighty drink from a jug which he thought contained liquor—and found it vinegar. Rattlesnake Dick was a mild-mannered man who was filled with abject terror at the sight of a rattlesnake. Calico Jack possessed a seersucker coat, which he sometimes wore. Woodbox Jim received his nickname when he returned to his home ranch, much the worse for drinking, and mistaking the woodbox for his bunk, slept in it until morning. Jerky Bill was a well-known small rancher, famous for his escapades, but the manner in which he received his name and was known throughout the country, has been forgotten.

—By Alice C. Guyol
W.P.A. Manuscripts Collection
Wyoming State Archives and Historical
Department

Fort Platte, Wyoming, 1841-1845: Rival of Fort Laramie

By

DAVID W. LUPTON

Bicentennial travelers following the Oregon Trail will undoubtedly include on their tour a visit to the exciting Fort Laramie National Historic Site. Just north of the fort they will pass a monument in stone to still another fort—Fort Platte. One hundred and twenty-five years earlier their predecessors also passed a monument to old Fort Platte, but in the form of crumbling, faded white-washed adobe walls. Few could know that this roadside marker heralds a site which can boast a long list of famous visitors, exciting frontier incidents and trading activities that rivaled its better known neighbor, Fort Laramie.

What was the origin of this little remembered trading post? The answer lies in a letter of October 5, 1879, in which Lancaster Platt Lupton wrote as follows:

"I left the Army in the year 1836. My resignation took effect on the 31st March 1836. In the fall of the same year about 15 Sept. I started on a trading expedition to the Rocky mountains. I established a trading post on the south fork of the Platt[e] river about 15 miles below Denver City, Colorado. A few years after I established another trading post on the north fork of the Platt[e] river near the site of Laramie City. In a few years I exten'd my' trade till my trading posts extended from the Arkansas Rivers to the Cheyenne River on the North, a distance of more than 500 miles."[1]

The post on the south fork of the Platte River was Fort Lancaster, later referred to as Fort Lupton, established in 1836. The trading post on the north fork of the Platte River near the so-called site of Laramie City was Fort Platte. The exact date that Fort Platte was built by Lupton is not recorded; however, in the sum-

---

[1]Lancaster P. Lupton to Lieut. Col. C. S. Stewart, October 5, 1879, in Archives, United States Military Academy, West Point, New York. (Lupton's reference to Laramie City is not to be confused with the present-day town of Laramie, founded as Laramie City in 1868 in southeastern Wyoming. Ed.)

mer of 1840 the missionary Pierre Jean De Smet mentions only one fort, Fort William, on the Laramie River in the vicinity of the North Platte River.[2] This fort, built by the American Fur Company in 1834, was soon to meet opposition from Lupton's independent trading post. In the fall of 1840 or spring of 1841 Lupton chose the site for his second fort on the south bank of the North Platte, about a mile and a half north of Fort William and three-fourths of a mile west of the mouth of the Laramie River.

The confluence of the North Platte and Laramie rivers was a point of great importance for overland travelers west as the trail left the plains here and entered mountainous country. Emigrants followed either the north or south bank of the North Platte until they reached the Laramie River, where they selected a suitable crossing to arrive at Fort Platte.[3]

Apparently Lupton's new adobe structure, the first adobe post on the North Platte, stimulated the rebuilding of Fort William's old wooden stockade, for in the summer of 1841 a new fort of New Mexican type adobe was under construction by the American Fur Company. Fort William's replacement was first known as Fort John, but later came to be called Fort Laramie after the river in the region.[4]

While the early history of Fort Laramie appears to be well documented by historians, few materials seem to have survived which can provide specific information regarding the early years of Fort Platte's existence. It has therefore been necessary to draw up the scattered records which have survived to date to form a composite picture of this fort.

The building of Fort Platte was probably completed in the spring of 1841, for on June 22 of that year the California emigrant John Bidwell was the first to mention its existence, stating that the post was owned by Lupton.[5] During late June the missionary Joseph Williams confirmed Bidwell's observation, writing that there were two forts in the area about one mile apart.[6] Fort Platte was firmly established by May 30, 1841, for by that date Lancaster P. Lupton was intending to set out with a caravan from

---

[2]Le Roy R. Hafen and Francis M. Young, *Fort Laramie and the Pageant of the West, 1834-1890*, (Glendale, Calif.: Arthur H. Clark Co., 1938), p. 69.

[3]Merrill J. Mattes, *The Great Platte River Road*, (Lincoln: Nebraska State Historical Society, 1969), map following p. 492.

[4]Hafen and Young, *op. cit.*, pp. 69-70. In an attempt to establish a clearer frame of reference for the reader, the contemporary name Fort Laramie is generally used throughout this article rather than the original name of Fort John.

[5]*Ibid.*, p. 69.

[6]*To the Rockies and Oregon, 1839-1842* . . . , (The Far West and Rockies Series, Vol. 3) ed. by LeRoy R. and Ann W. Hafen (Glendale: Arthur H. Clark Co., 1955), p. 226.

Independence, Missouri, for his northern Platte place of business. Accompanying Lupton's caravan as an employee at the rate of $20 to $25 per month was Rufus B. Sage, an author westbound for the first time to gather material for a book. Lupton's trading party departed on September 2.[7]

Sage gives us our first description of Fort Platte:

> This post occupies the left [right] bank of the North Fork of Platte river, three-fourths of a mile above the mouth of Larramie, in lat. 42° 12' 10" north, long, 105° 20' 13" west from Greenwich, and stands upon the direct waggon road to Oregon, via South Pass.
>
> It is situated in the immediate vicinity of the Oglallia and Brulé divisions of the Sioux nation, and but little remote from the Cheyennes and Arapaho tribes. Its structure is a fair specimen of most of the establishments employed in the Indian trade. Its walls are 'adobies,' [sun baked brick], four feet thick, by twenty high—enclosing an area of two hundred and fifty feet in length, by two hundred broad. At the northwest and southwest corners are bastions which command its approaches in all directions.
>
> Within the walls are some twelve buildings in all, consisting as follows: office, store, warehouse, meathouse, smith's shop, kitchen, and five dwellings, so arranged as to form a yard and corel, sufficiently large for the accommodation and security of more than two hundred head of animals. The number of men usually employed about the establishment is some thirty, whose chief duty it is to promote the interests of the trade, and otherwise act as circumstances require.
>
> The fort is located in a level plain, fertile and interesting, bounded upon all sides by hills, many of which present to view the nodding forms of pines and cedars, that bescatter their surface,—while the river bottoms, at various points, are thickly studded with proud growths of cottonwood, ash, willow, and box-elder, thus affording its needful supplies of timber and fuel.
>
> One mile south of it, upon the Larramie, is Fort John, a station of the American Fur company. Between these two posts a strong opposition is maintained in regard to the business of the country, little to the credit of either.[8]

It was Sage who stated that the party with whom he was traveling brought back twenty-four barrels of alcohol for the winter trade with the Indians. Reports from the mountains had brought word to Lupton's party that during his absence from Fort Platte a battle had ensued during a drunken spree between two factions of the Sioux, resulting in the death of Chief Schena-Chischille and several of the tribe. On October 24 the company was joined by two engagés from Fort Platte and after two months travel, Lupton's group reached Fort Platte on November 2. At this time another unfortunate incident regarding liquor and the Indians was

---

[7]Rufus B. Sage, *Scenes in the Rocky Mountains* as reprinted in *Rufus B. Sage . . .* , (The Far West and Rockies Series, Vol. 4), edited by LeRoy and Ann W. Hafen (Glendale: Arthur H. Clark Co., 1956), Vol. 1, pp. 84, 125.
[8]*Ibid.,* Vol. 1, pp. 219-220.

recorded by Sage.[9]   On the night of the party's arrival, a celebration was held which lasted into the next day.   Apparently one of the Brulé Sioux chiefs, Susu-ceicha, while riding at full speed from Fort Laramie to Fort Platte, being too drunk to maintain his balance, fell from his horse and died of a broken neck.[10]

Winter trade was thus fully opened with the Indians.   Parties were sent with goods from the fort to the different villages for barter, and the liquor trade apparently continued in brisk fashion. An expedition was detached to Lupton's post on the South Platte River, Fort Lancaster [Lupton], late in November and another to the White River (Nebraska), an affluent of the Missouri, northeast of Fort Platte.   The expedition to the White River included Sage, who recorded that on the last of November they were under way with two carts freighted with goods and liquor and accompanied by six whites, one Negro and an Indian.[11]

By the end of January, 1842, Sage's expedition had depleted its provisions and he and two engagés left for a return to Fort Platte for a fresh supply of horses, cattle and dried meat.   After a strenuous winter trip the company returned again to the North Platte post on February 12.   Sage recited several instances of quarrels and drunkenness at Fort Platte during his stay there.[12]

About the same time that Lupton and Sage were leaving Independence, September 1841, partners John Sybille [Sibille] and David Adams were taking their first trading outfit westward out the "Oregon Trail" route to the Laramie River fork area, arriving with their company by mid-November.   Sybille and Adams were free-lance traders, having been issued their first license at Saint Louis on July 31 to trade on Laramie's fork and the Cheyenne and Wind rivers.   John Adams, David's brother, served as one of the "sureties" for the partners and Bernard Pratte, Jr., a former partner of Pierre Choteau, Jr., was another of the backers.   As will be seen later, Sybille, Adams, and Pratte would play an important part in the history of Fort Platte.[13]

Although Fort Platte's business appeared to have been successful, Lupton could not maintain two trading posts, and according to Sage, apparently went bankrupt.[14]   Between February 12 and April 26, 1842, Fort Platte changed hands and the new owners were Sybille, Adams and Company.   Lupton's original reasons for building this post on the North Platte, other than for trade

[9]*Ibid.*, Vol. 1, pp. 149-150, 200, 218.
[10]*Ibid.*, Vol. 1, pp. 224-226.
[11]*Ibid.*, Vol. 1, p. 232.
[12]*Ibid.*, Vol. 1, pp. 279-291.
[13]Louise Barry, *The Beginning of the West,* (Topeka: Kansas State Historical Society, 1972), p. 437.
[14]Sage, *op. cit.,* Vol. 2, p. 46.

expansion, could possibly have been related to his marriage. His wife, Tomaz (Thomass), was the daughter of a Cheyenne chief. She had been born and raised in the Fort Laramie region as was their first child, John, born in 1837. Another son, George, was born at Fort Platte in 1841 or 1842.[15] Although her tribe may have convinced Lupton that a trading establishment at this place would be advantageous, six years of experience may have proven to him that the trade business was beginning to falter. He made his decision to settle at Fort Lancaster [Lupton] approximately 150 miles south of Fort Platte.

Although the exact date of the sale of Fort Platte is not recorded, Rufus Sage who had been on a hunting trip from February to late April, 1842, found the fort and its fixtures claimed by Sybille and Adams upon his return. Prior to this expedition, Sage had indicated that preparations had previously been underway to build a boat at Fort Platte for the transportation of furs and buffalo robes to St. Louis.[16] Apparently Lupton's sale included a fifty-foot keel boat as well as the cargo of sixty packs of robes (between two and three tons), and provisions for four weeks. Sage had consented in February to take charge of the boat when he returned, and therefore set off for Saint Louis from Fort Platte on May 7, 1842. By June they had reached a point only about two hundred miles below the fort, as the expected spring rise of the river had failed. The previous winter had been mild in the neighborhood of the fort. Navigation of the Platte having failed, the furs and robes were cached on the river bank and a portion of the crew returned to Fort Platte. It had apparently been decided that the fort would be left in command of the trader Joseph Bissonette, and an overland party of oxen teams and wagons accompanied by Sybille, Adams and John Baptiste Richard started for Saint Louis. The group arrived at that place with the furs and robes sometime in early August, 1842.[17] In the meantime Sage and several other crew members had continued on to Independence, Misouri, by foot and canoe, arriving there by July 21.[18]

The year 1842 had been one of unparalleled drought in the area, not only preventing the traders from carrying their furs by boat to the Missouri River, but also destroying the grass and vegetation necessary for horses and buffalo alike. Apparently these extremely dry conditions prompted greater movement of Indian war parties making travel unsafe for both Indians and white travelers. While Joseph Bissonette was in charge of the fort during the summer of

[15]Alan P. Bowman, *Index to the 1850 Census of the State of California*, (Baltimore: Genealogical Publishing Co., 1972), p. 85.

[16]Sage, *op cit.*, Vol. 1, pp. 292, 344-345.

[17]Hafen and Young, *op. cit.*, pp. 78-80.

[18]Sage, *op. cit.*, Vol. 2, pp. 19-45.

1842, a war party of some two hundred Crows invaded the Sioux country, penetrating as far as Fort Platte and beyond.[19] On July 1 Bissonette wrote a letter from Fort Platte to Lieutenant John Charles Fremont, who was leading his first expedition to the Rocky Mountains. The communication, written by a clerk at the fort, L. B. Chartrain, read as follows (translated from the French):

Fort Platte, July 1, 1842

Mr. Fremont: The [Sioux] chiefs, having assembled in council, have just told me to warn you not to set out before the party of young men which is now out shall have returned. Furthermore, they tell me that they are very sure they will fire upon you as soon as they meet you. They are expected back in seven or eight days. Excuse me for making these observations, but it seems my duty to warn you of danger. Moreover, the chiefs who prohibit your setting out before the return of the warriors are the bearers of this note.

I am your obedient servant,

Joseph Bissonette,

By L. B. Chartrain.

Names of some of the chiefs. - The Otter Hat, the Breaker of Arrows, the Black Night, the Bull's Tail.[20]

Bissonette, one of the principal Indian traders for Sybille, Adams and Company, did meet Fremont at Fort Platte two weeks after the above letter was written. Fremont also visited Fort Laramie and described both structures as follows:

Issuing from the river hills, we came first in view of Fort Platte, a post belonging to Messrs. Sybille, Adams and Co., situated immediately in the point of land at the junction of Laramie with the Platte. Like the post we had visited on the South fork [Fort Saint Vrain], it was built of earth and still unfinished, being enclosed with walls (or rather houses) on three of the sides, and open on the fourth to the river. A few hundred yards brought us in view of the post of the American Fur Company, called Fort John, or Laramie. This was a large post, having more the air of military construction than the fort at the mouth of the river. It is on the left bank [of the Laramie River], on a rising ground some twenty five feet above the water; and its lofty walls, whitewashed and picketed, with the large bastions at the angles, gave it quite an imposing appearance in the uncertain light of evening.[21]

Fremont's description of Fort Platte gives the impression that Fort Platte was rebuilt by Sybille and Adams after it was purchased from Lupton. Although circumstantial, this indeed seems to have been the case as Rufus Sage described the fort as a much larger

---

[19]*Ibid.*, Vol. 1, pp. 338-339.

[20]John C. Fremont, *Report of the Exploring Expedition to the Rocky Mountains in the Year 1842 . . .* , (Washington: 1845, Sen Doc. No. 174, 28th Cong., 2nd Sess., Ser. No. 461), pp. 44-45, 49-50.

[21]*Ibid.*, pp. 34-35.

structure, with fewer rooms, than did later travelers who made careful measurements shortly after it was abandoned.

On July 17, when Fremont dined at Fort Platte, Bissonette urged him to take along an interpreter in case their party was attacked by Indians. Accordingly, when Fremont departed from Fort Platte on July 21, he engaged Bissonette as a guide and interpreter for the remaining portion of his expedition westward to the Red Buttes (Wyoming).[22] The importance of Bissonette's position at the Fort as "manager" is attested to by the fact that Fremont's voucher for goods and services rendered between 20 July and 1 September referred to Fort Platte as Fort Bissonette. Charles Preuss, cartographer for Fremont, also referred to Fort Platte as "Fort Bissonet" in his diary. Preuss comments about two Mexicans who had run away from the fort in August because they had been treated badly. He further stated that the workers in forts Platte and Laramie were exploited unfairly, earning only six to ten dollars monthly with which they were forced to buy all necessities at the fort. Incidentally, a similar Fremont voucher of 17 July for services rendered from Fort Laramie referred to that post as Fort John (after its builder John B. Sarpy).[23] The trapper Antoine Ledoux [Ladeau], Jr., who was born and raised in the area claimed that Fort Laramie never bore the name of Fort John, but that there was a Fort John at the mouth of Laramie River occupied at one time by Sybille and Adams (Fort Platte—called Fort John after co-owner John Sybille?). Ledoux claimed that the confusion of names was simply a mistake of the trappers who mixed the names of the two forts.[24] Contradictory to this claim, however, is the evidence that the "official" name of Fort Laramie was Fort John, and that it was not called Fort Laramie by its owners. The latter name was generally applied to it by the public. Only upon its acquisition by the United States government in 1849 was the name Fort Laramie officially established.[25]

While Fremont was completing his journey, John Sybille had delivered the furs and robes to Saint Louis and was preparing the return trip to Fort Platte, accompanied by seven men, two wagons and a load of alcohol. On August 14, 1842, Lieutenant John W. T. Gardiner of the First Dragoons, with twenty men dispatched from Fort Leavenworth, overtook Sybille and his outfit, seizing

[22]Ibid., pp. 42-44.

[23]Donald Jackson and Mary Lee Spence, The Expeditions of John Charles Fremont, (Urbana: University of Illinois Press, 1970), Vol. 1, pp. 146-147; and Charles Preuss, Exploring with Fremont, (Norman: University of Oklahoma Press, 1958), pp. 34, 63-66.

[24]C. G. Coutant, The History of Wyoming, (Laramie: Chaplin, Spofford & Mathison, 1899), Vol. 1, p. 301.

[25]T. L. Green, "Scotts Bluffs, Fort John," Nebraska History, Vol. 19, July-September 1938, No. 3, p. 181.

and destroying eleven barrels of contraband alcohol. Sybille and his men with the confiscated wagons and other property were escorted to the military post and then taken to Platte City, Missouri, for confinement. After the local magistrate refused to act, the group was set free, and Sybille put his outfit back together again, including several barrels of alcohol and proceeded again for Fort Platte. They arrived there on October 12. Sybille's partner, David Adams, having delayed his start from Missouri, reached the fort about two weeks later.[26] By October 27 he had recorded in his diary that the fort was "oll finished and oll the boys well." The "boys" now included A. Lucier who was listed in August as an employe.[27]

Since the Indians did consider the area about the fort as an important trading center, transactions during the winter of 1842-1843 probably continued as in preceding years. The only outstanding recorded event for this winter period appears to be the ordeal of Raphael Carrofel, one of the emissaries from Fort Laramie to the Indian villages. He dragged himself back to Fort Platte after a long, suffering ordeal in the snow.[28] After an uneventful winter however, the spring heralded a numerous list of travelers who would visit Fort Platte in the summer of 1843.

In May, 1843, Sybille and Adams sent their friend and partner John Richard with "some cows & 6 Buffalo Calves & one young Elk also 5 or 6 One (horse) Waggons loaded with Robes" down the Oregon Trail, across "Kansas" apparently headed for Saint Louis. By the time Richard reached the Big Blue River (Nebraska) on June 6, he met a westbound party which included William L. Sublette, one of the founders of Fort Laramie in 1834. William and his brother Solomon P. Sublette arrived at forts Platte and Laramie on July 5 in the company of Sir William Drummond Stewart and approximately sixty or more hunters and health seekers.[29] Accompanying Sir William's expedition for his health was Matthew C. Field, a prominent actor and newspaperman of Saint Louis and New Orleans. He wrote interesting accounts of the company's adventures for the New Orleans *Picayune* and the Saint Louis *Reveille*.[30]

Field presents us with a brief description of Fort Platte during his stay there. Under the date of July 6 his diary stated "visited the yet unfinished fort of Messrs. Adams & Sibelle—100 by 100 feet in extent, strong, but not so complete in any appointment as LaRamee—4 young buffalo calves running tame outside the

[26]Barry, *op. cit.*, pp. 456-457.
[27]Jackson and Spence, *op. cit.*, Vol. 1, pp. 146-147.
[28]Hafen and Young, *op. cit.*, pp. 84-85.
[29]Barry, *op. cit.*, pp. 474-475, 486.
[30]Hafen and Young, *op. cit.*, pp. 102-103.

walls—75 mouths in all including squaws and children, who were outside in the air."[31] It is not known why Field referred to the fort as yet unfinished for in October of 1842 co-owner Adams stated that remodeling was finished.

In a letter to "Dear Friends" in the New Orleans *Daily Picayune* of September 6, Field wrote the following ode from Fort Platte, LaRamee Fork, July 8, 1843:

> Hurrah! for the prairie and mountain!
> Hurrah for the wilderness grand!
> The forest, the desert, the fountain-
> Hurrah! for our glorious land![32]

Other members of Sir William's expedition included Jefferson Kennerly Clark and William Clark Kennerly, son and nephew respectively of William Clark of the Lewis and Clark expedition, as well as the son of Sacajawea, Baptiste Charbonneau.[33] Sir William Drummond Stewart and his company remained at Fort Platte until July 8; however, Solomon P. Sublette stayed on until the autumn when he left with Indian trade goods for the South Platte and upper Arkansas river areas. On their eastbound return to Saint Louis, Sir William's party again stopped at Fort Platte for supplies and rest from September 7-13.[34]

Five days after Stewart's caravan left, Fort Laramie was visited by a small party of Oregon-bound emigrants, one of whom was John Boardman who left Kansas on May 29, 1843. The night after they arrived at Fort Laramie they attended a dance at Fort Platte. On July 15 another Oregon bound company under Captain William J. Martin arrived and another dance was held at the Fort.[35]

At the very same time in July, 1843, two other Oregon bound emigrants, Overton Johnson and William H. Winter, made their way to Forts Laramie and Platte. These travelers, like Sage, Fremont and Field, have contributed to history with a description of the posts:

> "We continued up the North Fork, and on the 13th came to Lauramie Fork, opposite Fort Lauramie. Finding it full, we were obliged to ferry, and for this purpose we procured two small boats from the Forts, lashed them together, and covered them with a platform made

---

[31]Matthew C. Field, *Prairie and Mountain Sketches* . . . , edited by Kate L. Gregg and John Francis McDermott (Norman: University of Oklahoma Press, 1957), pp. 79-80.

[32]*Ibid.*, pp. 85-87.

[33]Hafen and Young, *loc. cit.*

[34]John E. Sunder, *Bill Sublette, Mountain Man,* (Norman: University of Oklahoma Press, 1959), pp. 209, 214.

[35]"The Journal of John Boardman . . . ." *Utah Historical Quarterly,* October 1929, p. 103.

of wagon beds, which we had taken to pieces for the purpose. Upon this platform, we placed the loaded wagons by hand, and although the stream [Laramie River] was very rapid, all succeeded in crossing without much difficulty . . . . Fort Lauramie belongs to the American Fur Company, and is built for a protection against the Indians. The occupants of the Fort, who have been long there, being mostly French and having married wives of the Sioux, do not now apprehend any danger. The Fort is built of Dobies (unburnt bricks.)   A wall of six feet in thickness and fifteen in height, encloses an area of one hundred and fifty feet square. Within and around the wall are the buildings, constructed of the same material. Those are a Trading House, Ware Houses for storing goods and skins, Shops and Dwellings for the Traders and Men. In the centre, is a large open area. A portion of the enclosed space is cut off by a partition wall, forming a carell (enclosure), for the animals belonging to the Fort. About one mile below Fort Laurimie, is Fort Platte; which is built of the same materials and in the same manner, and belongs to a private Trading Company. On the morning of the 16th we left the Forts . . ."36

The next month another view of the Fort was given when Thomas Fitzpatrick's division of Fremont's second exploring expedition visited Fort Platte. Theodore Talbot, journalist of this party, wrote in his journal on August 5:

"I went down to Sybille & Adams' post at the mouth of the Laramie River a mile below Fort John. It is called Fort Platte or Bissonette's Fort: it is smaller than the Am. Fur company post [Fort Laramie] but seemingly more active & lively. Many indians round about it, whose portraits Sir W. D. Stewart has engaged a painter [Monsieur P. Pietierre of Paris] to remain here and take. Met here Sol. Sublette and John Smith, who frequently resides among the indians and speaks at present the purest Sheyenne. A fiddle was brought forth in the course of the evening . . ."37

Solomon P. Sublette has been identified earlier; however, it should be mentioned that John Simpson Smith was a trader in the employ of Bent's Fort on the Arkansas River.38   Pietierre's sketches and paintings are yet to be discovered.

While Talbot has indicated that Fort Platte was the smaller of the two neighboring posts, another writer has stated that "Lupton built one of the largest adobe trading posts, called Fort Platte . . .", apparently referring to the very large dimensions recorded by

---

36Overton Johnson and William H. Winter, *Route Across the Rocky Mountains,* (Ann Arbor: University Microfilms, 1966), pp 18-19.

37Charles H. Carey, editor, *The Journals of Theodore Talbot,* (Portland: Metropolitan Press, 1931), p. 34; Robert C. Warner, *The Fort Laramie of Albert Jacob Miller: a Catalogue of all the Known Illustrations of the First Fort Laramie,* (Laramie: University of Wyoming, 1973), pp. 29-30.

38Ann W. Hafen, "John Simpson Smith" in *The Mountain Men and the Fur Trade of the Far West* edited by LeRoy R. Hafen (Glendale: Arthur H. Clark Co., 1968), Vol. 5, p. 329.

Rufus Sage in 1841.[39] It should be mentioned, however, that the dimensions of Fort Platte as recorded by Sage (two hundred and fifty feet in length, by two hundred broad) appear to be suspect. Sage also stated that in September, 1842, Fort George (St. Vrain) in size "rather exceeds that of Fort Platte, previously described". As the remains of Fort St. Vrain measured 128 feet by 106 feet (exclusive of bastions) its size was comparable to that of Fort Platte, indicating that Sage's description of the size of Fort Platte was grossly overestimated.[40] Comments such as these, coupled with other references to the lively and effective competition of the forts, prompts this researcher to include a short comparative discussion of the dimensions of various fur trading posts in the region.

By 1847 the outside dimensions of Fort Platte were measured at 144 feet by 103.2 feet, with walls 11 feet high and about 30 inches thick. The same year Fort Laramie, also built of adobes and in similar shape, measured 167.11 feet by 121.9 feet. At this time its walls were measured at 9 feet high.[41] Joel Palmer, however, estimated that earlier in 1845, Fort Laramie's walls had been 12 or 14 feet high with the tops picketed or spiked. Palmer, who also estimated that the walls were about two feet thick, wrote that "Fort John [Fort Platte] stands about a mile below Fort Laramie, and is built of the same materials as the latter, but is not so extensive."[42] Notice the name problem again arises.

Fort Vasquez, one of several fur trading posts on the South Platte River about 150 miles south of Fort Platte, was also an active competitor of the day. Made of adobe bricks, this fort measured 100 feet by 98.5 feet inside the main walls, with height of the walls estimated at 14 feet, averaging 26.5 inches in thickness.[43]

Bent's Fort on the Arkansas River was of dominant importance and size as a trading post in the central portion of the western plains. While it was also built of adobe, there is considerable discrepancy as to the fort's exact dimensions. In 1846 two soldiers of the Army of the West gave almost identical measurements: 178-180 feet by 135-137 feet with walls 14 to 15 feet high and three or more feet thick.[44]

---

[39]Robert A. Murray, *Citadel on the Santa Fe Trail* (Bellevue, Neb.: Old Army Press, 1970), p. 17.

[40]Hafen, LeRoy R., "Fort St. Vrain," *Colorado Magazine,* October, 1952, pp. 245-249.

[41]Hafen and Young, *op. cit.,* pp. 125-137.

[42]Joel Palmer, *Journal of Travels over the Rocky Mountains,* as reprinted in *Early Western Travels . . . ,* edited by R. G. Thwaites (Cleveland: Arthur H. Clark Co., 1906), Vol. 30, pp. 60-61.

[43]W James Judge, "The Archaeology of Fort Vasquez," *Colorado Magazine,* Summer 1971, pp. 187-188.

[44]David Lavender, *Bent's Fort,* (New York: Doubleday & Co., Inc., 1954), p. 387.

Concluding the discussion concerning size, it appears that Fort Platte may have been somewhat larger in size than comparable posts on the South Platte River, but smaller than the major posts in the area—Fort Laramie and Bent's Fort. The walls were also somewhat shorter in height. It should be remembered that Sybille and Adams apparently rebuilt Fort Platte after purchasing it from Lupton in 1842.[45] Thus its final form consisted of a rectangular compound made up of four rows of fifteen rooms, including a store, which surrounded a yard; a horse corral with a tower attached at one corner for defense purposes, and a small building attached at the other corner, possibly a wagon room.[46]

While the travelers during the summer of 1843 were busy noting the activity and size of the posts, John Richard was re-crossing "Kansas" heading back to Fort Platte (from St. Louis?) with an outfit of eight or nine men and some fifteen pack animals. He carried principally kegs of alcohol said to total nearly 300 gallons.[47] When he arrived on about August 15 he found the Fort still under the charge of Joseph Bissonette.[48]

In the meantime, (August 17, 1843), David Adams, in the company of Dan Finch and Julius Cabanne, was also westbound for Fort Platte via the Oregon Trail.[49] They were reported to have with them about twenty traders (including John Charles Cabanne?) to scatter over the country, as well as approximately forty voyageurs and seventy head of horses, mules, oxen and wagons laden with goods, but no alcohol.[50] This group met Matt Field of Sir William Drummond Stewart's party, now eastbound, on September 23 near Ash Hollow.[51] It is interesting to note that Field has also added to the name confusion by referring once to Fort Platte as "Richard's fort," exemplifying, however, the important connection which John Richard had with the Fort at this time.[52]

---

[45]Fremont, op. cit., p. 35.
[46]Hafen and Young, loc. cit.
[47]Barry, op. cit., p. 486.
[48]Hafen and Young, op. cit., p. 85. It should be noted that Stewart's eastbound party stopped again at Fort Platte on September 8 where they purchased supplies, but the name of the proprietor is not mentioned. (Sunder, Bill Sublette . . . , p. 214).
[49]Barry, op. cit., p. 493.
[50]"Fort Tecumseh and Fort Pierre Journal and Letter Books," South Dakota Historical Collections, 1918, pp. 196-197.
[51]Field, op. cit., p. 202. In a letter from Joseph V. Hamilton to Andrew Drips, dated October 7, 1843, at Fort John, Hamilton stated that Mr. Cabania [Cabanne], of Pratt and Cabanne (this would be John Charles Cabanne) had arrived with wagons of goods, etc., from St. Louis. Was John Charles Cabanne in the same caravan as Adams, Dan Finch, and his brother Julius or did Matt Field confuse the identity of John Charles with his brother Julius?
[52]Ibid., p. 74. The reader is referred to the historical novel Chant of the Hawk, by John and Margaret Harris (New York: Random House, 1959).

The importance of relating this early fall activity lies in the fact that the fort again changed hands between August 5 and 10, 1843, while Bissonette and Richard were managing the business. Sybille and Adams must have sold the fort prior to the westward journey of Adams and Cabanne, for the fort is referred to as "the company of Pratt [Bernard Pratte, Jr.] and Cabenna [John Charles Cabanne][53] . . . on the Platte" in a letter from Indian Agent Andrew Drips, written September 7, 1843.[54]   In spite of this Sybille and Adams must have retained some ties with their former establishment. In September they agreed to sell hunter Lucien Maxwell, then in Taos, New Mexico, fifty head of cattle from Fort Platte.[55] Pratte and Cabanne had been issued a trading license at Saint Louis on July 27 of that year to trade (with twenty-six men) on the Upper Missouri, Laramie's Fork, South Platte, and other areas.[56]

With the August arrival of Richard and his 300 gallons of alcohol, it seems appropriate to mention briefly the liquor trade. In the early 1840s the ill effects of the liquor trade on the Indians was becoming so marked, and the competition of opposition traders to the American Fur Company at Fort Laramie so keen, that the American Fur Company suddenly championed strict enforcement of the law. During the earlier decade, prior to the competition of Fort Platte, the American Fur Company opposed the enactment of a prohibition law, contending that it undercut their competition with the British Hudson's Bay Company. Although the prohibition law was enacted, the traffic continued much as before primarily due to government negligence and tolerance.[57] On September 8, 1842, Major Andrew Drips had been appointed Indian agent for the upper Missouri region.[58]   Major Drips was

---

In this story centered around the rivalry of forts Platte and Laramie, Reeshar (apparently referring to Richard) is a major character and manager of Fort Platte.

[53]John E. Sunder, *Fur Trade on the Upper Missouri, 1840-1865,* (Norman: University of Oklahoma Press, 1965), p. 9.

[54]"Fort Tecumseh . . . ," *op. cit.,* p. 188; and OIA, Letters Received from SIA, St. Louis (Record Group 75, Micro 234, Roll No. 753), National Archives.

[55]Charles Hansen, Jr., "The Abalone Shell as a Trade Item," · *Museum of the Fur Trade Quarterly,* Fall, 1973, p. 8. Through the courtesy of Charles Hansen, Jr. it should be noted that a letter in the Adams Family Papers, Missouri Historical Society Library, St. Louis "from Ft. Platte to Adams on the South Fork December 19, 1843 notes that Cabanne had 'arrived from Missouri with a few goods' and that the balance of Richard Sibille's outfit (apparently on the Missouri) was to be transferred to Ft. Platte. The letter also mentions that Sibille had arrived with Cabanne but had then gone on the White River (Nebraska)."

[56]Barry, *op. cit.,* p. 486.

[57]Hafen and Young, *op. cit.,* p. 86.

[58]"Fort Tecumseh . . . ," *op. cit.,* p. 170.

especially commissioned to stop the liquor trade, including that at
Fort Platte. It should be noted that his instructions were given by
Superintendent of Indian Affairs at Saint Louis, David D. Mitchell,
who was a former employee of the American Fur Company![59]

Agent Drips was authorized to appoint sub-agents, and in April,
1843, he chose Major Joseph V. Hamilton, another American Fur
Company employee, to be stationed in the Laramie region. Three
months later, however, Superintendent of Indian Affairs Mitchell
dismissed Hamilton, who by then was determined to continue his
own investigation. Hamilton traveled overland from Fort Pierre
(South Dakota) to the upper Platte River region to examine for
himself Forts Laramie and Platte for smuggled alcohol.[60] The new
prohibition enforcement officers appeared to serve the American
Fur Company first and the government afterwards. On October 7
Hamilton wrote to Major Drips from Fort John [Laramie]. This
letter referred to an earlier communication in which Hamilton had
explained why he had not succeeded in finding the liquor cache
reported as belonging to Pratte and Cabanne at Fort Platte.[61]
Apparently the Fort Platte men had learned that he was coming
to confiscate the liquor and expel the traders. When Hamilton
arrived he found only empty caches within the fort. Although the
liquor had been moved, Hamilton procured affidavits that the
traders had sold liquor.[62] Nevertheless, after nine months of investigation, from September 1843 to May 1844, Hamilton found
nary a drop of "liquid evidence"; his mission failed for lack of
proof.[63]

Major Drips in the meantime continued his own investigation.
On October 16, 1843, he wrote to Major Mitchell, Superintendent
of Indian Affairs at Saint Louis, that the boat of Pratt [Pratte] &
Cabanna [Cabanne] had not yet arrived at Fort Pierre. Drips
stated that as soon as it arrived he was going to start on a circuit
over the trading posts.[64] As Hamilton had been certain that Pratte,
and Cabanne were guilty of breaking the liquor laws on the Platte,
he had strongly advised Drips to confiscate the Pratte and Cabanne
keelboat on the upper Missouri, probably enroute from Saint
Louis.[65] Three weeks later, on November 5, Pratte and Cabanne
stopped at Ebbett's [Abbott's] Wintering Ground[66]—a trading
post of John A. N. Ebbetts, Fulton Cutting and Charles Kelsey at
Little Bend on the Misouri River near the mouth of the Cheyenne

[59]Hafen and Young, *loc. cit.*
[60]Sunder, *Fur Trade* . . . , pp. 69-70.
[61]"Fort Tecumseh . . . ," *op. cit.,* pp. 196-197.
[62]Hafen and Young, *op. cit.,* p. 87.
[63]Sunder, *Fur Trade* . . . , p. 70.
[64]"Fort Tecumseh . . . ," *op. cit.,* p. 196.
[65]Sunder, *Fur Trade* . . . , *loc. cit.*
[66]"Fort Tecumseh, . . . ," *op. cit.,* p. 175.

(South Dakota) north of Fort Pierre.[67]   Shortly thereafter, Pratte and Cabanne apparently continued on past Fort Pierre.   It is not known if Drips stopped them or even made such an attempt, but by December 20, 1843, Major Drips had completed his tour of the trading posts in the interior and had returned to Fort Pierre.[68]   He continued his unproductive liquor hunt into the spring of 1884. His presence on the upper Platte must have jeopardized the illicit alcohol trade, for as long as he was there the liquor traffic was held down.

In order to visualize the efforts and frustrations which the government faced in their attempt to stop the liquor trade at Fort Platte, the following letters from the Office of Indian Affairs have been reproduced:

"Fort Pierre 7th Sep 1843

"To Major Andrew Drips Agent for Indian affairs for the District of Territory West of the Mississippi River attached to the State of Missouri

"The undersigned states that about the 10th day of August 1843 he arrived at Fort John on Larrimie's fork of Platte river.   That he remained there until the 20th August.   That during the time he was there he frequently visited Fort Platte, the property of a Company trading under the style & name of Pratte Cabanne & Co situated on the north fork of the Platte river.   He further states that about the 15th August a Mr. Richard one of the persons employed by said Company arived near the Fort with a party of 8 or 9 persons and 15 pack horses and mules.   That Mr Richard entered the Fort in the morning with a view of ascertaining whether any agent of the Government was there.   That finding there was none a Messenger was dispatched for the remainder of his party who came into the Fort with the pack animals.   That as soon as they entered the Fort the gates were closed and locked.   That said animals were loaded with Kegs of Alcohol Containing as he was informed near 300 gallons, which were taken off and carried into the Fort store room & there deposited.   He further states that during the time he remained at Fort John alcohol was traded to one indian in a quantity more than one half gallon by the officers of Fort Platte, and that he was informed by those belonging to the Fort that much more (a large quantity indeed) was during a short period previously traded to the indians.   He further states that a Village belonging to the Brule band of Sioux Indians encamped partly on the North & partly on the South side of Platte river near the said Fort.   That whilst encamped there a number of them were intoxicated and such intoxication was produced by spirits furnished them by Officers of said Fort.   He further states that he was informed by the Officers of said Fort and by Traders in their employ that Alcohol was frequently traded to them by said Company.   He desires and hereby requests you as an Officer of the Government fully empowered to act in the matter to proceed under the provisions of an act of the Congress of the United States approved 30th June 1834 and particularly the 20th Section thereof and in accordance with the Circular letter of Instruction addressed to you by the Commissioner of

[67]Sunder, *Fur Trade* . . . , pp. 39, 58.
[68]"Fort Tecumseh . . . ," *op. cit.*, p. 184.

Indian Affairs dated 6 December 1841 to have said Fort, the Boats
Stores packages and places of deposits belonging to said company of
Pratte and Cabanne to be thoroughly searched and if any liquor is
found to proceed to take into custody and deliver to the proper officer
of the Government all the goods boats waggons stock packages and
peltries belonging to said company within the Indian Territory and to
give such information to the Attorney of the United States as will
enable him to proceed and have the Same confiscated according to
law And also to give said Attorney such information as will authorize
him to put the Bond of said Company in Suit & prosecute the same;
and to recover all such penalties as the Law may inflict upon said
Company & those in their employ. He further states that he does not
positively know the names of each of the firm to whom said Fort
belongs but that it is the firm owning the Fort on the South side of
the N. fork of Platte river commonly known as Fort Platte. In conclusion he requests to have such proceedings so instituted as that he
may receive such compensation as Informer as the Act of Congress
provides; and so that the Attorney of the United States may be fully
informed to tender the Same to him in pursuance of the instruction
addressed to him by the Solicitor of the Treasury dated 6th November
1841. For the Substantiation of the facts herein set forth he refers
to Mr. J. Loughborough a Citizen of Liberty Missouri who was then
in Fort Platte to William D. Hodgkiss the Clerk of said Fort—to Mr.
Sigler Mr. John Smith & Mr. Parisier [or Parisiu?] Traders in the
employ of said Company And to Mr. Montgomery a person furnishing supplies from Touse [Taos] to said Company and a Mr. Richard
who is also employed by them, and a Mr. Dubois [Dubrais?] a person
acting as Steward for said company.

Signed J. Sarpy"

"Fort Pierre 7th Septr 1843
"All the facts stated in the forgoing Letter by Mr. Sarpy are written
within my Knowledge personally or communicated to me by the Officers and Traders at Fort Platte.

J. Loughborough"
"Fort John September 17th 1843
"To Major Andrew Drips Agent for Indian Affairs for the District
of Territory West of the Mississippi River attached to the State of
Missouri.

"Dear Sir
By the request of
Major J. V. Hamilton I take the liberty of addressing you on the
subject of licensed traders in this section of Indian Country trading
Spiritous Liquor and this is to certify that between the 9th and 15th
of this month I purchased from traders in a Fort called Fort Platte
now in charge of a Mr. Bissonett and belonging to Messers Pratte &
Cabina Spirited Liquors to the amount of Eighty dollars which I gave
my Draft for on Mr. J. B. Sarpy in favour of Messers Pratte and
Cabina of Saint Louis, I shall remain here this Winter and I think
likely shall return in the Spring to Saint Louis with Major Hamilton
when you can get my evidence.
Your Obedient Srevent

John Hill"[69]

---

[69]Sunder, *Fur Trade . . .* , p. 71; and OIA, Letters Received . . . , *op. cit.*

In spite of government agents in the area to harass the liquor traffic, trade at Fort Platte during the winter of 1843-1844 was brisk.[70] From Ebbett's Wintering Ground mentioned earlier, Pratte and Cabanne had written to Major Drips requesting permission to allow John Richard along with five other traders to be included in the licenses under which they were trading.[71] Richard had apparently been operating without a license and had reputedly gained a very bad reputation for smuggling whiskey from Santa Fe and Taos to the Fort Platte and Fort Laramie region.[72] That winter also saw the expansion of Pratte and Cabanne's trading activities. The company decided to open an upper Missouri outfit and had received a license from Superintendent Mitchell to trade with the Sioux in various new locations between Forts Pierre (South Dakota) and Clark [Osage] Missouri. By November of 1843 they had received permission from Drips to build trading houses on at least four new sites near the mouths of the Beaver, Grand, Moreau and Cheyenne Rivers[73] and to send out and trade meat but nothing else at these posts.[74]

One report of the following spring's activity appeared in the *Niles Register* of May 4, 1844: "Captain Cabanne, with a portion of his company has arrived at Saint Louis from the north fork of the River Platte. They report their trip as very successful."[75] Apparently Joseph Bissonette had accompanied Cabanne to Saint Louis, for later that month he had set out for a return trip to Fort Platte with a company of pack mules and ponies. On May 23 he passed the emigrant companies of James Clyman, also enroute to Fort Platte.[76]

That spring also saw unusually heavy rains and high flooding, bringing great distress to emigrants along the Oregon Trail. To the traders, however, it was a boon for they were able to bring their furs and robes down river by boat with little difficulty. One June 21 six mackinaw boats loaded with peltries from the North Platte arrived in Saint Louis. These were probably those of Pratte and Cabanne since the boats from Fort Laramie with seven hundred packs of buffalo robes did not arrive until June 27. On the

---

[70]Hafen and Young, *op. cit.,* p. 88.
[71]"Fort Tecumseh . . . ," *op. cit.,* p. 175.
[72]John D. McDermott, "John Baptiste Richard" in *The Mountain Men and the Fur Trade of the Far West,* edited by LeRoy R. Hafen (Glendale: Arthur H. Clark Co., 1965), Vol. 2, pp. 291-293.
[73]Sunder, *Fur Trade . . . ,* pp. 70-71.
[74]"Fort Tecumseh . . . ," *op. cit.,* p. 175-176.
[75]*Niles Register,* May 4, 1844, p. 160.
[76]Charles L. Camp, *James Clyman, Frontiersman,* (Portland: Champoeg Press, 1960), p. 69.

way to Saint Louis the Fort Platte traders had been attacked by a party of Pawnee Indians but repelled them without loss of life.[77]

During June, 1844, Joseph Bissonette had fortunately returned to Fort Platte. His services were needed to avert danger to an Oregon bound emgirant party of which one William M. Case was a member. As the emigrant train approached Fort Platte in late June or early July, word was received that there was a large war party of Sioux Indians at the Fort, and if anyone in the train knew the Sioux language they should be sent to the Fort. It is reported that the Indians wanted the emigrants' horses. To prevent destruction to the train, Bissonette met with the Sioux chiefs and told them that one of the emigrants had just died of smallpox. As the Indians understood only too well what smallpox was, the "chiefs slid out to their tents, and within fifteen minutes the whole army was on the move, going to the north, and not returning while the immigrants of that season were passing."[78] On August 1 when James Clyman and company came in sight of the whitewashed mud battlemènts of "Fort Larrimie & her twin Sister fort Piearre [Platte] "the walls were surrounded by only a few Indian lodges. The company remained only two days.[79]

An interesting event occurred during the period from August to September of this year. Whether by design or coincidence, three of the former owners of Fort Platte returned to that place. On September 3, David Adams, trader, with a small outfit set out from Hickory Grove, Kansas, near Fort Leavenworth, for the Laramie River. During the day he was joined by Lancaster P. Lupton, the original builder. On September 21 the combined Adams-"Anson"-Robidoux-Lupton pack horsè party, eleven men or more, proceeded to Frederick Choteau's trading post a few miles above present Topeka, Kansas, and eventually arrived at Fort Platte on October 24. When they arrived, they were met by John Sybille and Dan Finch who had come earlier in August.[80] One can only wonder as to what Lupton's, Sybille's and Adams' reminiscences were upon this visit to their former place of business.

June, 1845, was a prelude to the end of Fort Platte, a closing which symbolized the fading fortunes of the American fur trade business. On the morning of June 14, Fort Laramie and Fort Platte received their first visit from United States military troops. Colonel Stephen W. Kearney led five companies of the First Dragoons over the Oregon Trail to guard the emigrants and impress the Indians. The two forts vied for the distinction of having the

[77]Hafen and Young, *op. cit.,* p. 89.
[78]H. S. Lyman, "Reminiscences of Wm. M. Case," *Oregon Historical Quarterly,* September 1900, pp. 273-275
[79]Camp, *op. cit.,* pp. 89-90.
[80]Barry, *op. cit.,* pp. 526-527.

Dragoons camped in their vicinity. The good grass on the Laramie River bottoms three miles above Fort Laramie appears to have determined the choice of post. As some 1200 Bruleé and Oglala Sioux were assembled near the forts, Colonel Kearney arranged to meet in general council on the neutral ground between forts Platte and Laramie on June 16.[81]   In the meantime twelve men of Pratte and Cabanne's company had taken the steamer *Tobacco Plant* to Saint Louis;[82] however, the remaining traders at Fort Platte prepared chairs and benches backed with elk skins for the council leaders and carpeted the ground with buffalo robes.   The Indians seated themselves in a great semi-circle, with women and children making up the rear.[83]   Kearney's address was translated and interpreted by Joseph Bissonette who was still associated with Fort Platte.   Howitzers and rockets were fired to fully impress the Indians.[84]

The day after the council, Kearney and four of his companies departed the area to follow the North Platte to the Red Buttes, leaving Colonel William Eustis and A Company behind to keep an eye on the Sioux concentrated in the area.   Returning to forts Platte and Laramie on July 13, Kearney and his four companies found Company A not far from where they had left it on the Laramie River.   The campaign then continued south to Bent's Fort.[85]

While heading west, Colonel Kearney's summer campaign passed between 1300 and 3000 emigrants in 460 to 500 wagons along the Oregon Trail.   Between June 14 and 16, 1845, the foremost companies of travelers reached Fort Laramie.   It is interesting to note that during this month the traders in the Fort Laramie area had counted 550 wagons of Oregon bound settlers.[86] On September 4 the St. Louis *Reveille* had reported that a letter written from Fort Platte (in June?) said that 421 wagons of emigrants had passed the Fort and sixty were still behind.[87]

Among the emigrants was a company headed for Oregon led by Captain Joel Palmer.   The group reached the "twin" forts on June 24 and remained encamped for two days busying themselves with trading at the forts, shoeing horses and oxen and repairing their wagons.   On the 25th the emigrant families held a grand

---

[81]Hamilton Gardiner, "Captain Philip St. George Cooke and the March of the 1st Dragoons to the Rocky Mountains in 1845," *Colorado Magazine*, October 1953, p. 258.

[82]St. Louis *Reveille*, June 3, 1845.

[83]Hafen and Young, *op. cit.*, p. 110.

[84]Otis E. Young, *The West of Philip St. George Cooke, 1809-1895* (Glendale: Arthur H. Clark Co., 1955), pp. 160-161.

[85]*Ibid.*, pp. 161-167.

[86]Barry, *op. cit.*, pp. 552-553.

[87]St. Louis *Reveille*, September, 4, 1845.

feast for the Sioux Indians camped nearby, followed by council talks and smoking of the peace pipe. One of the fort traders (Bissonette?) interpreted the chief's speech and Palmer's response. Palmer wrote that "Fort Laramie, situated upon the west side of Laramie's fork, two miles from Platte river belongs to the North American Fur company. The fort is built of adobes . . . Fort John [Fort Platte] stands about a mile below Fort Laramie, and is built of the same material as the latter, but is not so extensive. Its present occupants are a company from St. Louis."[88]   Another recorded visit to this place was that of John E. Howells, who left Missouri for Oregon on April 11, passing both forts on June 27, 1845. In the company of one other emigrant, Howells traveled with one wagon, three yoke of oxen, and one horse.[89]

Shortly thereafter the Fort was apparently abandoned, for on August 31, 1845, Mr. Anthony A. Bouis wrote to Honore D. Picotte from Fort Pierre that

> "Mr. Cabanne has abandoned Fort Platte. Bissouet [Joseph Bissonette] is stationed a few miles below that fort with a few articles of trade that remained on hand last spring. It is supposed that if Cabanne comes up next fall it will be with a small outfit. The prospect of trade in that section of the country is very flattering, plenty of buff and there will be more Indians there this season than ever. Part of the Minniconajous and 200 lodges of Cheyennes will winter in the neighborhood of the fort. Joe [Picotte, who had been sent to take charge of Fort Laramie in June 1845] thinks he will trade 12 to 1500 packs."[90]

Shortly after Kearney's departure from Fort Platte in June 1845, Joseph Bissonette supervised the abandonment of the post, and in December Pratte and Cabanne sold their interest in the trade to the American Fur Company, ending the rivalry between Fort Laramie and Fort Platte.[91]   But what became of the principal figures in the history of Fort Platte: Lancaster P. Lupton, John Sybille, David Adams, Bernard Pratte, Jr., John C. Cabanne, Joseph Bissonette, and John Richard?

As mentioned earlier Lupton had another trading post on the South Platte River, Fort Lancaster (later known as Fort Lupton). He managed this establishment until 1845. The following year he moved to Hardscrabble (New Mexico Territory) near present-day Pueblo, Colorado. In 1849 Lupton and his family joined the

[88]Hafen and Young, op. cit., pp. 108-109.
[89]"Diary of an Emigrant of 1845," Washington Historical Quarterly, October 1906, pp. 138-139, 144.
[90]"Fort Tecumseh . . . ," op. cit., pp. 203, 206.
[91]Hafen and Young, op. cit., pp. 92-93 and John D. McDermott, "James Bordeaux," in The Mountain Men and the Fur Trade of the Far West, edited by LeRoy R. Hafen (Glendale: Arthur H. Clark Co., 1968), Vol. 5, p. 69.

'49ers for California. There he engaged in mercantile pursuits until 1852 when he moved near Coloma to do some gold mining. From 1852-1862 Lupton mined and farmed in El Dorado County, and from 1862-1868 he continued farming in San Joaquin County. Finally in December 1868 Lupton and his family moved to Humboldt County, near Arcata, where he continued farming until his death on October 1, 1885.[92]

John Sybille, after dissolving his ownership of Fort Platte in August/September 1843, apparently established a fur trading post at Little Bend on the Missouri River below the mouth of the Cheyenne River (near Fort Pierre).[93] In May 1846 he was in association with Joseph Bissonette bound from Missouri to the upper North Platte River (Fort Bernard?), and it is known that he continued in the fur trading business. Sybille subsequently lived in the Denver, Colorado, area in the 1860s, later moving to Saint Louis where he died in 1879.[94]

Upon relinquishing his part ownership in Fort Platte to Pratte and Cabanne in August/September of 1843, David Adams continued as a fur trader in the area.[95] In April, 1849, he guided a party of gold seekers to California from St. Joseph, Missouri, and tried his luck at the mines. The lure of the fur trade, however, brought him back and he plied the fur trade until it died. David Adams spent his impoverished last years in Saint Louis where he died in 1874.[96]

Bernard Pratte, Jr. apparently returned to Saint Louis in the spring of 1844, "actively" retiring from the fur trade business, and was elected mayor of that city for two terms, 1844-1846.[97] In the meantime he had maintained a partnership with John C. Cabanne, and after Fort Platte was abandoned in July or August of 1845, they moved eight miles east of Fort Laramie along the North Platte River to build and operate a post named for him, Fort Bernard. Apparently Cabanne, Bissonette, and Richard had been left behind at forts Platte and later Bernard to conduct business during his term of office in Saint Louis.[98] It has been indicated that Mayor

[92]Research in progress by the author, June 1975, on the book *Lancaster P. Lupton: Fur Trader on the Platte.*

[93]"Fort Tecumseh . . . ," *op. cit.,* p. 177.

[94]Statement of Francis W. Hammitt to F. W. Cragin, April 14, 1903, Early Far West Notebooks, V-51, Cragin Collection, El Paso County Pioneers Museum, Colorado Springs, Colo. and "The Reminiscences of General Bernard Pratte, Jr.," *Bulletin of the Missouri Historical Society,* October 1949, p. 69.

[95]Johnson and Winter, *op. cit.,* p. 132.

[96]" Trade Papers," *Bulletin of the Missouri Historical Society,* October 1956, Fur 101.

[97]Reuben Gold Thwaites, *Early Western Travels* (Cleveland: Arthur H. Clark Co., 1906), Vol. 22, p. 282.

[98]Hafen and Young, *op. cit.,* pp. 93-94, 118-119.

Pratte was most diligent in advancing improvements to that city.[99] By December 1845 Pratte and Cabanne had relinquished their interests in Fort Bernard leaving its management to John Richard.[100] During 1845 Pratte and Cabanne had also withdrawn from the fur trade on the upper Missouri River, as had the Union Fur Company, leaving the American Fur Company master of the upper Missouri fur trade.[101] In March 1849 Pratte was listed as a member of the original board of directors of the newly-formed Pacific Railroad Company,[102] and the next year he retired to a farm near Jonesboro, Montgomery County, Missouri, where he lived until his death in 1886.[103]

John Charles Cabanne, upon abandoning Fort Platte in July or August, 1845, apparently remained in business until the end of that year with Pratte, Bissonette, and Richard.[104] With the demise of the fur trade on both the North Platte and upper Missouri rivers, we lose track of the wanderings of John C. Cabanne until his death in Saint Louis in 1854.[105]

After Fort Platte was abandoned in July or August, 1845, Joseph Bissonette moved down the North Platte River to a point eight miles east of Fort Laramie. There, under the supervision of Pratte and Cabanne, he began the construction of a new post, Fort Bernard. After Pratte and Cabanne sold their interest in Fort Bernard, Bissonette stayed on with John Richard and they successfully continued the rivalry with Fort Laramie until Fort Bernard burned to the ground in July 1846. The roles which these two men played at Fort Platte, however, appear to have been reversed at Fort Bernard. At this post Richard ran the business and Bissonette visited the Indians in their camps. Bissonette continued to trade in the Laramie area in association with James Bordeaux and John Richard. For a while he acted as interpreter for the Indian Agency near Fort Laramie. In 1871 he lived with the Sioux in northwestern Nebraska, eventually moving to Wounded Knee Creek, South Dakota, where he died in August, 1894.[106]

John Baptiste Richard, after Fort Platte was abandoned in July or August of 1845, moved on to Fort Bernard. He served at this

[99]J. Thomas Scharf, *History of Saint Louis City and County* (Philadelphia: Louis H. Everts & Co., 1883), Vol. 1, p. 675.

[100]Sunder, *Fur Trade . . .* , p. 10.

[101]*Ibid.*, p. 80.

[102]Dorothy Jennings, "The Pacific Railroad Company," *Missouri Historical Society Collections,* 1928-1931, pp. 288, 292.

[103]"The Reminiscences of General Bernard Pratte, Jr.," *op. cit.,* p. 59.

[104]Sunder, *Fur Trade . . .* , pp. 9-10, 80.

[105]Paul E. Beckwtih, *Creoles of St. Louis* (St. Louis: Nixon-Jones Printing Co., 1893), p. 72.

[106]John D. McDermott, "Joseph Bissonette," in *The Mountain Men and the Fur Trade of the Far West,* edited by LeRoy R. Hafen (Glendale: Arthur H. Clark Co., 1966), Vol. 4, pp. 51-60.

post as manager, with Bissonette as trader, until July, 1846, when Fort Bernard burned down while he was away on a liquor buying trip to New Mexico.   Richard remained for a short time in the fur trade business, but during the 1850s he operated a toll bridge with Bissonette and others over the North Platte River near Fort Laramie.   In 1858 he was one of the first frontiersmen to bring news of the Pike's Peak gold discoveries to the Kansas-Nebraska settlements.   Two years later he opened a store and saloon in Denver, and in 1865 he was probably one of Jim Bridger's comrades-in-arms in the Powder River campaign.   He was killed by Indians on the upper crossing of the Niobrara River (Nebraska) in the winter of 1875.[107]

Although organized trading activity was discontinued at Fort Platte by mid-1845, it is important to note the early statements of the pioneers as they passed through the area.   Their information often included the only accurate measurements of the "twin forts" available.   The first reference to the abandoned Fort by emigrants on the "Great Platte River Road" in 1846 appears to be that of Francis Parkman who passed by on June 15.   Parkman and his company continued on to Fort Laramie, crossing the Laramie River fork at its highest ford.[108]

The following year, on April 16, 1847, headed by Brigham Young, a "pioneer" Mormon band of 148 persons, seventy-two wagons, and livestock headed for "Utah" from eastern "Nebraska".[109]   By June 1 the Mormon pioneers had arrived opposite abandoned Fort Platte's adobe ruins where they camped for the night on the north bank of the North Platte River, opposite the mouth of the Laramie.   On the next day Brigham Young and other leaders of the party crossed the North Platte River and examined the ruins of Fort Platte.   Elder Pratt measured the distance across the river at this spot, and being in flood stage found it to be 108 yards wide.[110]

Several Mormon pioneers on this journey kept diaries, including Lorenzo Dow Young, Thomas Bullock, and William Clayton. Fortunately, both Bullock and Clayton took tape measurements of Fort Platte and Fort Laramie, and Thomas Bullock included in his diary sketches of both forts.   William Clayton described Fort Platte as follows:

---

[107]John D. McDermott, "John Baptiste Richard," in *The Mountain Men and the Fur Trade of the Far West,* edited by LeRoy R. Hafen (Glendale: Arthur H. Clark Co., 1966), Vol. 2, pp. 294-303.
[108]*The Journals of Francis Parkman,* edited by Mason White (London: Eyre & Spottiswoode, 1949), Vol. 2, p. 439.
[109]Barry, *op. cit.,* pp. 672-673.
[110]*William Clayton's Journal,* published by the Clayton Family Association (Salt Lake City: Deseret News, 1921), pp. 205-208.

". . . we went up to the remains of an old fort called Fort Platte which is near the banks of the river, the outside walls still standing, but the inside is in ruins, having been burned up. The walls are built of adobes, or Spanish brick, being large pieces of tempered clay dried in the sun and apparently laid one on another without mortar or cement. The dimensions of this fort outside are 144 feet east to west, and from north to south 103 feet. There is a large door fronting to the south which has led to the dwellings which have been fourteen in number, built in the form of a parallelogram, leaving a large space in the center. The space occupied by the dwelling is not quite half of the whole fort. Fronting to the east is another large door which opens upon a large open space 98 3/4 feet by 47 feet where it is supposed they used to keep horses, etc. At the northwest corner is a tower projecting out from the line of the walls six feet each way, or, in other words it is twelve feet square with port holes for cannon. At the northeast corner has been another projection extending eastward 29 1/2 feet and is 19 1/2 feet wide. The walls are 11 feet high and 30 inches thick. We took the dimensions of this with a tape line and then proceeded to Fort Laramie about two miles farther west . . . . It stands on the bank of the Laramie fork. Laramie fork is a stream forty-one yards wide, a very swift current, but not deep."[111]

Thomas Bullock described the measurements of abandoned Fort Platte as follows:

"144 by 103.2 outside, the door on the east side 9 f. 9 in., height of walls 11 feet - the doorway on s. side 10.6 wide - all the walls were about 30 inches thick; around the inside of the walls were 15 rooms; the one on the s.w. corner appeared to have been a store - these small rooms 16x15 surrounded a yard 61 f. 9 in by 56 f. - On the chimney piece of the 2nd room on the west side were paintings of a horse and a buffalo but little defaced - on the north side was a yard for horses 98 f. 9 in. by 47 feet inside having on the n.w. corner a square tower with holes to shoot thro' on the sides - which was 9 f. 3 in. square - on the n.e. corner, was an attached building 29 f. 4 in. by 19 f. 6 in. outside dimensions . . . the Oregon trail runs one rod from the s.w. angle of the fort - running the River road, under the bluffs. The building was made with unburnt bricks & had been white-washed."[112]

Discrepancies between the number of rooms and measurements are evident but not serious.

On June 3, 1847 the Mormons hired the Fort Laramie flat boat from James Bordeaux for $18 and ferried their wagons across the North Platte River, completing the task by early morning on June 4 when the trek was continued.[113]

The Mormon emigrations continued past forts Platte and Laramie along the "Mormon trail" through the fall of 1847, with a smaller emigration heading west in 1848. As the year 1849 dawned the California gold craze was beginning to sweep the country. Thousands of adventurers converged on the Missouri border towns for the trip west to the mines via the "Great Platte

---

[111]*Ibid.*, pp. 208-209.
[112]Hafen and Young, *op. cit.*, pp. 125-127.
[113]Clayton, *op. cit.*, pp. 209-213.

River Road".[114]   The first Forty-niners reached Fort Platte and Fort Laramie in late May 1849.

On June 14, 1849, two Argonauts, Vincent Geiger and Joseph Wood, mentioned both forts in their diaries on their way to the gold fields.   The latter wrote: "Found the water in Laramie's Fk so deep as to cover the fore wheels of our Wagon . . . On our right from here was the bare mud walls of an old deserted fort [Fort Platte] and on our left & one mile up Laramie's fork was the Fort of that name."[115]   Geiger referred to Fort Platte as "old Fort John, now deserted."[116]   On June 16 Company E of the U.S. Mounted Riflemen under Major Winslow F. Sanderson arrived at Fort Laramie,[117] and on June 26 the American Fur Company sold Fort Laramie to the government for use as a military post.   Included in the sale were probably the remains of Fort Platte as the purchase deed states that ". . . Pierre Choteau, Jr. and Co. should release and transfer to the United States all the houses, buildings, and improvements by them at any time held or occupied as a trading Post at Fort John, commonly called Fort Laramie . . . including all permanent buildings . . . situated within ten miles of the junction . . . of said Laramie Fork with said Platte river . . ."[118]

July 6 and July 9, 1849, afford the last mention of Fort Platte by emigrants and Forty-niners before the trading post fades into history.   The report of the Boston-Newton Company stated that on July 6 "We crossed opposite Fort John [Fort Platte] one mile below Ft. Larima.   These places are nothing but a mud wall with quarters for a company of a hundred men."[119]   On July 9 the Washington City and California Mining Association arrived at Fort Laramie.   The J. Goldborough Bruff Journal states "Several hundred yards back from the river's bank, on the right, stood the old adobe walls of Fort Platte, the original post of the fur traders, now in ruin; and looks like an old Castle.   It is rectangular."[120]

After the military had established themselves at Fort Laramie, Capt. Howard Stansbury and Lieut. J. W. Gunnison of the Corps of Topographical Engineers arrived there on July 12, 1849.   Capt. Stansbury wrote in his private journal ". . . after a march of 13

---

[114]Mattes, *Great Platte River Road*, p. 487.
[115]*Ibid.*, p. 489.
[116]David M. Potter, ed., *Trail to California, the Overland Journal of Vincent Geiger and Wakeman Bryarly* (New Haven: Yale University Press, 1945), p. 106.
[117]Barry, *op. cit.*, pp. 851, 853.
[118]Merrill J. Mattes, *Fort Laramie and the Forty-Niners* (Estes Park, Colo.: Rocky Mountain Nature Association, 1949), pp. 22-23.
[119]Jessie Gould Hannon, *The Boston-Newton Company Venture* (Lincoln: University of Nebraska Press, 1969), pp. 124-125.
[120]Georgia W. Read and Ruth Gaines, eds. *Gold Rush - The Journals, Drawings, and Other Papers of J. Goldsborough Bruff* (New York: Columbia University Press, 1949), pp. 34-35.

miles crossed Laramie fork and drove up to this Fort [Lara-
mie] . . . Below us is a company of mounted rifles . . . The
Laramie river is quite a rapid stream about 3 feet deep where the
wagons crossed which was just opposite and old adobe Fort now
abandoned [Fort Platte]. The American Fur Company peo[pl]e
are encamped on the left bank having sold out Ft. Laramie to the
Govt. for $4000."[121]

The remains of Fort Platte were possibly torn down in the late
1850s to provide filler material for new construction at Fort Laramie.[122] Throughout the years the site of Old Fort Platte appears
to have remained unnoticed until July 1951. On this date the
Historical Landmark Commission of Wyoming erected a plaque
south of U.S. 26 on state highway 160 bearing the following
statement:

FORT PLATTE

A Trading Post, Built by

LANCASTER P. LUPTON

In 1841,

Stood Fifty Yards To The

North.

Placed By

The Historical Landmark Commission

Of Wyoming

. July 1951

---

[121]Mattes, *Fort Laramie* . . . , p. 27.
[122]*Ibid.*, p. 35.

William Wallace Cook: Dime Novelist

By

MABEL COOPER SKJELVER

William Wallace Cook was one of the prolific writers in the "stable" of the world's largest publishing house of dime novels and story papers, Street and Smith of New York City, at the turn of the century. Collectors of dime novels and story papers now seek the stories of this Marshall, Michigan, author. Wally, as he was known to his family and friends in Marshall, had little difficulty in turning out short stories, serials, and novelettes to the order of his main employer, Street and Smith.[1] A variety of pseudonyms has made it difficult to identify completely his vast output of adventure stories for boys, girls, and adults. His versatility was evident on reviewing his known work, for he was adept at writing adventure, love, mystery, detective as well as western stories. He is best known as one of the major contributors of the Diamond Dick, Rough Rider, Merriwell, and Buffalo Bill stories, as well as the Nick Carter stories. Much of his vast output remains unidentified in the numerous pulp story papers of Street and Smith, Munsey and other publishers.

William Wallace Cook was born in Marshall, Michigan, April 11, 1867, and was the only child of Charles Ruggles and Jane Elizabeth (Bull) Cook. According to Cook in his autobiography, *The Fiction Factory,* as a young lad he was encouraged in his writing by his mother, who in a limited way was also a writer, having written for *Harper's Magazine.* His father, however, thought his son was wasting time at scribbling, preferring that he follow a business career.[2]

The elder Cook came to Marshall in 1845 at the age of six years, grew up in the community, enlisted in the army, serving

---

[1]"Uncle Billy" was the affectionate name given Cook by younger writers who sought his advice on how to construct a plot or market their writings. Letters from T. T. Flynn, undated, [ca. August, 1928]; Erle Stanley Gardner, August 12, 1929.

[2]John Milton Edwards, *nom de plume* of William Wallace Cook, *The Fiction Factory, Being the Experiences of a Writer Who, For Twenty-Two Years, Has Kept A Story-Mill Grinding Successfully,* (Ridgewood, N. J.: The Editor Company, 1912), p. 21. Information about Cook's life and writing prior to 1912 was taken from this autobiographical account.

three and a half years as a government detective. His employment as an immigration agent for various railroads following the Civil War demanded frequent travel and the family lived for a time in Layfayette, Indiana, and Cleveland, Ohio.[3]   In 1870 the Cook family went to Ottawa, Kansas, and remained there for eleven years.   Here young Cook wrote plays at the age of twelve, in which he performed with his friends.   At fifteen he had won an award of merit from Frank Leslie's *Boys and Girls Weekly* for a composition he had submitted.[4]   These early incidents did much to spur young Cook to seek writing as a career.

In 1882 the Cook family moved to Chicago.   Upon the urging of his father, William Wallace enrolled in the Bryant and Stratton Business College for two years, but continued to write in his spare time.   After leaving school, he worked first as a stenographer for a firm of subscription book publishers, next as a ticket agent for a railroad company, then as a bill clerk for a boot and shoe firm. He returned to work for the railroad company and upon the closing of their Chicago office, Cook worked first in the office for a firm of coke and sewer pipe wholesalers, then as a reporter for the *Chicago Morning News,* finally as a paymaster for a Chicago contractor.

The death of his father in 1889 brought heavy family responsibilities and in an effort to earn extra income, Cook wrote in the evenings and submitted material to newspapers and story papers. The Chicago *Inter-Ocean* story paper accepted an article at space rates ($2.50), while the Chicago *Times* used one of his stories, without payment.   Yet having his material in print gave Cook pleasure and encouragement.   The Detroit *Free Press* published Cook's first story, a tale of the Kansas wheatfields, entitled "No 1 Hard," in the fall of 1889.   While he received only $8 for it, he was encouraged to enter the *Free Press* story contest.   Two of his short sketches that he entered were bought and published, although he did not win a prize.[5]   That settled it; he became more industrious than ever, determined to find a way to devote more time to his writing.   By persistence he found outlets for his short sketches and serial stories during the next two years in *Puck, Truth, The Ladies World, Yankee Blade, Leslie's Monthly, Chatter,* and *Figaro.*   In 1890 a serial published in the Philadelphia, *Saturday Night,* James Elverson, publisher, gave the young writer

---

[3]Railroad pass cards of Charles Ruggles Cook in a private collection are for the Grand Trunk Line Northern Pacific; Chicago and Western Michigan; Toledo, Peoria and Western; Rock Island and Peoria; Chicago Burlington and Northern; Chicago and Grand Trunk; and Albert Lea Route.
[4]Edwards (Cook), p. 17.
[5]*Ibid.,* p. 21; Marshall *Evening Chronicle,* July 20, 1933, obituary of William Wallace Cook. Marshall Public Library.

—University of Nebraska Photo Service

William Wallace Cook about 1925

confidence that he could be a commercial success as an author, and also pointed Cook toward sensational story papers.[6] Cook sought more outlets of this type for his work.

He married Anna Gertrude Slater, of Madison, Wisconsin, in 1891. Two years later William Wallace Cook decided, with the encouragement and approval of his wife, to make his living as a writer. Cook had sold many stories and sketches, since his first story for the Detroit *Free Press,* but it was not until 1893 that his earnings from writing exceeded his office salary. His paymaster salary was $25 a week ($1200 a year) and his earnings from writing in 1893 amounted to $1825 with $1675 of this from one

---

[6]Edwards, p 23.

firm, Street and Smith of New York City.[7]   While these figures
appear bleak today, a family then could live well on $800 a year
and with an income of $1500 could play the part of "a member
of society."[8]

In the spring of 1893, William Wallace Cook through a coincidence was given the opportunity to write for Street and Smith.
It came about in this manner.   Alfred B. Tozer, editor of *The
Chicago Ledger,* had unwittingly suggested such an opportunity
when Cook called upon the editor to inquire if that Chicago story
paper could use serial stories of his.[9]   Tozer had at that moment
received a letter from Street and Smith, along with a bundle of
newspaper clippings, requesting Tozer to use the news items as a
basis for stories. Cook decided to send a sample of his writing to
this well-known publishing firm.   After the return of several manuscripts for revisions, Cook was accepted to write novelettes for
their juvenile five- and ten-cent libraries.   Cook was elated since
Street and Smith was regarded as the "big time", as well as a
steady market.

Street and Smith had been publishing a fiction weekly, *The New
York Weekly,* since the 1850s.   In 1889 the firm entered the dime
novel field, competing with such well established publishers as
Beadle and Adam, the Munros (George and brother Norman),
and Frank Tousey.   By 1900 the Beadle and Munro outfits had
folded, leaving only Tousey and Street and Smith in command of
the dime novel field.   Street and Smith bought out Tousey and
turned the paper-covered novels into serials for pulp magazines.
These serials in turn were later re-issued as paper-covered novelettes (Libraries) to a new generation of readers.   As soon as a
weekly or a library began to lose money, Street and Smith created
another publication to take its place, although it too might have a
short life, dictated by the changing tastes of the reading public.
This practice did not provide security for their fleet of writers.[10]

---

[7]*Ibid.,* p. 8.

[8]Frederick Lewis Allen, *The Big Change,* (New York: Harper, 1952),
p. 45.

[9]Edwards, pp. 31-37.   Tozer was one of the new writers Frederick Mar-
maduke Van Rensselaer Dey broke in for the Nick Carter stories when the
burden of work became too heavy for Dey.

[10]At the time William Wallace Cook became one of the many writers
for Street and Smith, Ormond and George Smith, sons of one of the founders, Francis S. Smith, were the owners of the publishing house.   Francis
Scott Street and Francis Shubael Smith took over *The New York Weekly
Dispatch* in 1855, under the paternal guidance of the owner, Amos J. Wil-
liamson.   Two years later, having proved their ability, they became sole
owners and changed the name to *The New York Weekly.*   At Street's death
in 1883 Ormond Smith bought Street's interest from the estate.   Francis S.
Smith, with his sons' assistance, directed the firm until 1933.   A detailed
history of the Street and Smith firm can be found in Quentin Reynolds'

Quentin Reynolds attributed the long survival of Street and Smith in the pulp field to two basic principles—diversity and killing off publications as soon as their popularity waned.

The Street and Smith vast publishing enterprise included the *Buffalo Bill Stories, The Log Cabin Library, The Nick Carter Detective Library,* The Frank Merriwell stories, Jesse James stories, *The Tip-Top Weekly,* the *New Fiction Library, The Diamond Dick Library,* the *Rough Riders* (Ted Strong) stories and many others. Russel Nye contends that the last genuine dime novel publication was Street and Smith's *New Buffalo Bill Weekly* in 1912.[11] However, the *New Buffalo Bill Weekly* would best be called a serial story paper, for not until the 1920s were these serials compiled into a paper back book form. Even these reprinted serials were extensively edited or revised, a necessity to make the three (or more) parts blend together, and to remove the "cliff-hanging" devices required for a serial.[12]

To provide stories for their many pulp publications Street and Smith kept a stable of writers busy turning out adventure stories on order. Stock writer names that were the property of Street and Smith were used. Many a young writer grew to literary maturity during his tenure with Street and Smith. The following are a few of the better known authors who wrote for Street and Smith at various times:

John Russel Coryell, originator of "Nick Carter" name.
Frederick Van Rensselaer Dey, primary author of the Nick Carter detective stories.
Edward Zane Carroll Judson, "Ned Buntline," No. 1, author of Buffalo Bill stories.
Prentiss Ingraham, "Ned Buntline," No. 2, author of Buffalo Bill stories.
Horatio Alger, Jr.
Upton Sinclair
Edward B. Ellis
St. George Rathborne, author of Buffalo Bill stories.
William Gilbert Patten, "Burt L. Standish," creator of the Frank Merriwell stories.
W. Bert Foster, author of Buffalo Bill stories.
John H. Whitson, author of Buffalo Bill stories and Merriwell stories.
A. Conan Doyle
Bret Harte
Sidney Porter, (O. Henry)

Theodore Dreiser also wrote for this publishing firm and served a

---

The Fiction Factory or From Pulp Row to Quality Street, (New York: Random House, 1955). The similarity of Reynolds' title to the title of William Wallace Cook's book of 1912 is striking.

[11]Russel Nye, *The Unembarassed Muse,* (New York: Dial Press, 1970, p. 201.

[12]Frank Luther Mott, A History of the American Magazine, Vol. IV, 1885-1905, (Cambridge: Harvard University Press, 1957, p. 117.

year as editor of *Smith's Magazine* (1905), a Street and Smith publication.

William Wallace Cook, credited as one of the many authors of the Diamond Dick, Frank Merriwell, Nick Carter, Buffalo Bill and Ted Strong of the Rough Rider stories, wrote numerous stories for many Street and Smith publications.

Pulp literature in the form of dime novels and story papers, while fostering patriotism, conventional morality, and virtuous conduct, provided entertainment for the masses through swift action, dramatic tales. Yet these stories, strangely enough, were frowned upon by parents, because they thought the sensational, exciting incidents might have immoral affiliations. These dime novels and story papers make tame reading for today's youngster satiated with television's blood and crime of the 1970s. In retrospect they served an educational function for they provided the means and created the desire for reading that has been largely lost for today's television oriented youth.[13]

Pulp literature is criticized for its stilted, crude writing, yet some ten million Americans paid tribute to the dime novel and story papers each month. The pulps never suggested any possible satisfaction in ideas, in intellectual curiosity, or in esthetic pleasures, for their role was one of escape from a humdrum troubled life to one of romance and excitement.[14]

While Erastiuc F. Beadle, and his brother Erwin, are credited as the originators of the dime novel in 1860, an editorial in *Western Library Messenger* points out that cheap literature was viewed with disfavor as early as the 1840s.

> Riding on the cars through Michigan today, we have been half amused and half pained to see with what avidity "yellow covered literature" is here as elsewhere, devoured by travelers . . . men, with foreheads of respectable dimensions, have busied themselves for hours today . . . in perusing, page by page, the contacts of some shilling romance by [J. H.] Ingraham or some other equally stale and insipid novelist.[15]

The major pulp publishing firm, Street and Smith, found prosperity at the end of the century, and on into the 1920s and '30s by providing "the John Smith's of America" with a variety of inexpensive reading matter that chronicled the adventures of Nick Carter, Diamond Dick, Buffalo Bill, Ned Strong, and Frank Merriwell. The pulps at the turn of the century concentrated on virtuous characters and exciting adventures, but by the 1920s three

---

[13]Frank Schick, The *Paperbound Book in America,* (New York: R. R. Bowker, 1958), p. 51; Nye, p. 203.

[14]Merle Curti, *The Growth of American Thought,* (New York: Harper and Row, 1954), pp. 725, 726, 729.

[15]An editorial in the *Western Literary Messenger,* VIII, No. 16, May, 22, as quoted in Albert Johannesen, *The House of Beadle and Adam,* (Norman: University of Oklahoma Press, 1950), p. 3.

other broad categories began to emerge: love, detective and western. By the 1930s other pulp publishers were imitating Street and Smith's three most successful magazines, *Love Story, Detective Story* and *Western Story*. Early love stories titillated readers without being pornographic. Pulps dealing with raw sex emerged in the late 1920s when publishers took advantage of the new frankness that followed the war. The detective story remained as a clear cut category, but a distinction between a western and an adventure story came about. Adventure stories eventually were subcategorized into sea, sport, air, and spy themes. The science fiction pulp emerged as a separate category in the late 1920s, but its antecedents can be found in such early story papers as *Argosy* and others that ran tales based on supernatural phenomena, or with scientific or pseudo-scientific background. Street and Smith's *Western Story* created in 1927 was the last of their dime paperback novelettes. The firm rightly read the public pulse in the thirties and forties and turned to science fiction, comics, romance and women's fashion magazines.[16]

The fiction of William Wallace Cook by his own statement was one of clean ethics. In a newspaper interview he contended he never wrote a line in his stories but what he would permit his own son to read, feeling secure that the reading would do no harm, but would, on the other hand, be beneficial to the boy.[17] Cook's stories had a great variety of content, in which adventure, mystery and daring situations predominated. One of his novelettes, *A Quarter to Four, or The Secret of Fortune Island,* in the *New Fiction Library* (1908) serves to illustrate. Robert Lorry, the hero, inherits the estate of an uncle in which the sole property is an envelope, a "small packet of paper money" and instructions in regard to the meeting of three other individuals at the Palace Hotel in San Francisco, who would identify themselves with the phrase "A Quarter to Four". They were to have similar envelopes, then all were to go to the office of a San Francisco lawyer for further instruction. Another envelope conveyed directions to charter a boat and prepare for a long cruise. Additional envelopes were to be opened at specified times once the four were at sea. Adventure, mystery and daring situations were imaginatively devised, with the personality of the individuals playing a major role. Besides the hero, there was a complaining, older woman; a beautiful, virtuous young woman; and a treacherous, crafty young man. Each chapter was packed with excitement ending with a "cliff hanging" situation. All the while, the reader knows a treasure

---

[16]Theodore Peterson, *Magazines of the Twentieth Century,* (Urbana: University of Illinois Press, 1964, p. 201.
[17]Marshall *Evening Chronicle,* July 20, 1933.

will be found and the hero will wed Zelda, the beautiful, virtuous young woman. In an "O· Henry" ending, Lorry finds that his uncle is not dead but a very ill man and had used this adventurous means to get his part of an ill-gotten treasure to San Francisco and to convey the shares of his three dead comrades to their heirs without the heirs knowing of its tarnished source.

One of William Wallace's first tasks for his new employer was to construct a tale based on a prominent insurance case reported in the newspapers. The use of news items as a foundation for a plot was an accepted practice of pulp publishers at the turn of the century. Cook decided to build his own inspirational source material by clipping interesting news stories upon which he might build a fictional tale, these he categorized and filed in letter-files. The indexing was done in such a way to suggest the character or main theme of the news item and where the clipping could be found in the letter-files. This system was no doubt a partial inspiration for his last book, *Plotto*.

Cook also maintained an extensive personal library that aided him to obtain realism in his fictional tales. Jules Verne's book *Around the World in Eighty Days* (1873) was one of the classics found in Cook's library and served as the inspirational basis for one of Cook's novelettes *Around the World in Eighty Hours* (1925). Borrowing from a masterpiece was a form of admiration and little effort was made to disguise this fact.[18]

William Wallace Cook experienced early the insecurity of writing for a publishing firm that rapidly adapted to the ever-changing pulp fiction field. For almost a year he had been writing serials for Street and Smith exclusively when the publishing firm decided to use reprints for a time, leaving Cook without a market. This alerted him to the danger of concentrating on one type of story for a particular outlet. He sent copies to Street and Smith of two of his published stories which had appeared in *Saturday Night* to inquire if similar stories would be considered for their most popular story paper, *The New York Weekly*. Ormond Smith liked them well enough to give Cook the assignment of writing sentimental fiction for young women under the pseudonym of "Julia Edwards," a Street and Smith owned name. Many of the Julia Edwards stories were actually written by men, such as Cook, Edward Stratemeyer, and others. "Julia Edwards" according to her inventors was a poor orphan working girl who wrote stories of her bleak life. As the bicycle was the current fashion, Cook was to build a love story that exploited this current infatuation. "Bicycle Bell" was the title of Cook's first serial under the Julia

---

[18]William Wallace Cook's library and papers are preserved by a private collector.

Edwards *nom de plume*.[19]   While the *New York Weekly* assignment provided a somewhat steady income, Cook thought he needed
to seek other markets.

In July 1894, Cook made his first trip to New York City to
confer with his publishers, hoping for additional assignments.   He
was given the task of writing a novelette in serial form.   He wrote
the first two installments while visiting in Michigan, where he had
close relatives.   Upon completion of the novelette he received
$500 for it, considered a large sum, as typical rates were 1/2
cent per word.   Cook was elated as this was the most he had
received for a serial story.   He was commissioned to do two other
juvenile serials under a Street and Smith *nom de plume* that year.
Cook was now confident he had established himself as a productive
writer, for his year's work brought him $2750, more than he could
have earned in the business world, but what brought more satisfaction was the confidence that Ormond Smith had placed in his
work.[20]

The next few years brought hard times, and ill health.   When
his health permitted he continued to turn out "two 30,000 word
stories per week," but when his illness curtailed his output, Street
and Smith gave others his previous assignments.   Such were the
realities of the pulp publishing field.   Shortly after the beginning
of the year (1895), Street and Smith notified him that the nickel
library business was not flourishing and that he would receive $40
per novel, rather than the $50 he had been paid.   They did, how-
ever, suggest he submit a story for a new detective library, *Diamond Dick*.[21]   This character was to bring some fame to Cook,
and he took Diamond Dick through many a Western adventure.
Cook was one of the numerous writers of the Diamond Dick series
writing under the Street and Smith name of W. B. Lawson.   The
Dime Novel Roundup has reprinted one of Cook's Diamond Dick
stories, "Diamond Dick Jr's Call Down or the King of the Silver
Box." (1895)[22]

The Diamond Dick detective serial was conceived by Street and
Smith to rival the Deadwood Dick detective library of Beadle and
Adam.   Nye states that the originator of Diamond Dick was Samuel S. Hall.   However, William Wallace Cook was one of the
writers of these detective stories as early as 1895.   Quentin Reynolds contends that Diamond Dick was inspired by an old frontier

[19]Mary Noel, *Villains Galore: The Heyday of the Popular Story Weekly*,
(New York: MacMillian, 1954, p. 185; Edwards (Cook), pp. 43, 48.
[20]*Ibid.*, pp. 49-51.
[21]*Ibid.*, p. 57.
[22]*Dime Novel Round Up*, a magazine of the Dime Novel Club, first
issued in 1944, edited by Edward T. LeBlanc, 87 School St., Fall River,
Mass.

fighter, Richard Tanner, who, tradition states, served on the plains with Custer and then gave exhibitions of his shooting skill in wild west shows. Diamond Dick and his friend, "Handsome Harry," galloped through millions of pages in the Diamond Dick library.[23]

Cook now had many assignments entailing deadlines that must be met if he were to make up the loss of $10 per nickel novel. Although ill he thought he could increase his productivity with the aid of stenographers. Shortly, however, he discovered that his time was consumed with editing and revising so that little profit was gained. Dismissing the three helpers he returned reluctantly to his earlier system, a slower but proven formula.

Cook describes this efficient system in his autobiography. His rapid, neat typing skill, developed during newspaper reporter days, enabled him to compose directly on the typewriter, including a carbon copy as he typed the original. Stories were double spaced on 8½ x 11 inch paper, with four hundred words on one sheet. A serial of 60,000 words covered one hundred fifty sheets; those of 30,000, seventy-five sheets; with short stories averaging from fifteen to twenty pages. Cook believed in having the latest in typewriters, as it saved him time, thereby increasing his production, as well as producing neater copies. He admits to owning twenty-five typewriters, often two machines at the same time, and could change from one machine to another without hampering his flow of ideas.

Stories were sent to a publisher with a self-addressed return envelope. By using paper and envelopes of the same weight, postage or express charges were easily calculated. Records of his manuscripts were at first kept in a bound book of pre-printed stubs and from letters, containing the date sent, the date returned, refusals or payment received. A quick look through this book gave him an idea of his current manuscript inventory. This proven system was to serve him efficiently throughout his writing career. He later made one adjustment using index cards rather than the bound books, to keep track of his manuscripts.[24] High production was mandatory for the remuneration was usually at a given rate per word, varying through time from one-half cent, one or two cents, to two and one-half cents and finally to three and three and one-half cents per word; thus a 1000-word short story at one cent a word would be worth $10. Cook was receiving the top rate of two to two and one-half cents per word by 1910 and three and one-half cents per word in the late 1920s.

In the fall of 1895, the doctors identified his illness as tuberculosis and advised him to move to a southwest location. From

---

[23]Nye, p. 206; Reynolds, pp. 96-98.
[24]Edwards, pp. 25-30.

November, 1895, to April, 1896, Cook and his wife lived on a ranch near Phoenix, Arizona, with Cook turning out Diamond Dick five-cent libraries for Street and Smith, as well as writing sketches and short stories for other publications. This western experience, while it brought about financial insolvency, provided inspiration not only for the Diamond Dick stories but for later Buffalo Bill and Rough Rider (Ned Strong) stories.

One of Cook's western short sketches, that appeared in *Munsey's Magazine,* May, 1896, entitled "Peter: A Study in Red," brought forth a strange reader reaction. Cook, while in Arizona, was continually alert for story material and spent time exploring the countryside and checking out local news. On one of these excursions he was told about the building of a dam at a place called Walnut Grove. The dam when completed stored a great deal of water. However, one night the dam gave way and a number of laborers, working a gold mine by a hydraulic method below the dam, were drowned. Cook's sketch for Munsey related how a Maricopa Indian, riding his pony in the gulch below Walnut Grove, gave up his mount to a white girl to prevent her drowning in the flood waters of the broken dam. After the sketch was published, Cook received a letter from a young Indian on the Maricopa Indian Reservation, claiming the Maricopa Indian rescuer was his father.[25] Fiction had turned into fact for one reader.

While in Arizona, he became interested in the possibility of developing a gold mine, and went east to secure capital to form a company to purchase and develop the mine. Whether he obtained capital from other sources is unknown, but he invested his own reserve in the venture. In a few weeks the mining venture proved a failure, with a loss of $10,000 to Cook.[26]

Cook's finances were virtually exhausted and in desperation he and his wife made a "prospecting" trip to New York, hoping that Street and Smith would permit him to submit additional stories to the firm. Since other authors were turning out acceptable stories, the publisher informed Cook that work could not be taken out of their hands and for the present time no new, continuing assignment was possible. They did, however, give him an order for four nickel novelette stories to be held in reserve in case a regular contributor, then ill, failed to meet deadlines, as well as four sketches for their new publication, *Ainslee's Magazine.* However, within a few days the publisher informed Cook that the regular writer was well and anxious to regain his post. Cook was to complete the nickel novelettes he had started. Two were accepted at $40 each. Four

[25]*Ibid.,* p. 79.
[26]*Ibid.,* pp. 60-61.

sketches for *Ainslee's Magazine,* were accepted at $10 each, but this amount would not long pay their New York expenses.[27]

Cook, with his wife, returned to Chicago, bringing with him an order for a serial for *The New York Weekly.* Renting a flat on the north side, the Cooks took their household effects out of storage and faced the problem of a meager existence, as Cook could now work only a half-day. Writing became a chore and the results were unsatisfactory, yet he persevered. By October, 1897, a serial was accepted by Street and Smith. Cook expected to receive $300 for it, but was paid $200. His protest brought an additional check for $100. The year closed with another order from Street and Smith for a Julia Edwards story. At the end of the year his income totaled a meager $425 but the following year his fortunes took a slight upturn.[28]

Cook sold a Julia Edwards serial to *The New York Weekly* shortly after the new year. In the spring, although little improved in health, Cook decided to journey to New York, hoping his presence would secure commissions. His arrival was opportune, for Street and Smith had decided to initiate a library based on the Klondike gold rush. Cook was given the assignment to write stories for the *Klondike Kit Library,* a juvenile serial. Cook gave the hero, Klondike Kit, a beautiful heroine, Nugget Nell, a resourceful, brave companion in Klondike Kit's many adventures. The Cooks remained in New York for three months; while there he wrote Klondike Kit stories and another serial for *The New York Weekly.* Because of the heat at midsummer, they retreated to the Catskill Mountains, living in a hotel near Cairo. By late summer Cook received the discouraging news that since Klondike Kit was not successful as a weekly, it would be continued as a monthly. Up to that time Cook had written sixteen stories for this library.[29] Obviously a monthly check of $40 would not pay for a summer resort life, so Cook and his wife returned to Chicago, settling again on the north side. Although his health was far from good, Cook continued to write for the *Klondike Kit Library, The New York Weekly* (Julia Edwards stories) and *The New York Five-Cent Weekly.* The *Five-Cent Weekly* assignment had been given to Cook due to the fact that the regular writer was seriously ill.[30]

By this time Cook was confined to his bed, but a writing assignment could not be refused since the family finances were at low ebb. A stenographer was hired and Cook dictated his stories for two weeks, then resumed writing them in bed on an improvised table. Much to the wonder of his physician and his wife, Cook

[27]*Ibid.,* pp. 61 and 72; Reynolds, p. 273.
[28]Edwards, pp. 61-62, 72-75.
[29]*Ibid.,* pp. 81-82; Reynolds, p. 107.
[30]Edwards, pp. 82-84.

slowly improved. He began a story embracing his Arizona experiences. This serial served a year later to introduce Cook to Matthew White, Jr., editor of *The Argosy,* a Munsey publication.[31] Cook had increased his earnings, most of which came from the Klondike Kit series. In better health the following year Cook turned out thirty-five five-cent libraries for Street and Smith, three *Klondike Kit Libraries,* and a novelette.[32]

Up to the turn of the century Street and Smith had been the heaviest purchaser of Cook's fiction. The serial he had sold to *The Argosy* encouraged him to seek other publishers. Shortly he found a market for a serial with *The Western World,* through a gentleman with whom his wife had become acquainted while attending Frank Holmes School of Illustration. *The Western World* purchased another serial, a mystery story, which the editors planned to use to boom circulation; i.e., the solution was not revealed until the last chapter, and prizes were offered for the correct solution of the mystery.[33]

In 1900 the McClure syndicate bought one of Cook's serials, issuing it first in metropolitan newspapers, then sold it to the Kellogg Newspaper Union, who in turn issued it as a "patent" to be sent out to country newspapers. Several years later, G. W. Dillingham Company, a New York publisher, bought the story, *His Friend the Enemy,* and published it with a paper cover.[34] Cook continued to submit stories to *The New York Weekly* and *The New York Five-Cent Weekly.* He received a further assignment to write twenty-eight stories for *Do and Dare,* a Street and Smith juvenile weekly.[35] This weekly for young boys featured "Phil Rushington" as the hero. When Cook had finished fifteen stories, the original writer became sick, and Cook was given the task of completing an unfinished story and then writing the entire series. *Do and Dare* folded after some forty-seven issues.[36]

The story Cook had written during his illness was purchased by *The Argosy's* editor, Matthew White, Jr., for $250. On the proceeds of the sale Cook and his wife took an extended outing to Atlantic City, New York, Boston, Salem, Plymouth and other places in the New England states. Cook devoted his mornings to

---

[31]"He Was a Stranger," cited in Cook's autobiographical account, was later published as *His Friend the Enemy.*

[32]Edwards, pp. 85-87, 96-97.

[33]*Ibid.,* pp. 95-96.

[34]William Wallace Cook, *His Friend the Enemy,* (New York: G. W. Dillingham Company, 1903).

[35]Edwards, pp. 96-99, 102; Reynolds, p. 108.

[36]Stanley A. Pachon, "William Wallace Cook," *Dime Novel Round-Up,* September 15, 1957, p. 72. This article encompasses only the years prior to 1912, being based on Cook's autobiographical account in *The Fiction Factory.*

writing and his afternoons to sightseeing. Late that summer, the Cooks went west, first to Michigan, then on to Wisconsin. They returned to Michigan, "to the little town where Cook was born, bought an old place and settled down."[37] This property on North Kalamazoo Avenue in Marshall, Michigan, was a bracketed brick house in the Italian villa style, built in 1869 by Frederick Karstaedt, a clothing merchant. Cook purchased the property in 1900. Later he removed the original wide front stone steps and added a porch. The property is now owned by Garth Thick.[38]

During his thirty-three years in Marshall, Cook participated in many city and state affairs and organizations. He was a member of the Presbyterian church, a Knight Templar, the Shrine, and a faithful attendant of the Marshall Rotary Club. He was a first-class story teller at family and social gatherings. His generosity was relied upon by colleagues, friends, and family for assistance in time of need or emergencies. In 1923 he was a member of the City Commission that was appointed to revise the Marshall City Charter. In 1931 he was appointed a member of the Marshall Electric Light and Water Commission, an office which gave him great satisfaction. He was a Democrat although most of his relatives were Republicans. He was an active member of the Michigan Authors Association, The Chicago Press Club and the Battle Creek Writer's Club.[39]

Once established at Marshall, Cook continued to write for Street and Smith's *New York Five-Cent Weekly,* as well as to revise and lengthen some of his old stories for this publisher. A new boys serial library, *Boys of America,* was created by Street and Smith and Cook wrote many stories for it. Street and Smith again reduced the remuneration for their weeklies and discontinued all orders for their five-cent libraries. Reprints would be issued again since there was a new generation of juvenile readers. Cook met this turn of events by directing his output toward Munsey's publication, *The Argosy.* G. W. Dillingham brought out Cook's book *His Friend the Enemy,* as a hard bound book. A prospecting trip to New York city during the winter of 1904, brought an assignment to write for a new Street and Smith publication, *The Popular Magazine.*[40] He was told also that there would be a new weekly, *Young Rough Riders,* (later changed to *Rough Riders*), for which he was to create stories, along with St. George Rathborne. The rate was to be $50 for each, a nice advancement from the old $40

---

[37]Edwards, pp. 98-99.
[38]*Ibid.,* pp. 99-100; a private collector; Mabel C. Skjelver, *The Nineteenth Century Homes of Marshall, Michigan,* (Marshall: Marshall Historical Society, 1971), p. 148.
[39]Marshall *Evening Chronicle,* July 20, 1933.
[40]Edwards, pp. 100, 102.

rate.[41]   Ted Strong, the fictional hero of the Rough Rider stories, was one of the volunteers with Teddy Roosevelt, having fought in the Spanish American War in the Philippines.   Following the war he owned a ranch, Black Mountain, in the Bad Lands of Dakota. William Wallace Cook wrote for this series under the Street and Smith stock name of Edward C. Taylor or as Ned Taylor.   Cook took over the writing of the Ted Strong stories from Rathborne with issue No. 38 and continued through issue No. 123, when Cook was temporarily relieved by W. Bert Foster.   Cook and Foster shared authorship through issue No. 175.   *The Rough Rider Weekly* stories were reprinted in the *New Medal Library* under the byline of Edward C. Taylor from 1909 to 1915.   The Ted Strong stories in *New Medal Library* appeared as serials in the *New Buffalo Bill Weekly* from 1916 to 1919.   They were re-issued from 1923 to 1930 in a thick pulp book series known as *Western Story Library*.[42]   Street and Smith were not inclined to permit good material to lie idle if it could be fitted into one of their numerous publications.

Buffalo Bill Stories was a Street and Smith weekly for which William Wallace Cook wrote western stories after his move to Marshall.   This western weekly was Street and Smith's most long-lived story paper, having a total of 591 issues from 1901 to 1912 (the last nine issues were repeats of the earliest Buffalo Bill tales). It ceased publication for one week and came back as *The New Buffalo Bill Weekly,* running from September 12, 1912, to June 19, 1919.   Although hailed as "new", all the stories were re-issues of previous *Buffalo Bill Stories*.   There were periods when the reprinting from the originals was fairly well mixed up, with some of Cook's original stories deleted.   With issue No. 357 *The New Buffalo Bill Weekly* became *The Western Story Magazine*.   This title was also used for reprints of the Rough Rider stories, as previously stated.   *The Western Story Magazine* also reprinted from other early Street and Smith publications, such as *Golden Hours, Good News, Bound to Win Library, Boys of Liberty Library* and the new *Medal Library* to the extent that only dedicated collectors would be willing to expend the effort and time to identify the original sources.   Cook wrote a great many of the Buffalo Bill tales up to 1919, sharing the task with Prentice Ingraham, St. George Rathborne, W. Bert Foster and John H. Whitson.[43]

In 1904, Mead and Company brought out Cook's second hardback book, *Wilby's Dan* under his own name.   Like his first book,

[41]Reynolds, p. 116.

[42]J. Edward Leithead and Edward T. LeBlanc, "Rough Rider Weekly and the Ted Strong Saga," *Dime Novel Round-Up,* July 15, 1972.

[43]J. Edward Leithead, "New Buffalo Bill Weekly," *Dime Novel Round-Up,* May 15, 1970.

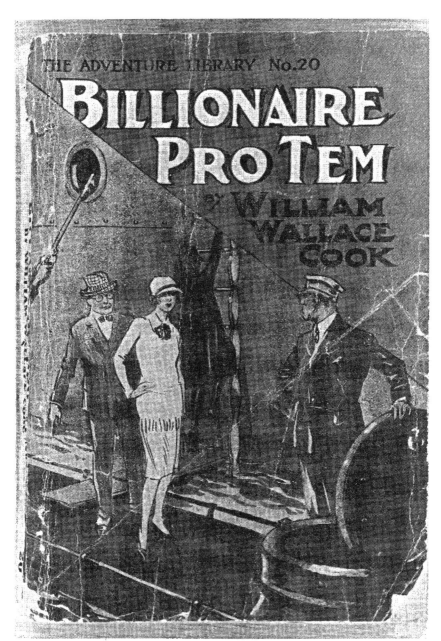

—University of Nebraska Photo Service

Cover of *Billionaire Pro Tem*, published in 1907

Wilby's Dan did not prove to be a great financial success, earning him only $250.[44] While Cook began to use his real name, pen names were still employed. A chance discovery of a Cook short story, "Bridget's Return", under the name of William Wallace Whitelock, which appeared in *Munsey's Magazine* for June, 1904, serves to illustrate the complexity of locating and identifying Cook's writings under various names.

Cook's continued output for Street and Smith did not deter him from writing for his old patron, *The Argosy*, and from seeking new outlets, such as *Woman's Home Companion, The Blue Book, The Red Book, The Railroad Man's Magazine, All-Story Magazine, The People's Magazine, The Popular Magazine* and *The Ocean*.[45] Through extensive reading he was able to write with realism on subjects removed from his personal experience. His technical knowledge on railroads was limited, despite his father's vocation, as was his knowledge of the sea, yet informed readers wrote favorably of his realistic familiarity with these subjects. In this his personal library and categorized reference material proved a great aid.

His production for 1908 was the largest so far in his career. His output in 1908 consisted of forty-four nickel novels for Street and Smith, (Buffalo Bill and Rough Rider stories), two novelettes for *The Blue Book,* four serials for Munsey publications, and a novelette for *The People's Magazine.* This averages one story per week. Two of his stories that year were purchased and translated by a German publisher, raising the hope that other European publishers might buy his stories, but this did not develop.[46]

That fall, Street and Smith offered to purchase the book rights of Cook's serials that he had written for Munsey and other publishers. Since Cook had failed to retain the book rights, he decided to go to New York to confer with editors White and Davis, of Munsey, as well as other publishers. Cook successfully obtained the required paper book rights with little difficulty. Of the serial stories only seven were long enough for immediate issue in paper book form. The others required lengthening and revision. These earlier serial stories from *The Argosy, All-Story, Ocean, Scrap-Book, Railroad Man's Magazine, Popular Magazine, People's Magazine, Blue Book* and *Woman's Home Companion* became Street and Smith's *New Fiction Series.*

In the fall of 1909 Street and Smith gave Cook "a new line of work", the *Motor Stories,* paying $75 for each. However, they were discontinued after thirty-two issues, although Cook wrote a total of thirty-four. Street and Smith rarely let stories remain in

---

[44]Edwards, pp. 115, 122, 124, 126.
[45]*Ibid.*, pp. 138-141, 176-180.
[46]*Ibid.*, pp. 147-150.

their files for long, so the extra two were published in *The Brave and Bold* weekly. Cook continued to write Buffalo Bill stories regularly.

A third hardback book, *A Quarter to Four,* was brought out by G. W. Dillingham Company in 1909.[47] Cook also tried his hand at writing scenarios for a company that had obtained the privilege of taking moving pictures of Buffalo Bill's Wild West Show and Pawnee Bill's Far East Show. While Cook furnished a great many scenarios, the remuneration was small, only $25 for all.[48]

From 1910 onwards Cook took on new assignments, although he continued to write for Street and Smith as well as for the Frank A. Munsey publications. Now stories carried his own name. A short story, "A Winged Victory," appeared in the May, 1910, issue of *Munsey's Magazine.* *Harper's Weekly,* August 5, 1911, published "Creshaw of the Gold Mill," a William Wallace Cook short story.

Street and Smith placed a new magazine, *Top-Notch,* in circulation in 1910. William Wallace Cook became a writer for it in 1911. Seward of Sacatone, a much loved desert character, was featured in Cook's countless adventure stories for *Top-Notch.*

That year he began to write his autobiography, using a pseudonym (John Milton Edwards) upon the advice of a friend.[49] *The Fiction Factory* was published in 1912 and must have sold reasonably well for the book is found in many college and public libraries.

The loss of his wife in 1912 briefly curtailed his output, yet he continued to write for *Top-Notch* magazine at the rate of one story a month from 1911 to 1915. He wrote Merriwell adventure stories under the Street and Smith owned name of Burt L. Standish.[50]

In 1916, Cook wrote several mystery stories for the *Detective* magazine, and continued with the *Top-Notch* assignment. When Gilbert Patten, the creator of the Merriwell stories, became editor of *Top-Notch* magazine in 1916, he ceased to write Merriwell tales. Cook, William Almon Wolff and John H. Whitson became the authors. From 1916 on *Top-Notch* featured new stories by these writers as well as many reprints of Patten's earlier Merriwell stories from *Tip-Top* weekly. The Merriwell stories continued to be so well received that reprints appeared in paper back form in the *New Metal Library* and *The Merriwell Series* during the 1920s.

Munsey publications and Street and Smith continued to be the main outlets of Cook's writings. By 1919 Cook indicated his gross earnings for the year were $10,707 in correspondence with the

---

[47]Edwards, pp. 155-156; Pachon, p. 74.
[48]Edwards, p. 166.
[49]*Ibid.,* p. 165.
[50]Archives of Street and Smith, now in the possession of Conde Nast Publications, Inc.

Collector of Internal Revenue. In an attempt to reduce his income tax for that year, Cook wished to have his inventory of publishable stories re-evaluated by the internal revenue. Shortly after the ratification of the sixteenth amendment in 1913 income tax rates ranged from 1% to 7% on incomes in excess of $3000 for a single individual. Cook's single status made him accountable for a higher rate, although his mother now resided with him and was dependent upon him for support.

Cook requested a "write off" of stories that had "exhausted their value," much as a business man writes off merchandise at a loss when it is no longer salable. He listed the stories in his inventory at their original sale price, two cents per word, estimating their current worth at half value, one cent per word, since Cook still held the second American serial rights, foreign serial rights, book rights and "moving picture" rights.[51] Cook's re-evaluated inventory of stories totaled more than $4000, a comfortable reserve.

The *Top-Notch* assignment continued to bring William Wallace Cook a measure of prosperity. He wrote serial and short stories for *Top-Notch* magazine steadily from July, 1921, to November, 1927, turning out on the average one story or one part of the serial each week.[52] Cook had a standing order each year for a football and a Christmas story from Street and Smith. He was often amused to find several of his stories in one magazine issue, some under assumed names, while one might be under his own name.

Cook wrote new stories for Street and Smith's *Adventure Library* from 1925 to 1927.[53] Thirty-eight were issued semi-monthly for fifteen cents under Cook's own name and were as follows:

The Desert Argonaut	In the Wake of the Scimitar
A Quarter to Four	His Audacious Highness
Thorndyke of the Bonita	At Daggers Dawn
A Round Trip to the Year 2000	The Eighth Wonder
The Gold Gleaners	The Cat's-Paw
The Spur of Necessity	The Cotton Bay
The Mysterious Mission	Cast Away at the Pole
The Goal of a Million	The Testing of Noyes
Marooned in 1492	The Fateful Seventh
Running the Signal	Montana
His Friend the Enemy	The Deserter
In the Web	The Sheriff of Broken Bow
A Deep Sea Game	Wanted: A Highwayman
The Paymaster's Special	Frisbie of San Antone
Adrift in the Unknown	His Last Dollar
Jim Dexter, Cattleman	Fools for Luck

---

[51]Letter to the Collector of Internal Revenue, Detroit, Michigan, dated June 4, 1920.

[52]Archives of Street and Smith.

[53]William Wallace Cook collection.

Juggling with Liberty   Dare of Darling & Co.
Back from Bedlam   Trailing *The Josephine*
A River Tangle
A Billionaire Pro Tem

The first eighteen were reprints of the *New Fiction Series, 1907-1909.* After the thirty-eighth issue, July, 1926, William Wallace Cook shared the *Adventure Series* with many others, or if he wrote additional stories for the series, they were issued under a Street and Smith company name. Only three stories in the *Adventure Series* were in Cook's own name after July, 1926. They were "Golden Bighorn," "The Innocent Outlaw" and "Rogers of Butte." Cook's stories for the *New Fiction Series* and *Adventure Library* were reprinted in the *Select Library,* 1928, under his own name.

Chelsea House, a subsidiary publishing house of Street and Smith, brought out William Wallace Cook's fourth hardback book, *Around the World in Eighty Hours,* in 1925. In that year Cook sold book rights for "The Skylark," "Harlequin, Ha" and "As the Sparks Fly Upward."[54]

Cook enjoyed seeing his stories transformed into film. Tom Mix appeared in "After Your Own Heart" and Douglas McLain in "Sunshine Trail." When a Cook story, "Speed Spook," was shown at the Garden Theater in Marshall, publicity was given the film by converting a regular passenger sedan so that the driver was for all appearance, invisible. Mr. Cook was both surprised and delighted to see a character and car he had created in fiction call at his home on North Kalamazoo Avenue.

He was married for the second time in 1927 to Mary A. Ackley. For some years they spent winters in California but returned to the Kalamazoo Avenue residence for the spring, summer and fall months.[55] In December of 1927 Charles Agnew MacLean, managing editor of Street and Smith's *Top-Notch Magazine,* wrote Cook to inquire about the possibility of writing additional Merriwell stories for *Top-Notch* on a more extended basis. MacLean pointed out that Patten was no longer writing for Street and Smith and that the company held the right to continue the stories under the Street and Smith owned name of Burt L. Standish. When Cook responded favorably, a file of earlier Merriwell stories were sent to Cook so that he could immerse himself with the proper background and take up Frank Merriwell, and his younger brother, Dick, where Cook had "left him off" earlier. The rates were now three and one-third cents a word so that a 30,000 word-story would bring $900.[56] When he began the series in January, 1928,

---

[54]Archives of Street and Smith.
[55]Marshall *Evening Chronicle,* July 20.
[56]Letters from Charles A. MacLean, editor for *Top-Notch Magazine,* dated December 6, 1927, and December 29, 1927.

his health was far from good and a new book, *Plotto,* absorbed his time, but he managed to write five stories by June, 1928, when ill health prevented him from continuing.

William Wallace Cook's last book, *Plotto, A New Method of Plot Suggestion For Writers of Creative Fiction* was published in 1928.[57] It was intended to be accompanied by class instruction. The author supplied standard skeleton plots and sub-plots that might be an inspiration for authors and by which they could embellish with their own imagination. Cook's ideas for this book had grown slowly through his years of writing. He had achieved much by his methodical, businesslike approach and diligent commitment to the task of composing. *Plotto* was the product of Cook's belief that writers did not need a great deal of inspiration; that stories resulted from hard work. A review of his life indicates he was a tireless worker.

Letters of inquiry from novice authors about the book brought great satisfaction for Cook, as did a testimonial from S. S. McClure, who stated *Plotto* provided everything but the soul of the story. This the author had to supply.[58] The limited edition book and the follow-up lessons cost $25. Cook hoped that this venture would provide enough income, along with the new Street and Smith contract for Merriwell stories for *Top-Notch* magazine, that he might enjoy a less demanding production schedule. The *Plotto* venture did not prove successful. His health problems returned and for the last years of his life a heart condition limited his output. After his death his widow sold the rights of *Plotto* to *Writer's Digest* for a specified number of years. A new cover was put on the book and it was again offered to the public, but with little success. Cook's heirs acquired the book, including the copper plates.

The last fiction tale of Cook was published in serial form in the Marshall *Evening Chronicle* from March 25, 1933, to May 4, 1933, just three months prior to his death. "Comrades of the Glory Road" was a novel of Marshall in which he vividly described the actual places in and around the city. The time of the story was just prior to World War I, on Decoration Day.[59] Although he stated the characters were imaginary, it seems likely they were a composite of family, friends and acquaintances that he had known through his years in Marshall.

An example of his description of places in the city is the passage

---

57Cook, William Wallace, *Plotto, A New Method of Plot Suggestion for Writers of Creative Fiction,* (Battle Creek: Ellis Publishing Company, 1928).

58Letters from T. T. Flynn, undated [ca. August, 1928], and Erle Stanley Gardner, dated August 12, 1929.

59Marshall *Evening Chronicle,* March 25, 1933 to April 22, 1933.

that .describes Exchange Square as the Decoration Day Parade pauses on its way to Oakridge cemetery. "At the corner of the lot by the GAR Hall is a cannon, nicely muzzled and painted a dull black. Close to the cannon is a pyramidal heap of solid shot, also veneered in dull black." Marshall residents would recognize these same objects today. Continuing on, the parade follows "the angling street that leads through Marshall to the home of the dead, crosses Rice Creek by the mill, surmounts a rise of ground, swings over the river by the power house and then climbs to an eminence covered with trees. And there among the white stones, bivouac the 'comrades' who have gone before."

The adventure and misadventure of two Civil War veterans provided the theme of the tale. The vivid realistic description of Marshall homes and social life lent authenticity that made the fictional tale appear true. The nostalgic sentimental tale of the two Marshall comrades seemed a fitting termination to W. W. Cook's career, although it was written for a scenario contest of the *Chicago Daily News* for which Cook was awarded a $500 prize.

William Wallace Cook died July 20, 1933, after a six-year illness. His editor and writer friends Frank Munsey, William Almon Wolff and Ormond and George Smith had preceded him in death.

With the death of the Smith brothers in April, 1933, the Street and Smith firm abandoned pulp fiction and turned to women's fashion magazines, such as *Mademoiselle* and *Charm,* and science fiction.[60]

The popularity of Cook's adventure stories carried on after his death. At least five of his stories were published in book form as late as 1940 by Wright and Brown, an English publisher.

---

[60]Reynolds, pp. 213, 215.

Wyoming State Historical Society

TWENTY-THIRD ANNUAL MEETING

Cheyenne, Wyoming   September 10-12, 1976

Registration for the twenty-third Annual Meeting of the Wyoming State Historical Society began at 7:00 p.m. in the American Room, Little America Motel, Cheyenne. Refreshments were served and the historical photographic exhibit entitled "The Spirit of '76 in the American West," prepared by the Museum Division, was on display. The exhibit was made possible by a grant from the Wyoming Bicentennial Commission. After the Annual Meeting the portable exhibit will be located in the west wing of the State Capitol for public viewing. It will be available later this fall to schools, libraries and museums in the state through the State Museum. Entertainment for the Get Acquainted Hour was provided by a guitarists' group named "The Unknown Quantity."

SATURDAY, SEPTEMBER 11

At 9:00 a.m. the president, Jay W. Brazelton, called the meeting to order in the American Room. Dave Wasden and Mable Womack were appointed to the auditing committee. The nominating committee, Henry Jensen, Henry Chadey and Dick Dumbrill, were given the ballots to count and to report to the membership at the Banquet.

A motion was made by Mr. Jensen to dispense with the reading of the minutes of the 1975 Annual Meeting. Motion seconded, carried. Copies of the minutes for 1975 were passed out to the membership.

The treasurer read the following report which was placed on file for audit:

TREASURER'S REPORT
September 7, 1975 - September 1, 1976

Operating Funds

Cash on hand, September 7, 1976		$ 3,266.88
Receipts:		
Dues	$5,546.00	
Sales & Miscellaneous	1,145.20	
Life Memberships	250.00	
From Savings	4,800.00	
		$15,008.08

Disbursements:
Annual Meeting	$ 259.67	
Awards		
Grant-in-Aid	500.00	
Junior Awards	85.00	
County Chapter	500.00	1,344.67
Trek		959.80
Officers' Expense		223.28
Postage for Annals		460.07
Supplies for Secretary		2.95
To Savings		5,500.00
Refund on dues		40.00
Incorporation Fee		3.00
Film Production		5,000.00
Painting (recondition)		249.89

	$13,783.66
Balance September 1, 1976	1,224.42
Investments	$15,624.69

Invested Funds

Balance Sept. 7, 1976	Deposits	Disbursements	Balance Sept. 7, 1975
Federal Bldg. & Loan #661:			
$4,867.74	$18,680.75	$14,800.00	$ 986.99
Federal Bldg. & Loan #2928-11 (Memorial):			
745.31	33.96		$ 702.35
F. Bldg. & Loan-Certificate #3203983:			
$2,514.83	165.90 Interest		$2,348.93
Capitol Savings & Loan-Certificate #870158:			
$7,496.81	471.75 Interest		$7,025.06
TOTAL INVESTMENTS			$15,624.69

Membership Report

583	Single memberships	
253	Joint memberships	
75	Life memberships (13 joint, 62 single)	
205	Institutional	1,116 total memberships

Bill Williams, Director of the Archives and Historical Department and Executive Secretary of the State Society, welcomed the members to Cheyenne and briefly discussed services provided by the department to assist the Society.

Glenn Sweem, Chairman of the Big Horn Forest Committee, reported completion of the book *Re-Discovering the Big Horns*. This was a Bicentennial project involving Big Horn, Johnson, Sheridan and Washakie Counties. The publication utilized the manuscript and photographs compiled in 1900 by Professor J. G. Jack, as well as current photos, and shows the environmental changes that have taken place in the Big Horns. Two thousand copies were printed and a few are still available from Glenn Sweem or Ray Pendergraft. Sweem stated that the U. S. Forest Service furnished film and provided brass cap markers for the project.

Bill Bragg reported the film, "Wyoming From the Beginning," will be completed on schedule and following a critique by the committee will be available for distribution to schools in the state through the Historical Research and Publications Division of the Archives and Historical Department.

Mrs. Violet Hord read the report of the Wyoming Historical Foundation. She reported that in 1966 the Foundation was formed to gather and administer private funds to be employed in the preservation, development and recognition of Wyoming's historical heritage. Ed Bille has been the moving spirit of the organization and has served as chairman for a number of years. Individual memorial contributions have been made and the county chapters have been asked to make contributions also. The largest contribution was $5000 from the Tom and Helen Tonkin Foundation with the stipulation that the money be used to further teaching of Wyoming history in the schools. With the help of a Wyoming Bicentennial Commission Grant to equal the amount already in the Foundation, "Wyoming From the Beginning," became a reality. A plaque will be made listing all who contributed $100 or more to the fund.

Dr. T. A. Larson reported for the Scholarship and Grant-in-Aid Committees. The committee consists of Dr. Larson, Dr. Robert Roripaugh and either Bill Williams or Katherine Halverson of the Wyoming State Archives and Historical Department. Mary E. Anders has completed her history of Iowa Center in Goshen County. Another project in progress is a biographical study of the famous naturalist, Olaus Murie.

Henry Jensen asked that the Society endorse a resolution to be submitted to Wyoming's Congressman and Senators, as well as to the Bureau of Land Management, that it has come to the attention of the Society that certain holders of coal leases in southern Montana propose to strip mine portions of the Rosebud Battlefield, which is on the National Register of Historic Places. A motion was made by Harry Brown that Mr. Jensen draw up a resolution to be submitted to all interested agencies. Motion seconded, carried.

A letter was read from Mrs. Alice E. Harrower, president of the Sublette County Historical Society, Inc., stating that she would not be able to attend the Annual Meeting but wished the Society a successful and interesting year. She reported that more than two thousand people attended the eleventh annual Green River Rendezvous in July. The directors are proceeding with construction of the Museum of the Mountain Men.

The president announced that chapter annual reports are to be sent to the Archives and Historical Department by September 1 of each year. The reports will be printed and distributed to the members at the annual meeting, and also may be of interest for "Wyoming History News."

Ned Frost, Wyoming Recreation Commission, historian, spoke about Fort Fred Steele State Park in Carbon County. The state legislature in 1976 appropriated $5857 for operation and maintenance of the park. There are many important considerations that are demanding the attention of the legislature and if the 1977 session does not appropriate a minimum of $50,000 toward restoration and development of Fort Steele the 112 acres donated to the state will revert back to the original owners, he said. The Recreation Commission asked the help of the Society to alert the legislature. The members asked that Ned Frost write to all the county chapters and request their support for his proposal.

Mr. Pendergraft moved that Article III, Membership, Sections 1, 2, 3 and 4, of the Constitution of the Wyoming State Historical Society be revised to read as follows:

Article III   Membership

Section 1—The organization shall be composed of the State Society and of chapters in each county of the state, upon each of which chapters will be the responsibility of collecting and preserving the items, documents and records of its area. Each chapter within each county will have its own officers and constitution and by-laws and charter and shall operate independently of any other chapter in the county.

Section 2—Membership in the society shall be open to all persons who will actively support the association, and upon payment of dues, as set forth in the by-laws of the society, provided, however, that persons residing in a county in which is located one or more duly chartered chapters shall affiliate only through membership in one of said chapters. Persons residing outside the state or in a county in which no chapter has been chartered shall affiliate directly with the state society.

Section 3—County chapters may be organized in counties in the State of Wyoming by application to the Executive Headquarters of the state society and fulfilling the requirements for affiliation. A county may have more than one chapter, provided upon application it has not less than fifteen (15) members and is to be located at least twenty (20) miles from any currently existing chapter within the county. A second chapter, within a county, may select its own name but may not use as its name the county unless designated by a number, as: Washakie County Chapter 2. The name of the chapter will be subject to approval by the Executive Committee.

Section 4—Affiliation of all chapters within a given county shall be by charter, to be granted by the Executive Committee of the society upon application, pursuant to the rules and regulations set forth in the by-laws of the society.

The motion was seconded. Following discussion, Mr. Pendergraft moved that the original motion be amended to provide that the name of a new chapter will be subject to approval by the Executive Committee. The motion was seconded and carried. The original motion was carried.

Mr. Pendergraft made a motion that Article VI, Annual Meeting, Section 2, be revised to read:

Time and place for the Annual Meeting shall be set by the Executive Committee at least six months prior to the date of said meeting, and written notice shall be given by the Executive Secretary to the president of each chartered chapter and to members residing in counties not chartered, at least one month prior to said meeting.

The motion was seconded and carried.

A motion was made by Mr. Pendergraft that the president of the Society be reimbursed for his expenses in travel around the state, including mileage, up to $1000 a year with an accounting of expenses to be made to the Society secretary-treasurer. Motion seconded. An amendment was made by Glenn Sweem to make it actual expenses and 15 cents per mile; seconded and carried.

A motion was made by Mr. Sweem to establish a cut-off date of April 1 each year for payment of dues. Motion carried.

No invitation for the 1977 Annual Meeting was submitted.

Bill Bragg submitted a resolution asking for help from the society to remove a rock crushing reduction company from infringing on land which is part of the Oregon Trail. The location is in Natrona County west of Casper. A discussion followed and it was determined that the resolution should be rewritten and sent to the Executive Committee.

The committee for the 1977 Trek is: Ray Pendergraft, Henry Jensen, Jay Brazelton and Dave Wasden. The dates for the Trek are July 16-17.

The meeting adjourned at 12:30 p.m. for luncheon in the American Room. Several door prizes were given.

Following luncheon Dr. Gordon Hendrickson of the Historical Research Division, presented a paper entitled "The Wyoming WPA Writers' Project: History and Collections."

Following this presentation the Friends of Fort Bridger, sponsored by the Museum Division, gave a Living History Demonstration, a melodrama based on Fort Bridger history.

CHAPTER REPORTS

Albany County. The Chapter has a membership of fifty-two this year, an increase over the previous year. A bequest was made by the Chapter to the Laramie Plains Museum in memory of Mrs. Alice Hardie Stevens, who had been instrumental in getting the museum established in its present location. · A variety of programs included history and development of the University Archives Department, early settlers in Centennial Valley, and early mining activities above Centennial.

Big Horn County. The most important activity centered around the Bicentennial Project of *Re-Discovering the Big Horns* and working with the other counties concerned with the project.

Campbell County. The Chapter has begun the collection of stories of early-day schools written by the teachers. Many pictures have been received and along with documentation will be placed in the files in the Museum. The Chapter won a blue ribbon at the county fair with its educational display, "Wyoming Firsts."

Carbon County. The Chapter assisted in the formal opening of the Carbon County Museum in February. Marian Geddes is curator, assisted by Marybelle Lambertson and Charlotte Vivion. A trek to Dexterville on the old stage route to the Dillon-Ferris-Haggerty mine was taken in June.

Fremont County. There are forty-three members in the Chapter this year. The outstanding programs included an oral history tape program by Harriett Bybee of her experiences as a young woman; attending the dedication ceremonies for the Houghton-Colter Store in South Pass City and helping with the evening reception at the annual Trek.

Goshen County. The Chapter's Bicentennial year project on school houses has been completed and is on display at the Homesteader's Museum in South Torrington. The project consists of some 200 pictures of schools and their classes from homestead days to the present. A map is part of the collection and identifies the location of the schools. The Chapter honored Chairwoman Ellen Smith of the Awards Committee for her encouragement and achievements with the junior members of the Chapter.

Hot Springs County. The most important event of the year was hosting the 1975 annual meeting and the tours. They also worked with the county Bicentennial committee to raise funds for a city Bicentennial Park in Thermopolis and presented Dorothy Milek's book *The Gift of Bah Guewana,* to the county library.

Laramie County. The Chapter completed plans for the third printing of the booklet, *Early Cheyenne Homes.* Another highlight of the year was the publishing of *Cheyenne Landmarks, 1976,* now at the printer. The research and writing was by Bill Dubois, editing and manuscript by Robert Larson and photography and layout design by James Ehernberger. An interesting program presented was Peggy Schumachers' opera, "Mini-aku, Daughter of Chief Spotted Tail."

Lincoln County. Main events were an Antique and Craft Fair held in LaBarge, and a Bicentennial meeting and the annual chuckwagon picnic in June, hosted by Kemmerer.

Natrona County. A preview showing of the film, "Wyoming From the Beginning," was one of the events of the year. A Bicentennial project was collecting Natrona County High School Annuals from 1913, the first year of publication, to the present, and presenting a set to the High School and one to Casper College. Some 200 books on Abraham Lincoln and the Civil War, a collection belonging to Kathleen Hemry, were given to the Rare Books Room at Casper College. Also Rose Mary Malone and Kathleen Hemry wrote histories of the schools and early day teaching.

Park County. Meetings are held alternately in Cody and Powell. Programs included a carry-in-dinner, guest speakers, placing a marker at Heart Mountain Relocation Center in memory of the Japanese boys who gave their lives in World War II, and slides of Fort Laramie presented by John Hinckley.

Sweetwater County. The membership is now 103, the highest in the history of the Chapter. They worked with the Green River Bicentennial Committee throughout the year raising money for the Sweetwater County Museum to gather and display historical pictures. Programs were a slide presentation on "Sweetwater Heritage-Melting Pot or Mosaic?", a history of newspapers of Sweetwater County by Adrian Reynolds and a tour of old homesteads on the Green River.

Teton County. On the Fourth of July, with the help of the Jackson Hole Outfitters, the Chapter staged a Bicentennial parade and barbecue with the proceeds going to the Chapter. The annual cook-out and bake sale was a great success.

Washakie County. The Chapter is formulating plans for a museum project but because of Worland's expansion the county expenses are too great to expect financial help from that source. Roger Inman from the Bureau of Land Management gave a presentation of the activities in the Shoshone Resource Area, telling of the caves and the findings. Another program was given by Jim Bell on range management in the Big Horn Basin.

Weston County. The Chapter had an enjoyable trek to Wyomings' newest town, Wright City. An old-fashioned fun night is planned at the old Beaver Creek School which has undergone remodeling recently.

Uinta County. The Chapter spent all of its time and money on the Bicentennial Chinese New Year that was held on January 30-31, 1976. All of 1975 was spent earning money for the project. Many members of the Chapter from Bridger Valley have spent long hours soliciting funds for the Evanston Museum. This will be finished in time for the tourist season next spring.

SATURDAY BANQUET

The evening started with a no-host Hospitality Hour, was well attended, and gave everyone the opportunity to say hello to old friends and make new friends.

The American Room was decorated with yellow chrysanthemum and gladiola arrangements. Individual tables had centerpieces of Bicentennial flags, sprays of greens and yellow carnations.

Jim Ehernberger, president of Laramie County Chapter, was master of ceremonies. Mayor Bill Nation welcomed the Society to Cheyenne. An Award of Merit from the American Association for State and Local History was presented by Mrs. Katherine Halverson, American Association for State and Local History Awards Chairman for Wyoming, to Dr. T. A. Larson, of the University of Wyoming, for his outstanding contributions on a national level as a historian, author and teacher.

Speaker Barry Combs, Public Relations Director of the Union Pacific Railroad, read emigrants' letters describing homesteaders' life in Nebraska and told of the many hardships endured by the families.

Henry Jensen, Chairman of the Nominating Committee, introduced the new officers for 1976-1977: Ray Pendergraft, president; Mrs. Mabel Brown, first vice-president; David Wasden, second vice-president; Mrs. Ellen Mueller, secretary-treasurer.

Historical awards were then presented by Mabel Brown, Awards Chairman:

Junior Historian Awards:

First place, Kent Hunter, Huntley, Huntley High School, "History of Hawk Springs."

Second place, Shane Stear, Huntley, Huntley High School, "History of Table Mountain."

Third place, Cathy Fix, Huntley, Huntley High School, "Great Grandad Morris."

Teacher Award:

Grace Grant, Newcastle, Gertrude Burns Grade School

Chapter Award:

Goshen County. Cash award to assist in the cost of a project of gathering pictures, history and location of the sites of as many of the county's schools as possible, and preparation of a large map showing locations.

Weston County. Cash award to assist with cost of mailing mini-museums to schools and other groups using the suitcase museums in educational projects.

Publications Awards:

Dorothy Milek, Thermopolis, book, *The Gift of Bah Guewana.*

Gene Downer, Jackson, magazine, *Teton, The Magazine of Jackson Hole Wyoming*

Adrian and Helen Reynolds, Green River, newspaper article, *"Patch of History."*

Dorothy Fifield, Torrington, numerous newspaper articles. Honorable Mention.

Activities Awards: ·

Nora Reimer, Sundance, museum activities.

Russ Arnold, Newcastle, tours.

Fine Arts Awards:

Mr. and Mrs. George Hufsmith, Jackson. For composing three-act opera, "The Sweetwater Lynching."

Marion Alexander, Casper, photography..

George Butler II, Newcastle, paintings.

Cumulative Award:

Mrs. Irene Brown, Jackson. For leadership in historical work and initiative in making taped interviews with old timers of Teton County and transcripts for the files of the Teton County Chapter.

SUNDAY MORNING

Members met for a breakfast at the Indian Village, Frontier Park, hosted by the Department and the Laramie County Chapter after which tours were conducted of the State Museum, Historical Research and Publications Division and the Archives and Records Management Division of the Department, in the Barrett Building. Personnel of all Divisions were on hand to explain the programs and facilities of each area, and to answer questions.

Many Society members also participated in a tour to the F. E. Warren Air Force Base Museum.

Book Reviews

William Clark: Jeffersonian Man on the Frontier. By Jerome O. Steffen. (Norman: University of Oklahoma Press, 1977). Index. Bib. 196 pp. $8.95, cloth.

Professor Steffen has written an intellectual biography of William Clark, a man who, ironically, left little material by which later scholars might discern what values he held. Consequently, the work deals with a man who was not an intellectual in the usual sense. That is, Clark reflected the ideological bent of the 18th Century Enlightenment by his actions, but wrote down very little. The author uses Clark's actions throughout his life to reflect on how the man dealt with a changing environment and, ultimately, how Clark's ideological predilections grew increasingly remote from a rapidly changing America.

Clark's professional career encompassed three major activities: exploration of the West, Missouri territorial politics, and administration of federal Indian policy. Throughout his career Clark, a native Virginian, reflected the values of the Jeffersonian Republicans, an Enlightenment belief in the interrelationship of all earthly matters. Intellectually, Clark relied heavily on self-education, using his older brother, classically-educated George Rogers Clark, as his model. Plantation Virginia imbued him with a belief in a natural aristocracy, but also with a commitment to equality of opportunity to permit that group of leaders to emerge. Central also to Clark's philosophy was a hatred of the British, largely due to the death of one brother during the American Revolution, but also due to continual trouble with Indians in the Northwest. Transplanted Kentuckian Clark served with Anthony Wayne in the latter's campaigns against the Indians. Clark's acquaintance with Indians and with the frontier alerted him to the potential within the region and among the Indian peoples for mercantile pursuits.

Professor Steffen argues that Clark's role in the Lewis and Clark expedition should not be minimized. The expedition sought scientific and commercial information which Clark was trained to record. The study of Indians provided further insight into the mechanical workings of God's intricately organized world. The possibilities for commercial ventures abounded. Clark sketched most of the geographical observations made during the expedition and handled much of the navigational data. Further indication of Clark's scientific mind is Jefferson's sending him to excavate fossils of Pleistocene mammals at Big Bones Lick, Kentucky, at a later date. Clark later established a museum of natural history in St. Louis and was eulogized in 1838 by the Academy of Natural

Science. The Lewis and Clark expedition in addition revealed Clark's abilities as a dependable administrator, in which capacity he would be used by the federal government for his remaining years.

As Jefferson's agent for Indian affairs in St. Louis, Clark worked towards the Enlightenment goal of minimizing environmental differences between the races, in the belief that Indians needed time for their civilization to advance to the stage already reached by the whites. Fearing the power of British fur traders, Clark continually argued for the establishment of an American fur trading monopoly to provide security and to promote racial interdependence. He attempted to use his government contacts to his advantage in co-founding the Missouri Fur Company (1809), but the War of 1812 created such uncertainty in the region that lack of capital caused the company to fail in 1814. The war's conclusion saw the influx of farmers into Missouri and a change in political philosophy with which Clark was unable to deal.

After the war, ignoring settlers who had flooded into the area, Clark once again argued for a government monopoly of the fur trade. This colonial notion of the status of the West failed to take into account the increasing political and economic independence of the agrarian interest which was by then dominant in Missouri. Consequently, Clark, who had been appointed governor of the territory in 1813, grew increasingly remote from his constituents. Settlers stressed individual, rather than national, interests. Upon statehood, leadership would be elected in the reflection of local values. Clark instead tied himself to old established families and merchants, seeing Missouri as part of a larger West.

Clark's unpopularity with Missourians originated in a questionable decision in 1816, when he decided a disputed election for the territorial delegate to Congress in favor of one of his friends. The election, voided by Congress, precipitated close federal scrutiny of all of Clark's subsequent actions. Clark ran for state governor in 1820, but by then he had become a symbol of the old order, even supporting a constitution that limited popular influence in state government. His overwhelming defeat was mitigated only by appointment in 1822 as Superintendent of Indian Affairs, permitting him to remain in St. Louis.

Clark regained his popularity through his vocal support of Indian removal. Clark's motives did not reflect those of many of his supporters, for Clark wished only to promote assimilation by creating a class of Indian yeoman farmers, away from white competition and influence. He felt that identical environmental influences would help to equalize the cultures. A measure to organize an Indian Department, introduced in Congress by Lewis Cass and conceived, in large part, by William Clark, failed. Clark hoped to delimit and centralize federal Indian authority, to distribute funds efficiently and to establish efficient accounting procedures. Thus, at the close of his career, Clark found himself unable to influence legislation concerning Indians, yet ironically he received considerable praise for his efforts to remove the Indians from proximity with white agrarians. The populace, in effect, bought removal only as a means towards subjugating the Indian, whereas Clark, a Jeffersonian to the end, hoped to provide some basis by which the two creations of God, the Indian and the white man, might eventually live in cultural harmony through parallel environmental influences.

Professor Steffen's book provides persuasive arguments as to the consistency of Clark's ideas throughout his career, though the author does not criticize the man's lack of flexibility. Clark's intellectual portrait reflects frustration if not failure, his political rejection demonstrating the anachronistic Jeffersonian Enlightenment dogma, his position on removal used by those who had rejected him to meet their own ends. The author's insight into his subject's mind and ideas offers valuable commentary not only on Clark, but also, one suspects, on many of his contemporaries.

University of Georgia   S. J. KARINA

The Adventures of Alexander Barclay, Mountain Man: A Narrative of His Career, 1810 to 1855; His Memorandum Diary, 1845 to 1850. By George P. Hammond. (Denver: Old West Publishing Company, 1976.) Maps. Illustrations. Notes. Appendices, Index. 246 pp. $17.50.

During the past sixty years the saga of the Rocky Mountain fur trade has received widespread attention from scholars who have rigorously analyzed its economic and social impact on American history. Just at this time when many person seem willing to close the door on future research possibilities, a new book appears indicating that the field is still ripe for further exploration. George Hammon's latest effort is one such work. Drawing upon a rather brief diary and some family correspondence, Hammond details the life of Alexander Barclay, an English immigrant who failed at farming, tired of a St. Louis bookkeeping job, and ultimately found the adventurous life along the Colorado-New Mexico border during the mid-nineteenth century.

Barclay's life was inextricably linked to the firm of Bent and St. Vrain between 1838 and 1842 when he served as superintendent at Bent's Fort. Following his resignation from that position, he spent two years as an independent trader on the Platte River, followed by a return to the Bent's Fort area where he continued an unsuccessful venture to provide buffalo for European zoos. In

1848 Barclay finally settled down to a life as land baron and trader when he established Barclay's Fort near present-day Watrous, New Mexico. The small fortress served as a welcome haven for trappers, Santa Fe-bound traders, and territorial officials who appear throughout the final chapters of the book.

Despite his boundless energy and enterprising instincts, Barclay faced financial disaster at the time of his death in 1855. The declining fur trade and shifting direction of the Santa Fe Trail cut deeply into his profits. More importantly, the Army established Fort Union not more than seven miles north of his post and it quickly replaced Barclay's Fort as the commercial center of the area. Thus the cycle of unrealized dreams was completed for Barclay who always seemed on the verge of prosperity, but who could never fully grasp it.

Readers who purchase this book will not only be rewarded with the history of the Southern Rockies fur trade, they will also receive a lesson on masterful detective work. Hammond has sifted through a variety of sources to fill the gaps left by Barclay's diary and correspondence. A less patient author would have given up the task long ago, but Hammond's detailed notes indicate the extensiveness of his search for corroborative materials. Three foldout maps of the region provide further understanding of this important region and a series of paintings, including several by Barclay, enhance the beautifully crafted book. In addition to the regular text, Hammond wisely includes the original diary and portions of the correspondence, all of which he has carefully edited for the general reader.

Few faults exist with this book, but perhaps a tying in of the broader story of the Southern Rockies fur trade and the Mexican War would have placed Barclay's story in a better context. Likewise, the inclusion of all notes at the end of the text rather than at the bottom of each page detracts from the utility of a book such as this which offers so much information in its notes. But be that as it may, Hammond has provided us with a unique and important glimpse at one aspect of American history.

University of Nebraska at Omaha MICHAEL L. TATE

Wyoming's Wealth: A History of Wyoming. By Bill Bragg. Edited by Dr. Amir Sancher. (Basin: Big Horn Publishers, 1976) Index. Map. Illus. 237 pp. $14.95.

William F. "Bill" Bragg, Jr. is a teller of tales *par excellance* and a lover of his native Wyoming. He has a fluid writing style that is probably patterned after his manner of speaking, which, in the main, makes for easy listening.

The book is divided into nineteen chapters, each of which are sub-divided and include an "epic" and a "vignette." Bill introduces the theme of the chapter, such as "Chapter Eleven: Railroad Wyoming", with an "epic" entitled "The Anvil Chorus," then deals with the subject matter at hand and climbs off the train by telling a "vignette" entitled "Wyoming Goldrush."

This particular style—of division and sub-division—while unusual, is certainly not unpleasant. And it probably facilitates the use of the book as a text, which is Bill's avowed purpose in writing *Wyoming's Wealth* in the first place.

I particularly liked one "vignette" about the meaning of color to the Plains Indians. Bill is at his best with passages such as:

> Blue came from blue mud. We call it bentonite. Some kinds of boiled roots were used for blue, also. Blue meant the sky, long life, or serenity.

> Red stood for warmth, the tipi, home, and Wyoming's red hills. In fact, red came from those very hills. Oxidation of iron helps turn the hills red-colored, so iron was the chief ingredient in the red dye.

I like short sentences, though I don't often write them myself. They are easy to read, and make a statement in a sensible manner. They are also more comprehensible for the average student.

Some other parts of the book, however, leave me baffled. I don't pretend to know anywhere near as much about Wyoming history as Bill knows, but there were a couple of chapters that sent me scurrying to other source material, just as reading *Time* magazine always sends me to the dictionary.

Take the Pony Express, for instance. Bill states that the transcontinental telegraph put the Pony Express out of business, which is certainly true. Exception should be taken, however, to the conclusion he draws that "Pony Express riders carried vital messages back and forth, each day their distance being cut down by the telegraph lines marching forward." In other words, the Pony Express, in its last days, rode only between the advancing termini of the telegraph line. The problem inherent in this conclusion is obvious. If true there should be no overland letters in existence following September, 1861, when the telegraph was marching across the plains toward completion. Yet, that was a busy period for the Pony and at least twenty envelopes are known that departed Placerville eastbound, and Atchison, Kansas, westbound from the period of September 2, 1861, to October 31, 1861.

The Pony Express, as conceived by the Central Overland California & Pike's Peak Express Company, was an overland operation. It carried the United States mails with a surcharge of $5.00 per half-ounce, from St. Joseph, Missouri, to Placerville, California. It continued to do so even *after* the completion of the telegraph. There are envelopes in existence cancelled in New York City on October 26, 1861 and St. Joseph a week later that were delivered in San Francisco on November 20, a month after the completion of the telegraph. Thus, it would seem that the "last kick of the Pony" brought mail overland that had crossed the entire continent.

And Bill isn't to blame for repeating the old legend that the big, bad cattlemen suppressed Asa Mercer's book, *Banditti of the Plains,* for almost everyone who ever wrote a word about the Johnson County Cattle War tells the same old, sad story. ". . . each copy was systematically hunted down and destroyed. Even the Library of Congress copy disappeared. Mercer's press was destroyed in a mysterious way."

The "evidence" that all of this really happened is parrotted hearsay and folklegend. The evidence that it did not is inferential, yet substantial. (See Asa Mercer and *The Banditti of the Plains: A Reappraisal,"* in this issue of *Annals of Wyoming.* Ed.)

It is my own conclusion that Bill has told a story about Wyoming in a chatty, interesting style, but the overall impact suffers from a lack of any footnotes at all. I would cite as one example the relating of the murder of "U.S. Deputy Marshall George Wellman" following the Johnson County Cattle War. Wellman was not a U.S. Deputy Marshall. He was the foreman of Henry Blair's Hoe Ranch, and had been deputized to help U.S. Marshall Joe Rankin serve warrants in the Buffalo area.

A footnote here would have allowed the author to explain the true situation without breaking up the flow of his writing style. And I think any work of history, no matter how informal, should have a bibliography. The author owes that to his readers.

The greatest criticism I have of *Wyoming's Wealth* is of the physical properties of the book itself. One would wish the publishers had taken as much effort in the type-setting and lay-out as the author did in the writing. Photographs and paintings are thrown in slap-dash, often with no identification and little reason for inclusion. One might wonder, for instance, why the "Mountain Man in Wyoming" chapter is headed by a colorful painting of a man, Winchester in hand and Colt on hip, who is evidently a cowboy of the 1890s period.

And who the balding gentleman on page 121 might be is anybody's guess. He certainly isn't John Allen Campbell, Wyoming's first territorial governor, as the publishers identification implies.

Ignoring the typos—and they are difficult to ignore—the printing style of the book has no consistency. Sub-heads are set in boldface type in one chapter and not in the next. Chapter titles are enclosed in quotation marks when they are not quotes. One photograph may be butchered to fit the blank space available on a given page, and still another page has nothing but white space staring at the reader.

As a former photographer and picture editor I suppose I am overly sensitive about the use of photographs and illustrations, but some of these used in Bill Bragg's book drove me to the wall. Unidentified paintings used simply because the printer had color available for that particular page are bad enough, but in some cases those same unidentified paintings are reproduced from out-of-focus color separations. That seems to be the final insult to the reader's intelligence.

It is not pedantic to criticize the printing of a book. If one pays today's high price for the printed word—or picture—then one has the right to expect some modicum of quality in the product.

Cheyenne   CHARLES "PAT" HALL

Montana. A History of Two Centuries. By Michael P. Malone and Richard B. Roeder. (Seattle and London: University of Washington Press, 1976). Index. Bib. Illus. 352 pp. $14.95.

This year numerous state histories are appearing as a result of the bicentennial "The States and the Nation" series. This new history of Montana is independent of that effort. And this is probably fortunate, for the authors, both professors of history at Montana State University, would have felt severely restricted by the criteria and space limitations of the state history series. What they felt was needed was a new comprehensive history of Montana which gives particular attention to important developments in the 20th century. In this respect they have succeeded admirably.

For those inclined to read of Montana's romantic 19th century past there is little that is startlingly new. The Indians of the Montana region, the early exploration, the fur trade, and the early mining and cattlemen's·frontiers are all treated in a solid but traditional fashion. In fact, general readers will find the rather dated *Montana: An Uncommon Land* (Norman: University of Oklahoma Press, 1959) by K. Ross·Toole, or the classic literary effort, *Montana: High, Wide and Handsome* (New Haven, Conn.: Yale University Press 1959, first ed., 1943) by Joseph Kinsey Howard, more enjoyable for their grace of style and provocative regional interpretation.

Yet it is the 20th century, and particularly the relationship of Montanans to the giant Anaconda Corporation, which has been of particular historic significance. The themes of exploitation of natural resources, corporate domination and political corruption have given Montana its unique, though somewhat sour, flavor. In interpreting this history Malone and Roeder are admirably objective in their analysis. While not discounting that Montana in the early 1900s "seemed to be the classic example of a 'one-company state,' a commonwealth where one corporation ruled supreme," their account is free from the polemical subjectivity which has marred previous histories. Certainly it is time for Montanans to analyze dispassionately their long love-hate relationship with the twin corporate powers of Anaconda and the Montana Power Company. This new history accomplishes that purpose.

Many readers will find interesting the authors' concluding chapter on "The Recent Political Scene: 1945-1975." Here Malone and Roeder discuss in a thoughtful manner the state's proclivity to send liberal Senators and Representatives to Washington, while insisting on electing conservatives to the statehouse at Helena. There is no easy explanation for this paradoxical, schizoid voting behavior, although the authors theorize that the urban areas of Montana have the voting power to elect liberals to Washington while the more conservative ranching communities can still muster the strength to control the state house.

Today there is no subject more controversial in the northern Rocky Mountain states than that of environmental quality. In Montana the debate over what environmental sacrifices should be made for economic gain is one of extreme intensity. The authors do not approach this issue with the fire-breathing passion of K. Ross Toole's *The Rape of the Great Plains* (Boston: Little, Brown, and Co., 1976), but they strive for a balanced account which leans toward the exploitation theme. It is clear that with historians the likes of O'Toole, Malone and Roeder jogging Montana's collective memory, the state is in no danger of repeating the mistakes of the past.

One cannot conclude a discussion of this new work without mentioning the bibliographic essay. It is a superlative effort and now becomes the most complete Montana history bibliography extant. Those interested in pursuing Montana history in depth will find the thirty-page bibliography a perfect starting point.

In summary, this new history is unabashedly a textbook, and as such, it will undoubtably capture the market. It is also a provocative history which is highly recommended to those interested in "Big Sky" history. It is also suggested reading for those intrigued by Wyoming history, for it is often through comparison and contrast that we gain new perspectives with regard to our own state history.

University of Wyoming   ROBERT W. RIGHTER

Learn to Love the Haze. By Robert Roripaugh. (Vermillion, S.D.: Spirit Mound Press, 1976). 60 pp. $2.95.

Bannack and Other Poems. By Wendell H. Maynard. (Philadelphia and Ardmore, Pa. Dorrance & Company, 1976). 84 pp. $4.95.

Stephen Vincent Benet, in his long, descriptive poem about New

York City, "Notes to Be Left in a Cornerstone", writes, "You will not get it from weather-reports". He means, of course, that only the eye and ear of the artist can recreate the true climate of a time or place.

In the same sense, the truth about the old or the modern West cannot be learned by studying town plats or annual records of snowpack measurements at the higher elevations. Nor can you get it from who-what-when-where newspaper accounts or wearily written trail diaries.

Only the artist, the poet, can pluck the facts from the shifting debris of past or present and weave these precise and perfect (arti)facts into a fabric, so that we can know, not only with our minds, but with our viscera, what it was or is to experience an incident, a human being, even an era. We who live in the West can also bring to the poetry of the West our own memories and experiences, so that the finished product of the poet is ours as well as his.

Most of us know, for example, about the 1865 battle fought within sight of Platte Bridge Station, in which Sergeant Amos Custard and his U. S. Army party of a dozen or so died at the hands of Sioux and Cheyenne warriors. We know the fort was later named for Lt. Caspar Collins who tried to ride out to rescue the party. But only in Wendell H. Maynard's narrative poem can we read:

> "Rescue
> And great hope registered itself once
> When Lt. Caspar Collins thundered
> Across the wooden bridge to ride up
> The stilted land.
>   Collins caught an arrow
> In his forehead and rode his crazy iron-gray
> Into the land's edge. He was seen to go
> Upright and cold of face and nearly
> Stiff as the bridle steel in his horses's mouth."

The reader has accompanied the little military band across the treeless plain on a hot July day; knows, because of the poet, their weariness and their fear when they encounter the warriors; he feels the leap of their hearts as Collins rides out onto that bridge, and the foreknowledge of their own deaths as the arrow finds its mark.

In similar ways, Maynard, who is an English teacher at Raceland High School in Kentucky, brings us to the experiences of real people (not always major characters, sometimes bit players in the drama) at Fort Laramie, at Independence Rock, other places we know; and in the title poem, at Bannack, Montana Territory, where vigilantes hanged a gang of ruffians who were robbing gold prospectors in the region.

This collection of poems enriches history by bringing its own poetic truth to the facts we know.

* * * * *

Robert Roripaugh, who teaches creative writing and Western Literature at the University of Wyoming, brings the same kind of truth to the current Wyoming scene. Read "Elegy for an Indian Girl" in which he explains:

> "Where I come from you look for Indian news
> In 'Hospital Notes' and the paper's
> Last-page square called 'Police Activities.' "

But then he takes you to a reservation barroom where young blood is restless, "For winter nights are long/ And still on tribal land." You go with an Indian maiden and two Indian boys in "a peeling Ford smoky/ With beer and breath" and you learn with sick horror the violence and tragedy of the night. No sociologist can tell you in a PhD thesis as much about the "problems of Indian youth" as Roripaugh tells you here in a few brief lines.

Roripaugh's poems are lyrical: they are deft watercolors, and when he uses symbols he uses them to help us see and hear, not to impress other poets. When he says in "Reservation Winter: Fort Washakie"

> "Two men are frozen to a storefront,
> Rolling cigarettes in wind."

we feel the gusts and really see the men through our frosted windshields.

This collection contains love lyrics, landscapes (with wildlife) and takes its title from a poem written to his mother. (Does it strike you as interesting that poets tell their fathers, "Do not go gentle into that good night" and tell their mothers, "Learn to love the haze"?)

Roripaugh has lived both in the Orient and in western states, including a ranch along the Wind River mountains of Wyoming. His two novels, "A Fever for Living" and "Honor Thy Father" (about the Indians of the Wind River reservation) thus have two radically different cultural settings. How different are they? Perhaps we should ask of Mr. Roripaugh another book which relates the two cultures, delineates the ethnic differences and the simple human bonds. We think it would be a "first".

Riverton, Wyoming   MARGARET PECK

The Czar's Germans. By Hattie Plum Williams. Edited by Emma
S. Haynes, Phillip B. Legler, and Gerda S. Walker. (Denver:
World Press, Inc., 1975, published under the auspices of the
American Historical Society of Germans from Russia, Lin-
coln, Nebraska). Index. Illus. Bib. 236 pp. $8.95.

Beginning in the early part of the twentieth century significant
numbers of Russian-German people started coming into Wyoming,
at first as summer migrant sugar beet workers, and later as permanent resident farmers. Many of these Russian-Germans, or
"Rooshuns" as they were commonly called, had first settled in
Lincoln, Nebraska, which had become a center and "jumping-off"
place for large numbers of Russian-German immigrants coming to
the United States. Following the demand for beet workers in the
opening years of the sugar beet industry, they migrated into other
western states, including Wyoming.

The Czar's Germans is a brief but fascinating account of the
history of Russian-German people in Russian prior to their settlement and dispersal in the United States. A comprehensive history
of the Russian-German people was first conceived and planned by
Hattie Plum Williams, a student at the University of Nebraska
before World War I. While failing to complete the task, Mrs.
Williams went on to receive her doctorate and serve as chairman
of the sociology department at the University of Nebraska from
1915 to 1945.

Recognizing the groundbreaking work of Williams, and the
value of her early research, the American Historical Society of
Germans from Russia (AHSGR) decided to sponsor the editing
and publication of her notes and manuscript. The result has been
an interesting and informative book that does credit not only to the
author, but to the editors and the AHSGR.

Following a rewarding introduction about the author, the book's
four chapters fulfill the limited purpose of the work with clarity
and skill. The reader first becomes aware that the German people
had already established a pattern of emigration prior to accepting
the invitation of Catherine II in 1762-1763, and migrating in large
numbers into Russia. Receiving favored status in Russia, which
included exemption from military service, the German colonists
maintained their ethnic identity for over a century in their auton-
omous rural villages. In the reading, Williams devotes special
attention to the Volga Germans since they furnished the bulk of
the Russian-German migration into Lincoln. The book's final
chapter reviews the Russian-German immigration to America, and
the subsequent pattern of settlement in the Dakotas, Kansas and
Nebraska.

The historian will appreciate the author's intent to provide more
than a chronological study of the Russian-German people. Wil-

liams discusses the formulation of Russian policy toward the German colonists, the various regions of German settlement in Russia, and the underlying causes that compelled these people to seek opportunity in America (the large majority of Russian-Germans remained in Russia). Nor has the author neglected the more human aspects of history, noting the hardships, struggles, failures. and successes of the German people in Russia. From her account, one recognizes similarities between these people and pioneer settlers moving Westward in eighteenth and nineteenth century America.

The reading gives an insight into the historical background of a people who were confronted with physical and political problems in Russia, and who eventually played an important role in the development of the sugar beet industry in our western states. In addition to the author's diligent scholarship, the reader gains the benefit of the views of an early observer of the Russian-German immigrants before they had become assimilated into American life. The book's carefully selected drawings, reprints, and photographs further enhance the quality of the text.

Later publications such as Adam Giesinger's *From Catherine to Khrushchev,* have provided additional and more detailed information about the Russian-German people. Yet, *The Czar's Germans* is an excellent source to become initially acquainted with these people. After reading the book, the reader should have little difficulty in accepting what Mrs. Williams concluded nearly seventy years ago, that the Russian-Germans were not Russian!

Eastern Wyoming Community College   DON HODGSON

John S. Gray. *Centennial Campaign: The Sioux War of 1876.* (Fort Collins, Colo.: The Old Army Press, 1976). Index. Bib. Maps. 392 pp. $20.

A few years ago, Vine Deloria, Jr. wondered aloud when historians would forsake their fascination with the Plains Indian wars and move, at last, into concerns of the twentieth century. Deloria's point is well-taken and given the plethora of material already available, one must wonder about the need for John S. Gray's study of "The Sioux War of 1876", *Centennial Campaign.* The enduring appeal possessed by the personalities and events of 101 years ago guarantees Gray's book a ready audience. More importantly, the volume succeeds for the most part in placing strategies, maneuvers, defeats and victories of that climactic year in a perspective we seldom have.

Gray attempts to describe the war's beginnings, present its strategy and tactics, and take the clash "to its dramatic and tragic conclusions"—in short, "for the first time to narrate the full story of the Sioux War of 1876." In trying to achieve these objectives, Gray divides his account in two parts: a narrative of 269 pages and "facets" comprising an additional 87 pages. The narrative, of course, reviews the chronicle of events in the war carried out against "hostile" Sioux in order to populate fully the reservation, to make available new land for whites, to legalize the invasion of the Black Hills, and to clear the way for the Northern Pacific railroad. The "facets" section covers such details as medical service, fatalities at Little Big Horn and the demography of Native American peoples faced by the army throughout the campaign.

This is a determinedly bipartisan account. Gray views the war as an inevitable clash between two widely different cultures. While the portrait of "the Indian" culture is as overgeneralized as the book's subtitle, it does help us to appreciate the desperate and ultimately unsuccessful battle waged by Native Americans. Gray devotes most of his attention, however, to the opponents of the Indians. Here emerges in blunt and uncompromising detail many elements which influenced the course of the war: the deceptive premise on which it was fought, the limited knowledge of the territory possessed by army leaders, the tentative and often mistaken decisions made by these leaders, and the stubborn and egocentric natures of many of these men. Crook, Terry, Gibbon and Reynolds, to mention some prominent examples, do not survive unscathed. On the other hand, Miles comes off relatively well, as does the much-maligned Custer. Gray concludes: "Custer's decisions, judged in the light of what he knew at the time, instead of by our hindsight, were neither disobediant [sic], rash, nor stupid. Granted his premises, all the rest follows rationally. It was what neither he, nor any other officer, knew that brought disaster."

Centennial Campaign is volume eight of the Old Army Press' Source Custeriana series. The book is augmented by eight three-color maps by John A. Popovich which will aid those grittily determined to follow the war every step of the way. The hefty price of the volume will deter some readers, while Gray's rather sluggish prose and simplistic form of documentation may disturb others.

University of Wyoming   PETER IVERSON

Pioneer Steelmaker in the West: The Colorado Fuel and Iron Company, 1872-1903. By H. Lee Scamehorn. (Boulder, Colo.: Pruett Publishing Company, 1972). Index. Bibliographical Essay. Illus. 231 pp. $19.95.

In the preface Scamehorn states that this volume "endeavors to place in historical perspective the origins and development of the Colorado Fuel and Iron Company and its predecessors during the years from 1872 to 1903." The study was undertaken at the request of officials of the company. In addition the company, through a gift to the Alumni Development Foundation of the University of Colorado, underwrote many of the expenses involved in conducting research. However, the company gave the author full access to all pertinent records and complete freedom in assessing their meaning.

Organized by topics, the book emphasizes the role of business entities and the men who ran them. Of secondary importance is the subject of labor-management relations. Highlighted by 142 photographs, this attractive volume traces the evolution of one of the principal heavy industries in the American West. The author presents a brief survey of the development of the iron and steel industry in the United States and its relationship with the Colorado-based company. Several chapters describe the complex development of the iron and steel portions of the company and the parallel development of its coal and coke-producing properties.

Other interesting subjects were the attempts of corporate officials to develop towns on land owned by the company. The chapter on the Southern Colorado Coal and Town Company scheme is an excellent example of these attempts. The chapters on industrial medicine and industrial sociology are fascinating and illustrate well-intentioned programs designed to alleviate the harsh conditions associated with the life of the miner and steelworker. It is an example of the practical recognition by company officials that a content, healthy worker was more useful to the corporation than a discontented, unhealthy employee. Although some of the methods implemented by the company may seem unsophisticated today, they were considered enlightened for the era. The book also examines the history of efforts made by individuals to manipulate and maintain control of the company. The rise and fall of some of these tycoons is quite interesting. The main corporate facilities were situated in and around Pueblo, Colorado, and gave the company a genuine western flavor. Other company holdings at Sunrise, Wyoming, and in the modern era in the eastern states made the corporation a national concern.

Most of the characters mentioned in the volume were individuals who held executive or professional positions within the company. Although some of these men were quite interesting, others were somewhat lifeless and quite similar to their contemporaries. It is regrettable that the author did not write more about the rank and file employees. Whenever the focus was shifted to the workers and their families, it was more readable. Perhaps the large number of statistics, dates and names could have been pruned without detracting from the final product. However, the author has achieved his purpose and the book is a contribution to the industrial history of the west.

Missouri Southern State College   ROBERT E. SMITH

Blacks in the West. Contributions in Afro-American and African
   Studies, #23. By W. Sherman Savage. (Westport, Conn.:
   Greenwood Press, 1977). Index. Bib. 231 pp. $14.95.

The existence of blacks in western American society and life during the nineteenth century, and their meaningful participation in social and economic activities, has been substantiated by a number of important books and monographs issued over the past decade. Historians such as Kenneth Wiggins Porter have described black involvement in the fur trade; John Millar Carroll and Arlene L. Fowler have discussed blacks in the frontier army; and William Loren Katz and others have provided overviews of the black western experience. Despite these endeavors, however, it is always useful to have another historian's appraisal of black participation in western events, especially that of W. Sherman Savage, Professor Emeritus at Lincoln University in Missouri and himself an outstanding representative of black achievement in western higher education and scholarship.

Dr. Savage's work covers the role of blacks from the days of the fur trade into the early twentieth century in such areas of human endeavor as economics, politics, legislation and the fight for civil rights, business and industry, the military and education. His definition of the West is a broad one, covering the area from Iowa, Wisconsin and Missouri westward to the Pacific Coast. Perhaps it is understandable that Savage's main focus of attention is on California, with its relatively significant black population from the days of the Gold Rush onward and its significant debates on slavery and black civil rights which are ably described in the author's book. Western states such as Montana, Wyoming, Idaho and Nevada receive lesser notice for the most part except for their location as scenes for the activities of black fur traders, soldiers and cowboys.

Savage depicts the West in rather favorable terms insofar as opportunities for blacks were concerned. He examines this situation in a relative fashion, of course, comparing the West as a haven for blacks against the more restrictive and onerous social structure of the East. Blacks were able, as he relates, to engage in important commercial ventures in California, including food wholesaling, real estate and newspaper publication. The black cowboy seems to have been at least tolerated by his white peers, probably, although Savage does not stress this point, because of the greater animosity displayed by whites towards the numerous Mexican cowboys.

As might be expected, given the scanty records of black Western endeavors available to the scholar, the author places greatest emphasis on records of individuals rising above their circumstances into positions of relative prominence. George Washington Bush, for instance, receives considerable space for his activities on the Washington frontier where he gained the respect and admiration of his white neighbors for his civic minded actions and keen sense of economic and political needs. William Alexander Leidesdorff was one of the first prominent black businessmen in California; his career is explicated by Savage as an example of business acumen resulting in an estate valued at $1,500,000 at the time of his death. The frantic scramble to acquire that estate on the part of Leidesdorff's real or alleged heirs is depicted in able fashion by the author.

Savage's book in sum is not a definitive history of all aspects of the black experience in the West during the nineteenth century, but it does touch on many of the most important facets of that experience. The author's readable narrative is fortified by research of the highest quality.

Camden County College   NORMAN LEDERER
Blackwood, New Jersey ·

Boots and Saddles at the Little Big Horn. By James S. Hutchins. (Fort Collins, Colo.: The Old Army Press, 1976). Illus. 81 pp. $3.50 paper.

To those of us who enjoy dabbling in the mysterious world of U. S. Army uniforms and equipage of the Indian Wars era, the name of James S. Hutchins is a familiar one. In 1956 he authored a landmark article in *The Military Collector and Historian* which presented the first realistic look at the frontier cavalry. This was followed in 1958 by a second article in the same journal which showed that Mr. Hutchins has the rare talent for combining research and writing with artistic ability to illustrate his work. He also wrote a valuable introduction to a reprint of Ordnance Memoranda No. 29, Horse Equipments and Cavalry Accoutrements, 1885. Furthermore, if you like to research this subject, his name will usually appear before your own on the check-out cards at the National Archives!

Almost since the final shot of the Battle of the Little Big Horn, the literary world has been bombarded with publications dealing with nearly every conceivable aspect of that fight. Artists, too, have had a heyday attempting to capture the "Last Stand" scene. Few have come even close to depicting how it really might have been. Over the past few decades Hollywood has contributed some, shall we say, "extraordinary" versions which bear little if any resemblance to the actual event.

However, amid all the dust that has been stirred up over Little Big Horn, there is one character who, ironically, has received little serious attention. Everyone has been so busy trying to place the blame for the disaster in one corner or another or with trying to reconstruct the events, that the lowly soldier in the ranks who died there has been nearly forgotten.

In *Boots and Saddles At The Little Big Horn,* James Hutchins uses a combination of text, art, and photography to aid the Custer student and the layman in visualizing just what cavalry soldiers of the 1870s looked like. The layman's impression, ingrained by the movie makers, disintegrates in *Boots and Saddles . . .* Hutchins' work presents brief piece-by-piece descriptions of the uniform items, accoutrements, weapons, and horse gear in use in 1876. He utilizes official records and personal accounts, supplemented by secondary sources to establish how the typical enlisted men and officers of the Seventh Cavalry were dressed and equipped.

At long last we have those Hollywood troopers, with yellow neckerchiefs and skin tight trousers, shown up for what they really are—fantasy. The soldiers of the Seventh Cavalry, as well as the other regiments on the frontier for that matter, campaigned in a duke's mixture of clothing, partly civilian and partly military. They were a rather rag-tag lot outfitted in a motley assortment of quartermaster goods ranging all the way back to the 1850s. In the field, officers and enlisted men were concerned only with having what it took to do the job, and, in Hutchins' words, "appearances counted for nothing."

For those who like Custer nostalgia, there is a chapter devoted to officers' clothing and accessories. Several items alleged to have belonged to General Custer are pictured and described.

Perhaps the most interesting chapter deals with the items which went to make up the saddle pack. These were the pieces of equipment carried by each soldier to enable him to survive in the field. Although the cup was briefly mentioned, in the discussion of the haversack there was nothing said about the other mess gear, utensils and meat can or plate. These could have been treated with little difficulty. Certainly they would have been scattered about the field of action and any artist using this work as a guide should know about them.

Other chapters in the book describe the horses, horse equipments, weapons, and flags in use by the Seventh at the peak of the Indian campaigns. Much of the information can be applied to all of the cavalry serving in the West at the time. Therein lies one of the mose subtle values of the work.

Hutchins' *Boots and Saddles . . .* is a good primer on the subject, but the collector and "buff" will find it lacking in enough detail for their own intense interests. Brevity is the main short-coming. Assuming that the author intended only to write an introductory work, even the novice may find himself left out here and there when the author does not elaborate in more detail.

Many pages throughout the book are occupied with photos of single items surrounded by an abundance of blank space. In the horse equipment chapter, for instance, six of the eight pages are devoted entirely to illustrations of this type. The old adage about a picture being worth a thousand words may have some truth in it, but it would seem that a better arrangement or more text or both could have made this book more effective.

James Hutchins set out to tackle a complicated and rather elusive subject and to present it to a general audience; a popular approach if you wish. Overall he has made a commendable effort and has opened the door for further work in this area. We can only hope that Hollywood costume designers and producers will discover it. If you still envision Custer's troopers in blue cotton shirts decorated with chevrons and flashy yellow neckerchiefs, or if you are simply interested in the frontier cavalry, then this book is for you.

Fort Laramie National Historic Site   DOUG MCCHRISTIAN

The Story of the Latter-day Saints. By James B. Allen and Glen M. Leonard. (Salt Lake City: Deseret Book Company, 1976). Index. Bib. Illus. 722 pp.

The Story of the Latter-day Saints is a narrative history of the Church of Jesus Christ of Latter-day Saints from its beginnings in the early 1800s to the present. The authors elaborate on four definable characteristics of Latter-day Saints: their religiosity, their being influenced by the world around them, their self-view of a worldwide institution, and finally the dynamic nature of the institution of Mormonism itself.

To tell this story, Allen and Leonard divide their book into five parts. The first lays the foundations of Zion and reviews the early influences, beginnings, and developments from New England and upper New York State to Kirtland, Ohio, and Missouri. The second section discusses developments of the church in Illinois, Joseph Smith's leadership and eventual martyrdom, Brigham Young's succession to leadership and his move to Zion to the Valley of the Great Salt Lake.

Next the authors look at the Mormons making a defense of the kingdom in the midst of the mountains, where the institutions peculiarities flowered, were attacked, and succumbed as part of the price of statehood for Utah and full rights of citizenship for Mormons.

The fourth part is seen as the transition period from opposition to incorporation within American society including its problems. Joseph F. Smith is shown as the first of the new generation leadership. The final section traces the institution's expansion into a worldwide church with missionary programs, area conferences, and reorganization of church leadership to that purpose.

It is readily apparent to the reader that the authors are writing an in-house history, a basic statement of historic faith to Latter-day Saints. Their narrative style serves them well once the church is established and its role and authority assumed. The chapters dealing with the Kirtland conflict, the Missouri unrest, the move to Utah, the post-Brigham Young leadership, and the twentieth century represent the best work in the book. The latter portion is particularly valuable since it is the first good LDS general history on this time period.

The book contains a wealth of information, but is uneven in both style and content. The first three chapters are especially troublesome. In them the book's concept of history is shown as the unfolding of the will of God, while the authors' roles are advanced as defenders of the faith. While some attempt is made to review historical challenges to Joseph Smith's own early history, no serious historical review of his claims is made. The divine mission of Mormonism is finally simply assumed. Once the position is established that God has restored his church, then the authors move quite deftly to deal with the historical forces that impacted the people and the institution.

Unfortunately, the early Utah period is treated primarily as early Utah history. Little effort is made to see what "setting up the Kingdom" did for or to the basic policies, practices, and doctrines of the church. How significant to Mormonism was Brigham Young's leadership? Later the authors do show clearly the impact of modern business values and leadership on the present-day church.

Overall the book makes major contributions to Mormon history. Its index and bibliography are excellent. Students of Mormon history and the general reader will find it useful and enjoyable.

Utah State Historical Society   MELVIN T. SMITH

Charles Boettcher: A Study in Pioneer Western Enterprise. By Geraldine B. Bean. (Boulder: Westview Press, 1976). Index. Bib. Notes. Illus. 220 pp. $15.00.

In a year marked by the appearance of so many glossy publications, the University of Colorado Centennial Commission fortunately chose to sponsor this volume, in which Mrs. Bean with careful scholarship traces the life of a businessman whom she hails as a pioneer prototype for the novels of Horatio Alger, Jr.

At age seventeen in 1869, Charles Boettcher came from Kolleda, Germany, to Cheyenne to join his brother, Herman, a storekeeper. The next ten years were a prologue to his later success. He engaged in business with his brother in Cheyenne and in three towns in Colorado—Greeley, Evans, and Fort Collins, where he married Fannie A. Cowan of Kansas. The newlyweds relocated in Boulder and built a substantial trade for their hardware store, but in 1879 Boettcher abruptly moved his operations to booming Leadville.

Mercantile success in Leadville made the enterprising German a speculator in mining stocks and a director of the Carbonate National Bank. He moved to Denver in 1890 after his election to a directorship of that city's National Bank of Commerce, of which he became president in 1897. Boettcher was a controversial figure in the Ibex Mining Company, which surreptitiously accumulated mining properties in Leadville. He built himself a modest mansion on Capitol Hill. He attempted to retire in 1900 and toured Europe for six months, only to return to Colorado resolving to remain at work and carrying a supply of sugar beet seed.

In his second career Boettcher was instrumental in the founding of the Great Western Sugar Company, a momentous event in the economic history of the Northern Plains. Next he organized a firm to manufacture cement, formed a holding company to absorb competitive plants, and eventually consolidated them into the Ideal Cement Company. He also twice was a receiver of the Denver and Salt Lake Railway Company. Prior to his death in 1948 he saw portions of his fortune benefit worthy causes through the Boettcher Foundation.

Mrs. Bean does an ingenious job of reconstructing the life of Boettcher from diverse and disconnected sources, including the Boettcher Collection of the State Historical Society of Colorado. The "life and times" approach which she adopts, however, sometimes relegates him to the role of a vehicle used to weave together strands of the economic history of Colorado. The style of writing is straightforward, smooth, and interesting.

The greatest strength of the book is the author's evenhanded verdicts on controversial issues. She is careful to highlight her subject's considerable contributions to the regional economy, but when relating his occasional foibles she neither condemns nor rationalizes. Issues such as the Ibex Mining Company and violations of antitrust laws receive scrupulous treatment; judgements are made only in the light of the times in which the events occurred. Although the sources leave teasing gaps as to Boetcher's personal life—for instance why his marriage collapsed in 1915— his businesslike attributes of innovativeness and industriousness

emerge clearly.   Mrs. Bean may not justify her hyperbole that
"The West, in truth, was won by men at roll-top desks" (p. ix),
but she ably delineates the accomplishments of one such figure.

Oklahoma State University   THOMAS D. ISERN

*A Governor's Wife on the Mining Frontier.   The Letters of Mary
    Edgerton from Montana, 1863-1865.*   Number Seven of the
    Series Utah, The Mormons and the West.   By James L.
    Thane, Jr.   (Salt Lake City: University of Utah Library,
    1976).   Index. Bib. Illus. 148 pp. $8.50.

The comment has often been made that it was the *ladies* who
dared to live on the Frontier that civilized the West.   If this statement is true, then *A Governor's Wife on the Mining Frontier* by
Dr. James L. Thane, Jr., reflects that civilizing influence.   It is
the story of the two years Mary Wright Edgerton spent in Idaho
Territory and as the wife of the First Governor of Montana.

The few documents surviving which tell the story of this lady
are not as revealing of the life around her as one might wish.
Either that, or the movies and TV have shown us a side of life
on the frontier which is not altogether a true picture.

Mrs. Edgerton's letters show a formality of living which would
cause a lady to call her husband Mr. Edgerton always, even to her
own family, and they show restrictions on her life in the community because of her position.   If she saw the type of life we so
often have been exposed to, she did not write about it because her
family might not understand, or she chose to ignore it as beneath
a lady and the wife of an official.

Mrs. Edgerton does mention the hangings of the outlaws in
Bannock, but with no emotion whatever other than the statement
that now her husband would be safer on his trip to Washington.
She mentions dancing as the only form of entertainment and that
the people of the community thought the reason she did not allow
her daughter and niece to attend was that her husband was governor and she thought them not her equal.   Her daughter was fourteen, but she said the public would not believe that because the
girl was large for her age.

Most of her letters are concerned with the every day ailments,
such as colds, and the everyday problems of frontier living, such
as foods, the problems of getting clothing, and their costs.   She
did not describe her home, nor complain that she had no servants
although she had been used to having help in the house before
she came to the frontier.

There was more description of the prairie and life on the trek
than of her life in Bannock after they got there.

Little comment is made of Mr. Edgerton's problems as chief

justice and as governor. If he confided in her, this was private business and not to be told to the family in letters.

Mrs. Edgerton is an educated woman and the letters are well-written, but their chief interest lies in the fact that so few of the women of the frontier preserved their history in letters.

Dr. Thane spent the first two chapters reviewing the history before he inserted the letters, which may account for the fact that this reviewer felt they did not say as much as they could have. Certainly they are a part of the history of the times and place and will be read with interest by historians and researchers.

Cheyenne   LOUISE F. UNDERHILL

$10 Horse, $40 Saddle. Cowboy Clothing, Arms, Tools and Horse Gear of the 1880's. By Don Rickey, Jr. (Ft. Collins, Colo.: The Old Army Press, 1976). Index. Illus. 135 pp. $10.

$10 HORSE $40 SADDLE is an extremely well-researched, illustrated, documented book. Rickey gets down to the basics in a hurry about cowboy clothing, arms and equipment and cowboy gear.

To the student of Western Americana and especially the student of the 1880's cowboy, Rickey superbly details for the reader why cowboys had and needed the clothing they wore, why the 1880's cowboy used the arms and equipment they did and why they preferred certain types of cowboy gear.

In choosing to write about the free grass cowboy of the 1890's, Rickey has chosen a subject that Western buffs will continue to study for a long time. Our society cannot get enough of this kind of educational/informational material and thus Rickey's book is much needed and wanted.

I highly recommend $10 HORSE $40 SADDLE be used by students in Western history and Western art classes. As our society becomes more urban we urgently need books such as Rickey's to reflect back and intelligently document what the range riders used to fight and cope with the elements of the out-of-doors. Range riders lived continuously in the elements and on horseback moving and driving cattle herds.

Every piece of garb or type of hardware that Rickey has chosen to write about was a necessary tool that evolved through the outright nature of the range riders' occupation. The old raw-hiders had to have these special kinds of gear that Rickey describes literally to survive as a range cowboy. Rickey has meticulously researched and documented what these tools of the range riders trade were. If you delight in knowing detail about types of hats or types of boots that were worn by the 1880's cowboy, then read this book.

The illustrations by Dale Crawford of cowboy clothing and gear are well done. The illustrations in the book really give meaning to the entire objective Rickey is trying to achieve. One needs both the narrative and the illustrations to properly document this subject and Rickey has got just that. Crawford has shown detail in his illustrations and that definitely has more meaning for the reader. Crawford simply has done a good job.

The most impressive one thing about Rickey's book is the approach he used to obtain historical accuracy about how the cowboys dressed and the paraphernalia they used. He went to the source, interviewing men who had been cowboys in the eighties and nineties, making their living on the range. What better source can one ask for than the individuals who were truly bonafide cowmen of the 1880's era?

Wyoming Stock Growers Association   JOHN D. PEARSON

The Sioux Uprising of 1862. By Kenneth Carley. (St. Paul: Minnesota Historical Society, 1976.) Index. Illus. Bib. Maps. 102 pp. $7.50 cloth; $3.50 paper.

The Sioux Uprising began in August, 1862, when some bands of Santee Sioux lashed out at farms and towns and at Fort Ridgely in the Minnesota River Valley. This short but bloody war that finally cost the Sioux their Minnesota lands has long been of great popular interest and literature about it abounds.

Carley's excellent illustrated history was first published in 1961. The author stated in the preface to the first edition that his work was intended "to present an accurate, concise narrative in words and pictures of the Sioux Uprising . . . ." The second edition, he explains "is an amplification of its predecessor in terms of text, pictures, and, in a few instances, interpretation. Two wholly new chapters, as well as numerous illustrations, have been added, and the entire text has been carefully reviewed and revised in the light of recently discovered source materials and the research of other scholars since 1961." In the two new sections Carley describes the siege of Fort Abercrombie (in present North Dakota on the Red River) and the banishment of the Sioux from Minnesota.

Carley has fulfilled his stated purpose admirably. The text is concise and lucid and the numerous photographs and drawings of participants and historic sites not only complement the narrative but add to its impact. Every page has at least one illustration. The principal participants are all shown including Little Crow, the Sioux War leader; Shakopee and Medicine Bottle; Henry H. Sibley, commander of state militiamen dispatched to quell the Indians; and Charles Flandrau, the defender of New Ulm. The text is prefaced by a chronology which outlines the main features of the war and a colored centerfold map shows settlers' forts, Indian villages, battle sites and commemorative monuments. An outstanding feature is the lengthy bibliography which is without doubt the best and most up-to-date available.

In this work, Carley achieved more than his stated purpose, for he succeeded in producing a balanced, judicious and objective account. He places no blame on Indian or frontiersman, but instead dispassionately describes the causes of the war, its military phases and its aftermath. Quite obviously, in this short book much specific detail had to be sacrificed; nonetheless, readers will find it to be the best single source on Minnesota's Sioux War.

Mankato State University   WILLIAM E. LASS

Contributors

BARTON R. VOIGT is a student in the College of Law, University of Wyoming. He is a former research historian with the Wyoming State Archives and Historical Department and served for two years as manuscripts curator at the South Dakota State Historical Resource Center. He has previously had historical articles published in *Annals of Wyoming* and *South Dakota History.*

JOHN S. GRAY, of Fort Collins, has researched and written about American frontier history full time since his retirement in 1974 as professor and department chairman, Department of Physiology at Northwestern University Medical School. He is a member of Chicago Westerners, Fort Collins Westerners, the Western History Association and numerous biomedical societies. He has published widely in historical journals, and his book, *Centennial Campaign. The Sioux War of 1876,* was published in 1976 by The Old Army Press.

CHARLES (PAT) HALL served as executive director of the Wyoming Bicentennial Commission for its duration. He previously had a long career in journalism as a photographer and picture editor for newspapers in the mid-west. He came to Wyoming in 1967 to become editor of the Wyoming Game and Fish Commission's magazine, *Wyoming Wildlife.* A specialist in postal history, he has recently planned the development of the Wyoming Postal History Galley, a new permanent exhibit of the Wyoming State Museum, Cheyenne.

GRANT K. ANDERSON teaches American history in LeCenter, Minnesota. He holds an M.S. degree in history from the University of North Dakota. He belongs to several historical societies, including Western History Association and has had articles published in *South Dakota History* and *Nebraska History.* Anderson has presented papers at the last eight Dakota History Conferences at Dakota State College.

DAVID W. LUPTON, librarian and associate professor, is head of the serials department at Colorado State University, Fort Collins. He is currently working on a book about historic Fort Lupton, Colorado, and its founder, Lancaster Platt Lupton. He holds degrees in library science, entomology and zoology from the University of Wisconsin. Lupton belongs to various historical, entomological and archaeological organizations.

MABEL COOPER SKJELVER is a Nebraska native. She has been on the faculty of the University of Nebraska since 1973. She holds a B.S. degree from the University of Nebraska, the M.S. from Michigan State University and the Ph.D. from Florida State University.

Index

WYOMING STATE ARCHIVES AND HISTORICAL DEPARTMENT

The Wyoming State Archives and Historical Department has as its function the collection and preservation of the record of the people of Wyoming. It maintains the state's historical library and research center, the Wyoming State Museum and branch museums, the Wyoming State Art Gallery and the State archives.

The aid of the citizens of Wyoming is solicited in the carrying out of its function. The Department is anxious to secure and preserve records and materials now in private hands where they cannot be long preserved. Such records and materials include:

Biographical materials of pioneers: diaries, letters, account books, autobiographical accounts.

Business records of industries of the state: livestock, mining, agriculture, railroads, manufacturers, merchants, small business establishments and of professional men such as bankers, lawyers, physicians, dentists, ministers and educators.

Private records of individual citizens, such as correspondence, manuscript materials and scrapbooks.

Records of organizations active in the religious, educational, social, economic and political life of the state, including their publications such as yearbooks and reports.

Manuscript and printed articles on towns, counties and any significant topic dealing with the history of the state.

Early newspapers, maps, pictures, pamphlets, and books on western subjects.

Current publications by individuals or organizations throughout the state.

Museum materials with historic significance: early equipment, Indian artifacts, relics dealing with the activities of persons in Wyoming and with special events in the state's history.

Original art works of a western flavor including, but not limited to, etchings, paintings in all media, sculpture and other art forms.

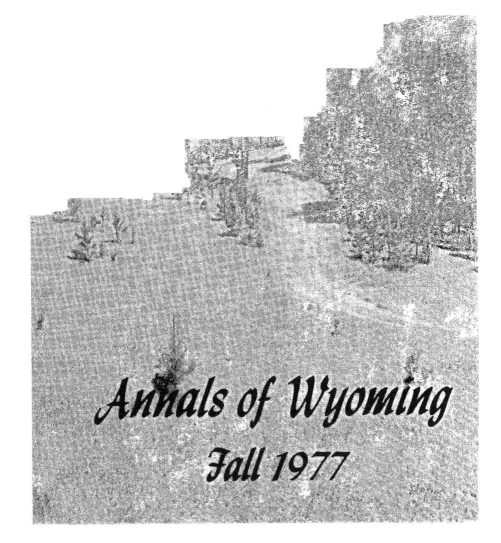

Annals of Wyoming

Fall 1977

ANNALS OF WYOMING

The ANNALS OF WYOMING is published biannually in the spring and fall and is received by all members of the Wyoming State Historical Society. Copies of previous and current issues also are available for sale to the public and a price list may be obtained by writing to the Editor.

Communications should be addressed to the Editor. The Editor does not assume responsibility for statements of fact or opinion made by the contributors.

ANNALS OF WYOMING articles are abstracted in Historical Abstracts. America: History of Life

Annals of Wyoming

Volume 49   Fall, 1977   Number 2

KATHERINE A. HALVERSON
Editor

JOHN C. PAIGE
WILLIAM H. BARTON
ELLEN E. GLOVER
Editorial Assistants

Published biannually by the
WYOMING STATE ARCHIVES AND HISTORICAL
DEPARTMENT

Official Publication of the Wyoming State Historical Society

WYOMING STATE HISTORICAL SOCIETY

OFFICERS 1977-1978

The Wyoming State Historical Society was organized in October, 1953. Membership is open to anyone interested in history. County Historical Society Chapters have been organized in Albany, Big Horn, Campbell, Carbon, Crook, Fremont, Goshen, Hot Springs, Johnson, Laramie, Lincoln, Natrona, Niobrara, Park, Platte, Sheridan, Sweetwater, Teton, Uinta, Washakie and Weston Counties.

Table of Contents

COVER NOTES

Devils Tower, the nation's first national monument, was designated by a presidential proclamation signed by Theodore Roosevelt on September 24, 1906. Following are excerpts from that proclamation:

"WHEREAS, It is provided by section two of the Act of Congress entitled 'An Act for the preservation of American Antiquities, 'That the President of the United States is hereby authorized, in his discretion, to declare by public proclamation historic landmarks, historic and prehistoric structures, and other objects of historic or scientific interest that are situated upon the lands owned or controlled by the Government of the United States to be National Monuments, and may reserve as a part thereof parcels of land, the limits of which in all cases shall be confined to the smallest area compatible with the proper care and management of the object to be protected;'

"And, whereas, the lofty and isolated rock in the State of Wyoming known as the 'Devils Tower,' . . . is such an extraordinary example of the effect of erosion in the higher mountains as to be a natural wonder and an object of historic and great scientific interest, and it appears that the public good would be promoted by reserving this tower as a National monument with as much land as may be necessary for the proper protection thereof;

"Now, therefore, I THEODORE ROOSEVELT, President of the United States . . . do hereby set aside as the Devils Tower National Monument the lofty and isolated rock situated in Crook County, Wyoming, . . .

"Warning is hereby expressly given to all unauthorized persons not to appropriate, injure or destroy any feature of the natural tower or to locate or settle upon any of the lands reserved and made a part of said monument by this proclamation . . ."

The cover photograph is from the Stimson Photo Collection, Wyoming State Archives and Historical Department.

The WPA Writers' Project in Wyoming: History and Collections

By

GORDON O. HENDRICKSON

The crash of the Wall Street stock market on October 24, 1929, signaled the end of the apparent American economic boom of the 1920s. The following twelve years brought to the United States an unprecedented depression — a depression which affected not simply the economic giants of the nation, but each and every American. In a day before unemployment benefits, social security, federal deposit insurance, and innumerable other federally sponsored programs, the man in the street found himself not only without work, but with no prospect for work or financial support.

After nearly four years, during which Herbert Hoover and his presidential administration attempted to reverse the economic stagnation, Franklin Delano Roosevelt took office as president of the United States. Within the first one hundred days of his administration, a number of executive actions and congressional enactments altered considerably the focus of the federal relief attempt.[1] These new programs were successful in alleviating some of America's fears concerning the depression, and they provided employment and relief for some Americans. A number of programs such as the Agricultural Adjustment Act, the Tennessee Valley Authority, the Public Works Administration, and the National Industrial Recovery Act were enacted during the memorable hundred days, but perhaps the most widely remembered New Deal program waited two years before enactment.

On May 6, 1935, President Franklin Roosevelt issued Executive

---

[1] For a discussion of the Hoover administration's attempts to combat the Depression, see Albert U. Romasco, *The Poverty of Abundance: Hoover, The Nation, The Depression* (New York: Oxford University Press, 1965); William E. Leuchtenberg, *The Perils of Prosperity* (Chicago: University of Chicago Press, 1958), pp. 249-268; and, John D. Hicks, *Republican Ascendancy, 1921-1933* (New York: Harper & Row, 1960), pp. 260-280. An excellent overview of the New Deal period is William E. Leuchtenberg, *Franklin D. Roosevelt and the New Deal* (New York: Harper & Row, 1963). His fourth chapter deals specifically with the "Hundred Days."

Order No. 7034 which established the Works Progress Administration (WPA) as a part of the New Deal attempt to stymy the Great Depression.[2] The WPA sought to provide work to unemployed persons throughout the country by supporting them in gainful occupations which would provide benefit to the general public. WPA projects were to meet a number of criteria prior to receiving full approval. Only those projects which afforded "permanent improvement in living conditions or created future new wealth for the nation" would be approved. These new projects were also required to be

> such as involved a large percentage of direct labor; they should be planned and selected to compete as little as possible with private enterprise; they should be so located as to serve the greatest employment needs; and they should be compensated for on a scale larger than the amount received as a relief dole, but not so large as to encourage the rejection of opportunities for private employment or the leaving of private employment to engage in government work.[3]

With these guidelines clearly in mind, a number of WPA projects were undertaken. Roads and streets, sidewalks, public buildings, sewer systems, and conservation and recreation facilities were among the types of projects which the WPA sponsored. These construction projects are among the most widely known of the WPA activities.[4]

Since not only manual laborers were affected by the Great Depression, something had to be done for the white-collar and professional workers. With these people in mind, special projects were developed under the auspices of the WPA for their benefit. The Federal Artists' Project, the Federal Theatre Project, the Federal Music Project, and the Federal Writers' Project all provided employment opportunities for unemployed professionals in their respective fields. These individual projects were all part of a multi-faceted program of WPA activities for professionals known collectively as Federal Project No. 1.[5]

While Congress authorized funds for the WPA in April, 1935, many months passed before relief for white-collar workers in the form of Federal One actually got off the ground. Fully four months passed before WPA officials announced a forthcoming program of work relief for unemployed professionals. The exact

---

[2]William F. McDonald, *Federal Relief Administration and the Arts* (Columbus, Ohio: Ohio State University Press, 1969), p. 104. The Emergency Relief Appropriation Act of April 8, 1935, 115 Stat. 49, provided the funding for the agency Roosevelt created nearly a month later.

[3]Dexter Perkins, *The New Age of Franklin Roosevelt, 1932-1945* (Chicago: University of Chicago Press, 1957), p. 30.

[4]Leuchtenberg, *Franklin D. Roosevelt and the New Deal*, p. 126.

[5]McDonald, *Federal Relief Administration and the Arts*, provides a historical review of these federal programs.

organizational plan for the program had not been fully developed by August, but state WPA officials were asked to "submit for approval, through the regular channels, such additional State and local projects in these fields as are warranted by the availability of relief workers." In addition to previously solicited projects for blue-collar workers, new programs related to art, music, theatre, and writing were requested in August, 1935.[6]

Wyoming officials responded to the call for new projects by devising a plan for the systematic collection of "sundry historical data, including diaries, relics, first hand accounts and any other historical material available."[7] Alice Lyman, Wyoming state librarian and ex-officio state historian, in submitting the Statewide Historical Project to the WPA for approval, called for the placement of at least one previously jobless employee in each of Wyoming's counties for the purpose of gathering this historical data.[8] The suggested program, being statewide in scope and being designed to utilize the talents of relief workers, seemed to correspond closely to the August WPA guidelines. The requested funding for the Statewide Historical Project was apparently sidetracked in Washington while federal administrative officials worked to organize a much broader national program for writers.

Whereas the August, 1935, guidelines suggested programs of "State and local" scope, administrative officials were working to establish a nationwide project for writers in all of the states. Henry G. Alsberg, national director of the Federal Writers' Project, conceived of an American guide book which could be published under the auspices of the WPA. Suggestions for a publication reviewing the historical and tourist attractions of the United States had been circulating in Washington for some time before the WPA adopted the idea.[9] Alsberg felt that workers on the local and state level could research, write, and edit material for inclusion in a book which would help Americans in the "discovery of the roots from which America had grown," and which would serve as a "signpost of America's potentialities for the future." The American guide which Alsberg hoped to create through the Writers' Project was to be "an appreciation of America and a revelation of the democratic tradition, which, though it had

---

[6]*Ibid.*, p. 129, citing WPA Letter WP-7, August 2, 1935.

[7]Letter, Lester C. Hunt to Agnes Wright Spring, no place, August 7, 1935. Wyoming Work Projects Administration's Federal Writers' Project Collection, Wyoming State Archives and Historical Department, Part III, Administrative Files, Folder 51, "Correspondence, 1935." (Hereafter cited as: WPA Collection, part number, folder number, and title.)

[8]*Ibid.*

[9]McDonald, *Federal Relief Administration and the Arts*, chapter 28, *passim*.

never ceased to exist, had been obscured" in America.[10]   After adoption by the WPA Writers' Project, Alsberg viewed completion of the American guide as being the primary concern of the state and national Writers' Projects.   State and local workers were to study their local areas and filter their written material up through the system so a single American guide could be produced. Alsberg assumed the project leading to the American guide would not necessarily call for the preparation and publication of local, or state guide books.   The final product would consist of five sections, each dealing with a specific region of the country.[11]   Any other products would be secondary to the major objective.

As the Federal Writers' Project became organized, state administrators for the project, including Mart Christensen of Wyoming, received descriptions of duties which included directing "the field force in the state and [acting] as editor of collected material for a potential state book, which will be a by-product of the Federal project.   Further by-products," the instruction continued, "will be local guides for every locality in which we shall be working."[12] Like all major research undertakings, the format and structure of the project changed considerably before its termination.   The proposed by-products of the major publication became the major publications themselves.

By the end of the entire relief project, some local guides were produced, and each of the then forty-eight states, the District of Columbia, New York City, and Puerto Rico all produced "state" guide books.   These publications preceded the production of the American guide by as much as twelve years.   The publication of the national study was delayed long beyond the termination of the Works Progress Administration.   In 1949, Henry G. Alsberg, who had left the WPA Writers' Project in 1938, edited *The American Guide*.   While receiving no funding or support from the federal government, Alsberg credited the Federal Writers' Project with the production of much of the material he used in the national guide book.[13]

Even though Wyoming officials had presented the plans for a Statewide Historical Project prior to having received instructions concerning the production of material for the American guide, the initial work of the WPA Writers' Project in the state was oriented

---

[10]*Ibid.*, p. 665.

[11]Katherin H. Davidson, (comp.), *Records of the Federal Writers' Project Work Projects Administration, 1935-1944* (Washington, D. C.: National Archives and Record Service, 1953), p. 3.

[12]McDonald, *Federal Relief Administration and the Arts*, p. 147, citing Letter, Jacob Baker to Thad Holt, October 5, 1935, no place.

[13]Davidson, *Records of the Federal Writers' Project*, p. 3.

—Wyoming State Archives and
Historical Department Photo

Mart Christensen

to the American guide.[14]   In fact, throughout the history of the
Writers' Project, the most important project, both in the eyes of
state and national officials, was the guide book.[15]   In Wyoming,
Mart Christensen, after being appointed state director of the Federal Writers' Project, commenced work in late October, 1935, on
the collection of data for use in writing the guide book.   He hoped,
through the production of this guide book, to "tell the rest of the
United States what we have in Wyoming and where to find it."[16]

---

[14]Letter, Mart Christensen to Alice Lyman, Cheyenne, Wyoming, November 25, 1935. WPA Collection, Part III, Administrative Files, Folder 51,
"Correspondence, 1935."
   [15]McDonald, *Federal Relief Administration and the Arts,* p. 693.
   [16]Letter, Mart Christensen to Alice Lyman, Cheyenne, Wyoming, November 25, 1935. WPA Collection, Part III, Administrative Files, Folder 51,
"Correspondence, 1935."

After authorization for the project, work commenced almost immediately and continued through the final production of the desired guide.

By November 25, 1935, Christensen had ten writers on the project who, with assistance from others added in coming months, continued to gather material for the Wyoming guide through the next two years.[17] Under Christensen's guidance, workers collected data according to the formulas and guidelines set down by the federal office in Washington, D. C.[18] By early 1937, Christensen was submitting copy for the final book to the national office for review and editing.[19] Apparently he worked hard on the guide, but his production never received full approval of the Writers' Project editors in Washington. Editorial comments returned to Christensen's office indicated a strong degree of displeasure with the presentations submitted.[20] The only section of Christensen's writing which received approval from Washington was the compilation of a chronology for the book. However, even that section was redone prior to the book's final production.[21]

While Christensen was working on the preparation of the Wyoming guide book, Alice Lyman's Statewide Historical Project received a green light from the national office of the WPA Writers' Project.[22] This project, as indicated earlier, was designed to collect Wyoming historical data for preservation and future use. The operation of the Statewide Historical Project was distinct from that portion of the Writers' Project concerned with production of

------

[17]*Ibid.*

[18]The instructional materials for preparation of the American Guide were some 694 pages in length. WPA Collection, Part III, Administrative Files, Folders 116-121, "American Guide - Instructions."

[19]Copies of the materials Christensen submitted to Washington for review prior to incorporation into the Wyoming state guide are contained in the WPA Collection, Part II, Subject Files, Folders 1562-1599.

[20]Letters of comment from the central office in Washington concerning the materials Christensen submitted are preserved in *Ibid.* An example of the editorial criticisms of Christensen's writings is the following comment of George Cronyn, Associate Director of the Federal Writers' Project. "I have re-read the Contemporary Scene and although it is improved, it seems to me that it will be a rather colorless introduction to a book of unusually vivid interest." Letter, George Cronyn to Mart Christensen, Washington, D. C., March 17, 1937. WPA Collection, Part II, Subject Files, Folder 1572, "Wyoming Guide - Contemporary Scene."

[21]Letter, Henry G. Alsberg to Mart Christensen, Washington, D. C., March 8, 1938, with handwritten annotation. WPA Collection, Part II, Subject Files, Folder 1571, "Wyoming Guide—Chronology."

[22]Memorandum, "Wyoming Statewide Historical Project," no author, no date. WPA Collection, Part III, Administrative Files, Folder 53, "Correspondence, 1937."

the Wyoming guide. Some of the materials collected under the auspices of the Historical Project were used when preparing the state guide book, and the sources of funding were the same, but the two projects remained basically separate. As will be seen, when a decision was made between the two projects as to which would continue, the Statewide Historical Project fell by the wayside.

Maude Sholty was placed in charge of the Statewide Historical Project when it finally received approval early in 1936. Under her direction, workers in all Wyoming counties interviewed pioneers, collected historical materials such as diaries, journals, and letters, and wrote up the results of their research. After compilation on the county level, the materials were sent to Sholty in Cheyenne to be processed for inclusion in the holdings of the State Historical Library. The manuscripts written in the field were given a final editing in the state office, were retyped according to subject, author, and title. When a manuscript had been completely processed, it was ready for accessioning into the holdings of the Library.

Sholty and her workers compiled an impressive amount of historical material, but the final editing and indexing of that material was long and tedious. By the end of 1937, some 1900 manuscripts had been gathered under the auspices of the Statewide Historical Project. Nina Moran, then Wyoming's State Librarian, indicated that even though the manuscripts had been collected and were physically in the State Library, they had not all been indexed or catalogued. Only ninety-seven manuscripts had been completely processed by that time.[23] Despite the amount of clerical work which remained in the project, not to mention the numerous historical sources in the field which had not been tapped, a decision between funding for the Statewide Historical Project and the other projects of the Federal Writers' Project was necessary near the end of 1937.

WPA officials drew a clear distinction between federal and non-federal projects, terming anything which "supplements some normal activity of the State, municipality or other public body" as a non-federal project.[24] The Historical Project clearly fell within this category, as it served to collect materials for inclusion in the regular holdings of the State Historical Library. When a decision concerning project funding was necessary, the decision fell in favor of the federal project in Wyoming. By September 8, 1937, Maude Sholty had resigned her post as director of the Statewide Historical

[23]Letter, State Librarian to Louis Ash, no place, March 28, 1938. WPA Collection, Part III, Administrative Files, Folder 54, "Correspondence, 1938."

[24]McDonald, *Federal Relief Administration and the Arts,* p. 127.

Project, and no one was appointed as her replacement.[25]   With Sholty's resignation, the Historical Project drew to a close as a separate project of the Federal Writers' Project in Wyoming.   The project was officially discontinued in October, 1937.[26]

Nina Moran worked throughout early 1938 to obtain additional clerical help financed through the WPA to continue the cataloguing and indexing of the nearly 1900 manuscripts which had not been completed.   Moran contacted both local and regional officials of the Historical Records Survey suggesting that some means of support be located.   Louis Ash, then Acting State Director of the Historical Records Survey in Wyoming, suggested to his superiors that something be worked out since some of the material consisted of "collections of a public and semi-public nature which undoubtedly contain imprints such as we desire."[27]   By August, a plan for the loan of workers from the Historical Records Survey to the State Library to complete the processing of the Historical Project manuscripts had been finalized.   By October, at least one worker, Harry J. Shad, had begun verifying the manuscripts, overseeing their typing, and indexing and cataloguing the manuscripts.[28]   Shad's efforts resulted in the preparation of an unknown number of additional manuscripts for library use.

In addition to the projects discussed above, the production of the Wyoming guide book and the Statewide Historical Project, federal officials developed a third program for the Federal Writers' Project.[29]   The Historical Records Survey, as conceived at the national level, called for workers to go into each and every county in the nation to survey and inventory existing federal records, state and local records, church records, manuscript collections, and imprints.   A printed inventory of the records of each county was then to be published so future historians and other researchers could know exactly what records existed in the states and counties which would be of value to their historical researches.   Following official

---

[25]Letter, State Librarian to Harry Strong, no place, September 8, 1937. WPA Collection, Part III, Administrative Files, Folder 53, "Correspondence, 1938."

[26]Letter, State Librarian to Louis Ash, no place, March 28, 1938. WPA Collection, Part III, Administrative Files, Folder 54, "Correspondence, 1938."

[27]Letter, Louis Ash to Robert H. Slover, Cheyenne, Wyoming, April 1, 1928 [1938]. WPA Collection, Part III, Administrative Files, Folder 54, "Correspondence, 1938."

[28]Letter, Robert H. Slover to Nina Moran, Missoula, Montana, August 4, 1938; Letter, Harry J. Shad to Mildred Nelson, Cheyenne, Wyoming, October 6, 1938. WPA Collection, Part III, Administrative Files, Folder 54, "Correspondence, 1938."

[29]For a detailed study of the Historical Records Survey in Wyoming, see James A. Hanson, "The Historical Records Survey in Wyoming: 1936-1942," *Annals of Wyoming*, Spring, 1973, pp. 69-91.

appointment of Luther K. Evans as National Director of the Historical Records Survey on October 1, 1935, the several states commenced work to establish a survey in their jurisdictions.[30]   In each state, the Historical Records Survey was to function as a project under the supervision and guidance of the State Director of the Federal Writers' Project. After an Historical Records Survey Project had been authorized for Wyoming on January 4, 1936, Mart Christensen, State Director of the Federal Writers' Project, began preparing a project outline for submission to Washington for approval.   Dan W. Greenburg worked closely with Christensen in preparing the project format.   Together they developed a plan which seemed reasonable and submitted it to Washington for approval in March, 1936.[31]

—Wyoming State Archives and
Historical Department Photo

Dan Greenburg

---

[30]McDonald, *Federal Relief Administration and the Arts*, pp. 791-827.
[31]Hanson, *"Historical Records Survey in Wyoming,"* pp. 73-76.

Officials in the national office of the Historical Records Survey granted approval for the project to commence on March 11, 1936. Work proceeded at that time under the direction of Mart Christensen but with considerable unofficial assistance from Greenburg.[32] Greenburg was, for all intents and purposes, the director of the Historical Records Survey in Wyoming even though he did not officially assume that position until December 15, 1936. From March to December of 1936, Greenburg was able, through his political connections with Governor Leslie A. Miller, to solidify his influence on the Historical Records Survey. He was able, for example, to obtain offices for the Survey, which were located next door to his own in the State Planning Board. Once the offices had been moved, Greenburg assumed "quasi-direction" of the entire project.[33] Christensen, always more interested in production of the state guide, gradually lost control of the entire project.

Problems of direction for the Historical Records Survey were present in other parts of the country as well. As a result, in October, 1936, the Historical Records Survey was officially separated from the Federal Writers' Project.[34] Following that time, separate state directors in each state would administer the Historical Records Survey and the Federal Writers' Project. Since Christensen was infinitely more interested in the work of the Writers' Project, a new director had to be located for the Records Survey in Wyoming. Greenburg, in many respects the logical choice for the position, was passed over for the post, since he did not fit the requirements for a "relief" worker. Leon Frazier, Greenburg's assistant, was appointed to fill the position, but when he resigned due to illness, Greenburg was appointed. Thus, for the period from December 15, 1936, to September 30, 1937, Greenburg served as state director of the Wyoming Historical Records Survey.[35]

During the period of activity from the start of the project in Wyoming to Greenburg's appointment as director, eleven county surveys had been completed, but only three were on schedule for publication by December 15, 1936.[36] The work was slow and tedious, and the results were not uniformly of a high standard. This is not terribly surprising when one considers that the skills needed to do a thorough job of inventorying public records was noticeably lacking among the workers for the Historical Records Survey in Wyoming. Coupled with the lack of necessary skills was a lack of adequate statewide and nationwide guidance for the

---

[32]Ibid., p. 76.
[33]Ibid., p. 78.
[34]McDonald, Federal Relief Administration and the Arts, p. 765.
[35]Hanson, "Historical Records Survey in Wyoming," p. 80.
[36]Ibid.

project. Mart Christensen, the first official Director of the Survey in Wyoming, was more concerned with the production of the Wyoming guide than with the Historical Records Survey. The second state director lasted only about three months, and even when Greenburg assumed the post of state director, the administrative problems were not resolved. Greenburg was not noted for abiding by all requirements sent down from the Washington office and was eventually asked to resign from the post. During the life of the Records Survey in Wyoming, only about five and one-half years, a total of eight different men served as state director.[37] With such a record, it is not surprising that, when manuscripts were prepared for publication, much editing was required in Washington. While three manuscripts were on schedule for publication by December 15, 1936, nearly eighteen months passed before the actual printing of the first Wyoming county inventory in July, 1938.[38]

Publication of the first county inventory in July, 1938, was but one step in the work of the Historical Records Survey. Despite the problems of research, direction, and delays in publication, six county inventories were eventually published under the auspices of the Wyoming Historical Records Survey. Goshen, Laramie, Lincoln, Park, Platte, and Sweetwater county inventories were published prior to the termination of the project in June, 1942. Material for other county inventories was collected but was not put into final form for publication.

The Wyoming Federal Writers' Project reached a turning point in early 1938. The three programs of the Project had all undergone considerable changes by that time. The Historical Records Survey, as mentioned above, had been separated from the Writers' Project in late 1936. The Statewide Historical Project, while accomplishing much in its short lifetime, had been cancelled in October, 1937. The only viable project under control of the Federal Writers' Project in the state, therefore, was the program leading to the production of the state guide book. But, even that portion of the Writers' Project was altered in early 1938 when Mart Christensen resigned his post as state director in order to run for political office.

Following Christensen's resignation, Agnes Wright Spring was

[37]Mart Christensen, Leon D. Frazier, Dan Greenburg, Donald Snyder, Louis Ash, Claude Campbell, Benjamin H. McIntosh, and Henry Challender, all served as State Directors of the Historical Records Survey in Wyoming. Hanson, "Historical Records Survey in Wyoming," *passim.*

[38]Historical Records Survey, Division of Women's and Professional Projects, Works Progress Administration, *Inventory of the County Archives of Wyoming: Number 11, Laramie County* (Cheyenne, Wyoming: The Historical Records Survey, July, 1938).

appointed to his post.[39]   As indicated earlier, Mart Christensen had written some manuscripts to be used in the Wyoming guide which were not fully acceptable to the Washington editorial office. As a result, when Agnes Wright Spring assumed the directorship of the Wyoming Writers' Project, she commenced to rewrite all sections of the Wyoming state guide book.   Under her direction, workers throughout the state continued to collect material for use in the book.   She especially sought local assistance in the writing of the "tours" section of the guide book.   Local writers throughout the state wrote guided tours of the points of particular historical or scenic interest in their areas.   Representatives of the state office in Cheyenne then reviewed these manuscripts, submitted them to Washington for further editorial criticism, and prepared them for inclusion in the final Wyoming guide.   The portion of the book consisting of essays on general subjects and individual cities was written, for the most part, by Agnes Wright Spring and/ or her chief assistant Dee Linford.[40]

By 1940 the Wyoming guide was ready for publication.   The material had all been edited and had received approval from the national office of the Writer's Project.   Lester C. Hunt, then Wyoming's secretary of state and official sponsor of the Writers Project in Wyoming, wrote an introduction to the book in which he related the nature of Wyoming's heritage and he called upon visitors and citizens alike to enjoy and to understand Wyoming.   Hunt presented the Wyoming guide as a literary map to the state's unique historical and scenic attractions.[41]

When the Wyoming guide was published and available to the public early in 1941, the primary undertaking of the WPA Writers' Project in Wyoming was completed.   As the time of publication approached, however, writers were still available in the field for work on yet other projects.   As early as 1938, when some states were completing their guide books, the Washington office of the Writers' Project suggested additional projects for qualified writers.

Henry G. Alsberg, national director of the Federal Writers' Project proposed the production of state place name studies in

---

[39]Letter, Alice Guyol to Agnes Wright Spring, Hartville, Wyoming, March 3, 1938. WPA Collection, Part III, Administrative Files, Folder 54, "Correspondence, 1938."

[40]WPA Collection, Part II, Subject Files, Folders 1562-1599. Numerous drafts of the tours sections of the Wyoming guide are included in these folders as well as in the various folders of the Subject Files under each county.

[41]Writers' Program of the Work Projects Administration in the State of Wyoming, *Wyoming: A Guide to Its History, Highways, and People* (New York: Oxford University Press, 1941), pp. v-vi.

July, 1938.[42]   He suggested that the state directors see that such a work be carried forth, and in September, 1938, he offered a format for the collection and preparation of place name material. He emphasized, however, that "the work should, under no circumstances, delay work on the State Guide."[43]   Agnes Wright Spring, in Wyoming, apparently took this advice to heart.   While interested in such a study, Spring delayed work on the place names until the guide neared completion.[44]

In December, 1939, when the field work for the Wyoming guide was nearly completed, another project outline came forth from the Washington office.   George F. Willison had prepared an outline for the production of a "History of Grazing" in the seventeen western states.   The research project called for the collection of data in each of the western states, with the data to be prepared and sent to Washington where a final book on the history of grazing would be prepared, presumably under Willison's direction.[45]   Mrs. Spring, with the assistance of workers in the Department of the Interior's Bureau of Grazing, launched the new project almost immediately.[46] Workers for the Writers' Project in Wyoming scoured the newspapers, interviewed ranchers, and researched secondary works to collect data on grazing activities in the state.   Mrs. Spring reviewed the material, supervised the typing and final preparation of the data, and forwarded it to the Washington office.   Unfortunately, the study was never published.

In 1940, the Writers' Project in Wyoming undertook yet another project which proved to be more successful than the grazing history.   The Wyoming National Guard did not have a current history of its activities in the state, and in 1940 the Writer's Project of the WPA undertook preparation of just such a history.[47]   Consequently, the field workers employed by the Writer's Project again searched the newspapers and other sources for information relating to the National Guard and its activities in the state.   This data was

---

[42]Memorandum, Henry G. Alsberg to All State Directors, no place, September 23, 1938.   WPA Collection, Part III, Administrative Files, Folder 54, "Correspondence, 1938."

[43]*Ibid.*

[44]"Instructions to Mrs. Alice Guyol: Geographic Names in Wyoming," no author, June 10, 1940.   WPA Collection, Part III, Administrative Files, Folder 56, "Correspondence, 1940."

[45]Letter, C. E. Triggs to L. G. Flannery, Washington, D. C., December 5, 1939.   WPA Collection, Part III, Administrative Files, Folder 55, "Correspondence, 1939."

[46]Letter, Harold J. Burbank to Agnes Wright Spring, Rawlins, Wyoming, January 4, 1940.   WPA Collection, Part III, Administrative Files, Folder 56, "Correspondence, 1940."

[47]Letter, R. L. Esmay to All Organization Commanders, Cheyenne, Wyoming, February 17, 1940.   WPA Collection, Part III, Administrative Files, Folder 56, "Correspondence, 1940."

—Courtesy of Agnes Wright Spring

Agnes Wright Spring

sent to Cheyenne where workers in the state office, more than likely Agnes Wright Spring, reviewed the data and prepared a narrative history of the Wyoming National Guard to accompany a profusely illustrated yearbook-type history.[48]

Other projects suggested to the leaders of the Writers' Project in Wyoming included a work on Esther Morris, a small nationwide study entitled "America Eats," and, under the auspices of the Historical Records Survey, the preparation and reproduction of an index to C. G. Coutant's *History of Wyoming*. The Morris work never got off the ground, but Wyoming contributed several recipes

---

[48]*Historical and Pictorial Review: National Guard of the State of Wyoming, 1940* (Baton Rouge, Louisiana: Army and Navy Publishing Company, Inc., 1940).

to the national work on regional foods and eating habits, and the Coutant index was prepared and distributed in mimeographed form.[49]

The Federal Writers' Project in Wyoming, therefore, was a broad program of federally-sponsored relief projects designed to provide employment for persons unable to find work in their professional capacities. Unfortunately, the Writers' Project, as a whole, was not particularly suited to a state such as Wyoming. Wyoming did not have a high percentage of unemployed professional workers. As a result, those persons who found employment with the Writers' Project and the Historical Records Survey were not necessarily trained as historians, writers, or archivists. They learned the profession as they worked. For the most part they learned quite well. Despite their lack of prior training, these workers collected and preserved much material of historical interest. They prepared a respectable history of the Wyoming National Guard, and, perhaps most importantly, published a fine state guide book. While Agnes Wright Spring and her assistant, Dee Linford, almost single-handedly wrote the Wyoming guide, they could not have done so without the assistance of numerous and nameless field researchers and writers.

The published works of the Writers' Project, however, do not represent the sole remaining evidence of the federally funded project. Materials gathered by the field workers of the Statewide Historical Project included much valuable information about the state's pioneer period. Manuscripts written by Wyoming pioneers; diaries, journals, and other original materials from the pioneer period; and interviews conducted and preserved by researchers for the Historical Project are equally, if not more, important than the published works. The materials collected under the auspices of the Historical Records Survey, which were to be used in preparing inventories of county records, also include much material of historic interest, as well as provide an accurate accounting of the existing county records in the late 1930s. These materials have been preserved.

In 1976, a detailed inventory of the WPA Writers' Project materials in the Historical Research and Publications Division of the Wyoming State Archives and Historical Department was com-

---

[49]Letter, Supervisor to William C. Snow, no place, June 14, 1940. WPA Collection, Part III, Administrative Files, Folder 56, "Correspondence, 1940"; Memorandum, Michael Kennedy to All State Editors of the Region, no place, October 28, 1941. WPA Collection, Part III, Administrative Files, Folder 57, "Correspondence, 1941"; Historical Records Survey, Division of Writers' Program Work Projects Administration, *Index to History of Wyoming by* C. G. *Coutant* (Cheyenne, Wyoming: Wyoming State Library, 1941).

pleted.[50]   The collection consists of some sixty-five boxes of manuscripts, photographs, and administrative papers.   These materials
have been reviewed, organized, inventoried, and catalogued, so
they are available for researcher use.   Materials from the Statewide Historical Project account for the vast majority of the material.   This is not surprising when one remembers that this project
was designed specifically to augment the holdings of the state historical library.   The pioneer interviews and manuscripts in this
portion of the collection provide a valuable record of how the
early settlers in Wyoming viewed their own lives and their personal
accomplishments.   Many of the early residents of Wyoming were
interviewed in 1936 and 1937 to relate their impressions of the
early days in the state.   These predecessors of our modern oral
history interviewers wrote up the pioneer interviews and filed them
with the State Historical Library.   These interviews, coupled with
other biographical data collected under the auspices of the Historical Project, resulted in some 2600 pioneer biographies.   These
biographies and biographical materials were preserved and are now
indexed, so they can be retrieved for historical and genealogical
research.

A second portion of the WPA collection consists of the materials
collected in preparation for the Wyoming guide and other programs of the Writers' Project in the state as well as material collected by the Statewide Historical Project which was not strictly
biographical or autobiographical in nature.   Prior to 1975, only
about seven hundred of these manuscripts had been fully catalogued.   These manuscripts were about the only materials from
the entire WPA collection which were then readily available to
researchers.   As a result of recent work, all of the manuscript
material has been reviewed and indexed.   The collection is fully
available for researcher use.   An inventory of the collection includes nearly 250 typed pages of references to assorted manuscripts on Wyoming history topics.   This inventory includes reference to the newspaper transcriptions which workers compiled in
preparation for the history of the National Guard and the study
of grazing in the western states, as well as the numerous notes
taken in preparation for the Wyoming place name study and the
massive amount of research conducted for use in the Wyoming
guide.

Another portion of the WPA collection which is particularly
valuable to researchers is the records of the Historical Records

---

[50]Gordon Olaf Hendrickson, (comp.), *Wyoming Works Projects Administration Federal Writers Project Collection Inventory* (Cheyenne, Wyoming: Wyoming State Archives and Historical Department, 1977).

Survey in the state. The workers for the Records Survey investigated the holdings of local court houses, churches, and libraries to determine exactly what historical materials were available for research. The data were collected and stored in Cheyenne for a number of years. The entire collection was transferred from its storage area in the State Library to the holdings of the Wyoming State Archives in 1954.[51] The materials were given a cursory inventory and stored in the State Archives until transferred to the Historical Research and Publications Division in August, 1975.[52] These records provide the best survey available of the material present in the various Wyoming counties for historical research. The records included mention of existing records of churches in the state, local library holdings, as well as the more standard information concerning the archives of county court houses.

A final portion of the WPA collection consists of the administrative papers of the project. While not necessarily complete, these records include all that remains of the Project's operation within the state. Letters and other materials which passed from the state director to the field workers have been preserved. The records concerning the location of pioneers, solicitation of historical manuscripts, and some of the financial records for the project are also present in the collection. Not all of the administrative papers are preserved in Cheyenne. A complete, detailed administrative history of the Wyoming WPA Writers' Project cannot be compiled through exclusive use of this collection. Fortunately, many of the records of the Washington office of the Federal Writers' Project have been preserved in the National Archives.[53] When the sources in Cheyenne and Washington are thoroughly researched, an accurate understanding of the administrative operation of the Wyoming Writers' Project will be possible.

The study of Wyoming's history has been aided considerably by the efforts of the WPA Writers' Project workers. Many of these essentially amateur historians diligently collected materials throughout the state, which shed considerable light on the pioneer period of Wyoming history. The biographical data they collected add considerably to the body of material available on the early stages of Wyoming's development. Likewise, the manuscripts which pioneers wrote or narrated to field workers provide some unique insights into the self image of the early Wyoming settlers.

---

[51]Hanson, "Historical Records Survey in Wyoming," p. 86.

[52]"Transfer of Records," MA #7161, Historical Research and Publications Division, Wyoming State Archives and Historical Department, Transfer File.

[53]RG 69, "Records of the Works Projects Administration," National Archives, Washington, D. C.

These materials will add substance and vitality to future histories of the state. The recently completed inventory of the Writers' Project collection permits greater use of these valuable papers in the future.

Editor's Note: Agnes Wright Spring, who now lives in Fort Collins, Colorado, was invited to read this manuscript before its publication and to make any comments she felt might implement the information available to the author in his research.

She provided the following information which the editors feel is of interest and gives a clearer understanding of the Wyoming WPA program, as well. The editors are most appreciative of her interest and assistance.

After Mart Christensen resigned his position as state director of the WPA, Mrs. Spring was appointed to the post. She immediately concentrated on obtaining correct data for the "Tours" section of the *Guide*. Accompanied by her husband, A. T. Spring, as chauffeur, she began the logging of all the highways and by-ways that were to be contained in the book. On the numerous field trips Mrs. Spring visited every field worker, varying in number from twenty to forty. She encouraged the workers in their duties of gathering data relative to historic and scenic points that might interest tourists. Mrs. Spring collected photographs and made notes for the *Guide's* essays. These final essays, data on cities and the many tours, plus an index, were all written and prepared for publication in the *Guide* by Mrs. Spring, her chief assistant, Dee Linford, and Assistant Editor Richard Rossiter.

In regard to the history of the Wyoming National Guard, Mrs. Spring provided the additional information that the history was published with the cooperation of the Adjutant General's office.

Finally, according to Mrs. Spring, after the United States entered World War II, she resigned her position to join her husband who had been called to defense work with Remington Arms in Denver. The files of the project were turned over to George O. Houser and the $18,000 left in the budget was turned over to the Wyoming Historical Blue Book project.

Wyoming's Senator
Joseph C. O'Mahoney

By

THOMAS R. NINNEMAN

The following two political studies, "The Making of a Senator" and "Confrontation in Cheyenne," are revised portions of the author's doctoral dissertation which dealt with Senator O'Mahoney's early life, introduction to Wyoming politics, Postmaster Generalship and New Deal Senatorial career, with the main thrust on his role in the 1937 Court Fight.

THE MAKING OF A SENATOR

Ernie Pyle, beloved correspondent of the Second World War, was stranded in Chadron, Nebraska, at the end of August, 1936. The evening was uncomfortably warm, and Pyle ventured into the town seeking diversion. A political rally in behalf of Congressman Harry Coffee caught his passing interest. To his astonishment, sharing the platform with Coffee was the familiar bushy-browed visage of Joseph C. O'Mahoney, United States senator from Wyoming. Pyle settled down in the back of the park.

> It was one of the most reasonable political meetings I have ever heard. Exaggeration and villification were not invited in. The speakers actually sounded as tho they meant what they said. . . . Senator O'Mahoney made an excellent speech. He did not use notes, he did not hesitate, he did not 'ah' or 'er' a single time. He is thin and doesn't look like a politician and his voice is rich.[1]

O'Mahoney, curiously enough, originally rode out of the east, not the west, and it was only after half of a lifetime of obscurity that he catapulted into the public eye.[2] Massachusetts-born, he was near thirty when he took a job with Wyoming Governor John B. Kendrick's *Cheyenne State Leader* in 1916 and settled in Wyoming. After Kendrick's election to the United States Senate later that year, O'Mahoney accompanied him to Washington, serving as secretary to the new senator and at night studying law at Georgetown University. O'Mahoney returned to Cheyenne in

---

[1] *Washington Daily News*, Sept. 25, 1936.

[2] O'Mahoney's rise to the Senate and role in the Supreme Court packing controversy of 1937 is the subject of the writer's doctoral dissertation, "Joseph C. O'Mahoney: The New Deal and the Court Fight" (University of Wyoming, 1972).

1922, partly to practice law, partly to manage Kendrick's re-election bid, and partly to promote his own political ambitions. He was successful in all three.

The hubbub of the 1922 campaign had scarcely subsided when the politically-minded began to consider 1924. The aging Senator Francis E. Warren, Republican, must defend his seat, and he was reported vulnerable. O'Mahoney reckoned that ". . . it would be the easiest thing in the world to unhorse the old man . . . ."[3] The question was, who would be the Democratic contender? Governor William B. Ross was a possibility:

> I have been unable to make up my mind whether Ross would really like to run, but I think he would. As it happens, however, he is getting no encouragement from Democrats. They feel he should stay where he is, because they do not see any benefit to the party in turning the governorship over to the Republicans in exchange for another Senatorship.[4]

O'Mahoney's own name was bandied about, but he had misgivings, especially about the powerful and hostile Ku Klux Klan.[5] He would have had further misgivings if he had known that Harry H. Schwartz, Casper attorney, was whispering; some Democrats feared an O'Mahoney candidacy would trigger a "religious row"; Catholics thought it "not a good year" for the likes of an O'Mahoney; others questioned O'Mahoney's oil connections; many feared he would forestall a better nominee.[6] Curiously, none of the objections reported by Schwartz centered on residency. Save for some months in 1916, the O'Mahoneys had actually resided

---

[3]O'Mahoney to oilman John D. Clark, Chicago, Oct. 9, 1923, Joseph C. O'Mahoney Papers, Western History Research Center, University of Wyoming (hereafter cited as O'M. Mss.), file drawer 1, "All of 1933 and before . . ." (hereafter cited as #1), file "John C. Clark."

[4]Ibid.

[5]Ibid. O'Mahoney to speculator and developer Daniel J. Danker, Boston, Dec. 8, 1923; Dec. 15, 1923, O'M. Mss. #1, file "Daniel J. Danker." O'Mahoney's Dec. 8, 1923, letter to Danker indicated that he would have Ross's support if he made the race.

[6]Schwartz to Kendrick, Apr. 20, 1924, John B. Kendrick Papers, Western History Research Center, University of Wyoming (hereafter cited as Kendrick Mss.), file drawer (hereafter cited as #) 40. Schwartz added that some said O'Mahoney ". . . came back from Washington with an official benediction. Didn't say who gave it to him." Kendrick replied May 27, 1924, ignoring the crudely phrased query as to whether the O'Mahoney candidacy had his blessing, but cooly observing that he agreed "almost entirely" with Schwartz's appraisal of the vote-getting capabilities of the potential nominees, ibid. Governor Ross, however, was of the opinion that O'Mahoney, after his late winter Washington trip and apparent meeting with Kendrick, had decided not to seek the nomination, Ross to Cheyenne editor Tracy S. McCraken, Apr. 15, 1924, "Personal Scrapbooks of Tracy S. McCraken," Wyoming State Archives and Historical Department, Cheyenne (hereafter cited as McCraken Scrapbooks), real #1.

in Wyoming only from the spring of 1922. O'Mahoney's claims on the West rested squarely on his tenure in Kendrick's office. Friends cautioned him to play the waiting game, lest he prove the stalking horse for another. He obliged.

The Democratic state convention was held at Casper in mid-April. O'Mahoney was keynote speaker and temporary chairman Governor Ross reported:

> Joe O'Mahoney was given a great ovation. He made a fine speech, and at its conclusion the whole auditorium rose and applauded him for at least five minutes. He made his speech from the floor, and when he finished the applause began. He went behind the curtain and the applause continued, and he came out on the platform and the applause continued. He was entitled to it. He is one of the best men we have and one of the ablest, and deserved this ovation.[7]

O'Mahoney announced his candidacy for the Senate June 11, 1924.

Appealing to progressives in both parties, the candidate courted farmers with a demand for reduced freight rates, workers by calling for recognition of the right of collective bargaining, the general citizenry by pledging economy in government.[8] However, the Republican *Wyoming State Tribune* observed:

> Mr. O'Mahoney has been a newspaper worker, secretary to Senator Kendrick for a period and attorney in Cheyenne. He has been the vice chairman of the Democratic State Committee. A leap into the United States Senate from these somewhat humble positions would be a mighty one.[9]

Cagey old Francis E. Warren complained that the proliferation of Democratic hopefuls suggested ". . . I am a 'has been,' too old and too incompetent for action."[10]

---

[7]Ross to McCraken, Apr. 15, 1924, McCraken Scrapbooks, Reel #1. Probably more to O'Mahoney's liking than the ovation was the failure of the convention to endorse a candidate for Warren's seat, thus affording him time in which to reconsider his own role. Very much to his liking was his appointment to be alternate delegate to the national convention in New York City. He attended, but a speaking engagement at Superior, Wyo., necessitated his departure before the balloting for the party's presidential nominee was concluded.

[8]Hope for Republican support had been heightened by a visit from a Republican county chairman the previous winter: ". . . this gentleman is of the progressive type and he represents what appears to be a fairly numerous faction in the Republican party, who seem to be about ready to support a liberal Democrat in preference to Warren," O'Mahoney to Danker, Dec. 16, 1923, O'M. Mss. #1, file "Daniel J. Danker."

[9]Editorial, June 15, 1924.

[10]Warren to P. C. Spencer, chairman, state Republican central committee, June 21, 1924, Francis E. Warren Collection, Western History Research Center, University of Wyoming (hereafter cited as Warren Mss.), letter book #101, p. 288.

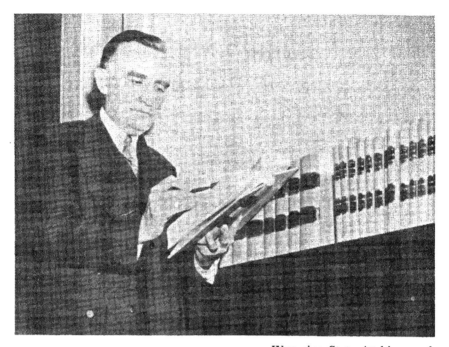

—Wyoming State Archives and
Historical Department Photo

Joseph C. O'Mahoney

Democrats who had feared the O'Mahoney candidacy would preclude a bid by the party favorite, Judge Robert E. Rose, were relieved when that gentleman filed. L. E. Laird, state highway commissioner, also opposed O'Mahoney in the primary. An important factor was the attitude of Kendrick. Warren was confident he would not intervene in the primary, possibly not even in the general election.[11] He was right on both counts.

The three-way race attracted little attention that summer. Warren, however, followed the proceedings with keen interest. He noted, with satisfaction, the preoccupation of O'Mahoney (and Judge Rose as well) with the labor vote, dismissed his call for a "living wage" as unreasonable, and marked him as a La Follette

---

[11]*Ibid.* Professor T. A. Larson marked the apparent understanding, after the 1913 struggle, noting that ". . . when one stood for election, the other offered only token opposition." T. A. Larson, *History of Wyoming* (Lincoln: University of Nebraska Press, 1965), pp. 449-450. O'Mahoney himself complained: "Warren's friends are sedulously cultivating the idea that Kendrick is behind Warren and that he will throw his influence against making any real campaign against the old man," O'Mahoney to Clark, Oct. 9, 1913, O'M. Mss. #1, file "John D. Clark."

man in Democratic clothing.[12]   August 19, the O'Mahoney bid was decisively rejected by Wyoming Democrats.[13]

In 1928, O'Mahoney, reflecting upon Wyoming's rejection of the Al Smith candidacy by a margin of nearly two to one, and, likely, of his own unsuccessful bid in 1924, sadly concluded that ". . . a Catholic has no real chance in Wyoming."[14]   However, there is no evidence that O'Mahoney's religion was a factor in his loss.   He carried every precinct in Laramie County (Cheyenne), and Sweetwater County (Rock Springs) as well, despite the fact that the Klan was reputed strong all along the Union Pacific line.[15] Further, by all accounts, the race was dull, which is usually not the case with a bigoted campaign.   Even more convinving, two months after the primary, the Republicans nominated a Catholic for the unexpected gubernatorial race.   However, O'Mahoney thought his religion had alienated voters in 1924, and that was important. Kendrick long before had reasoned that a Democrat in Wyoming must enter the lists not once but twice or thrice before anticipating success.[16]   After 1924, O'Mahoney shrank from a popular test for a decade.

On October 2, 1924, Governor Ross died in office.   Secretary of State Frank E. Lucas, thereupon acting governor, ordered a special election coincident with the general election to fill the unexpired term.   The Republicans quickly nominated Eugene J. Sullivan, New Hampshire native, Catholic, Casper attorney with oil connections, and graduate of the Jesuit-operated Creighton University law school, Omaha.   The contest was made to order for O'Mahoney, Massachusetts native, Catholic, Cheyenne attor-

---

[12]Warren to G. O. Houser, Guernsey, Wyo., Aug. 20, 1924, Warren Mss. letter book #101, p. 719.

[13]Rose, 6,906; O'Mahoney, 4,480; Laird, 3,400. O'Mahoney carried only four of the twenty-three counties. *1925 Official Directory of Wyoming and Election Returns for 1924* (compiled by the Secretary of State, Cheyenne), p. 39.

[14]O'Mahoney to law partner Michael A. Rattigan, Washington, Dec. 19, 1928, O'M. Mss. #1, file "Rattigan." Larson reported that later O'Mahoney aides recalled that their chief had attributed his 1924 defeat to the Klan, *History of Wyoming*, pp. 457-458. Leslie A. Miller, Democratic candidate for the state Senate in 1924, later governor of Wyoming, repudiated the Klan's support and attributed his 1924 defeat to that action. Leslie A. Miller, "Autobiography of Leslie A. Miller, Governor of Wyoming, 1933-1939" (bound collection of newspaper clippings in possession of T. A. Larson, Laramie, Wyo.), p. 40. Decades later, O'Mahoney, from the vantage point of a senior stateman, generously denied that he had ever been the victim of religious prejudice, to Mrs. William E. Gosdin, Oklahoma City, Aug. 11, 1960, O'M. Mss., file drawer "Retirement, Post-retirement & Personal Correspondence" (no number, and hereafter cited as "Retirement, Post-retirement"), file "O'Mahoney Personal."

[15]McCraken to Kendrick, Nov. 20, 1926, Kendrick Mss. #44.

[16]Kendrick to State Senator Theodore C. Diers, Sheridan, Aug. 16, 1917, Kendrick Mss. #22.

ney with important oil connections, and graduate of the Jesuit operated Georgetown University law school. However, O'Mahoney was ineligible by virtue of a law barring defeated primary candidates from competing in the next general election, and so he had to be content with stumping for the Democratic nominee, Mrs. Ross. The widow, riding a strong tide of public sympathy, easily succeeded to her husband's office even though the party lost both the senate and congressional races.[17]

Early in 1927, O'Mahoney confided to Mrs. Kendrick that Mrs. Ross, now a lame duck, had asked him to coordinate her pending speaking engagements in the east.[18] The truth was that Wyoming had suspected O'Mahoney of handling far more than her speaking arrangements. O'Mahoney, so the word went, really was the behind-the-scenes governor, and Mrs. Ross intended to appoint him to the Senate should Warren die in office.[19] The resultant charge of "invisible government" turned back Mrs. Ross' bid for re-election in 1926.[20] Her defeat was a disaster for O'Mahoney, coming as it did in the wake of his own defeat in 1924. Although he attempted to shrug off the matter as a natural reaction to women in high office,[21] even his closest friends feared the O'Mahoney embrace was a kiss of death:

> The day before the election Republicans took around handbills advertising the Ross rally that night. Joe O'Mahoney's name was on it,

[17]Barbara Jean Aslakson, "Nellie T. Ross: First Woman Governor" (unpublished master's thesis, Department of History, University of Wyoming, 1960), p. 6. "O'Mahoney Transcript," p. 56. Mrs. Ross defeated Sullivan, 43,323 to 35,275; Warren overwhelmed Rose, 41,293, to 33,536, *1925 Official Directory*, p. 41. O'Mahoney, shaken by the Republican ground swell, confided to Danker, Nov. 14, 1924, that Mrs. Ross was probably the only Democrat in the State who could have saved the governor's seat for the party, O'M. Mss. #1, file "Daniel J. Danker." More than likely, the margin of Sullivan's defeat, especially since the rest of the Republican ticket won handily, strengthened O'Mahoney's fears that a Catholic could not win in Wyoming.

[18]Jan. 27, 1927, Kendrick Mss. #45.

[19]McCraken to Kendrick, Nov. 20, 1926, Kendrick Mss. #44. Aslakson, "Nellie T. Ross," p. 80. Larson reported that Mrs. Ross had told him that O'Mahoney and Attorney General David J. Howell were in fact her principal advisers, *History of Wyoming*, p. 460. Warren did die in office and Republican Governor Frank C. Emerson appointed Patrick J. Sullivan to the seat.

[20]Aslakson, "Nellie T. Ross," p. 80. Mrs. Ross was defeated by Emerson, 35,286 to 35,651, *1927 Official Directory of Wyoming and Election Returns for 1926* (compiled by the Secretary of State, Cheyenne), p. 43.

[21]O'Mahoney to Mrs. J. B. Kendrick, Nov. 14, 1926, Kendrick Mss. #44. *The Wyoming Eagle*, Nov. 19, 1926, was probably closer to the truth when, observing that Emerson garnered fewer votes in winning than had Sullivan in 1924 in losing, it attributed the setback to the failure of the Democrats to get out the vote.

and the Republican Klansmen would point to it and say, "See, that's the fellow—a Catholic—who will really be the Governor."[22]

O'Mahoney turned his attention to the presidential aspirations of Al Smith. He had supported the New York governor at the Democratic national convention in 1924, and now labored long and hard to woo western Democrats to the easterner's cause. Mrs. O'Mahoney, in the capacity of executive secretary to Mrs. Ross, accompanied the former first lady on a visit to Smith headquarters in New York City.[23]

Ought not hard-driving Joe O'Mahoney, queried McCraken of Kendrick, rather than quarrelsome, divisive Harry H. Schwartz, then boosted by the Casper Democrats, be designated the party's state chairman? Kendrick, himself seeking re-election, demurred: "You of all men know not only my feeling toward Joe but my appreciation of his ability and his friendship and his attitude of helpfulness." However, Schwartz, he argued, was more generally acceptable to Wyoming Democrats.[24] So it was done. O'Mahoney continued to serve, as he had since 1922, as vice chaiman. Kendrick, gratified by the margin of his victory despite Smith's crushing defeat, subsequently saluted Schwartz's "splendid contribution."[25]

The winter of 1928 was the nadir of O'Mahoney's fortunes. Business correspondents reproached him for past neglect. Cheyenne partner, D. Avery Haggard, prepared to retire. Washington associate, Rattigan, requested a greater share in the profits of that office. O'Mahoney sadly contemplated his unbuilt castles:

You know, of course, that my principal motive in coming to Cheyenne

---

[22]McCraken to Kendrick, Nov. 20, 1926, Kendrick Mss. #44. McCraken added that the irony of it all was that Republican candidate Emerson's "right hand man," John Dillon, also was a Catholic.

[23]Unidentified newspaper clipping, dated Aug. 27, 1928, O'M. Mss, file drawer 2-A (no other identification, and hereafter cited as #2-A), file "Danker Misc. 1929." Danker, who had sent the clipping to O'Mahoney, observed: "That should prove a very interesting experience, make possible many attractive acquaintances and give her a close contact with the main works. It should work to your own advantage and if Smith should win it would appear that the O'Mahoney family was in line for something worthwhile," Danker to O'Mahoney, Aug. 27, 1928, ibid.

[24]McCraken to Kendrick, Aug. 6, 1928; Kendrick to McCraken, Aug. 8, 1928, Kendrick Mss. #48. Kendrick, although apprehensive that the head of the ticket would drag him down to defeat, valiantly promoted Smith, Kendrick to Senator Millard E. Tydings, Democratic National Headquarters, New York City, Sept. 28, 1928. Son-in-law [Hubert Harmon] to Kendrick, Nov. 17, 1928, Kendrick Mss. #48.

[25]Kendrick to Schwartz, Nov. 10, 1928, Kendrick Mss. #48. Wyoming voters cast 29,299 ballots for Smith, and 52,748 for Herbert C. Hoover; Kendrick defeated Charles E. Winter, 43,032 to 37,076, 1929 Official Directory of Wyoming and Election Returns for 1928 (compiled by the Secretary of State, Cheyenne), p. 41.

was political although I thought that the oil business would be more profitable than it has turned out to be. I was confident that the Leasing Act would bring the development of some of the fields in which I was interested, but only Oregon Basin has panned out. Agnes always felt that it was a mistake. Her judgment proved much better than mine particularly so far as politics is concerned. The result of the election last month pretty well demonstrates that a Catholic has no real chance in Wyoming. Cheyenne is really not the best town in the world in which to live—it has two seasons, they say, July and winter, but I've laid a pretty good foundation here and I suppose the wise thing to do is to stay, although with our relatives on both sides all back in the East, the thought of returning East not infrequently turns up. It would be too great a sacrifice just now, but in another year or so, by sticking close to business and passing up politics, I might be able to do some such thing.[26]

"Sticking close to business and passing up politics" was not a realistic goal for O'Mahoney. As the decade ended, he could be regularly espied huddled over a luncheon table at the Plains Hotel with businessman Miller and newspaperman McCraken, and Miller subsequently allowed only that politics was not the only topic of conversation.[27] In time, the trio was dubbed the "M.O.M.," and their initial goal was to seat Miller in the governor's chair.[28] O'Mahoney himself still aspired to a national office. An appointee of Governor Emerson occupied the senate seat of Warren after the old man's death, November 24, 1929, and the seat would be contested in the elections of 1930. However, it appears that McCraken advised O'Mahoney against a move, and that Kendrick proposed O'Mahoney bid for Kendrick's own seat in 1934.[29] O'Mahoney agreed: "There is a rather wide spread impression that this may be a pretty good year for a Democrat but I think it would take a pretty big revolution to induce this State to send two Democrats to the United States Senate."[30] The decision was fortuitous. O'Mahoney was spared the ill fame concomitant with a second defeat, and Schwartz, who ambitiously seized upon the opportunity, was set back by former Governor Robert D. Carey.[31]

---

[26]O'Mahoney to Rattigan, Dec. 19, 1928, O'M. Mss. #1, file "Rattigan."
[27]Miller, "Autobiography," p. 44.
[28]Ibid. Time magazine recognized the sobriquet: ". . . Wyoming's famed political steam roller, the 'M.O.M.,' " Nov. 15, 1937, p. 28.
[29]Rattigan to O'Mahoney, Dec. 16, 1929, O'M. Mss. #1, file "Rattigan." Kendrick to Miller, June 10, 1930, Kendrick Mss. #52.
[30]O'Mahoney to George B. Kerper, May 14, 1930, O'M Mss. #1, file "School Lease T. 56-98."
[31]Schwartz, quarreling with party powers such as Democratic National Committeeman Patrick J. Quealy, Kemmerer, pleaded for Kendrick's support. Kendrick replied with the rather unnerving request that Schwartz file only for the regular six year term (against Carey) and that he not file for the remainder of the Warren term against Emerson's appointee, Sullivan. Kendrick explained that he and Sullivan had gotten along so nicely in the last session of the Congress that he would like his appointment ratified at the polls. Schwartz to Kendrick, May 24, 1930; June 17, 1930; Sept. 13,

The Democratic ticket in 1930, with the exception of Miller, who was but narrowly edged by Governor Emerson, was swamped.[32]   A disappointed O'Mahoney, who had found it impossible to keep his "neck out of the yoke" of politics, struggled to untangle neglected business interests.   Then, on November 17, 1930, Wyoming's Democratic national committeeman, Patrick J. Quealy, Kemmerer, died.   O'Mahoney, an honorary pallbearer, joined numerous state and national dignitaries at the wake.   McCraken's *Wyoming Eagle* soon boosted O'Mahoney as a fitting successor,[33] and it was done.   On January 16, 1931, the party's state central committee designated O'Mahoney temporary national committeeman.[34]   The appointment was "temporary" only in the sense that it was to be referred to the membership at the next (1932) state convention.

Early in March, 1931, the new committeeman set out for Washington and his first meeting with the Democratic National Committee.   Doubtless, the adventure moved him mightily.   He had attained the highest position in the power of a state political organization to bestow.   Returning, he whiled away long hours as the train rolled across Iowa and Nebraska laboring over an account of the proceedings.[35]   Ostensibly addressed "To the Members of

---

1930; Kendrick to Schwartz, May 30, 1930, Kendrick Mss. #52.   Meanwhile, back at the Kendrick ranch, Mrs. J. B. Kendrick was receiving the cordial thanks of Carey for her privately expressed good wishes, Carey to Mrs. Kendrick, Sept. 9, 1930, *ibid.*   Schwartz assured Kendrick that O'Mahoney had been offered the chairmanship of the party's state central committee at its June 16 meeting, but that position had been declined; the office thereupon was filled by O'Mahoney's good friend, Dr. Thomas K. Cassidy. Schwartz also passed along to Kendrick the rumor that O'Mahoney was interested in the nomination for the state's lone congressional seat. Schwartz to Kendrick, June 17, 1930, *ibid.*   Kendrick, of course, was far more likely to be informed of O'Mahoney's plans than Schwartz.   However, O'Mahoney apparently did give some thought to a house seat.   Rattigan warned him Dec. 16, 1929: "So far as the House is concerned, that means a fight every two years, and being the one Representative from the State would mean a continuous fight . . . and it seems to me that you would have to spend most of your time keeping your political fences in repair, assuming of course you run next year and win out," O'M. Mss. #1, file "Rattigan."
[32]Miller, 37,188, Emerson, 38,058; Schwartz, 30,259, Carey, 43,626. *1931 Official Directory of Wyoming and Election Returns for 1930* (compiled by the Secretary of State, Cheyenne), p. 49.   The hand of the Cheyenne group was thus enormously strengthened by Miller's excellent showing, that of the Casper group weakened by Schwartz's relatively poor showing. This would be very much to O'Mahoney's advantage as the decisive years of his life drew near.
[33]"Political and Otherwise," editorial page, *Wyoming Eagle*, Jan. 16, 1931.   *Wyoming State Tribune—Cheyenne State Leader*, Jan. 16, 1931.
[34]Mrs. Ross was the national committeewoman.
[35]"Report on the Washington Meeting of the DEMOCRATIC NATIONAL COMMITTEE," O'M. Mss. #1, file "Campaign of 1932."   O'Mahoney to Danker, Apr. 16, 1932, O'M. Mss. #2-A, file "Danker—1930-33."

the Democratic State Committee of Wyoming," the brilliant, incisive report was set to type by McCraken and found its way all over America. Franklin D. Roosevelt, governor of New York, read it with interest, and invited the author to correspond with him ". . . at any time in regard to matters concerning our Party in Wyoming."[36]

O'Mahoney looked forward to the 1932 meeting of the National Committee with great anticipation. Then, two days before his departure in January, a recurrence of his old nemesis, the grippe, laid him low, and Miller went in his stead. It was a bitter disappointment. He had made the acquaintance of James A. Farley, shepherd of the Roosevelt candidacy, in Cheyenne the previous summer, and subsequently had been identified as a Roosevelt supporter. A national committee meeting would have enabled him to advance the candidate's interest. However, there remained the state convention. On May 9, 1932, at Casper, he helped to secure Wyoming's six convention votes for Roosevelt. The measure was modest but the moment timely.[37] From Farley came recognition that ". . . the West had done its part," and a warning: "Be prepared for a busy time [at the national convention], because we will put you on the job, and you will have lots to do."[38]

The Democratic National Convention opened in late June in Chicago, and, to his delight, O'Mahoney learned he had for some weeks been scheduled for a substantial role. His assignment was to the platform committee (committee on resolutions), whence he rubbed shoulders with Senators Carter Glass, David I. Walsh, Burton K. Wheeler and Cordell Hull, former Attorney General A. Palmer Mitchell, and the controversial William G. McAdoo. He was a member of the subcommittee of three which cast the platform in its final form. Farley was appreciative.[39]

Farley, now party chairman, clearly was increasingly impressed with O'Mahoney: "Joe had a cool head, was a good organizer, and most of all was intimately informed on the mining, farming and livestock problems of the Western states, an invaluable asset."[40] O'Mahoney joined other party leaders at Democratic headquarters in New York early in August. His job was to help with

---

[36]Roosevelt to O'Mahoney (copy), Apr. 13, 1931, O'M. Mss., file drawer 2, "Old old material, Georgetown . . ." (hereafter cited as #2), unfiled.

[37]Thanks to O'Mahoney's good work, the loss of California's 44 votes on May 3 ". . . turned out not to be the beginning of the end for Roosevelt but rather the low ebb in his tide," Frank Freidel, *Franklin D. Roosevelt,* Vol. III: *The Triumph* (Boston, 1956), p. 288.

[38]Farley to O'Mahoney, June 4, 1932, O'M. Mss. #1, file "Becker, L. D."

[39]James A. Farley, *Behind the Ballots: The Personal History of a Politician* (New York, 1938), p. 107. O'M. Mss. Scrapbook "A." Farley to O'Mahoney, July 27, 1932, O'M. Mss. #1, file "Campaign of 1932."

[40]Farley, *Behind the Ballots,* pp. 161-62.

the briefing of state chairmen on the forthcoming campaign. At the end of the two weeks, Farley asked him to remain on in the capacity of his first assistant. O'Mahoney agreed. The title "Vice Chairman of the Democratic National Campaign Committee" was concocted for him.

> Democratic national headquarters was a seething bedlam. Wild-eyed Progressive Republicans, burly Tammany men, long-winded, ancient Democrats who hadn't peered out of their holes for 12 long years, milled around the Biltmore Hotel. In the midst of this agitated mass sat Mr. O'Mahoney, serene, tactful, impeccably efficient. On his desk were two telephones, always busy; in his waiting room, obscured in a fog of cigar smoke were state committeemen, national committeemen, and future ambassadors; downstairs were dozens of typists, working hour after hour to send out the voluminous correspondence. His motto was, every one must be attended to and there must be no mistakes.[41]

O'Mahoney's duties were not exactly earthshaking, but his proximity to Farley lent stature and prominence.[42] He joined the candidate at Albany for the planning of FDR's western campaign swing, and then went along on the trip. He carefully scheduled a tour of Cheyenne, and stops at Laramie, Rawlins, Rock Springs (belatedly), and Green River for Roosevelt, and then appeared with him. He secured invitations from Roosevelt's secretary, Marvin H. McIntyre, to Wyoming party leaders to board the train and travel through the state with the candidate. In short, his involvement on the national level yielded rich dividends on the state level.

Near the end of the campaign, O'Mahoney returned to Wyoming. Governor Emerson had died the previous year, and Miller was a candidate for the balance (two years) of the unexpired term.[43] O'Mahoney strove strenuously the final week to deliver the state ticket to the Democrats, and had the satisfaction of telling Farley and Roosevelt, in the course of their election night telephone conversation with him, that Wyoming at long last had voted for both a Democratic president and Democratic governor.

---

[41]Grace Hendrick Eustis, *The Wyoming Eagle*, Nov. 17, 1933.

[42]For the lighter side of O'Mahoney's role, see Farley, *Behind the Ballots*, pp. 1-0-82.

[43]The special election to fill the vacant post coincided with the general elections of 1932. The Miller candidacy had been subjected to some criticism in party circles. Kendrick's own choice for the race had been Nels A. Pearson, Sheridan. Pearson, in turn, hesitated to make the plunge, allegedly because success would place two Sheridan Democrats, himself and Kendrick, in Wyoming's top political offices. Kendrick dismissed the possible imbalance, arguing that ". . . I doubt if I'll run [in 1934]," Kendrick to Pearson, Apr. 25, 1932, Kendrick Mss. #55. Pearson's procrastination prompted Miller to write out two statements: in one, Miller announced he was a gubernatorial candidate; in the other, Miller disclaimed the nomination. Miller signed each and gave both to Pearson, to be

"WYOMING MAY HAVE MAN IN THE NEXT CABINET," speculated the Republican *Wyoming State Tribune.*

O'Mahoney, a shrewd politician and able advocate, may be rewarded with appointment to the portfolio of attorney general of the United States. . . . There is suggestion also that O'Mahoney, if not made attorney general, may be appointed commissioner of the general land office, a place which generally goes to a western man, or failing this may be named as assistant attorney general, assistant secretary of state or a secretary to the president.

The Wyoming national committeeman, it is assumed, might have the United States attorneyship for the district of Wyoming for the asking, but Democratic officialdom is believed to hold a higher place for him than this.[44]

The Wyoming legislature, however, had something else in mind for the state's adopted son. By joint resolution, January 23, 1933, the Republican Senate and Democratic House unanimously urged Roosevelt to appoint O'Mahoney Secretary of the Interior. Kendrick concurred.[45] O'Mahoney was delighted with the uproar, but well aware that the post had been a highly sensitive appointment for a generation. Anyway, he knew that a cabinet choice was a particularly personal matter for the president-elect. Rather, when he refused reimbursement for his personal expenses in August, September and October, he had in mind a less assuming position, preferably that of solicitor general, or, if needs be, assistant attorney general. However, if an appointment of such distinction was not forthcoming, it was his intention to return to the east and practice law through the Washington office.[46]

---

released at the latter's discretion. When Pearson continued to delay, Miller, exasperated, announced his candidacy. Pearson never did make a move. Kendrick thereupon was reconciled to the Miller candidacy. Miller to Kendrick, May 31, 1932; Kendrick to Miller, June 11, 1932, Kendrick Mss. #55. Nevertheless, Miller was forced to fight for the nomination, defeating Thomas D. O'Neil, Big Piney, in the primary, Aug. 16, 1932. T. A. Larson, *History of Wyoming,* (Lincoln: University of Nebraska Press, 1965), p. 463.

[44]Nov. 12, 1932, p. 1.

[45]O'M. Mss. #1, file "Campaign of 1932." Kendrick to Farley (copy) Jan. 12, 1933, O'M. Mss., "Of utmost importance—Presidential files" (hereafter cited as #9), file "Special Personal Letters." Farley to O'Mahoney, Feb. 4, 1937, *ibid.* Farley advised O'Mahoney: "I am for it 1000 per cent," Farley to O'Mahoney, Jan. 28, 1933, O'M. Mss. #1, file "Campaign of 1932." Danker to O'Mahoney, Jan. 14, 1933, O'M. Mss. #2-A, file "Danker 1932-33."

[46]O'Mahoney to Rattigan, Nov. 17, 1932; Dec. 13, 1932, O'M. Mss. #1, file "Rattigan." O'Mahoney disavowed the efforts to make him Secretary of the Interior, protesting that ". . . a position in the cabinet is altogether too great a distinction to justify any persons 'logging' for it," to Farley, January 28, 1933, *ibid.,* file "Campaign of 1932." "Joseph C. O'Mahoney Transcript," Columbia University Oral History Collection (hereafter cited as "O'Mahoney Transcript"), p. 14.

November and December passed. O'Mahoney remained in Cheyenne, struggling with an accumulation of legal work. Rattigan, from Washington, protested that O'Mahoney was isolating himself from the struggle for power and position going on in New York, and urged his partner to fly east and claim his reward.[47] Rattigan may have been right. O'Mahoney waited. He expected a summons from Farley surely before the end of the year, but, not until the end of February was the invitation forthcoming. To his keen disappointment, one bleak early March morning Farley proposed that he and O'Mahoney continue their fine working relationship with the latter in the $6500 a year position of First Assistant Postmaster General. Quietly O'Mahoney queried the big man: " 'Jim, who's the First Assistant Postmaster General now?' There was a great silence . . . 'I get what you mean, but I still want you to be First Assistant Postmaster General.' "[48] The oath of office was administered March 6, 1933.

In the first hectic months of the new administration, O'Mahoney practically ran the Post Office Department. Observers of the national scene came to know and respect him. Perhaps because newspapermen recognized one of their own, perhaps because he knew how to make news, he enjoyed a good press. Then, too, Farley generously directed attention to him. Certain it is that he was close to the center of political power. However, all this notwithstanding, O'Mahoney carefully maintained his political fences back on the prairie.[49]

. O'Mahoney's Cheyenne connections loomed large on the night of November 1, 1933, when John B. Kendrick was felled by a stroke. O'Mahoney quickly made arrangements for the long trip home. In Cheyenne, still uncertain as to Kendrick's condition, Governor Miller summoned John D. Clark and Tracy McCraken to the executive mansion for an early morning conference.

> A vacancy would have to be filled and it appealed to me as wise that the appointment be made as quickly as decently possible . . . an early disposal of the matter would prevent the build up of rival ambitions and the consequent disturbing situations. As I had anticipated, we three had no difficulty in arriving at a meeting of minds. Only a few hours of discussion were needed to agree that Joe O'Mahoney was the logical choice.[50]

Several hours later, he learned that Kendrick's illness was indeed

---

[47]Rattigan to O'Mahoney, Nov. 16, 1932, O'M. Mss. #1, file "Rattigan."
[48]"O'Mahoney Transcript," p. 14.

[49]June 3, 1933, Wyoming toasted O'Mahoney at a testimonial dinner celebrated at the Plains Hotel, Cheyenne, O'M. Mss., file drawer "5" (no other identification).

[50]Miller, "Autobiography," p. 51. O'Mahoney to McCraken, Dec. 28, 1960, O'M. Mss. "Retirement, Postretirement," unmarked file.

mortal. The seventy-six-year-old senator died November 3. On November 8, the day following the interment at Sheridan, noting O'Mahoney's ". . . position of established influence in the Roosevelt Administration," Miller appointed him to serve in the Senate until a successor could properly be elected. The election was thereupon deferred until the next general election, November 6, 1934.

Miller's scarcely decent haste not at all stifled rival ambitions. Indignant Casper supporters of Harry Schwartz ". . . raised quite a fuss."[51] Further, there was more than a little suspicion in the minds of thoughtful men that Miller and possibly O'Mahoney himself had contrived to circumvent the law. The law seemed clear enough: if the vacancy occurred less than a year before the next general election, the vacancy was to be filled at that election; if it occurred more than a year before the next general election, the vacancy was to be filled by a special election on a day appointed by the Governor.[52] Kendrick had died a year and three days before the next general election (Nov. 6, 1934). Thus, the vacancy must be filled by special election rather than by the next general election. What Miller did was to order a special election, but postpone it until the time of the next general election. His action had the effect of erasing the distinction between vacancies of less than one year and vacancies of more than one year. It also necessitated the appointment of a man to represent Wyoming in the ensuing twelve months, and assured him of a full session of Congress in which to establish his reputation. Miller lamely defended his action on the grounds that Wyoming could not afford to hold a special election. Secretary of State Alonzo M. Clark, a Republican, announced he would contest the decision in the courts.[53]

The first move of the beleaguered Miller was to quell discontent within party ranks. On the eve of the announcement of the O'Mahoney appointment, Senator Joseph Robinson, powerful majority leader, in Sheridan for the Kendrick funeral, had artfully allowed that O'Mahoney was fit to fill Kendrick's boots. From Vice President Garner came congratulations on the appointment,

---

[51]Miller, "Autobiography," p. 51.

[52]Section 36-105, *Wyoming Revised Statutes,* 1931.

[53]November 11, 1933. Clark noted that Miller, then a state senator, had voted for the law in 1929, and that in 1933, Miller had actually invoked the law in ordering a special election to fill a vacancy in the State Senate from Niobrara County, *Basin Republican-Rustler,* clipping, Nov. 16, 1933, O'M. Mss., file drawer 7, "Pictures, Albums, Diplomas, and Robes," manila envelope of miscellaneous clippings. Miller had acted without consulting Attorney General Ray E. Lee.

affectionately addressed to "Old Top."[54]   Miller himself hastened to Washington, returning with the endorsement of Franklin Roosevelt: ". . . I want to tell you how pleased I am that you are going to send Joe O'Mahoney down here as Wyoming's Senator. He'll do well for Wyoming and the nation."[55]   And, as if all that wasn't enough for Harry Schwartz, there was a promise that the Cheyenne clique would give him a second chance against Senator Carey in 1936.[56]

The second step was to reconcile the Republicans to the appointment before December 9, 1933, the day on which Miller was ordered by the State Supreme Court to respond to the *mandamus* initiated by Clark. The approach had been established in the appointment announcement, namely O'Mahoney's Washington connections. November 17, *The Wyoming Eagle* reported that the "Senator-Designate" had secured both the early opening and full utilization of the then-in-construction veterans hospital at Cheyenne. Bi-partisan editorial support for the appointment quickly set in. Further, the value of having a person acceptable to the Washington administration was recognized by politicians in both parties. O'Mahoney obviously was more acceptable than any other Wyoming Democrat, and would doubtless be worth his weight in gold as the federal government's spending increased. Most important of all was the role of Charles S. Hill. The veteran Republican and one-time State Commissioner of Immigration, then ". . . broke or worse than broke,"[57] and hopeful that a grateful O'Mahoney would ". . . give a sympathetic ear to a Wyomingite" involved in an oil controversy,[58] hastened to Cheyenne from Washington. Hill hit upon the simple maneuver of amending the law, and engaged in such a frenzy of arm twisting that on December 9, 1933, both houses of the Legislature,[59] with the rules suspended, unanimously adopted a measure authorizing the governor to fill a vacancy in the U. S. Senate when it occurs and to hold the subsequent special

---

[54]Garner to O'Mahoney, Nov. 20, 1933, O'M. Mss., file drawer 3, "O'Mahoney: Early stuff—1933 and before . . . ," unlabeled file of congratulatory messages.

[55]*The Laramie Republican Boomerang,* Nov. 20, 1933, p. 1.

[56]Miller, "Autobiography," p. 51. They did, and Schwartz won.

[57]Warwick M. Downing, Denver, to O'Mahoney, Dec. 11, 1933, O'M. Mss., #2-A, file "Personal of O'Mahoney."

[58]Downing to Hill, Nov. 27, 1933, O'M. Mss., file drawer 11, "Statehood for Hawaii . . ." (hereafter cited as #11), file "Divide Creek Case." Downing warned Hill that there was no possibility of a "deal" or a "trade" with O'Mahoney, but that the latter in the Senate ". . . would do a million times more for Wyoming than any Republican, and much more than any other Democrat."

[59]Republicans controlled the Senate by a margin of 16-11; Democrats controlled the House by a margin of 41-20.

election at the time of the next general election. Thereupon, the appointment was formalized.[60]

A decade of politicking on the prairie had propelled the eloquent easterner into the place of a champion of the west. O'Mahoney had the satisfaction of knowing that the seeming usurpation was in fact a legitimate inheritance. Kendrick himself had confirmed the spiritual kinship:

> As the years have gone by I have been reminded many times of what I believe to be true in connection with our relationship; that is that more than any man with whom I have been closely associated you have glimpsed my real attitude of mind and my motives.[61]

However, the former First Assistant Postmaster General, having abandoned a position of influence and prominence, had but a single session of the Senate in which to gain the popular support that hitherto had escaped him. It was a gamble he won. Wyoming returned him to the Senate not once but four times, and upon his retirement in 1960 hailed his extrordinary career.

CONFRONTATION IN CHEYENNE

Senator Joseph C. O'Mahoney, Wyoming Democrat, was a key figure in the most important and dramatic domestic imbroglio between the wars, the Supreme Court packing controversy of 1937.[1] The Massachusetts-born O'Mahoney, who as Wyoming National Committeeman helped advance the presidential candidacy of Franklin D. Roosevelt, and who as First Assistant Postmaster General joined Roosevelt's official family, had been appointed to the United States Senate by Governor Leslie A. Miller at the end of 1933. Roosevelt was delighted: "I am looking forward to a

---

[60]"I want you to know that Charlie Hill is entitled to the sole and exclusive credit, if it be a credit, of amending the Wyoming statute to make appointment by the Governor beyond question," Downing to O'Mahoney, Dec. 11, 1933, O'M. Mss. #2-A, file "Personal of O'Mahoney." O'Mahoney, properly grateful, endeavored to introduce Hill to administration figures in a position to be of assistance, O'Mahoney to Downing, Mar. 5, 1934, O'M. Mss. #11, file "Divide Creek Case." There is not the slightest suggestion, however, that O'Mahoney acted improperly. Indeed, Hill's success with the Republican legislators led O'Mahoney to suspect that the opposition to his appointment had its roots in the fury of Harry Schwartz and a bi-partisan collection of Casperites rather than in Republican partisanship, Downing to O'Mahoney, Dec. 11, 1933, *loc. cit.* O'Mahoney to Julian Snow, Cheyenne, Dec. 1, 1933, O'M. Mss. #9, file "Personal, 1934."

[61]Kendrick to O'Mahoney, Nov. 11, 1932, Kendrick Mss. #55. Also see Kendrick to Miller, June 10, 1930, Kendrick Mss. #52.

[1]O'Mahoney's rise to the Senate and role in the Court Fight is the subject of the writer's doctoral dissertation, "Joseph C. O'Mahoney: The New Deal and the Court Fight" (University of Wyoming, 1972).

continuation of our very pleasant relationship . . . ," he wrote O'Mahoney.[2]

The relationship between the President and the Senator was extremely cordial. Indeed, nothing in O'Mahoney's performance suggested that he was anything but loyal to the Chief, and Roosevelt particularly prized the virtue of loyalty in his associates. Then, on February 5, 1937, Roosevelt unveiled the Court Bill, a request for six additional Supreme Court justices of his own appointment.[3] The move, ostensibly to aid the overworked and overage justices, actually to safeguard the constitutionality of certain social legislation, astonished O'Mahoney. When his efforts to dissuade Roosevelt failed, he publicly assailed the President's proposal as a threat to the people's liberties.

The Court Bill failed in the Senate Judiciary Committee, in large part due to O'Mahoney's efforts, and he personally prepared the *Adverse Report,* a lucid, logical, damning indictment which called upon the Senate to reject the measure so emphatically that ". . . its parallel will never again be presented to the free representatives of the free people of America."[4] One presidential intimate termed the document ". . . the worst public humiliation he [Roosevelt] had ever had."[5] In the subsequent struggle on the Senate floor, O'Mahoney's contribution to the final defeat of the Court Bill was again enormously important.

The President's supporters capitulated on July 22. Back in Cheyenne, the Democratic-oriented *Wyoming Eagle,* published by O'Mahoney's close friend, Tracy S. McCraken,[6] assured the party faithful:

> The administration has graciously yielded to its first major defeat in Congress. The threatened breech in the ranks of the Democratic party has been averted. Once more, all's quiet on the Potomac.[7]

However, those privy to the President knew full well that his mood was anything but gracious. They doubted that the battle was over,

---

[2]Roosevelt to O'Mahoney, Jan. 5, 1934, Joseph C. O'Mahoney Papers, Western History Research Center, University of Wyoming (hereafter cited as O'M. Mss.), file drawer 9, "Of utmost importance—Presidential files" (hereafter cited as #9), file "Roosevelt, President Franklin D."

[3]U. S. Congress, Senate, *A Bill to Reorganize the Judicial Branch of the Government,* S. 1392, 75th Cong., 1st Sess.

[4]U. S. Congress, Senate, Committee on the Judiciary, *Reorganization of the Federal Judiciary: Adverse Report,* S. Doc. 911, 75th Cong., 1st Sess. (hereafter cited as *Adverse Report*), p. 23.

[5]Rexford G. Tugwell, *The Democratic Roosevelt* (New York, 1957), p. 406.

[6]With Governor Miller, O'Mahoney and McCraken made up the "M.O.M." previously mentioned.

[7]Editorial, Aug. 11, 1937.

and they wondered what form the almost certain reprisals would take.[8]

The first order of business for O'Mahoney was sugar, specifically the O'Mahoney Sugar Bill. The Jones-Costigan Sugar Act of 1934, amended by O'Mahoney in order to advance the interests of Wyoming beet sugar growers, expired December 31, 1937. The pending O'Mahoney measure increased the production quotas of the continental growers of both beet and cane sugar, but left the production quotas of the insular (principally Hawaiian) cane growers untouched. Harold L. Ickes, Secretary of the Interior, was *ex officio* champion of the Islands, and he was determined to defeat the O'Mahoney measure. It all added up to an excellent test of the Wyoming senator's ability to deliver in the wake of the Court Fight.[9]

The O'Mahoney Sugar Bill was laid on Roosevelt's desk August 20. It appeared destined for ". . . an almost certain veto, either in written form tomorrow or by the pocket method later."[10] Ickes prepared a veto message. Unexpectedly, on September 1, although scoring the intransigence of the measure's sponsors on several of its more controversial aspects, the President signed it into law.

Wyoming cheered. Its senior senator had demonstrated that despite his role in the Court Fight, he could still deliver the kind of legislation Wyoming demanded. Not only was the Sugar Bill "generally satisfactory," acknowledged the Republican press, but the amount of money appropriated by the Congress for state projects was most impressive.[11] Apparently, the Senator's independence had not hurt his state; had it hurt himself?

Postmaster General James A. Farley, chairman of the Democratic National Committee, seemed to make it official August 4: there would be no reprisals. Reports that opponents of the Court Bill were going to be punished politically were dismissed as nothing but Republican "moonshine."[12] As though acting on his words, Senate Democrats, August 10, broke bread at a "harmony dinner"

---

[8]"He had an elephant's recall for injury," recalled Tugwell, *The Democratic Roosevelt,* p. 192. Also see Frances Perkins, *The Roosevelt I Knew* (New York, 1946), p. 158, and Samuel I. Rosenman, *Working with Roosevelt* (New York, 1952), p. 54.

[9]O'M. Mss., file drawer 28, "Sugar, 1937-38," file "Legislation, 1938 Sugar." O'M. Mss., file drawer 11, "Statehood for Hawaii + much more," file "Sugar." Ickes privately indicated surprise that the Wyomingite would expect any consideration from the Administration for his bill. See *The Secret Diary of Harold L. Ickes,* Vol. II: *The Inside Struggle, 1936-1939* (New York, 1954), p. 141.

[10]*New York Times,* Aug. 21, 1937, p. 4.

[11]Richard Cowell, *Wyoming State Tribune-Cheyenne State Leader,* Aug. 23, 1937, p. 6. Also see *New York Times,* Sept. 24, 1937, p. 3.

[12]Farley speech to the Summit County Democratic Organizations, Akron, Ohio, Aug. 4, 1937, *New York Times,* Aug. 5, 1937, p. 1.

honoring Alben W. Barkley, new Majority Leader. Good fellowship allegedly was very much in evidence as a live dove darted above the diners' tables. Roosevelt, however, chose to absent himself. The President, it was explained somewhat ominously, feared that ". . . if he attended, he would have to make a speech, and he might unintentionally make statements which some members of the warring factions in the majority party might resent."[13]

Ten days later, the peace was broken. Senator Joseph F. Guffey, chairman of the Democratic senators' campaign committee, bitterly denounced opponents of the Court Bill in a nationwide radio address. The Pennsylvania Democrat's cruelest remarks were reserved for O'Mahoney. Asserting that the Wyomingite owed his appointment to the Senate in 1933 to the influence of the late Senator Joseph T. Robinson, floor manager of the Court Bill, and his election to the Senate in 1934 to the popularity of the President, Guffey snorted:

> I dislike ingrates and ingratitude. I now predict that when the voters of Wyoming next cast their ballots in the Democratic primaries of 1940, the new senior senator from Wyoming will be returned to his home on the range where the deer and the antelope roam.[14]

Governor Miller quickly denied that Robinson had influenced the O'Mahoney appointment.[15] McCraken's newspaper noted that Roosevelt owed his 1932 nomination to men like O'Mahoney.[16] The latter counterattacked. Face to face with his red-necked, unsmiling assailant, he protested to equally outraged colleagues, ". . . I would rather walk out of the door of this chamber and

---

[13]*Ibid.*, Aug. 11, 1937, p. 1.

[14]*The Wyoming Eagle,* Aug. 21, 1937, p. 1. The speech was sponsored by the Pennsylvania Democratic Committee. In 1946, Guffey was characterized as "a machine politician of the lowest order who's made a big thing of New Dealism," "Senators Face Election," *Life,* Mar. 11, 1946, p. 100. The same article represented O'Mahoney as ". . . a Senator of importance and stature," p. 99. Robinson, literally a victim of the Court Fight, died of a heart attack on July 14, two days after O'Mahoney had delivered a particularly effective and eloquent speech against the Court Bill before ninety of his fellow senators and many of the House. Joseph Alsop, and Turner Catledge, *The 168 Days* (New York, 1938), provide an indispensable account of the entire struggle.

[15]Miller's statement in part: "The appointment of Joe was agreed upon without benefit of consultation with Senator Robinson whatever, as could be amply proven were it necessary. Furthermore, it is proper here to say that Joe O'Mahoney's proven capabilities and his accomplishments as a Senator of the United States have justified his appointment beyond argument—I am proud of the judgment exercised in his care." O'M. Mss., file drawer 25, "Supreme Court, 1937" (hereafter cited as #25), unfiled. It is a fact that Robinson's endorsement after the appointment was welcomed by O'Mahoney.

[16]". . . the men who organized the west for Roosevelt in the pre-convention days of 1932, and who went down to Chicago and held the line for

never return than to surrender any honest conviction I have."[17]
Then, in a rare concession to personal feeling, he lashed out:

> I say here in the presence of the gentleman who spoke on the radio
> last night, and in the presence of those Democrats who are likely to
> be candidates for office in 1938, the sooner we get that man out of
> the position he now occupies by virtue of the acquiescence of his
> fellows [chairmanship of the Democratic senators campaign commit-
> tee], the better it will be for the Democratic Party.[18]

What was the significance of the Guffey speech? How could it
be squared with Farley's pledge of "no reprisals?"[19] O'Mahoney
insisted Roosevelt had nothing to do with Guffey's stance, implying that the President was linked to Farley's position.[20] Washington correspondents, noting that Guffey conferred with Roosevelt
only hours before his speech, concluded that it was the other way
around.[21] Perhaps closest to the truth was an Associated Press
dispatch:

> One of the New Deal's most trusted strategists . . . described as "trial
> balloons" two contradictory speeches made almost simultaneously
> last week by men often regarded as White House spokesmen [Farley
> and Guffey]: . . . Reaction to their pronouncements . . . will guide,
> in large measure, the president's future policy.[22]

Roosevelt until he had won the nomination owe no apology to anybody.
Without their aid, President Roosevelt might never have been nominated,
and they have justly been entitled to all the administration's support they
later received in behalf of their own candidacies." R. F. MacPherson,
"Political and Otherwise," *Wyoming Eagle,* Aug. 24, 1937, editorial page.
The influence of Roosevelt on O'Mahoney's election to the Senate in 1934
was never denied.

[17]*Cong. Rec.,* 75th Cong., 1st Sess., Senate, p. 9560.

[18]*Ibid.,* p. 9559. When a petition was circulated to remove Guffey from
the chairmanship of the campaign committee, Barkley revealed Guffey had
already resigned the office.

[19]On Aug. 20, the very night of the Guffey attack, Farley renewed the
pledge before the Indiana State Convention of Young Democratic Clubs,
Indianapolis, *New York Times,* Aug. 21, 1937, p. 6.

[20]*Cong. Rec.,* 75th Cong., 1st Sess., Senate, p. 9559. "You can ask me
whether I think the Guffey statement was inspired by the President. The
answer is no." O'Mahoney interview, *The Wyoming Eagle,* Sept. 3, 1937,
p. 1.

[21]Pearson and Allen, "The Washington Merry-Go-Round," *The Wyoming
Eagle,* Aug. 25, 1937, editorial page. David Lawrence, *Washington Evening
Star,* clipping, Aug. 26, 1937, O'M. Mss. file drawer 6, "Miscellaneous let-
ters, articles, and speeches . . ." (hereafter cited as #6), unfiled. Also see
New York Times, Aug. 21, 1937, p. 5.

[22]*Wyoming State Tribune-Cheyenne State Leader,* Aug. 24, 1937, p. 1.
Cf. Tugwell: ". . . no predecessor [of Roosevelt's] would have been more
adept, as a matter of fact, in the use of the trial balloon or of this even
more extreme settlement by controversy," *The Democratic Roosevelt,* pp.
100-01. Also see Arthur M. Schlesinger, Jr., *The Age of Roosevelt,* Vol. II:
The Coming of the New Deal (Boston, 1959), pp. 562-63.

The Guffey trial balloon, if indeed such it was, caused O'Mahoney considerable anxiety before it was shot down. In late September and early October of 1937, hundreds of copies of the Guffey speech were mailed to Wyoming Democrats, apparently by Guffey, or Iowa's Democratic Senator Clyde L. Herring.[23] The effect on O'Mahoney's party standing was minimal, although it likely was a factor in his decision to downgrade the court fight.[24]

On September 13, what may have been another trial balloon was released. L. G. "Pat" Flannery, Wyoming's state chairman of the Democratic party, in Washington a party business, issued a statement: ". . . those who have been Democrats in the past, but who are reactionary and conservative at heart, can properly take their places in the Republican ranks where they will feel more at home."[25] Apparently, Flannery had O'Mahoney in mind, and the latter's friends took angry exception.[26] The state's most important Democratic newspaper warned:

> Should the state chairman desire to dismiss from party councils those who disagreed with the president on that issue [the Court Bill], those so dismissed would constitute a notable gathering. Not only would nearly every Wyoming Democratic newspaper be 'read out of the party," but in every precinct and county organization, men who carried the banner of Democracy through the lean years would find themselves classed as outcasts, disowned by the very organization which they created and perpetuated.[27]

The furor quickly subsided. Flannery protested that a perfectly innocent observation had been misconstrued; he had had no particular person in mind and had proposed no purge. O'Mahoney sniffed the political winds, and took stock of his position. Some-

---

[23]Mills Astin to Julian Snow, Sept. 27, 1937, O'M. Mss. #25, unified. *The Wyoming Eagle,* Oct. 1, 1937. O'Mahoney was particularly mystified as to who, either in the state or national office of the party, had supplied Guffey with the mailing list.

[24]A. N. Gabbey, Jenny Lake, Wyo., advised O'Mahoney Oct. 7, 1937: "A few days ago, as Chairman of the County Central Committee of Teton County, I received fifty of the attached folders of the recent radio address of Senator Guffey. I was requested to distribute these folders in Teton County. Personally, I have never approved the stand you have taken regarding the additional United States Supreme Court Judges, however, for your information will state that I shall not distribute the Guffey folders." O'M. Mss. #25, unfiled.

[25]*The Wyoming Eagle,* Sept. 14, 1937, p. 1.

[26]State Treasurer J. Kirk Baldwin denounced Flannery's attempt ". . . to start a campaign of purging the party of such liberals as U. S. Sen. J. C. O'Mahoney who, at the cost of losing his own party prestige and power, defied dictation of others by following his own convictions and expressing them openly in opposing President Roosevelt's supreme court bill," *ibid.,* Sept. 15, 1937, p. 1.

[27]Editorial, *ibid.,* Sept. 17, 1937.

thing was going to happen.[28]   Roosevelt, it may be assumed, likewise took stock of the Senator's Wyoming support, and, possibly as early as this time, determined that something was not going to happen.

In the course of his reply to Guffey, O'Mahoney had pledged: "If anybody undertakes to 'go out on the range' into my home state, no matter who it may be, I shall be willing to meet him there and discuss what I have done and what I intend to do."[29]   Suddenly, it appeared that the Senator's challenger would be the President himself.

In late July, Ickes had proposed to the President that the latter visit the northernmost tier of western states and then swing down the California coast, returning through Colorado, Nebraska and Missouri.   The purpose of it all would be to renew his personal contact with the people.   Roosevelt liked the general idea but not the specific itinerary: "He thought it would be very helpful if, for instance, he could go into Wyoming, which is Senator O'Mahoney's state, without inviting O'Mahoney onto his train."[30]

By late August, reports of a pending presidential trip reached the west.   Governor Miller wired Roosevelt August 30 inviting the Chief Executive to visit Wyoming and promising a "royal welcome."[31]   However, the President's unofficial itinerary indicated that although he expected to pass through northern Wyoming enroute to Yellowstone National Park, which he had never seen, Cheyenne and even Casper would be bypassed.[32]

Cheyenne! Suddenly Cheyenne was the name of the game.   On the eve of the President's departure for the west, it was revealed that he would both pass through and stop at Cheyenne.   Indeed, to the astonishment of veteran political observers, Cheyenne was the first scheduled appearance of the President on the trip.[33]

---

[28]The *Wyoming State Tribune-Cheyenne State Leader*, in an editorial, Sept. 29, 1937, reported that Flannery's statement had tipped off the M.O.M. to the possibility of an attack on O'Mahoney by Roosevelt himself, and they thereupon began to consider their course should the President stop at Cheyenne on his western trip.

[29]*Cong. Rec.*, 75th Cong., 1st Sess., Senate, p. 9560.

[30]Ickes, *The Inside Struggle*, pp. 176-77.   Rosenman described Roosevelt's "keen personal interest" in the details of his various visits, especially in the matter of which local politicians would be invited on board the train, *Working with Roosevelt*, pp. 112-13.

[31]Franklin D. Roosevelt Library, Official Files (hereafter cited as Official Files), 200-SS, box 55.

[32]*The Wyoming Eagle*, Sept. 2, 1937, p. 1.   Apart from his interest in the Park, Roosevelt reportedly was traveling west to visit his grandchildren in Seattle, and to sound out the people on various matters including the court fight, *New York Times*, Sept. 6, 1937, p. 1.

[33]Roosevelt actually made five unscheduled stops in Iowa, and spoke briefly to a crowd at the Union Pacific station in Omaha.

Roosevelt intended to travel three-fourths of the way across the country in order to give a speech on the morning of Friday, September 24, in the prairie capital of a thinly-populated state.

. O'Mahoney first learned of the new development Sunday afternoon, September 19. The Senator was in Chicago. He had a speaking engagement in the Windy City September 20, and he had intended to remain there the greater part of the week. Instead, he set out for Cheyenne by automobile September 21, the very day on which Roosevelt left Hyde Park. That same September 21, Miller wired Marvin H. McIntyre, the President's secretary:

> SENATOR O'MAHONEY ON WAY HERE FROM CHICAGO EXPECTED TO ARRIVE THURSDAY STOP SINCERELY TRUST I AM NOT INTRUDING WHEN I SUGGEST THAT IF AT ALL POSSIBLE WORD BE SENT HIS SECRETARY HERE THAT JOE WILL BE WELCOMED TO THE PRESIDENTIAL TRAIN IN WYOMING.[34]

There was no reply.

As O'Mahoney and Roosevelt converged on Cheyenne, interest in the confrontation intensified. Governor Miller, fellow Democrats Harry H. Schwartz, Wyoming's junior senator, and Congressman Paul R. Greever, together with a number of lesser dignitaries, were invited to board the presidential train at Cheyenne, and accompany the President to Casper. The slight to O'Mahoney was obvious. What did the President intend to say in Cheyenne? How would he receive the author of the *Adverse Report?* It was a foregone conclusion that the state's senior Senator would be publicly spanked. Wyoming was enormously excited.

O'Mahoney reached Cheyenne early in the afternoon of Thursday, September 23. The President would not arrive until morning. The M.O.M. conferred, coordinating the counterstroke which they had contemplated since the first warning of the President's intention.[35] Doubtless the Senator acquainted his colleagues with the not-yet-released Gallup Poll for September 26, proofs of which had been privately provided him by the editor of the *Washington Post*.[36] The poll revealed that 56 per cent of Wyoming's Democrats and 92 per cent of the State's Republicans approved of his fight against the Court Bill.[37]

---

[34]Official Files, 200-SS, box 55.

[35]For a first hand account, see Governor Miller's "Autobiography of Leslie A. Miller, Governor of Wyoming, 1933-1939" (bound collection of newspaper clippings in the possession of T. A. Larson, Laramie, Wyoming), p. 71.

[36]Eugene Meyer to O'Mahoney, Sept. 22, 1937, O'M. Mss. #25, unfiled.

[37]*The Wyoming Eagle,* Oct. 7, 1937, p. 1: Simultaneously, another poll revealed an erosion, particularly marked in the Rocky Mountain States, of the President's popularity, "The Fortune Quarterly Survey: X," *Fortune,* XVI (October, 1937), p. 109. O'Mahoney's own files bulged with testimonials to the popularity of his court fight role.

How was the President's challenge to be handled? O'Mahoney's carefully correct public posture provided the answer. When the presidential train stopped in Omaha enroute to Cheyenne, Senator Edward R. Burke, Nebraska Democrat and bitter foe of the Court Bill, refused to go down on the station. When word reached Senator Burton K. Wheeler, another adversary of the President, that Roosevelt would exit from Yellowstone National Park by way of Montana, the Montana Democrat made plans to be out of the state. O'Mahoney, on the contrary, unlike the other Democratic opponents of the Court Bill, had driven hard for a long distance across the country to be on hand when Roosevelt arrived, ostensibly to extend a western welcome to his chief. Wyoming Democrats were not compelled, at least by O'Mahoney, to choose between their president and their senior Senator.

> If there is a split, it will be forced by the president, for O'Mahoney upon his arrival from the east yesterday issued a statement in which he said: "I have hurried home in order that I might be on hand to join with the people of the state and their official representatives in welcoming him." A split between the two would create a paradoxical political situation for, it is generally conceded, both Senator O'Mahoney and President Roosevelt are supported by a great majority of people in Wyoming.[38]

The details were quickly worked out with Miller and McCraken. The governor appointed O'Mahoney chairman of the Wyoming welcoming committee, and the editor placed the front page of a special September 24 presidential edition of *The Wyoming Eagle* at his disposal.

The paper was put together with great care. Emblazoned across the front page was astonishing news. "STATE TENSE AS F. R. NEARS CHEYENNE." The anxiety was ascribed to Roosevelt's failure to acknowledge the senior Senator. Another caption cautioned the President that some kind of a confrontation could not be avoided:

O'MAHONEY TO GREET CHIEF EXECUTIVE
THIS MORNING IN ROLE OF PRIVATE CITIZEN

> The Wyoming senator, who cancelled a Chicago engagement for Wednesday evening in order to be in Cheyenne in time to greet the chief executive when he arrived in Cheyenne, last night accepted appointment as a member of the citizens' welcoming committee named

---

[38]Editorial, *The Wyoming Eagle*, Sept. 24, 1937, p. 1. Newspaperman Warren Moscow reported under a Cheyenne dateline: ". . . if the President believes that support for him inevitably means punishment for those Senators who opposed his Supreme Court plan, he will find an exception to that here. Wyoming is . . . also for Joseph C. O'Mahoney. . . . the President cannot help himself particularly by campaigning for the Court Bill in Wyoming and may hurt himself if he does it too vigorously." *New York Times*, Sept. 24, 1937, p. 1.

by Governor Miller and it is in that role, rather than as an outstanding national figure, that he will greet the president.

Elsewhere on the front page was another story:

DEMOCRATS TO HONOR SEN. O'MAHONEY AT BANQUET

As a testimonial to their faith in him and in appreciation of the outstanding service he has rendered both state and nation, Democrats of Cheyenne and vicinity will gather in Cheyenne Monday night, Sept. 27, at a banquet in honor of Sen. J. C. O'Mahoney. . . . the distinguished solon has faithfully and ably served all the citizens of his state. It was he, along with a small handful of others, who kept the Democratic party alive in Wyoming during the long years there wasn't a ghost of a chance for success at the polls.

Then the presses rolled. The first twenty-five copies of the edition were rushed by automobile to Sidney, Nebraska, to be placed aboard the presidential train in the early morning hours.

Friday, September 24, 1937, dawned. About nine o'clock in the morning, the train approached the outskirts of Cheyenne, and stopped. Governor Miller swung himself aboard, subsequently recalling:

I saw the President first and before he saw me. He was seated near the rear door with a copy of the *Eagle* across his knees. When he heard our approach, he looked up, saw me, and hastily brushed the paper behind him.[39]

Roosevelt then prepared to receive the welcoming committee and, inevitably, the committee chairman. Determinedly, deliberately, with dignity, without defiance, O'Mahoney advanced. The greeting was slightly cool, sufficiently cordial.[40]

Afterwards, historians, only half aware of what had happened, perhaps misled by the scarcely objective pen of Harold Ickes,[41] represented the confrontation as a capitulation: "Many Democratic Congressmen who had voted against . . . the Judiciary Reorganization Bill made haste to show their loyalty by rousing speeches and eager jostling for place at the President's side and a word of approval from him before their constituents";[42] "Congress-

---

[39]Miller, "Autobiography," p. 71.

[40]Thomas L. Stokes, *Washington Daily News*, clipping, Sept. 25, 1937, O'M. Mss. #25, unfiled. *The Wyoming Eagle*, Sept. 25, 1937, p. 1. *Wyoming State Tribune-Cheyenne State Leader*, Sept. 25, 1937, p. 1.

[41]Ickes confided to his not-so-secret diary: "He [Roosevelt] was especially amused at the manner in which Senator O'Mahoney had crashed the gate in Wyoming, although O'Mahoney had not been invited to his train. He thinks O'Mahoney is very eager to be on good terms again with the Administration on everything except the Court issue." Ickes, *The Inside Struggle*, p. 223.

[42]Basil Rauch, *History of the New Deal, 1933-1938* (New York, 1944), p. 293.

men who had opposed Court reform and other New Deal measures fought for a place on his train";[43] ". . . the politicians who had just refused him the support he asked, who had checked and cheated him through the bitter months of the regular session, had crowded and jostled each other to appear by his side before their constituents."[44] They were wrong. What really happened in the Union Pacific Railroad yards at Cheyenne was that O'Mahoney humbled himself in the best interests of the party which he genuinely believed to be the hope of America.

O'Mahoney was not content to shift the responsibility for an open rupture to Roosevelt. Rather, he was determined that a break be avoided. There would be no legislative progress until there was party peace. As O'Mahoney manfully advanced, hat in hand, arm extended, it was peace which he offered.[45]

The train resumed its progress into the city, coming to rest in the center of the Wyoming capital. O'Mahoney swung down from the rear platform and was immediately engulfed in a great crowd of well-wishers. Newspapermen, until then unaware that the confrontation had already taken place, observed his progress with astonishment and admiration. "Mr. Roosevelt and I," he explained to the press, "had a perfectly normal greeting."[46]

Mrs. Roosevelt approached O'Mahoney, greeting him warmly, and inquiring about the health of Mrs. O'Mahoney.[47] He, in turn,

---

[43]William E. Leuchtenburg, Franklin D. Roosevelt and the New Deal, 1932-1940 (New York, 1963), p. 251.

[44]Tugwell, The Democratic Roosevelt, p. 434.

[45]Oct. 7, 1937, Senator David I. Walsh wrote O'Mahoney: "It is difficult for me to express my feelings of resentment over the manner in which the President and his party treated you on his Western trip through Wyoming. It was all so petty and so unbecoming the exalted office of President. It is most regrettable that conscientious public service is unrecognized where it ought to be applauded." O'M. Mss. #25, unfiled. One can only speculate how deep the Massachusetts Democrat's resentment would have run if the President had, indeed, spoken against O'Mahoney. Roosevelt received a "Summary of Editorial Reaction to President Roosevelt's Recent Tour Through Northwestern States," dated Oct. 12, 1937, from the Division of Press Intelligence for the U. S. Government: "Many of the editorials relating to the President's Wyoming trip comment on his treatment of Senator O'Mahoney. All of these approve the President's failure to attack Senator O'Mahoney in his speeches, and the Senator's action in boarding the President's train is generally approved as a smart political move." Official Files, 200-SS, box 51.

[46]The Wyoming Eagle, Sept. 25, 1937, p. 1. Also see Jay G. Hayden, Daily Oklahoman, clipping, Sept. 25, 1937, "Personal Scrapbooks of Tracy S. McCraken," Wyoming State Archives and Historical Department, Cheyenne (hereafter cited as McCraken Scrapbooks), reel 1.

[47]New York Times, Sept. 25, 1937, p. 1. O'Mahoney afterwards assured a niece: "Agnes is standing the excitement very well. It was rather tough that she was advised to get out of Washington in order to get away from the excitement of the court fight only to be plunged into it worse than ever

introduced his colleague, Senator Schwartz. The First Lady had not recognized Schwartz, an oversight which some reported afforded O'Mahoney perceptible pleasure.[48]

Then the crowd settled down to hear what the President was going to say about their obviously popular senior senator. He said nothing. Grimly observing that "some people wonder why I am here," Roosevelt discoursed at length upon the importance of every president keeping in touch with the people, and promised that he was not going to coast through the remainder of his term. An uneasy silence hung over the gathering until suddenly it was crystal clear that Roosevelt was not going to say anything about O'Mahony or the Court Bill. Then the crowd cheered. As the President finished speaking, McIntyre drew near O'Mahoney, and whispered an invitation to board the train for the trip to Casper. O'Mahoney accepted.[49]

O'Mahoney, and Miller as well, was convinced that Roosevelt did not deliver the speech that had been prepared for Cheyenne.[50] Indeed, the former long afterwards recalled that the President had at hand a folder marked "Cheyenne Speech" which he left on the arm of his chair when he went to the platform to address the crowd.[51] Newspapermen accompanying the President agreed; at the last minute, Roosevelt had decided to spare the Senator.[52]

O'Mahoney joined Miller in the coach occupied by the Wyoming delegation. However, shortly after the train got underway, Miller was invited to join Roosevelt for a discussion of state matters and lunch. There was no invitation for O'Mahoney. Nor was he invited to appear on the platform with the President at the

---

here." O'Mahoney to Katherine Sheehan, Salem, Mass., Sept. 27, 1937, O'M. Mss., file drawer 16, "General Legislation 1935-1936, Sen. Jos. C. O'Mahoney" (hereafter cited as #16), file "O'Mahoney Personal."

[48]Jay G. Hayden, *Daily Oklahoman*, clipping, Sept. 25, 1937, McCraken Scrapbooks, reel 1.

[49]"WYOMING HAS A BOX SEAT BUT SHOW IS FLOP" headlined one account, *ibid.* Newspaper reports generally agree on the details of the day's events.

[50]Miller, "Autobiography," p. 71. Miller to Mrs. John B. Kendrick, Sept. 25, 1937, John B. Kendrick Papers, Western History Research Center, University of Wyoming, file drawer 62. O'Mahoney to Katherine Sheehan, Sept. 27, 1937, O'M. Mss. #16, file "O'Mahoney Personal."

[51]O'Mahoney to McCraken, June 9, 1960, O'M. Mss., file drawer "Retirement, Post-retirement & Personal Correspondence" (no number, and hereafter cited as "Retirement, Post-retirement"), file "Personal." No such speech has turned up among the papers of the President.

[52]Typical was the account by Joe Alex Morris of the United Press: "The president, quick to sense public reaction, apparently altered his plans for opening a fight in Wyoming for revival of the court bill," *The Wyoming Eagle*, Sept. 29, 1937, p. 1.

various stops along the way. However, Schwartz, a resolute supporter of the Court Bill, was likewise ignored.[53]

In Casper, Roosevelt was scheduled to tour old Fort Caspar before addressing the citizens of Wyoming's second largest city. Miller and O'Mahoney settled themselves in car number four of the entourage for the drive to the ruins. Suddenly, an aide approached, conveying Roosevelt's request that the Governor ride with the President. Although Miller interpreted the several generous gestures toward him as an attempt to spite O'Mahoney, he good-naturedly honored the request.[54]

O'Mahoney listened attentively to the President's speech. Was it what the President said or how he said it that momentarily struck an unfriendly note?

> Yes, I am pretty well convinced that the rank and file of the people of this country approve the objectives of their government. They approve and support those who work for objectives—by present methods to obtain the objectives . . . but they do not become very enthusiastic about those who give only lip service to the objectives, and do nothing toward attaining them.[55]

That was all. The moment passed.

The President shook hands cordially with O'Mahoney when the latter took his leave at Casper. Later in the afternoon, a change in the President's itinerary was announced. He would not go into Montana. Instead, he would leave the train at Cody, drive through the Park to West Yellowstone, board the train, and continue to Seattle by way of Idaho. It was still Friday, September 24.

What did it all mean? First of all, it meant that Roosevelt did not intend to turn the western trip into a speaking tour against opponents of the Court Bill. Even more significant, it meant that the Court Bill was indeed dead. Until O'Mahoney confronted Roosevelt in Cheyenne, it was widely believed that Roosevelt intended to renew his drive for a Court Bill in the near future. That issue, at long last, appeared to be laid to rest.[56] Finally, perhaps most important, O'Mahoney offered Roosevelt the opportunity to heal the grievously hurt party, an opportunity which if not exactly capitalized upon was at the same time not specifically spurned.

As the days passed, some observers began to wonder whether

---

[53]Miller, "Autobiography," p. 71. Also see Robert P. Post, *New York Times,* Sept. 25, 1937, p. 1.

[54]Miller, "Autobiography," p. 71. It was, of course, quite appropriate that the Governor ride with the President.

[55]*New York Times,* Sept. 25, 1937, p. 1. Also see James MacGregor Burns, *Roosevelt: The Lion and the Fox* (New York, 1956), p. 317.

[56]Tugwell was not so sure: ". . . I have often wondered whether, if he had lived on into the post-war period, he would have tried again," *The Democratic Roosevelt,* p. 407.

Roosevelt had ever intended to challenge O'Mahoney in Cheyenne: "Politicians and hostile commentators who had confidently expected President Roosevelt to unleash his scalping knife when he visited the bailiwick of Senator O'Mahoney of Wyoming yesterday must have been temporarily forgetful of the President's political acumen."[57] Farley suspected that Roosevelt had deliberately encouraged apprehension and speculation over the nature of his stop in Cheyenne, and recalled that the President had laughingly told him, "They'll know I was there, Jim." However, although Farley was not sure what was going to happen in Cheyenne, he did not believe that Roosevelt was going to read O'Mahoney out of the party.[58]

The suspicion that Roosevelt did not intend to attack O'Mahoney in Cheyenne is reinforced by McIntyre's reply, three days before the encounter, to the request of radio station KLZ, Denver, for permission to carry the Cheyenne speech live if the President's talk was to be a major address: "CONFIDENTIALLY PRESIDENT MAKING VERY BRIEF IMPROMPTU TALK CHEYENNE NO OBJECTION AT ALL TO LOCAL BROADCAST."[59] It might very well be that if Guffey's and Farley's August 20 remarks, and Flannery's September 13 statement, were "trial balloons," Roosevelt thereupon concluded that O'Mahoney's Wyoming support was strong and decided to leave him alone. The M.O.M., however, went to their graves believing that the confrontation in Cheyenne ". . . really was an event"; they had outmaneuvered the master.[60] As the Republicans enviously admitted, "the Democratic boys at Cheyenne can play the game right shrewdly when the occasion challenges their guile."[61]

The testimonial dinner in honor of O'Mahoney was held Monday evening, September 27. Although hastily arranged the previous Thursday, and somewhat anticlimactic, it was, nevertheless, a huge success. O'Mahoney conducted himself like the true Democrat that he was, and, perhaps to the dismay of some of the 350 diners who jammed the Wyoming Room of the Plains Hotel, paid respectful tribute to Roosevelt.[62] Then the Senator and Mrs. O'Mahoney sailed for Hawaii.

It was over. Or was it? Governor Miller's bid for re-election

---

[57]Delbert Clark, *New York Times,* Sept. 26, 1937, p. E3.

[58]James A. Farley, *Jim Farley's Story: The Roosevelt Years* (New York, 1938), pp. 96-97.

[59]F. W. Meyer, manager, to McIntyre, Sept. 21, 1937; McIntyre to Meyer, Sept. 21, 1937, Official Files, 200-SS, box 51.

[60]O'Mahoney to McCraken, June 9, 1960, O'M. Mss. "Retirement, Post-retirement," file "Personal."

[61] dito ia, *Wyoming State Tribune-Cheyenne State Leader,* Sept. 29, 1937E   r l

[62]For an account of the festivities, see *The Wyoming Eagle,* Sept. 28, 1937, p. 1. O'Mahoney accepted the acclaim of the assemblage with

failed in 1938. November 10, 1938, O'Mahoney asked Roosevelt to appoint him to some kind of executive position in the Administration. Roosevelt agreed to consider the request. Months, and then years elapsed. O'Mahoney renewed his request repeatedly but there was no room in the Roosevelt administration for O'Mahoney's friend.[63]

On December 28, 1938, Roosevelt sought Farley's opinion regarding the vacancy on the court caused by the resignation of Justice Sutherland. Farley proposed O'Mahoney. Roosevelt smiled: "Black has dissented many times since I put him on the bench, but his dissents would be a drop in the bucket to what O'Mahoney would do if he were on the Court."[64] The following year, December 14, 1939, Roosevelt again asked Farley's advice regarding the court, this time for Justice Butler's replacement. Farley again proposed O'Mahoney. Roosevelt cooly brushed the suggestion aside with the words, "Joe is your friend."[65] Farley really was not surprised:

> I knew he was disappointed, even incensed with some Democrats. His attitude was that he had been double-crossed and let down by men who should have rallied to his support. I was certain that he would not dismiss it all as part of the game.[66]

Farley was right; Roosevelt neither forgave nor forgot O'Mahoney's opposition to the Court Bill. Although the Wyomingite, in the wake of the confrontation at Cheyenne, succeeded in reestablishing a working relationship with Roosevelt that for some years stood both Wyoming and the nation in good stead, his previous friendship with the President was never renewed. Perhaps it was for that reason that O'Mahoney was to occupy no higher office than that of United States Senator.

---

aplomb, but afterwards sent his secretary around the state to find out what Democrats really thought of him. The consequent county-by-county analysis, thirteen crowded pages, replete with the observations and opinions of a good many local politicians, revealed that O'Mahoney really was stronger than ever. O'M. Mss., file drawer 23, "Supreme Court, 1937." This conclusion was verified by the general election of 1940. O'Mahoney ran well ahead of the presidential ticket, defeating Milward L. Simpson 65,022 to 45,682, while Roosevelt outdistanced Wendell Willkie 59,287 to 52,633. *1941 Official Directory of Wyoming and Election Returns of 1940* (compiled by the Secretary of State: Cheyenne), p. 75.

[63]O'Mahoney to Roosevelt, Nov. 10, 1938, Jan. 21, 1941, July 10, 1941; Roosevelt to O'Mahoney, Nov. 14, 1938, O'M. Mss. #9, file "Roosevelt, President Franklin." In 1942, O'Mahoney prevailed upon War Production Board Chairman Donald Nelson to appoint Miller director of the Board's region #9 (Mont., Wyo., Colo., Utah, and N. Mex.), Miller, "Autobiography," p. 70.

[64]*Jim Farley's Story*, p. 162.

[65]*Ibid.*, p. 216.

[66]James A. Farley, 'Why I Broke with Roosevelt," *Colliers*, June 21, 1947, p. 89.

The Black Legend in Wyoming High School Textbooks: Anti-Hispanic Attitudes in Their Treatment of the Period 1492-1848

By

GREG SCHEURMAN*

Part of the Anglo-Saxon heritage enjoyed by many of the persons in this country has unfortunately contained within it a predilection for viewing those of Spanish or Mexican descent in undesirable or degrading terms. A number of history textbook authors have inherited such views, and thus unwittingly perpetuate them in our classrooms. This study accordingly examines the treatment given to the Spanish and Mexican people in United States history textbooks. Many of the American history texts presently used in Wyoming high schools have come under scrutiny. The principal object of this examination has been to deduce the historical validity of the information contained in the texts. Questions kept in mind throughout have been: Is the treatment a fair one? Are unwarranted stereotypes likely to be fostered by the treatment?

A mail survey conducted during the latter part of 1976 revealed that at least twenty-one different American history texts are used in Wyoming high schools. Seventeen of these, or roughly 81% of the texts identified by the survey, have been examined in this study. Recent figures indicate that there are between 25,000 and 30,000 Wyoming students enrolled in grades nine through twelve. On the assumption that each high school student takes at least one American history class during the time he or she is in high school, the texts examined in this study will affect at least 16,500 students,

*This article was originally written as part of a graduate program in history at the University of Wyoming under the direction of Lawrence A. Cardosa.

or approximately 55-66% of the total. This figure is large enough to allow generalizations to be made regarding Wyoming American history textbooks as a whole.[1]

The justification for a study such as this one is predicated on the realization that, for many high school students, the single exposure given a people in a history textbook is the sole contact that the students will have with its history. Thus, a misinformed or poorly-worded text contains the unfortunate potential of stereotyping an ethnic group in a student's mind thenceforward. At the outset it would be appropriate to say that a fair amount of the material examined was less than historically accurate. Some of it contains information that is downright misleading, and it consequently might well lead to unjust stereotyping by Wyoming students.

The findings of this study become more meaningful if preceded by a brief statement about the traditional ways in which the Spanish and Mexican people have been portrayed in Europe and in the United States. For over four hundred years, there has been a decidedly anti-Spanish tone in much of the literature and history written about Spain by other Europeans. This tone accompanied the European colonists to North America, and became a part of the American outlook toward Spaniards and Mexicans. The reasons why anti-Spanish attitudes became prevalent are many, but it is reasonable to conjecture that they parallel many of the anti-United States feelings abundant throughout the world today. The Spanish empire of the fifteenth, sixteenth, and seventeenth centuries was comprised of a strongly-united, powerful, and wealthy set of sub-kingdoms. It was a far-flung enterprise which excited emotions of hate, fear, envy, or jealousy in its sister European peoples. Many consider the United States likewise to be a reactionary stronghold of material wealth and conservative ideals situated on a globe of political unrest.

The term *leyenda negra* ("Black Legend") was coined early in this century to describe the plethora of denigrating attitudes held about the Spanish people. Philip Wayne Powell has described some of the undesirable traits which have been attributed either with or without malice to the Spaniard:

---

[1]School enrollment figures derived from the State Department of Education report, "Wyoming Fall Enrollment By School, As Reported September 10, 1974." Current enrollment figures are available in the Education Directory, published annually. The ninth grade is not considered to be "high school" in some districts, thereby reducing the total potential number of textbooks identified in the survey which are utilized by adolescents. Schools using more than one text have been counted only once in determining the total number of students affected by the texts examined. Detailed information gleaned from the survey is found in the appendix.

The stereotyped Spaniard as portrayed in our schoolbooks, popular literature, movies and television, is usually a swarthy fellow with black, pointed beard, morion, and wicked Toledo blade. He is, of course, treacherous, lecherous, cruel, greedy, and thoroughly bigoted. Sometimes he takes the form of a cowled, grim-visaged Inquisitor. In more recent times, and with somewhat better humor, he has appeared as a kind of slippery, mildly sinister, donjuanesque gigolo. But whatever the guise, he is most likely to be cast as foil for the Nordic ego.[2]

Charles Gibson recently identified a number of broad areas in which the Black Legend plays a part: his "eight key issues" include "Spanish Decadence, Authoritarian Government, Political Corruption, Bigotry, Indolence, Cruelty in the American Conquests, Native American Civilizations, and Indians in the Established Colony." Gibson's eight issues illustrate the all-pervasive nature of the Black Legend.[3]

Anti-Mexican attitudes joined the anti-Spanish thinking in this country to form a sort of dual Legend. The infusion of Spanish blood and culture into the primordial Indian civilizations of the New World had produced a mongrelized race. These half-breeds exhibited traits as undesirable as those the Spanish had shown by themselves. Now there were two nationalities to which Black Legend precepts could be applied. Cecil Robinson, author of the definitive examination of literary treatment of Mexicans in the United States, described these attitudes:

> Americans, in their Protestant individualism, in their ideas of thrift and hard work, in their faith in progress through technology, in their insistence upon personal hygiene, in puritanism and racial pride, found Mexico much to their distaste because of its hierarchical Catholicism and the extent of priestly power, its social stratification with pronounced sense of caste, its apparent devotion to pleasure and its seeming avoidance of work, its technological backwardness and its alleged ineptness with machinery, its reported indifference to cleanliness, and its reputation for pervasive sensuality.[4]

With attitudes such as these well in mind, many Americans found it relatively easy to justify both the Mexican War and the Spanish-

---

[2]*Tree of Hate: Propaganda and Prejudices Affecting United States Relations with the Hispanic World* (New York: Basic Books, 1971), p. 6.

[3]*The Black Legend: Anti-Spanish Attitudes in the Old World and the New* (New York: Knopf, 1971), pp. 18-27. Another work in English on the Black Legend is William S. Maltby, *The Black Legend in England: The Development of Anti-Spanish Sentiment, 1558-1660* (Durham: Duke University Press, 1971), which surveys the origins of some stereotypes.

[4]*With the Ears of Strangers: The Mexican in American Literature* (Tucson: University of Arizona Press, 1963), p. vii. An article dealing with the merging of Anglo and Mexican cultures is David J. Weber, "Stereotyping of Mexico's Far Northern Frontier," *An Awakened Minority: The Mexican-Americans,* 2nd ed., edited by Manuel P. Servin (Beverly Hills: Glencoe, 1974), pp. 18-26.

American War in terms of "bringing civilization" to backward racial types.

A former Chilean ambassador to Washington and a provisional president of Chile, Carlos Davila, provided an interesting analogy:

> To get an idea of a present-day version of the Black Legend, imagine the history of the United States for the next three centuries written exclusively on the basis of what is published in *Pravda* or *Izvestia*. Suppose *Tobacco Road* and *The Grapes of Wrath* were the only documents on how the North American people lived in the twentieth century. And picture the whole history of race relations in this country reduced to a single animated cartoon—which Disney has not produced—graphically perpetuating the story of lynching.
>
> This distortion of the truth could not be more grotesque. Yet it would not be very different from what the Black Legend did to the Conquest and the colonial period in Spanish America.[5]

Davila then compares the Moscow papers and the novels to sixteenth-century writings condemning the Spanish, and equates the Disney creation with the gruesome drawings which illustrated many of the anti-Spanish tracts.[6] His comments were made at the beginning of the Cold War period (hence the Russian examples), but they serve admirably to sum up what has been said about the evolution of the Black Legend.

This study does not seek to condemn interpretation or to urge suspension of moral judgments in textbooks. Rather, its aim is to help create a more professional and less nationalistic approach to the writing of them. Speaking of the extreme examples of nationalistic bias found in the previous generations' texts, Ray Allen Billington has made some remarks applicable to this study. "Today's bias," he says, "is more subtle, more persuasive, and far less easy to detect, partly because it often mirrors subconscious prejudices of which the textbook author himself is aware." Billington cites two kinds of bias found in texts. The first of these he calls "bias by inertia," and says that authors "have shown a regrettable disinclination to keep abreast of the findings of modern historical scholarship, relying instead on discredited legends and outworn viewpoints that more often than not perpetuate the nationalistic prejudices of a bygone day." The second fallacy Billington calls "bias by omission." With regard to this he states: "When an author chooses *only* information that will reflect credit on his personal heroes, he is violating the canons of sound historical writing no less than the writer who openly distorts the truth."[7] The authors of the textbooks included in this study are guilty at

---

[5]"The Black Legend," *Americas* 1 (August 1949): 12.
[6]*Ibid.*
[7]"History is a Dangerous Subject," *Saturday Review*, 49, January 15, 1966, pp. 59, 60.

times of both of these biases. Incidentally, the Black Legend cannot exist in their absence.

Billington's remarks may be supplemented with some of the criteria for evaluation of textbooks found in earlier studies. Together, they form the basis for the questions directed at each of the texts examined in this study. These questions are: In quantitative terms, are Hispanic topics adequately dealt with? Is the material presented accurate in terms of presently-accepted fact? Are the contributions of the Spanish and Mexican people presented along with the more exciting military aspects of their history? Finally, are there specific areas in need of revision, and if so, how might this be accomplished?[8] As will be seen, when these questions are applied to the texts in a topic-by-topic manner, there generally emerge three types of treatments: in a strictly historical sense, they are "unacceptable," "acceptable," or "desirable." The following topical evaluation of textbooks provides examples of each treatment whenever possible.

The first theme to be examined is that of "motives for colonization." Under this general theme the textbooks suggest various reasons why Spain established colonies in the New World. The Black Legend holds that the one overriding motive was greed for gold, on a hit-and-run basis. That is, the Spanish allegedly came to America for the sole purpose of plundering it of precious metals; they then sailed back to Europe for enjoyment of the booty, hardly to think of the New World again. Some of the textbooks sustain this theme, while others offer additional reasons for colonization such as missionary motive and settlement for agricultural purposes. The various motives will be examined separately.

According to Powell, the trend has been for textbooks to give "disproportionate attention to the more exciting conquest phase, with all its 'blood-and-thunder' cruelties, gold-seeking, and sheer romance."[9] This is certainly the case in many of the texts used in Wyoming. Although it is not incorrect, for example, to say that gold was a very important motive for Spanish colonization, a student who reads little else is apt to equate the words "Spanish" and "gold" long after the rest of the lesson is forgotten. Leon H. Canfield and Howard B. Wilder in *The Making of Modern America* offer an example of a single-minded treatment of the motive of gold:

---

[8]These criteria have been adapted from a study done by the American Council on Education entitled *Latin America in School and College Teaching Materials: Report of the Committee on the Study of Teaching Materials on Inter-American Subjects* (Washington, D.C.: American Council on Education, 1944), p. 22; and a study by the American Indian Historical Society, *Textbooks and the American Indian* (San Francisco: Indian Historian Press, 1970). pp. 14-23.

[9]Powell, *Tree of Hate*, p. 22.

Led by soldiers of fortune called conquistadors (conquerors), large
numbers of Spanish adventurers invaded the New World . . . Most of
them were looking for riches, and a route to Asia . . . . The Spaniards tore down Aztec temples, where human sacrifices had been made
to the Aztec gods, and carried off untold wealth, which they shipped
back to Spain.

Adventurers from Europe continued to flock into New Spain, as
Mexico was called. They came for just one reason: to get rich.[10]

The book does mention religious conversion of the natives as a
motive, but the implication is clear that the authors consider that
of gold to be primary. In speaking of Pizarro's conquest of the
Incas, the book continues: "He had no interest in their fine civilization. He was interested only in the booty he could strip from
their temples, tombs, and palaces."[11] And after a brief comment
on Spanish agriculture, the text reads:

The New World settlements, however, were important to Spain chiefly
as a source of gold and silver. Huge amounts of the precious metals,
plundered from the Aztecs and Incas and later obtained by working
the mines of Peru and Mexico, were shipped to Spain.[12]

Gold was, in fact, a primary motive for Spanish colonization. But
reliance solely upon the gold theme does injustice to other aspects
of Spanish America. This part of the Black Legend is easily over-
come by saying that, in addition to his thirst for gold, a Spaniard
had *additional* motives and purposes in the New World. Some of
the texts do offer this more balanced view, and will be dealt with
later.

One additional excerpt from Canfield and Wilder illustrates just
how far this theme of gold can go. With reference to the English
motives for colonization, a reason offered is:

(2) Prices were high. Much of the gold and silver from the mines
in New Spain found its way into England either through trade or
piracy. This meant more money with which to buy the limited
supply of goods—inflation we would call it today. The resulting high
prices made life harder for the common people.[13]

Now the Spanish gold is being blamed for English inflation, even
though it entered the British Isles through legitimate trade or
officially-sanctioned piracy!

The Pageant of American History by Gerald Leinwand puts the
matter this way: "In 1519 Hernando Cortez, along with 550 men,
conquered the Aztecs, stole their gold, and enslaved the people.
Francisco Pizarro was even more brutal in the conquest of the

---

[10](Boston: Houghton Mifflin, 1966), p. 30. For localities where this
and the other textbooks are used, see appendix.

[11]*Ibid.*, p. 31.

[12]*Ibid.*, p. 32.

[13]*Ibid.*, pp. 39-40.

Incas of Peru in 1533."[14]   The impression upon a novice historian made by this passage is quite apparent.   It is erroneous, however, to imply that Cortes and 550 men conquered the Aztecs single-handedly.   What a brutal lot, indeed, if it were true that half a thousand Spanish soldiers could do in millions of Aztecs by themselves.   The facts of the matter are that Cortes intelligently played off the Aztecs against some of their subjected tribes.

Another text merits attention with regard to the theme of "gold."   *This is America's Story,* by Howard B. Wilder, Robert P. Ludlam and Harriett McCune Brown, appears to be fixated on the idea of gold as it states:

> High up in the crow's nest a sailor looks anxiously in all directions for swift-sailing pirate ships.   For this is a treasure galleon of the Spanish fleet, carrying riches to Spain.   Piled in the hold is treasure to stagger the imagination—heavy bars of gold and silver, boxes of pearls and emeralds.   What a prize for a bold pirate![15]

The book continues:

> What was more important to the gold-hungry Spaniards, the Incas were said to wear golden shoes and to eat from golden dishes.   Here, indeed, was a land worth finding![16]

And finally, there appears a possible misuse of words bordering on the ridiculous:

> As smaller children may fear a bigger boy who is a bully, so the countries of Europe feared Spain.   They were also jealous of her huge possessions in the New World.   They believed that Spain had no more right to the riches of the new lands than they themselves had.[17]

As written, the passage could imply that *no* country of Europe thought it had a right to the riches, which is absurd.

This is not to belabor a point, but one last example of this theme needs to be examined.   Bernard A. Weisberger's *The Impact of Our Past: A History of the United States* offers the expected comments, such as those dealing with the golden ear plugs of the Incas: "The Spaniards laughed at how the ornaments stretched the flesh, called the Incan noblemen *orejones* ('big ears'), and greedily eyed the gold."[18]   Add to this: "The magnet that attracted Spain's great explorer-conquerors was gold, which Columbus had seen islanders wearing as jewelry."[19]   Weisberger's work is more original, however, in this statement:

---

[14](Boston: Allyn and Bacon, 1975), pp. 8-9.
[15]Third edition, (Boston: Houghton Mifflin, 1970), p. 58.
[16]*Ibid.,* p. 64.
[17]*Ibid.,* p. 75.
[18](New York: American Heritage Publishing Co., 1972), p. 36.
[19]*Ibid.,* p. 62.

The conquistadors believed that their amazing victories were signs of God's approval. They thought of the wealth of the conquered lands as a feast for them to enjoy. They saw no reason to respect the customs of the defeated natives. They did not think of themselves as robbers but as among the most civilized people on earth. In this spirit of conquest and plunder, Spain pushed its new empire into the heart of North as well as South and Central America.[20]

Leaving aside the questionable assertion that the Spanish did not respect the customs of the natives, it is interesting to note what Weisberger says about the forceful acquisition of half of Mexico by the United States in 1848:

Most Americans thought that this speedy expansion was a sign of God's pleasure with the United States. They were given further reasons for this view by an amazing coincidence. Nine days before the treaty [of Guadalupe Hidalgo] was signed, gold was discovered in California's American River Valley . . . . Soon gold-hungry pioneers swarmed westward in droves . . . . Such sudden growth was exciting, but it also proved deeply upsetting.[21]

Here he is admiring in the American pioneer the very things he decried as barbaric in the Spaniard. Further qualities of the American are seen in a rhetorical question regarding the Americans in Texas prior to this: "Could the Mexicans govern these hardy, adventurous, aggressive newcomers?"[22] Perhaps the most ironic statement Weisberger makes is concerning the California gold rush: "It seemed as if Coronado's fabled cities had been found at last."[23] As was said earlier, it is not unappropriate to make moral judgments in textbooks. But one group of people should be judged on the same terms as another. A text which makes judgments any other way is only helping Billington prove his ideas about nationalism in the writing of history.

In all, eleven of the seventeen texts were sorely lacking on this theme. They either tended to play up the "goldlust" of the Spaniard, or they neglected to say anything about him at all. Five of the texts could be considered acceptable in that they included extensive coverage of other motives, and one stood above the others in its singular refusal to single out Spain as being the only gold-hungry nation in Europe:

"Barter" or the exchange of one type of goods for another, was too clumsy for trading large quantities over long distances. So, the barter system gave way to paying gold for products. Since gold was highly valued by all European nations, it was readily accepted in exchange for goods. Europeans came to believe that the welfare of a nation depended upon the amount of gold it possessed. They thought that

---

[20]*Ibid.*, p. 63.
[21]*Ibid.*, p. 297.
[22]*Ibid.*, p. 284.
[23]*Ibid.*, p. 298.

the more gold a nation had, the greater was its power and well-being. Thus, nations wanted to find new lands rich in gold.[24]

This treatment is essentially a "neutral" one, but it still manages to get across the point. It is highly doubtful that any one nationality has more of a propensity for greed than another, and even if it did, how is an empirical proof of this made? It is simply more sensible to describe a continental trend like this than it is to run through the tired, old nationalistic platitudes: the Spanish are inhumane warlords, catalytically-driven by gold, while the English are refined, humble folk whose desire for land and money are only reflections of an "inner energy."

The other primary motive attributed to Spanish colonization in some of the texts is that of religion. The Black Legend has it that the Roman Catholic Church and its affiliation with the state produced an "oppressive obscurantism" which hindered progressive thought in Spanish America. This is not the case, says Powell, who points to "Indian education, encouragement of literature, history, scientific investigations, and university instruction" as being exemplary of just the opposite.[25] Catholic obscurantism does seem rather unlikely in light of recent scholarship which supports statements like: "In colonial times the Church was a house of intellect as well as a house of worship. Surely those in the clerical establishment were the best-educated group in the Spanish and Portuguese Empires."[26]

The textbooks are on the whole more complimentary toward the Church and its functionaries than not. There is a trend toward lessening the role of missionaries as a motive for colonization in the more recent ones. Accusations of obscurantism are non-existent, and Billington's "bias by inertia" is not apparent. However, there may be signs of a "bias by omission" in some of the works, because there is no mention in them of the deep religious convictions of the king and the conquistadors. If there is any correlation between conquistadors and clerics, it is one of opposition and not of shared interests. However, a standard work in the area of New World religion asserted as early as 1933 that one example, Cortes,

was greedy, debauched, a politician without scruples, but he had his quixotic moments, for, despite his weaknesses, of which he later humbly repented, he had deep Christian convictions.
If one can reproach Cortes, it is not for laxness in the conversion

---

[24]Allan O. Kownslar and Donald B. Frizzle, *Discovering American History*, (New York: Holt, Rinehart, and Winston, 1974), p. 39.
[25]Powell, *Tree of Hate*, p. 25.
[26]Richard E. Greenleaf, ed., *The Roman Catholic Church in Colonial Latin America* (New York: Knopf, 1971), p. 14.

of the natives, but on the contrary, for having undertaken it hastily, without method, and for having forged ahead without pause.[27]

There is also a "bias by omission" in four of the texts in that neither missionary motive nor the Catholic Church are even mentioned. Nine textbooks very briefly ascribe religious motives to the Spanish, often relegating it to a single sentence. Religious savants would naturally claim that the treatment is far too brief, and it does seem reasonable to expect that a motive as important as this one should probably warrant more than mere mention. Three texts may be considered "acceptable" in a quantitative sense in that they devote at least a paragraph to the theme, but one of them fails to be non-biased:

> Along with the soldiers went a host of priests. They intended to Christianize the natives and bring them within the fold of the Catholic Church. All over the Americas, Catholic priests from Spain explored the country. They ministered to others and converted the natives. But the priests came mainly as missionaries and members of religious orders who could not marry. They did not build settlements of people of European origin like those which Protestant ministers and their congregations built in English-speaking colonies farther north.[28]

This is true, of course, but the wording implies that the Anglo-Saxon Protestant method of religion is superior to the Spanish Catholic one. The authors evidently do not take into account the facts that, first of all, the Spanish considered the Indian to be owner of a soul worth saving (and therefore devoted much of their energy to that end); and second, there were simply not enough Spaniards in the Americas to congregate around clergy-founded settlements. Thus, the preponderantly Indian-populated missions of the Spanish.

The Canfield and Wilder text fails to meet acceptability for another reason. It states:

> In general only the priests cared about the rights and feelings of the natives. The Spanish government, though aware that the natives were being treated shamefully, did not have enough control over the conquistadors to prevent their cruelty.[29]

The statement says that only the priests cared about the natives, and promptly goes on to say that the Spanish government did as well. In actual fact, the government cared a great deal about the

---

[27]Robert Ricard, *The Spiritual Conquest of Mexico: An Essay on the Apostolate and the Evangelizing Methods of the Mendicant Orders in New Spain: 1523-1572*, 1933 ed. tr. L. B. Simpson (Berkeley: University of California Press, 1966), pp. 15-16.

[28]Irving Bartlett, Edwin Fenton, David Fowler, and Seymour Mandelbaum, *A New History of the United States: An Inquiry Approach* (New York: Holt, Rinehart, and Winston, 1975), pp. 23-24.

[29]*The Making of Modern America*, p. 30.

natives, and passed numerous laws in their behalf.[30]   Although enforcement of these laws was lax at times, often owing to the sheer distance between New Spain and the mother country, the laws nevertheless existed.   The situation parallels that often found in the present-day United States, where civil rights legislation is ignored by certain sectors of the populace.   The government's humanitarian aims have been stated, but rely upon popular support for their success.   Canfield and Wilder add that "only around the many missions founded by the priests was the life of the natives easier."[31]   This assertion, too, raises questions.   Compare it with Gibson's claim that "forced labor for religious purposes developed in the 1530s and 1540s through various devices that bear a close relationship to encomienda and to the early labor organization in Mexico City."[32]   The encomienda was the most important Spanish institution in Mexico in the first fifty years after the conquest.   It involved a "contract" between a Spaniard and the king, whereby the Spaniard would be granted a number of Indians which he was to protect and Christianize.   In return, the Indians would pay for these privileges with tribute and forced labor.   The system approached that of slavery in its abuses, although enslavement of the Indian was officially forbidden.

The single textbook offering an equitable treatment of religion as a vital motive for colonization is, not surprisingly, by Kownslar and Frizzle.   Although too extensive to quote here, the book has students locate the major missions on a map, describes the architectural layout of the mission and its functions, and tells in some detail of the success of those which were in California and Texas.[33]

A third aspect of the "motives for colonization" deals with the settlement practices themselves.   A Black Legend tenet maintains that whereas all classes of good Englishmen came to the New World for permanent settlement and sturdy yeoman agriculture, the Spanish stayed only long enough to loot the country of gold and silver.   Such an appraisal is inaccurate, and who but Cortes himself serves to point up its fallacy.   After his victories in Mexico, he did not, as the Legend suggests, finish his life in golden retreat back in Spain.   Rather, he remained in the vast area of Morelos in Mexico and instituted as well as directed a system of agricultural management for the region until his death twenty-five years later.

---

[30]The good intentions of the Spanish government are detailed in Lewis Hanke, *The Spanish Struggle for Justice in the Conquest of America* (Philadelphia: University of Pennsylvania Press, 1949).

[31]Canfield and Wilder, *The Making of Modern America*, p. 30.

[32]Charles Gibson, *The Aztecs Under Spanish Rule: A History of the Indians of the Valley of Mexico, 1519-1810* (Stanford: Stanford University Press, 1964), p. 119.

[33]*Discovering American History*, pp. 45-46.

He added his own European natural products to the native ones, and was particularly successful in raising sugar cane and live- stock.[34]   The churchman, Bartolome de Las Casas (who, inci- dentally, was responsible for much of the Black Legend because of his widely-published criticisms of Spain), stands as another refutation of this aspect of the Legend.   He attempted to colonize the northern coast of Venezuela in 1521, and his plan called for "Spanish farmers who would till the soil, treat the Indians kindly, and thus lay the basis for an ideal Christian community in the New World."   The Indians, according to the plan, would learn the farmers' skill and industry through direct observation.   Although ultimately unsuccessful, the desire was still there.[35]

Notwithstanding the fact, then, that blanket generalizations con- cerning settlement are risky business, some of the texts neverthe- less make rather sharp distinctions between English and Spanish settlers.   There were major differences, certainly, but some of the generalizations give wrong impressions.   Contradictions also exist in the various accounts.   For example, *A People and a Nation* by Clarence L. Ver Steeg and Richard Hofstadter includes a compar- ative chart of English and Spanish colonial characteristics.   Under the heading "Types of Emigrants" the English are described as "Yeomen, artisans, indentured laborers—a middle-class element, forming the base for a self-governing society; mostly families." The Spanish are labeled "Soldiers, missionaries, and administra- tors—ruling class; mostly men."[36]   Compare this to what is said in *A New History of the United States: An Inquiry Approach,* which states that

> the countryside was filled with thousands of restless men.   They were the sons of petty nobles, without estates and with slim hopes for the future.   Spain obtained its soldiers and settlers from among these men . . . . They emigrated as conquerors in small numbers, and also women stayed at home.[37]

Foundations of Freedom: United States History to 1877 by Har old H. Eibling, Carlton Jackson, and Vito Perrone says it this way: "During the first half of the sixteenth century, Spaniards flocked to the New World.   Most of those who came were government officials, noblemen, merchants, or missionaries."[38]   As is becom- ing apparent, there are confusing and irregular accounts in dealing

---

[34]G. Micheal Riley, *Fernando Cortes and the Marquesado in Morelos, 1522-1547: A Case Study in the Socioeconomic Development of Sixteenth- Century Mexico* (Albuquerque: University of New Mexico Press, 1973), pp. 92-96.

[35]Hanke, *The Spanish Struggle for Justice,* p. 54.

[36](New York: Harper and Row, 1971), p. 10.

[37]Bartlett, Fenton, Fowler, and Manderbaum, *A New History of the United States,* p. 23.

[38](River Forest, Ill.: Laidlaw Brothers, 1973), pp. 70-71.

with the characteristics of Spanish settlement.   How is a student to form a clear idea about the subject?   Even an interested student, who consults more than one of these texts for clarification, is likely to become more confused than before.   At one point, for instance, he is told that early in the sixteenth century Spaniards "emigrated in small numbers," and at another point that they "flocked" to the New World.   The issue is further complicated in *The Pageant of American History*.   Here we read:

> The explorers we have thus far described cannot really be referred to as immigrants.   They had little intention of staying in the land they explored.   However, many of their followers did stay.   They prepared the way for immigrants who arrived shortly.[39]

Still another variation on this theme comes from *A History of the United States* by Richard C. Wade, Howard B. Wilder, and Louise C. Wade:

> The English settlements along the Atlantic seaboard were late in starting but in time outstripped the Spanish and French territories in population.   One reason was the different pattern of settlement. English families came to America to build a new life for themselves and their children.[40]

If the Spanish did not come to America to build new lives for themselves and their children, then this author is at a loss to explain what they did intend to accomplish by the trip over here.

It is difficult to evaluate the texts in terms of acceptability in this area, simply because the experts themselves do not always agree.   For example, observe Powell's opinion when he notes that

> after 1500, ships and fleets going from Spain to the New World regularly carried Spanish women, children, servants, officials; in short, nearly every imaginable type of human cargo.   On the farthest frontiers, even when Spaniards first arrived, Spanish women and families commonly accompanied their men, facing all the dangers and hardships that our ancestors encountered in frontier expansion.[41]

One could not ask for a stronger denial of this than that provided by the demographer Peter Boyd-Bowman: *"It is not altogether surprising that the entire dangerous Northern Frontier initially attracted not a single one of our women!"*[42]   (Italics his.)   What, then, represents the proper approach to the subject of Spanish

---

[39]Leinwand, *The Pageant of American History*, p. 9.

[40](Boston: Houghton Mifflin, 1972), p. 1.

[41]Powell, *Tree of Hate*, p. 19.

[42]"Patterns of Spanish Emigration to the Indies, 1579-1600," *The Americas: A Quarterly Review of Inter-American Cultural History* 33 (July 1976):   88.   Boyd-Bowman does corroborate the fact, though, that women were not left behind in Spain by noting that "in the last two decades of the 16th Century the percentage of women emigrants fell off slightly, though it was *still over one in four*."   Italics his, p. 84.

settlement in the New World?   The safest method appears to be the simple one of avoiding overgeneralization.   Grouping similar entities together to provide comparisons is one of the roles of the historian, but he must be careful not to be misleading when doing so.   It is one thing to praise the Spanish for bringing their women and families to America, as many did, but quite another to imply that the majority did so.   The answer in this particular case does not call for a monolithic interpretation of Spanish settlement in the New World; certainly, nothing short of government coercion would be able to produce one.   Variety and individuality are the corner-stones of American education.   But writers of textbooks would do well to avoid simplistic characterizations of the English as family-minded farmers and of the Spanish as upper-class bachelor mal-contents.   There were elements of both in each of the emigrating nationalities.

Another part of colonial Spain which the Black Legend seeks to malign is the government.   According to the Legend, the system was backward, inflexible, autocratic, and despotic, although evi-dence exists to show these words to be excessively strong.   The government intervened, for example, to stave the effects of the famine in New Spain of the 1570s.   Royal control was extended over prices, labor supply, production quotas, and even the tribute grain of the *encomenderos* (those holding the encomienda grant.)[43] The monarchy permitted and even encouraged criticism pertaining to the running of the colonial empire.[44]   Further, there was ample opportunity for subordinate officials to exercise subjective judg-ment.   Standards set by the imperial government which were con-flicting with each other afforded subordinates the option of relating each standard to each particular situation.   The end result in many instances appeared to be outright non-compliance with the law, but was actually a process of selecting which of the conflicting standards was applicable to any given situation.[45]   The grasp of the imperial hand was not, therefore, closed tightly around every administrative decision made in Spanish America.   It is even con-ceivable that this kind of "home-rule" rivaled that of many of the English colonies.

Overwhelmingly, the texts do not admit such a possibility. Those which do mention the Spanish government tend once again to make simplistic generalizations.   Many of them compare the

[43]Raymond L. Lee, "Grain Legislation in Colonial Mexico, 1575-1585," *Hispanic American Historical Review* 27 (1947): 647-60.   (This journal hereafter cited as *HAHR*.)

[44]Lewis Hanke, "Free Speech in Sixteenth-Century Spanish America," *HAHR* 26 (1946): 135-49.

[45]John L. Phelan, "Authority and Flexibility in the Spanish Imperial Bureaucracy," *Administrative Science Quarterly* 5 (June 1960): 47-65.

iron-fisted "autocratic" Spanish with the more democratic English, often implying that self-government in the English colonies was warmly received by the English government, which in numerous cases was clearly not true.   Only three of the seventeen texts did a fair treatment of this theme. *A New History of the United States: An Inquiry Approach* does an equitable job, although one senses that it refers more to the English than to the Spanish:

> Both long distances and slow communications forced colonial rulers to make decisions without consulting the home government.   And colonists who grew up in the sight of the forest and never saw the homeland became more and more inclined to make their own decisions.   In addition, the harsh conditions of the new land required new types of decisions about new issues.[46]

Weisberger intimates this also, and *History of a Free People* by Henry W. Bragdon and Samuel P. McCutcheon attempts to be more fair than the others in the majority as well.

The decline of the empire has been attributed to internal factors such as greed, economic incompetence, and lack of foresight.   Important factors like the English contraband trade, however, are often neglected.[47].   Very few of the texts specifically spend any time on the English role in weakening the empire.   One which does merits attention.   *This is America's Story* states:

> Drake felt a bitter hatred for the Spaniards.   For many years he proved his boldness and skill by capturing Spanish vessels and attacking Spanish towns.   Once he and his men landed on the Isthmus of Panama and cooly seized a Spanish mule-train bearing costly treasure! After this the Spanish called him "Drake the Dragon," and the king of Spain offered a sum equal to $200,000 to anyone who could kill him.[48]

One wonders if a Spanish pirate attacking English shipping would be "bold" and "skillful."   More likely, he would be pictured as being "wicked" and "treacherous."   And surely no Spaniard would be so warmly thought of for "coolly" seizing a treasure convoy. Ironically, the very same authors who so flagrantly throw around objectives warn in the margin of the teacher's edition to "bring out the Spanish and English viewpoints regarding Drake.   This is an example of why it is difficult to write history which will not be regarded as biased by some group."[49]

Although this area, the decline of the Spanish empire, contains less of a questionable nature than some of the others, there are

---

[46]Bartlett, Fenton, Fowler, and Mandelbaum, *A New History of the United States,* p. 27.

[47]See Vera Lee Brown, "Contraband Trade: A Factor in the Decline of Spain's Empire in America," *HAHR* 8 (1928): 178-89.

[48]Wilder, Ludlam, and Brown, *This is America's Story,* pp. 76-77.

[49]*Ibid.*

still comments such as "the people living in Spain and in the Spanish colonies had almost no voice in the government."[50] *Foundations of Freedom* states: "There was little self-government in Spain. All political power and authority were held by the king. And no self-government was allowed in the Spanish colonies."[51] Another text offers a rather vague, if unhelpful, "unwise policies of the Spanish king further weakened Spain."[52] *History of a Free People* gives the best account of the Spanish decline:

> Although the founding of the Spanish Empire was one of the great achievements of history, it was not followed by vigorous development after the first century of conquest and settlement. There are several reasons for this.
> (1) Spain tried to do too much in the "Spanish century . . . ."
> (2) The Spanish kept colonial trade in a straight jacket . . . .
> (3) Society in the Spanish colonies became fixed in a pyramid . . . .
> Despite these drawbacks, the Spanish extended their culture over an area many times larger than their own, and kept control for three centuries or more. Furthermore, they protected the native population from extermination and from the worst forms of oppression.[53]

Many of the texts seize upon the defeat of the Armada in 1588 as the turning point of Spain's fortunes. Whether this as a single event was that critical is a matter of judgment, but a much-used text, *Rise of the American Nation* by Lewis Paul Todd and Merle Curti, makes much of the defeat:

> The English defeat of the Spanish Armada was a decisive moment in world history—and in the history of the land that later became the United States. For nearly 100 years, Spain had been growing rich and powerful from trade and plunder in the New World. Unchecked, Spain might have gone on to build strong colonies along the Atlantic seaboard of North America from Florida to what is now Maine.
> The sea battle in the English Channel in 1588 marked the turning point of Spain's fortunes in the New World.[54]

The passage contains what may be construed as anti-Spanish sentiment. The word "plunder" (a favorite in the majority of texts) is essentially correct, but in reference to similar English actions further north the word is not used. After the sentence describing what Spain might have done "unchecked," one might imagine the authors saying to themselves, "Horrid fate!" There is relief in the next sentence, though, when the English do "check" the Spanish.

Other texts offer differing descriptions of the Armada itself. A student's perception of the Spanish navy could either be favorable

---

[50]Lewis Paul Todd and Merle Curti, *Rise of the American Nation*, 3rd ed. (New York: Harcourt, Brace, Jovanovich, 1972), p. 15
[51]Eibling, Jackson, and Perrone, *Foundations of Freedom*, p. 71.
[52]Canfield and Wilder, *The Making of Modern America*, p. 32.
[53]Bragdon and McCutcheon, *History of a Free People*, p. 7.
[54]Todd and Curti, *Rise of the American Nation*, pp. 4-5.

or unfavorable, depending upon which book he read. For instance, Canfield and Wilder state: "The attacking Spanish ships were big and clumsy. The defending English ships were smaller but skillfully handled."[55] *History of a Free People,* on the other hand, says that "comprising 130 ships manned by 27,000 men, this was the greatest naval expedition the world had ever seen."[56] Both views are correct, but one is clearly complimentary and the other not so. A fairer description would probably combine the two.

Most of the textbooks spend little time in the area of the Spanish treatment of the Indian. The Black Legend emphasizes the extreme cruelty with which the Spaniards treated him, to the exclusion of all else, including the fact that many Indians were not any worse off than they had been in pre-conquest days. The Legend also speaks of the planned and deliberate slaughter of millions of Indians, when in fact the vast majority of those millions died of disease. The Spanish had no desire to annihilate their labor supply.

> We know now that Indian depopulation was an ecological phenomenon, uncontrollable in sixteenth- and seventeenth-century terms. Humanitarian enactments were powerless against it . . . . Even casual contacts between Spaniards and Indians meant that Indians died, for they immediately became victims of the diseases that Spaniards carried.[57]

Weisberger offers the novel if dubious analogy that if Americans could as they did in 1938 to the radio broadcast of *War of the Worlds,* "imagine the reactions of Indians who had never seen an oceangoing ship, a horse, or a gun. The wonder is that some Indians had the courage to fight back at all."[58] This is somewhat like saying that if violence on television incites children, imagine what would happen if they saw their favorite program magnified hundreds of times in a movie theater. There is a possible, but not probable, connection. Of the textbooks examined, only *History: USA* by Jack Allen and John L. Betts provides a commentary which is not debatable one way or the other:

> From the earliest days of conquest and settlement, the Indian provided most of the labor which built the colonial empire. Although rarely enslaved, he generally lived and worked in communities without freedom of movement, without civil and political rights, and generally

---

[55]Canfield and Wilder, *The Making of Modern America,* p. 32.

[56]Bragdon and McCutcheon, *History of a Free People,* p. 12.

[57]Charles Gibson, *Spain in America* (New York: Harper and Row, 1966), p. 64. Lesley Byrd Simpson speaks of a developing "feudal relationship" between Spaniard and Indian in *The Ecomienda in New Spain: The Beginning of Spanish Mexico,* rev. ed. (Berkeley: University of California Press, 1966).

[58]Weisberger, *The Impact of Our Past,* p. 53.

without adequate pay. Such leaders as did develop were either slain
in revolts, executed, or bought off with an office, or title of rank.[59]

Historical interpretations on this theme vary. Some are likely
to show that the Spanish conquest did not disrupt Indian life as
much as might be imagined. William B. Taylor develops this
theme in his book, *Landlord and Peasant in Colonial Oaxaca.*
Here we learn that in the Valley of Oaxaca, Mexico, the Spanish
generally respected Indian titles to the land.[60] On the other hand,
Charles Gibson asserts that

> The Black Legend provides a gross but essentially accurate interpre-
> tation of relations between Spaniards and Indians. The Legend builds
> upon the record of deliberate sadism . . . . [T]he substantive content
> of the Black Legend asserts that Indians were exploited by Spaniards,
> and in empirical fact they were.[61]

This aspect of the Black Legend thus probably has more credence
than the others.

A last comment upon this theme illustrates two ways in which
the racial combination of Spaniards and Indians is presented in
the texts. One reads:

> Racially there is a wide difference between the people of the United
> States and their southern neighbors. For the most part, the Spanish
> conquerors of Latin America did not bring their families with them.
> As a result, a mixed race developed in many parts of Latin America,
> partly mestizo (white and Indian), partly mulatto (white and Negro).[62]

Essentially the same factual information contained in this con-
demnation of Spanish adultery is presented succinctly and neu-
trally in another: "In the United States today probably less
than one per cent of the population has any Indian ancestry; in
Mexico, however, *mestizos* (those people who are of mixed Indian
and white descent) form the great majority of the population."[63]
A New History of the United States: An Inquiry Approach approximates this treatment in its own, and perhaps Weisberger says it
best of all: "If they took Indian wives and had children, as they
often did, the youngsters were part of a new breed—Americans."[64]
The Indians, of course, were Americans before they encountered
the Spanish, but the passage is important in its placement of the
mestizo in the category of "American." Black Legend adherents
consider him to be neither American nor European, a "man without a country."

[59](New York: American Book Co., 1971), p. 19.
[60](Stanford: Stanford University Press, 1972), pp. 195-202.
[61]Gibson, *The Aztecs Under Spanish Rule*, p. 403.
[62]Canfield and Wilder, *The Making of Modern America*, p. 632.
[63]Bragdon and McCutcheon, *History of a Free People*, p. 7.
[64]Weisberger, *The Impact of Our Past*, p. 65.

Related to the Spanish treatment of the Indian is the subject of how they treated the black person.   Roughly half of the texts comment upon Negroes in the Spanish colonies.   The great majority of these make a distinction between Spanish and Anglo-American slavery, with the Spanish version generally emerging as being less harsh than its northern counterpart.   Todd and Curti in *Rise of the American Nation* present a well-balanced and thorough treatment of the phenomenon, stressing both the harshness, and at times comparative laxity, of Spanish slavery.[65]   There appears to be a singular absence of the Black Legend in this area, possibly owing to the fact that potential critics found it difficult to condemn an institution of theirs that was so treasured it caused a civil war. Nevertheless, those texts which say nothing about Spanish enslavement of the Negro are practicing a "bias by omission" in their refusal to deal with an important part of the social history of America.

Up to this point the discussion has centered solely in the Spanish colonial period, and consequently has dealt primarily with the Black Legend as applied to the Spanish.   As has been seen, the Legend continues to exist in much of the textbooks' treatment of the period.   As Billington intimated, much of it is of a subtle rather than glaring nature.   Even a wary reader is likely to leave parts of it unnoticed, because some of these attitudes have become ingrained into the very psyche of most Americans.   The following section illustrates what was said earlier about the Legend being applied not only to the Spanish, but to the Mexicans as well.

The Mexican War, and preceding it, the American occupation of Texas, provide most of the remaining material occurring in a sizeable number of texts which reflects Black Legend thinking. All of the texts are pro-Texan, as indicated by their sympathetic treatment of the Alamo, Goliad, Sam Houston, and so forth. There is probably nothing wrong in this, as these names are equated in most Americans' minds with heroism and determination. There should be, however, a reciprocal look at the position of the Mexicans.   This is not attempted by most of the books.   *This is America's Story* illustrates this point:

> Mexico realized too late that it had been a mistake to allow Americans to settle in her territory.   They did not get along well with the government or with the Spanish people in Texas.   The Americans were different in language, religion, and ways of living.   Furthermore, they were independent in spirit and disliked living under Mexican law.[66]

Historical inaccuracy exists in the second sentence.   The people referred to are not Spanish; they are Mexican, and there is a

[65]Todd and Curti, *Rise of the American Nation*, pp. 14-15.
[66]Wilder, Ludlam, and Brown, *This is America's Story*, p. 353.

difference. Once again, turn the passage around; the Americans living on Mexican soil are "independent in spirit" and thus do not like to obey Mexican law; but picture the description most likely given to Mexicans living on American soil. Here we would probably see words such as "rebellious," "anarchical," or "ungrateful." In actual fact, millions of Mexicans do at the present time live illegally in the United States. Are they "independent in spirit"? No, they are "wetbacks." Another text, *The Impact of Our Past: A History of the United States,* provides a potentially dangerous quotation:

> Revolutions brought frequent changes of rulers, leading the Texans
> to the harsh judgment expressed by one of them in a letter: "The
> Mexicans are never at peace with each other; ignorant and degraded
> as many of them are, they are not capable of ruling, nor yet of being
> ruled."[67]

There is nothing inherently wrong with this passage, and it is conceivably a good idea for students to know firsthand what the feelings of many Texans were. However, a teacher should point out to students exactly what the passage is attempting to convey. Otherwise, a light reading of the text is apt to implant the words "ignorant" and "degraded" to the exclusion of the substantive meaning of the excerpt. Again, all seventeen texts could stand improvement in this area if they wish to appear less biased.

The Mexican War of 1846-1848 is treated less uniformly than the above, reflecting the varied interpretations of its causes which have followed it to the present day. Since there is little consensus on the precise causes of the war, it is not possible to single out any particular texts as being historically inaccurate. At least half of them point to more than one cause, and none have been so bold as to affix sole blame upon Mexico. This is encouraging in light of the fact that this is an area one would think to be especially prone to jingoistic assaults upon those people "south of the border." Notwithstanding that fact, the texts do need to justify words such as "massacred," "slaughtered," or "mercilessly destroyed" in speaking of the plight of the Americans. Although the terms are emotionally strong, they may be considered justifiable—but only if similarly applied to American actions against others where appropriate. Other terms referring to Santa Anna as "wily," "crafty," and a "dictator" are sprinkled generously throughout. These are stereotypes commonly used to describe all Mexicans, and their use is justified only if they are perceived by students as serving this purpose. Finally, several of the texts allude to some of the "contributions" of civilization which the United States hoped to bring Mexican culture through the war. The teacher would do

---

[67]Weisberger, *The Impact of Our Past,* p. 287.

well to offer examples showing that these Anglo-Saxon contributions had existed in Latin America hundreds of years before.[68]

Pictures and captions are also capable of creating attitudes in the minds of students, especially in this age of "functional illiteracy" which has spawned such a number of illustrations in some texts that the narrative becomes seemingly secondary. Most of the pictures in the texts avoided the Black Legend stereotype of portraying Cortes in full battle regalia bearing down upon helpless Indians. In fact, one book labelled its picture of him "Hernando Cortes, explorer."[69] Many of the pictures dealt with contributions, such as architecture, rather than stereotypes. However, two of the seventeen included reproductions of engravings by Theodore de Bry. According to one authority, "no publisher did more to popularize the so-called Black Legend in Germany and throughout Europe than Theodore de Bry and his sons Jean Theodore and Jean Israel."[70] Powell tells why the family's engravings are seen with disfavor in Spain:

> In 1598 the De Brys of Frankfurt issued an edition of the *Brief Relation* [by Bartolome de Las Casas] with a new twist. The work contained seventeen engravings illustrating specific episodes of purported Spanish torture and killing of Indians, as described in Las Casas' text. These pictures were extremely gruesome, obviously catering to the general public and its common appetite for horrors. From this time on editions of the *Brief Relation* often contained all or some of the De Bry engravings. And the pictures themselves were dignified by separate publication, thus indicating their original propaganda aims.[71]

Although the pictures in the textbooks are not these particularly gruesome ones, it does seem out of place to use any of de Bry's work without an accompanying explanation of what he is most famous for. Not doing this is the equivalent of sending a sincerely cheery note to a Jewish person on a National Socialist White People's Party letterhead. Needless to say, no matter how cheerful the greeting, it will not excite a cheerful reaction on the part of the recipient.

Generally, undesirable traits have not been intentionally attributed to Mexicans and Spaniards by the authors. However, one ironic inclusion in *The American Experience: A Study of Themes and Issues in American History* by Robert F. Madgic, Stanley S. Seaberg, Fred H. Stopsky, and Robin W. Winks, is an excerpt from Philip Frenau's eighteenth-century poem, "The Rising Glory

[68]Herbert E. Bolton, "Some Cultural Assets of Latin America," *HAHR* 20 (1940): 3-11; rpt. New York: Kraus Reprint Corp., 1965.

[69]Ver Steeg and Hofstadter, *A People and a Nation*, p. 11.

[70]Benjamin Keen, *The Aztec Image in Western Thought* (New Brunswick: Rutgers University Press, 1971), p. 163.

[71]Powell, *Tree of Hate*, p. 80.

of America." Charles Gibson included the poem in his collection of representative Black Legend writings.[72] *Rise of the American Nation* includes a statement which sustains a rather unflattering stereotype: "Against this frontier of Spanish culture with its leisurely tempo of life pressed an irresistible tide of energetic, land-hungry Americans."[73] One wonders whether an irresistible tide of land-hungry Mexicans would be "energetic" or simply "greedy." *This is America's Story* describes Balboa as "a tall and haughty man and an excellent swordsman."[74] One wonders if knowledge of Balboa's haughtiness adds appreciably to a student's understanding of the story, but in any case the word is not applied to Americans. Andrew Jackson, surely one of the most haughty public figures of all time, is recorded in the same text as being bold, courageous, a man of action, honest, and hard-working, if prone at times to an uncontrollable temper.[75]

As was observed before, the Black Legend is selective in its use of historical fact. It concentrates on the alarming and undesirable actions of the Spanish and neglects the contributions they made to the areas now within the United States. Half of the textbooks do not mention any Spanish contribution to our country. One of them gives us a simplistic time-line which indirectly gives Spain all of three words:

"American Events"
1492   Columbus discovered America
1607   Jamestown settled[76]

The other texts do an accurate job of describing our Spanish inheritance. Todd and Curti provide one of the best treatments:

To their American colonies, the Portuguese and Spaniards brought domestic animals, plants, and seeds never before seen in the New World. In pens and crates on the decks of their ships, they transported horses, donkeys, cattle, pigs, sheep, goats, and poultry. Using barrels cut in half and filled with earth they carried fruit and nut trees—olive, lemon, orange, lime, apple, cherry, pear, fig, apricot, almond, and walnut. In bags they brought seeds of wheat, barley, rye, rice, peas, lentils, and flax. They also transplanted sugar cane and flowers.[77]

The authors also tell of farms, ranches, cities, books, colleges, and churches. This text and the others like it deserve to stand as

---

[72](Menlo Park, Calif.: Addison-Wesley, 1975), p. 50; and Gibson, *The Black Legend*, pp. 151-54.

[73]Todd and Curti, *Rise of the American Nation*, p. 324.

[74]Wilder, Ludlam, and Brown, *This is America's Story*, p. 60.

[75]*Ibid.*, p. 322.

[76]Boyd C. Shafer, Everett Augspurger, and Richard A. McLemore, *United States History for High Schools* (River Forest, Ill.: Laidlaw Brothers, 1973), p. 12.

[77]Todd and Curti, *Rise of the American Nation*, p. 14.

examples for forthcoming high school histories, if the Black Legend is to be ultimately erased.

One group of authors thought that including examples of Spanish contributions was a good idea, but would not allow them without reservations: "Because the Spanish settlements north of the lower Rio Grande were little more than military and mission posts on a distant frontier, Spanish civilization did not greatly influence the development of United States history."[78]   The authors then proceed to list some of the things such as religion, language, foods, and livestock which "did not greatly influence" our history.

To sum up, it should be clear by now that the Black Legend is "alive and well" in the United States history textbooks used in Wyoming high schools. Although the "Equality State" prides itself upon being less racially troubled than other parts of the country, it is obvious that teaching misconceptions in public classrooms are an inevitable by-product of the utilization of less-than-accurate textbooks.   To simplify the task of determining which books are responsible and which are not for transmitting unwarranted stereotypes, the seventeen examined in this study have been grouped under three headings, as follow.   It should be remembered that no single book is "all good" or "all bad," and a text guilty of incorporating the Black Legend can still be an excellent work in other areas.   For conciseness, only the titles are given below. More information may be obtained by consulting the appendix.

The *"Traditional"* texts are the ones most prone to abuse their responsibility of transmitting accurate history.   These are the "Black Legend" texts: *The Free and the Brave: The Story of the American People; The Impact of Our Past: A History of the United States; A History of the United States; The Making of Modern America;* and *This is America's Story.*   These textbooks need to be revised.

A second school of thought may be appropriately entitled the *"Omission"* school.   One might theorize that these authors are indeed aware of the Black Legend, and wish to avoid its complications by avoiding treatment of the Spanish and Mexican people altogether.   In any event, this denial of the cultural influence of the Hispanic peoples upon the history of the United States constitutes the most flagrant "bias by omission" imaginable.   The books are: *The American Experience: A Study of Themes and Issues in American History; The People Make a Nation; United States History;* and *United States History for High Schools.*   These too need revision.

---

[78]Allen and Betts, *History: USA*, p. 19.   For detailed treatment of some contributions, see Harry Bernstein, "Spanish Influence in the United States: Economic Aspects," *HAHR* 18 (1938): 43-65.

The third group of textbooks constitute a *"Revisionist"* school of thought. These authors, while guilty at times of injecting unintentional bias, at least make an effort to include a fair representation of Hispanic influence upon our history. At the same time, they do not "sugar-coat" the treatment in an effort to be all things to all people. They are represented by: *Discovering American History; Foundations of Freedom: United States History to 1877; History of a Free People; History: USA; A New History of the United States: An Inquiry Approach; The Pageant of American History; A People and a Nation;* and *Rise of the American Nation.* Although some of their coverage is scanty, it is accurate. One of the better texts, *Rise of the American Nation,* is used in most high schools along the southern tier of counties in the state. This is fortunate, because these counties contain by far the highest percentage of Mexican-American students, who are thus able to receive a more well-rounded picture than that offered by some of the texts. However, schools using the *"Traditional"* texts, especially in the northern part of the state with few Mexican-Americans, should not feel smug in their choices. After all, stereotypes are most often fostered by those who have little contact with the people they malign.

The American Council on Education made a number of conclusions based on its study of 1944. It said that it was reasonably optimistic about the whole matter, and that there was no desire by any of the authors to intentionally distort the truth. There were inaccuracies in some of the factual detail, but were considered correctable. However, there was widespread residue of the Black Legend, especially in the treatment of the colonial period, and racial prejudices were also evident. Sometimes a "Kiplingesque condescension" existed toward Latin America. Periods of conflict rather than of cooperation are stressed by the authors. Finally, the authors use terms like "dictator" without understanding their Latin American connotations. This study is in basic agreement with these conclusions, and differs from them in only one instance. While the Council thought that adequate quantitative material existed in the United States history books, that is clearly not the case with several of those presently examined.[79]

This study concludes with an example of what is being done in the case of one text as far as revision. The text is Henry F. Graff's *The Free and the Brave: The Story of the American People.* The second edition of the book is the one used by a Wyoming high school, but since that edition was not available for examination, the first and third editions were examined (1967 and 1977 respec-

---

[79]American Council on Education, *Latin America in School and College Teaching Materials,* pp. 27-37.

tively.) Since there was a ten-year span between the two editions, changes stick out quite readily. For example, in the first edition, motives for colonization include, "a fierce search for gold and silver" while in the third edition it is simply "to search for gold and silver."[80] Another example is this excerpt from the first edition:

> Despite the fact that his men died like flies, Balboa pressed on toward his goal. When he faced Indian enemies on the way, he turned on them the dozen ferocious dogs he had brought along. They could tear a man limb from limb and needed little encouragement in their work, which they performed often.[81]

Compare this to the newer edition:

> Even though his men died like flies, Balboa kept on toward his goal. When he faced Indian enemies along the way, he sometimes turned loose on them the dozen mean dogs he had brought along. The animals could easily kill a man, and often did.[82]

The passage was revised, although not substantially. What is amazing is that it was kept at all. Balboa's twelve dogs are historically unimportant in a survey of this nature which should spend its time on the really vital issues. Another change made in the text was to cease calling Pizarro "an ignorant man."[83] This is a sound revision. Although Pizarro might well have been ignorant, this is no place to say it. A further change was made in this passage: "The Spanish were affected by their contact with the Indians, too. They fell into the habit of refusing to work with their hands—a usual vice of conquerors."[84] The new edition states only that the Spanish did not want to work any more with their hands.

The book is still virulently anti-Hispanic even after revisions have been made, for the most part. This last quote, which is anachronistic and anti-historical, proves that more must yet be done:

> The Crusades taught the Spaniards and other Europeans now skills at waging war. The crusaders learned methods of attack which few people in the world—possibly only the Japanese—could match. So it was that the history of Europe and the Middle East affected the way in which conquistadors, wearing armor and carrying destructive halberds (two-handed swords), faced American Indians.[85]

The "revised" version of this passage is only slightly altered:

> The Crusades taught the Spaniards and other Europeans new ways of fighting. The men learned ways of attacking that few other people in the world—perhaps only the Japanese—could equal. So the his-

---

[80](Chicago: Rand McNally, 1967 and 1977), pp. 25, 26.
[81]*Ibid.*, p. 29.
[82]*Ibid.*
[83]*Ibid.*, p. 34.
[84]*Ibid.*, pp. 39, 40.
[85]*Ibid.*, p. 42.

tory of Europe and Southwest Asia helped *conquistadors,* who wore armor and carried two-handed swords, to conquer Indians.[86]

The book is still in the *"Traditional"* school.

APPENDIX

Information concerning the principal American history textbooks used in Wyoming high schools was obtained by questionnaire in the fall of 1976. The textbooks and the schools where they are used are listed below, in descending order according to frequency of use. The specific edition(s) of each text examined in this study follows the title.

The data following each school reveals: location (if not apparent in the school name); county; grade levels in which the text is used; approximate enrollment; average percentage of Mexican-Americans in a class; and the specific edition of the text which is used in the school.

Todd, Lewis Paul, and Merle Curti. *Rise of the American Nation,* 3rd ed. New York: Harcourt, Brace, Jovanovich, 1972.
1. Burns; Laramie County; 9-12; 170; 1%; 1972.
2. Campbell County; Gillette; Campbell County; 10-12; 900; unknown; 1972.
3. Central; Cheyenne; Laramie County; 10-12; 1300; 15%; 1974.
4. East; Cheyenne; Laramie County; 10-12; 1550; 5%; 1972.
5. Evanston; Uinta County; 10-12; 300; 1%; 1972.
6. Laramie; Albany County; 10-12; 1000 12.6% 1974.
7. Natrona County; Casper; Natrona County; 10-12; 2100; 2%; 1969.
8. Rawlins; Carbon County; 9-12; 780; 22%; 1972.
9. Star Valley; Afton; Lincoln County; 9-12; 480; none; 1972.
10. Torrington; Goshen County; 10-12; 475; 7%; 1974.
11. W. Wesly Morrow; Baggs; Carbon County; 7-12; 2; unknown; 1968.

Bragdon, Henry W., and Samuel P. McCutcheon. *History of a People.* New York: Macmillan, 1969.
1. Cowley; Big Horn County; 9-12; unknown; none; 1969 (with supplements in Mexican-American area).

---

[86]*Ibid.,* p. 41. There is irony in the fact that Henry F. Graff co-authored with Jacques Barzun a research and writing manual entitled *The Modern Researcher,* rev. ed. (New York: Harcourt, Brace and World, 1970). The manual stresses care in scholarship and clarity in exposition.

2. Greybull; Big Horn County; 9-12; 225; none; 1973.
3. Guernsey-Sunrise; Guernsey; Platte County; 9-12; 125; 2%; 1967.
4. Hot Springs County; Thermopolis; Hot Springs County; 9-12; 400; none; 1973.
5. Medicine Bow-Shirley Basin; Medicine Bow; Carbon County; 9-12; 125; .5%; 1973.

Current, Richard N., Alexander DeConde, and Harris L. Dante. *United States History: Search for Freedom.* Glenview, Illinois: Scott, Foresman, 1967.
1. Byron; Big Horn County; 7-12; 70; 11%; 1967.
2. Dubois; Fremont County; 9-12; unknown; 1%; 1967.
3. Kaycee; Johnson County; 9-12; 50; none; 1970.
4. Niobrara County; Lusk; Niobrara County; 9-12; 200; none; 1974.
5. Powell; Park County; 9-12; 735;5%; 1974.

Ver Steeg, Clarence L., and Richard Hofstadter. *A People and a Nation.* New York: Harper and Row, 1971.
1. Burlington; Big Horn County; 9-12; 75; 2-3%; 1971.
2. Cokeville; Lincoln County; 9-12; 66; 1%; 1971.
3. Hulett, Crook County; 9-12; 79; none; 1971.
4. Mountain View; Uinta County; 9-12; 154; none; 1974.
5. Newcastle; Weston County; 9-12; 450; 1%; 1971.

Shafer, Boyd C., Everett Augspurger, and Richard A. McLemore. *United States History for High Schools,* 2nd ed. River Forest, Illinois: Laidlaw Brothers, 1973.
1. Lagrange; Goshen County; 9-12; 60; 7%; 1966.
2. Moorcroft; Crook County; 9-12; 175; none; 1973.
3. Shoshoni; Fremont County; 9-12; 335; 1.5%; 1973.
4. Sundance; Crook County; 9-12; 250; none; 1973.

Leinwand, Gerald. *The Pageant of American History.* Boston: Allyn and Bacon, 1975.
1. Lingle-Ft. Laramie; Lingle; Goshen County; 9-12; 137; 1-2%; 1975.
2. Lovell; Big Horn County; 9-12; 270; 10-15%; 1975.
3. Pine Bluffs; Laramie County; 9-12; 150; .8%; 1975.

Wade, Richard C., Howard B. Wilder, and Louise C. Wade. *A History of the United States.* Boston: Houghton Mifflin, 1972.
1. Chugwater; Platte County; 7-12; unknown; none; 1972.
2. Glendo; Platte County; 7-12; 60; none; 1969.
3. Hanna-Elk Mountain; Hanna; Carbon County; 9-12; 112; 2%; 1972.

Allen, Jack, and John L. Betts. *History: USA.* New York: American Book Company, 1971.
1. Cody; Park County; 10-12; 608; 1%; 1976.
2. Glenrock; Converse County; 9-12; 235; 1%; 1971.

Graff, Henry F., and John A. Krout. *The Adventure of the American People.* Chicago: Rand McNally, 1971. (Not Examined in this Study)
1. Basin; Big Horn County; 9-12; 40; 2.5%; 1971.
2. Big Horn; Sheridan County; 9-12; 107; none; 1970.

Sandler, Martin W., Edwin C. Rozwenc, and Edward C. Martin. *The People Make a Nation.* Boston: Allyn and Bacon, 1975.
1. Buffalo; Johnson County; 9-12; 400; 2%; 1975.
2. Wheatland; Platte County; 9-12; 385; 5%; 1975.

Madgic, Robert F., Stanley S. Seaberg, Fred H. Stopsky, and Robin W. Winks. *The American Experience: A Study of Themes and Issues in American History,* 2nd ed. Menlo Park, California: Addison-Wesley, 1975.
1. Big Piney; Sublette County; 9-12; 60; 2%; 1975.
2. Central; Cheyenne; Laramie County; 10-12; 1300; 15%; 1975.

Weisberger, Bernard A. *The Impact of Our Past: A History of the United States.* New York: American Heritage Publishing Company, 1972.
1. Manderson-Hyattville; Manderson; Big Horn County; 9-12; 48; 6%; 1976.
2. Upton; Weston County; 9-12; 120; none; 1972.

Abramowitz, Jack. *American History,* rev. ed. Chicago: Follett Educational Corporation, 1971. (Not Examined in this Study)
1. Meeteetse; Park County; 9-12; 90; 8%; 1971.

Bartlett, Irving, Edwin Fenton, David Fowler, and Seymour Mandelbaum. *A New History of the United States: An Inquiry Approach.* New York: Holt, Rinehart, and Winston, 1975.
1. Wind River; Kinnear; Fremont County; 9-12; 155; 0-5%; 1975.

Branson, Margaret Stimmann. *American History for Today.* Boston: Ginn, 1970. (Not Examined in this Study)
1. Huntley; Goshen County; 9-12; 70; 2%; 1970.

Canfield, Leon H., and Howard B. Wilder. *The Making of Modern America,* 2nd ed.   Boston: Houghton Mifflin, 1966.
1. Riverton; Fremont County; 10-12; 750; 2-3%; 1966.

Eibling, Harold H., Carlton Jackson, and Vito Perrone. *Foundations of Freedom: United States History to 1877.* River Forest, Illinois: Laidlaw Brothers, 1973.
1. Lagrange; Goshen County; 9-12; 60; 7%; 1973.

Graff, Henry F. *The Free and the Brave: The Story of the American People,* 1st and 3rd eds.   Chicago: Rand McNally, 1967 and 1977.
1. Lyman; Uinta County; 9-12; 400; unknown; 1972 (2nd ed.).

Kownslar, Allan O., and Donald B. Frizzle. *Discovering American History.* New York: Holt, Rinehart, and Winston, 1974.
1. Central; Cheyenne; Laramie County; 10-12; 1300; 15%; 1974.

Sandler, Martin W. *In Search of America.* Boston: Ginn, 1975. (Not Examined in this Study)
1. Sheridan; Sheridan County; 9-12; 1100; 1%; 1975 (with supplements).

Wilder, Howard B., Robert P. Ludlam, and Harriet McCune Brown. *This is America's Story,* 3rd ed.   Boston: Houghton Mifflin, 1966 and 1970
1. Ten Sleep; Washakie County; 9-12; 60; none; 1968.

The following schools either had no standard text, returned partially invalid data, or divided United States history teaching into various classifications:

Arvada-Clearmont
Encampment
Green River
Kelly Walsh (Casper)
Lyman
The following schools chose not to respond to the survey:
Albin
Converse County (Douglas)
Deaver-Frannie (Deaver)
Farson-Eden (Farson)
Goshen Hole (Veteran)
Jackson Hole (Jackson)
Jeffrey City

Kemmerer
Lander Valley (Lander)
Midwest
Pinedale
Platte Valley (Saratoga)
Rock River
Rock Springs
Tongue River (Dayton)
Worland

The Bug Juice War

By

DOUGLAS C. MCCHRISTIAN

> He drank up all the bug juice
> The whiskey man would sell.
> They rammed him in the mill;
> They've got him in there still.
> His bobtail's comin' back by mail.
> O'Reilly's gone to hell.

These lines, taken from an old army barracks song, describe the plight of one soldier who fell victim to "demon rum." Inevitably, he was arrested and thrown into the guardhouse, or "mill," to sleep it off and to await charges. The scene was all too common to the regular army during the years after the Civil War.

The hard-drinking, hard-fighting Irish soldier has become a stock character associated with the army serving on the frontier. The fact that he existed is well supported by army records, including those of Fort Laramie. However, he certainly was not always Irish nor was he always a hard-fighter, at least in real combat. Some of his greatest "battles" took place in the bar at the post trader's store, in the barracks, or in one of the so-called "hog ranches" located just off the military reservation.

Although the degree of drinking varied somewhat from one post to another, it was always a problem. The environment under which it spawned and thrived was generally the same at any western post. Fort Laramie, far from being a bad duty station, had many of these conditions present.

Army life itself, no matter what the station, was conducive to liberal alcoholic consumption. The army of the Indian Wars era relied solely upon volunteers, who signed away five years of their lives to be soldiers. Many of these men had been tempered by experiences in the Civil War, by discouraging economic conditions, and by crime. In a word, they were tough. If they weren't when they joined, they became so long before their enlistment's end.

In most instances, military posts were far in advance of white settlement, usually to protect routes of travel or to stand watch over Indian reservations. Often they were located in harsh, barren terrain far from any town or city. In the case of Fort Laramie, the city of Cheyenne developed during 1867 on the Union Pacific ninety miles to the south. Prior to that the nearest settlement of any note had been Denver. Even at that, the distance was far enough to effectively bar Cheyenne as a source of recreation. Had the two been in close proximity, the result would have been much the same due to the rowdy and mostly-male nature of railroad boom towns. Wholesome recreation was scarce indeed anywhere on the frontier. Whatever soldiers found to do in their off-duty hours was done at or very near the post.

Life in the regular army was anything but glamorous. Those who joined to find excitement, as an alternative to watching the hind-sides of a plow team, were nearly always profoundly disappointed. For one recruit, Pvt. John E. Cox, this occurred as soon as he was issued his uniform at Newport Barracks in 1872.

> I was tall and slender, and of course drew a blouse big enough for Barnum's fat man, while my trousers could not be coaxed within six inches of my heels! United States soldier, indeed! U. S. scarecrows would be nearer the truth!

For others the letdown came more slowly. A day at Fort Laramie normally began at 5:45 a.m. with the first of three daily roll calls fifteen minutes later. From then until evening a soldier's life was a treadmill of drills, fatigues, and inspections. Then of course there were the ever-unpopular rotating tours of guard duty which ran twenty-four hours a day, fair weather and foul. Being a cavalry trooper brought the extra joys of at least two additional hours of horse care each day. When priorities had to be established, the drills were omitted in favor of work details which were the life blood sustaining a fort. The principal fuel, of course, was wood and it took several dozen cords monthly to supply a post the size of Fort Laramie. Men were detailed to construction and repair work, ice-cutting, warehouse duties, stable police, water hauling and a host of other non-military assignments. Small wonder that the rank and file termed the post a "Government workhouse."

The practice of utilizing soldiers to do work which might have been accomplished by contract or day labor became a major source of discontent among the men. Such a routine day in and day out for months on end in an isolated place bred monotony and pent-up energy which sought escape at any opportunity.

There were, certainly, alternatives to drinking. Again, the location of the post had a great deal to do with the variety of these alternatives. At Fort Laramie soldiers could usually obtain permission to go hunting, the object being to bring back meat for the company mess. In the 1880s, as game became more scarce in the vicinity of the fort, the army's increased emphasis upon target practice provided recreation as well as training.

Some soldiers also fished in the Laramie and North Platte Rivers. Baseball was very popular among the enlisted men and Reynolds J. Burt, son of Lt. Col. Andrew Burt, wrote that foot racing became quite a fad during the late 1880s. Horse racing, cards, reading, practical joking, and talking were all diversions used by soldiers to combat the loneliness and monotony of garrison life.

Many officers, like Brig. Gen. C. C. Augur, placed the blame for the army's drinking problem squarely upon its own system. In an 1870 report he stated:

> I desire, respectively, to state here that in my opinion, after twenty-seven years of experience, most of the drunkenness among soldiers in the army, and a large majority of desertions, is due to our system of paying the troops at long intervals of two months. Pay-day becomes an event which affords means for its own celebration, and is almost universally followed by days of drunkenness and disorder and desertions.

General Augur might have been even more candid by stating that it was not unusual for the troops to go even longer without pay. Weather, bad roads, hostiles, and bandits often delayed the paymaster so that four to six months between paydays was not uncommon. As might be expected, the delays only increased the intensity of the great event when it finally did arrive. A post trader's clerk at Fort Ellis, Montana, described one such occasion:

> Yesterday was a perfect pandemonium in the saloon, it was crowded all the time, everybody drunk and trying to outtalk everybody else. Every few minutes somebody would get knocked down, and occasionally they were having a free fight, that shook the whole house. When it got too bad, the officer of the guard would send down a squad of men and march the worst ones away to the guard house . . .

A soldier's pay did not allow extravagance; prior to 1870 it was fixed at $16 per month for a private. An economy-minded Congress in that year cut the monthly pay to $13 and as a result, at least in part, nearly one-third of the enlisted men deserted. The pay was meager by any standards, even for those times. At Fort Laramie in 1867 beer sold for fifteen cents a glass or two for twenty-five cents. Bottled beer usually went for fifty cents to one dollar and whiskey for ten cents a glass.

Some soldiers saved some of their pay or even invested it, while others sent a few dollars home to aid their families. For many, possibly the majority, it only burned holes in their pockets. Payday provided a chance to "live it up" and escape, for a while at least, the boredom and unyielding discipline of army life.

The post trader provided the most readily accessible source of alcoholic beverage at most frontier posts, including Fort Laramie. The trader was a civilian licensed by the Secretary of War to conduct business on the government reserve. His primary role was that of providing the soldiers, officers, and their families with such goods as the army did not supply through regular channels. In reality, he brought a touch of the East to these far-flung western outposts. Here one could purchase nearly anything, within reason, that he might need or desire.

Although the trader had no competition on the post, he did not possess a pure monopoly. Army regulations specified that prices would be established by a board of officers under the authority of the post commander. The board, using the trader's invoices to establish his costs, would fix the prices to be charged. A reasonable margin of profit would be included in the retail price, even though the merchant did not always agree. This method insured that the trader could not charge exorbitant prices and thereby take advantage of his captive market.

In order to maintain the army's traditional class distinction, the post trader normally operated two bars, one for officers, another for soldiers. Frequently the former was termed a "club room," a sophisticated name for what was still a frontier saloon. These drinking establishments were also subject to the authority of the post commander. Just how much latitude was allowed depended, to a great degree, upon the personality and morals of that officer.

As stated earlier, a soldier was normally kept busy doing something during most of each day. This held true, at least until he began to learn the ropes of soldiering. Surprisingly, the army established reasonable limits to the work-day long before labor unions brought about reforms to private industry. Regulations stipulated that during the winter soldiers could be worked up to eight hours and in the summer ten hours. This left free time before and after evening retreat parade, once a man learned that steady maintenance of his accouterments and "brass" would save him time in the long run. At times there were spare minutes during the day between duties when a dry throat could be satisfied. Some non-commissioned officers even chanced to slip away from supervising fatigue parties in order to have a quick refreshment at the enlisted men's bar. "Coffee Coolers" (goldbricks) went to greater extremes, like Pvt. Charles Pemberton of the 9th Infantry band. After reporting for sick call and being ordered to stay "in quarters" by the post surgeon, Pemberton proceeded to get "spiflicated" at the trader's bar. He was hauled off by the guard and later court-martialed for shirking duty in order to get drunk.

Americans have always been quick to seize upon a business opportunity and to turn it into profit. So it was with the entrepreneurs who established the so-called "hog ranches" near Fort Laramie. By law these men were prohibited from conducting business inside the six-by-nine-mile reservation in order to protect the rights of the post trader.

By the same token, these ranches were not hindered by army rules. For instance, at Ecoffey and Cuny's Ranch, just over the boundary to the west, a soldier could get all of the action he wanted. The owners served meals, stocked a good selection of liquor and cigars and usually had in residence a half dozen of the vilest sort of prostitutes. The only hitch was that a written pass was required for a soldier to be more than a mile from the flagstaff.

Many men took their chances as evidenced by a number of recorded trials. The "Three Mile," as it was also called, was only one of several such wicked dens that catered to Fort Laramie's garrison. The "Six Mile," christened with a similar lack of imagination, was also located on the road to Cheyenne. Its reputation was even worse than its neighbor, being a hangout for horse thieves and transient gamblers. The girls there allegedly wore old soldier clothes (probably taken in trade) and helped with the passing stages and other chores. Over the years, at least six men met violent deaths there including, ironically, Adolph Cuny, owner of the "Three Mile."

Owing to its distance from the post, it was usually necessary to obtain a mounted pass to go to the "Six Mile." But, there are always some who must overdo a good thing. On April 21, 1867, Sgt. Kesner of Company A, 2nd Cavalry, decided to take on the "Six Mile" in style. The officers who later sat in judgement of him decided that his "borrowing" an ambulance with a team and then returning roaring drunk was simply going too far. He forfeited his stripes and $10 of his pay.

A number of other sources for "bug juice" sprang up around Fort Laramie during its active years. Places like The Coon Dive, The Brewery and Brown's Hotel were familiar haunts of soldiers who served at the post during the 1860s, '70s and '80s. Now and then these establishments may have offered various enticements to attract business, but they existed primarily to supply one demand—liquor.

It was with good cause that many army officers were alarmed and distressed by the misuse of alcohol in the ranks. It was the single most nagging problem to plague post commanders during the frontier era. In fact, many other problems stemmed from alcoholic abuse.

Morale suffered at Fort Laramie as a consequence of intemperence. Boredom and the lure of the debauchery at the hog ranches led many soldiers to cease caring about proper military order. There were numerous cases like that of Pvt. William McCormick, Company E, 9th Infantry, who left the post without permission one evening in April, 1876, to go on a spree. When he returned the next afternoon about one o'clock, still inebriated, he may have had some regrets. The night out cost him $12 and twenty days at hard labor.

Drunkenness, however, was not confined merely to enlisted men. Although officers were expected to remain above such conduct, they contended with the same basic living conditions imposed upon the rank and file. Instances of alcoholism among officers were certainly not discussed as openly as with soldiers, but they existed nevertheless. Col. A. G. Brackett, commanding Fort Laramie in 1880, requested the department commander to order Capt.

William S. Collins before a retiring board. Brackett complained that Collins was frequently intoxicated to the degree that he could not effectively carry out his duties. Collins was also reported to have been drunk on duty four times while acting as post commander in Brackett's absence. The order to retire the captain was not long in coming. Obviously, officers such as Collins could hardly inspire temperance among their men.

Discipline was rigid; it had to be to keep order among the diverse types of men who comprised the army. When a soldier erred, the ironfisted system made certain that he would not soon forget his mistake. Even so, liquor often caused men to do things which they otherwise would have weighed more carefully. In May, 1876, Trumpeter Antone Blitz reportedly reached a "beastly state of intoxication" at the sutler's store. When a sergeant and several members of the guard attempted to arrest him, Blitz cursed them with a shocking array of foul language and fought with them until he was finally subdued and carried off to the "mill."

Eugene McGee, 2nd Cavalry private, got "loaded" while assigned to the post headquarters as a mounted orderly. The quartermaster sergeant, seeing that McGee was quickly getting out of hand, ordered the man to go with him to the guardhouse. The private unwisely replied, "I'll break your head! You're a god dam Dutch son of a bitch." His actions and poor choice of words cost him $10 plus twenty days behind bars.

Spending time in Fort Laramie's guardhouse was anything but pleasant. The structure used up until 1876 accommodated about two dozen prisoners in an unheated and unlighted sub-story room. No furniture was provided and bedding consisted only of the blankets which the prisoners brought with them. Food was provided by the messes of the respective companies to which the soldiers belonged. Some, however, were sentenced to a bread and water diet.

In many instances, the effects of overindulgence were much more serious. In 1877 two 3rd Cavalry soldiers, Privates McGuire and Browne, tangled at The Brewery near the fort. During the fight McGuire shattered a bottle over Browne's head then, seizing a second one, continued to cudgel Browne until he was severely injured. On another occasion a 5th Cavalry trooper, John Robinson, fell from his horse while drunk, caught his foot in the stirrup, and was dragged. Before the horse could be stopped, Robinson's skull was crushed.

Although drinking was a serious problem at Fort Laramie, there were most certainly attempts to control it. The ineffectiveness of these local measures is evidenced by the fact that cases of recognized alcoholism averaged three to four percent at the fort during the 1870s. This figure, however, reflects neither the actual extent nor the complexity of the situation. Taking the year 1876 as an arbitrary example, we find that of 114 courts-martial, sixty-seven (or 60%) were alcohol-related cases. Of course, these represent only those who were actually arrested and tried. During that year, then, the boards heard an average of over five cases monthly which arose from alcohol abuse. The time of three officers was consumed on each trial prompting one officer to pen his discontent in the following bit of poetry:

> The worst of our dreary routine
> Upon the bleak frontier,
> Is to meet in solemn conclave
> And these stupid cases hear.

The job of controlling the use of liquor usually fell to the post commander. In his omnipotent position, he held ultimate authority over his post and the surrounding vicinity. His primary target was the post trader, since his place of business was located on government property. The various COs tried a number of strategies to curb liquor consumption. Lt. Col. Palmer, for example, issued an 1867 order which required enlisted men to obtain the COs written permission to purchase liquor at the bar. A year later this was modified to allow for the purchase of a "moderate" amount of beer without an order. Down through succeeding years other commanders issued their own orders restricting the quantities and types of beverages to be sold at the establishment, as well as his hours of operation. One of the more interesting ones authorized the trader to sell to each man "two (2) drinks of whiskey each day (Sunday excepted) one between Reveille at 12 P.M. and the other between 1 P.M. and Retreat, neither drink to exceed one gill." Soldiers, challenged to find "loopholes," undoubtedly calculated that with a bit of timing they could obtain the equivalent of a half-pint of whiskey within about an hour's time.

Another way to beat the system was to "import" booze via incoming wagon trains and stages. When this scheme was discovered, the commander saw to it that all such vehicles from Cheyenne were searched by special sentinels.

Chapters of organizations such as the Order of Good Templars sometimes formed at frontier posts and were a great asset in improving the morals of the men who joined. Individuals and even entire companies pledged to abstain from liquor. At Fort Laramie members of the garrison obtained permission to use an old school building for a meeting place.

The month of March, 1881, brought to Fort Laramie the news that President Rutherford B. Hayes had placed prohibition on the sale of liquor at military posts. This proclamation was the strongest reaction yet to habitual drinking in the service.

Anticipating a loss of regular income, the post traders united their efforts to have the order revoked. Even though they were unsuccessful, they did manage to get it "clarified" to exclude the sale of beer, ale, cider, and light wines.

The enlisted men were not, of course, restricted from taking their business to the hog ranches outside the reservations. But the order at least alleviated the extent of drunkenness and disorder at the fort proper by forcing the men to go some distance away for higher-priced booze. There was also a greater possibility that the time and distance factors would tend to sober them on the return trip.

The presidential order would have worked splendidly had it not been for an unforeseen pitfall, that of liquor substitutes. Traders suddenly began doing an increased business in selling Jamaica ginger, bitters, and flavoring extracts—most of which contained 70 to 80% alcohol. These concoctions were certainly not new to soldiers, but when there were better things available to drink it was unnecessary to go on a "cheap drunk." It was inevitable that Fort Laramie's commander had to issue an order to stop the sale of such products.

The fact that some soldiers would drink almost anything and that unscrupulous ranch owners would sell it to them, sometimes spelled tragedy. A 7th Infantry private, James Collins, serving at Fort Laramie in 1887 was found dead on the road north of the post. An autopsy determined the cause of his death to be alcoholic poisoning. Evidently, someone in the area was selling a bad batch of home-brewed "forty-rod."

Another major reform appeared in the mid-1880s with the appearance of post canteens which sold beer, wine, sandwiches and canned delicacies. The canteen idea was effective in curbing drunkenness and it was popular among the soldiers because the business was owned and operated by the men themselves. Margins of profit were intentionally small to allow the soldier's pay to stretch farther and the money which was realized was divided among the shareholding company units. These funds were in turn used to purchase non-issue foods for the messes, sports equipment, barracks furnishings, and whatever else the company might desire. The canteens conflicted with the rights of the traders, but investigation proved that the new clubs were of such great benefit to the men and to discipline that they were allowed to flourish. Thus, at last, the enlisted men had a wholesome place to drink, eat, play games, and relax and at the same time receive the benefits of profits which otherwise would have gone to the pockets of post traders.

By 1890, when the sun finally set on Fort Laramie's long military career and, indeed, the "old" West itself, the army had become the harbinger of a new age. With the Indian Wars all but over, posts would be maintained in more populated locations, recruiting standards would demand higher quality men, soldiers would begin to achieve a degree of respect, and the war with "bug juice" would assume a lesser priority through ensuing years. Possibly drinking to excess was a product of the age and the West itself, a common malady to soldiers and civilians alike. As one old soldier who had served at Fort Laramie put it, "That good old ancient time was an era of drinking. There was no such thing known as 'prohibition,' and nearly everybody drank a little."

Freight and Stage Road from Rawlins to Red Lodge, Montana

THIRD SEGMENT OF TRAIL—MEETEETSE TO CHANCE, MONTANA

Trek No. 28 of the Historical Trail Treks

Sponsored by the Wyoming State Historical Society, the Wyoming State Archives and Historical Department and the Park County Chapter of the Society, the trek was under the direction of David J. Wasden of Cody, second vice president of the Society.

On Friday evening, July 15, the Park County Chapter hosted a get-together at the Cody Auditorium.

More than 160 people boarded busses at 8 a.m. Saturday morning at the Auditorium and traveled south to the L.U. Ranch on Gooseberry Creek. An announcer on each bus read a paper prepared by Mr. Wasden on historical highlights along the route.

A map drawn by Bob Edgar, Cody, was handed to each trekker. While not made to scale, the map clearly showed the relative locations of the sites to be visited.

TRAVEL LOG FOR SATURDAY, JULY 16

By David J. Wasden

On this two-day trek of the Wyoming State Historical Society, with the Park County Chapter acting as host, we will review portions of the original mail, stage and freight routes in use by the early settlers in the western portion of the Big Horn Basin.

This morning we leave the original Stinking Water, going south some forty-six miles to Gooseberry Creek, where the Angus Mc-

---

(Photo opposite page)

—Courtesy of David J. Wasden

This photograph was taken in the summer of 1899 at the ferry at Clark's Fork River at Sirrine, when Edith Anna Wiley Sherwin of Minneapolis, daughter of Solon L. Wiley, and wife of William Henry Sherwin, with her two daughters visited Wiley on the Germania Bench. The trip was made to Red Lodge by train and then by buckboard across country, according to Mrs. Marion Sherwin Chapman, granddaughter of Wiley. In the picture Marion stands next to her mother on the ferry and her sister Helen is next to her. The other two persons in the picture are unidentified.

Donald ranch was located. We are passing Beck Lake, used by
Cody for water storage. Alkali Lake is to the east. The Cody
Canal, started in 1895, was some twelve years in building. George
T. Beck conceived the idea and served as manager during its con-
struction. The system, which diverts water from the South Fork,
irrigates some 12,000 acres.

Sage Creek, to the east of us, was originally named Meeteetse
Creek in 1873 by Captain William A. Jones. (The first mail and
freight road, after leaving the Stinking Water at Corbett, followed
up this stream channel on the way south.)

Carter Mountain, coming into view, was named for Judge William A. Carter of Fort Bridger, who sent a herd of cattle into the
Basin in the fall of 1879 under the management of Peter McCul-
lough. This was one of the first herds to enter the Basin.

Sage Creek crossing is about the point where Solon L. Wiley
intended to cross with his canal, bringing water from the South
Fork to a storage reservoir in Oregon Basin, to reclaim about
200,000 acres of land lying to the east and extending to the Big
Horn River. This work was started soon after the turn of the
century. After sinking a half million dollars in the project, he
ran out of money and the project was never finished. The U.S.
Bureau of Reclamation has since made soil surveys and determined
that only about one-tenth of the intended acreage is suitable for
farming. Wiley's first canal venture, on the Germania Bench,
was very successful.

The Oregon Basin oil field, east of the highway, has been one
of the most productive fields in the entire state.

According to legend, Josh Dean once took refuge from unfriendly Indians on Elk Butte, to the east, when he was carrying
the mail, before the days of regular mail service.

When the Carter cattle were being trailed to the Stinking Water
drainage for grazing, one obstreperous bull, upon reaching this
point, decided he had migrated far enough and refused to go any
farther. The men left him, thinking he would die there, but in the
spring he was found in good shape. Since the bull came from
Oregon, the Basin took the name of the "Oregon Basin".

(We cross the North and South Forks of Dry Creek, which drains
into the Big Horn River at Greybull. This is Meeteetse Creek.
Old Meeteetse, with a cemetery to mark its location, is up the
creek about three miles. Five miles farther up the creek is where
Victor Arland and John Corbett established their last trading post
in 1884. It remained a gathering and trading location for a large
area until about 1890)

The range of mountains to the west, running north and south,
was first named "Yellowstone," following the name given to the
river that drains the area. In 1873 Captain William A. Jones
changed the name to "Sierra Shoshone". This name quickly came
into public use and had practically replaced the original name by

1880. In 1883 the U.S. Geological Survey disregarded both of the previous names and substituted "Absaroka," the Indian name for the Crow nation. This was later confirmed by the U.S. Board on Geographical Names.

About fifteen miles up the Greybull River, west of Meeteetse, Otto Franc located the famous Pitchfork ranch in 1878. The next season he brought in a herd of 1200 to 1500 head of cattle, via South Pass, which he had purchased in western Montana.

The names "Stinking Water" and "Shoshone", referring to the same river, have been used interchangeably. There can be little doubt as to why the Crow Indians, who had a favorite camping spot near the east side of the canyon, gave the stream the name of "Stinking Water". A sulphurous odor came from the springs near the canyon. This name was used by early trappers and mountain men and appeared on early maps. It is not certain who changed the name to Shoshone, but it may have been George T. Beck. The company he organized to build the Cody Canal in 1895 was called The Shoshone Land and Irrigation Company. A year later, in 1896, he referred to the Shoshone River when promoting Cody for the county seat of the new county of Big Horn, just being organized. Some local color was lost when the Wyoming State Legislature changed the name from Stinking Water to Shoshone in 1901. The bill effecting the change was introduced by Atwood C. Thomas of Meeteetse, senator from Big Horn County at the time.

Count Otto Franc von Lichenstein, of German royalty, became a stellar figure in the cattle business. He was a good business manager, progressive and far-seeing. Small in stature and known as "the little man", he was a dynamo of action. He bought a bicycle and was the first cowboy on wheels as he rode considerable distances over the range. He was far ahead of his time in the conservation practices he initiated on his ranch. He ran between six and seven thousand head of cattle, depending on feed and market conditions. He died in 1903 and is buried in the Meeteetse cemetery.

At the site of Half Way House Stage Stop on the North Fork of Dry Creek a rock dug-out near a fresh water spring in the hill side was established in 1903 as a stage "noon stop", where horses were changed and meals served. This was halfway between Corbett Crossing and the frontier town of Meeteetse. In 1904 Half Way Stop had a newfangled telephone complete with a large "Public Telephone" sign. The station was abandoned in 1908 after automobiles began to use the route, but the spring remained in use for many years.

After the railroad arrived in Cody in November, 1901, travel originated there rather than at Corbett. The Red Lodge to Corbett road was no longer needed. A road was located from Meeteetse to Thermopolis via Kirby, and "Bronco Nell,'" a character in her own right, is credited with driving the first load of freight from Cody to Thermopolis. This route left from southwest of Cody and went through the hills to Sage Creek. At the Frost ranch, instead of following the old road via Arland, it veered to the east as it proceeded south.

The Stockgrower and Farmer in June, 1903, tells of the improved mail and passenger service from Cody, and admonished: "Let no smooth-mouth, mild mannered individuals at any side track between Toluca and Cody delude you." This was a dirty dig at Garland, which for five years was the gateway for the greater portion of the Basin.

Cedar Mountain was first called "Spirit Mountain" by the Crow Indians. But Captain William A. Jones, on his reconnaissance trip in 1873, in deference to his Shoshone scouts, changed the name to Cedar Mountain.

The first stop of the morning was at the LU Ranch, where the following paper was read.

THE EARLY MAIL AND FREIGHT ROUTE IN WESTERN BIG HORN BASIN

By David J. Wasden

The problem of locating and defining early roads in the western portion of the Big Horn Basin is confusing because alternate routes were used. Roads would sometimes be changed to accommodate a new ranch or to service a new post office. The Angus McDonald Ranch, which later became part of the LU, is one which has remained fairly consistently on the road.

The question often arises as to how the mountain men found their way around in a new and unmapped country. They followed stream courses, made note of directions by way of the sun and the stars, and received guidance from the Indians who knew the country and unerringly located trails along the easiest grades and most direct routes.

While much argument centers around the exact path of John Colter's historic trip in the winter of 1807-1808, it is reasonable to accept the premise that he followed a much-used Indian trail on his journey south from the Stinking Water near Cody over the Owl Creek Mountains on his way to Jackson Hole and the Teton Basin. It is logical to assume he passed near the LU Ranch. This route could also have been used by early trappers and miners. Josh Dean, who instituted the first mail service in the Basin in 1876, used this route to bring mail from Camp Brown on a pack horse.

An attempt was made to locate a wagon road connecting Point of Rocks on the Union Pacific railroad with Fort Ellis, Montana. On May 15, 1873, the War Department issued an order to Captain

William A. Jones, Corps of Engineers. He was to "proceed as soon as practical to Northwestern Wyoming and there make a reconnaissance of the country within the territory about the headwaters of the Snake, Green, Big Horn, Greybull, Clark's Fork and Yellowstone Rivers. He will organize and equip his party at Fort Bridger." Second Lieutenant S. E. Blant was to accompany him as assistant and Assistant Surgeon C. L. Heizman as medical officer. Company I, Second Cavalry, was detailed as escort for the expedition. The party included a geologist, a botanist and meteorologist, a chemist, an astronomer and four topographers. The War Department allowed $8000 for the survey, which Captain Jones felt "was ample." The party measured the distance traveled by three odometers carried on a wheel attached to a pair of shafts arranged for moving over rough ground and through timber. Captain Jones kept a complete account of each day's activities, of the terrain passed over, vegetation encountered, and temperatures. Following are some notes taken from his journals, "Reconnaissance of Northwestern Wyoming 1873."

"June 13, after breaking camp on Big Muddy, trouble was experienced crossing that stream because of the high spring runoff. Later that day more trouble was encountered at Ham's Fork. It took the rest of that day and all the next to effect a crossing because of boggy lowlands which necessitated the unloading of the wagons and the men carrying the goods to firm ground."

"June 21. Broke camp 5:30 a.m. in a driving rain storm which turned to snow. Made stage station at Pacific Spring."

Here the party received word from Fort Stambaugh of hostile Indians in the neighborhood. Three wagons and teams were turned in at Fort Stambaugh before proceeding north. On June 28 Murphy's "ranch" on Little Popo Agie River was reached, where the Captain noted vegetables and cereals were being raised. The next day the company arrived at the site of Old Camp Brown on the North Fork of Big Popo Agie River where there was a small settlement of white people, including several women. Shortly afterward Indians killed two of the women. On June 30 the company reached Camp Brown, situated on the right bank of Little Wind River. The Captain learned that "Bryan is the chief point of shipping supplies to the Wind River posts—the distance being 146 miles."

Several days were spent at Camp Brown making preparations for continuing the journey to Fort Ellis, Montana, by pack outfit. Ten Shoshone Indians, hired as guides, insisted on taking their families along. This seemed a good idea, as hostile Indians would be less likely to attack a party with women and children.

On July 9 the expedition was ready to leave Camp Brown for Fort Ellis, but the army mules objected to being used as pack animals, and it was possible to move the camp only a half mile that day, across the river. Most of the next day was spent repairing broken packs and gathering up the contents so only the 8.4 miles to Sage Creek were traveled.

On July 16 the foothills of the Owl Creek Mountains were reached. The country was described as "desolate." The following day the mountains were crossed and camp made on the Middle Fork of Owl Creek. Some time was spent at this camp exploring the mountain peaks to the west, and on the 19th Captain Jones named the "Washakee Needles—a terrible crag 12,250 feet elevation." Three of the party succeeded in climbing within 200 feet of the top.

Captain Jones gave to Cottonwood Creek the Shoshone name of "Mee-yer-o" Creek. He noted an outcropping of coal nearby and also that this was a favorite range for buffalo and other game. On July 22 the party reached Beaver Creek. This was renamed Goosberry—"feeling little apprehension the name would be duplicated." Some Shoshone Indians who had come from the Stinking Water met them here and reported vast herds of buffalo.

Wednesday, July 23, they reached the Greybull River—"a stream of considerable size." The next day the party crossed the divide between the two rivers, the Greybull and the Stinking Water, and "Mee-tee-tse" Creek was named. This creek empties into the Stinking Water, and today is called Sage Creek.

On Friday, July 25, the group came to Chief Washakie's main hunting camp in the foothills of Carter Mountain. Seven more Shoshones were recruited here for the journey to Fort Ellis. The height of the mountain was estimated at 8607 feet. Present day U.S.G.S. records give this point as 8550 feet. The next day, July 26, the area around the junction of the North and South Forks of the Stinking Water was reconnoitered. The Captain gave the name "Ish-a-woo-a- River" to the South Fork. "I have given this stream the Indian name of a peculiar-shape rock, by means of which they distinguish it."

The party proceeded up the North River, through the Park to Fort Ellis, and then made the return via the Wind River to Camp Brown. Captain Jones gave a good report on the possibility of establishing a military road from the Point of Rocks on the Union Pacific to Fort Ellis going up the Wind River and entering the Park from the south, rather than attempting a road over the Owl Creek Mountains. This was looked upon with favor by his immediate superiors, but not so by an authority farther up the line of command, as evidenced by a latter date Chicago, May 16, 1874, to W. D. Whipple, Assistant Adjutant General, Headquarters for the Army, Washington, D.C.

"Colonel: The enclosed order was issued in order to give Captain William A. Jones, Engineer's Corps, a chance to have his work of last summer published; but I wish it to be distinctly understood that I in no manner can endorse the contemplated road from the Point of Rocks on the Union Pacific Railroad to Fort Ellis, via Yellowstone Lake, as a military necessity.

"If the Government desire to make appropriations for the benefit of the mining population at Atlantic City, and the settlers in and about Camp Brown in the Popo Agie Valley, I have no objection; but I am not prepared to give even a shadow of support to anything so absurd as the military necessity for such a road.

"The land transportation now via Carroll on the Missouri River to Fort Ellis is only two hundred and twenty miles over a good road.

"I am, Colonel, very respectfully, your obedient servant,
P. H. Sheridan, Lieutenant General, Commanding"

The earliest reference found to a wagon traversing the entire western sector of the Basin was in the fall of 1878. Fincelius G. Burnett and some associates left Fort Washakie in the summer for Bozeman and Virginia City to buy cattle, as Burnett had a contract to furnish beef to the Indian Agency. A wagon and two yoke of oxen were purchased to carry supplies for the return trip. Arrangements had been made with Chief Washakie for Shoshone Indians to act as guides and help with the return drive. After leaving Clark's Fork, the route led up Pat O'Hara Creek, across Skull Creek divide, then down Cottonwood creek to the Stinking Water at present day Cody. After crossing the river the trail went up Sage Creek (or Meeteetse Creek, as it was still known) and over the divide to the Greybull River. The course held south to Gooseberry Creek and on to Owl Creek. At times the Indians reported back that it was impossible to take the wagon any farther over the rugged terrain, but somehow a way was always found to move the wagon along with the herd of cattle.

There was no established road nor need for one on the western side of the Basin until 1879 when the cattle interests began moving in and making permanent settlements. They looked not only to Lander, but increasingly to Coulson on the Yellowstone River, for supplies.

Coulson, which was the forerunner of Billings, was named for S. B. Coulson, who had a government contract for moving freight on the upper Missouri River. On May 26, 1874, his steamboat, "Josephine", started up the Yellowstone River and reached a point two miles above present-day Billings on June 7 before turning around. The settlement of Coulson was started in 1876 when a man named Freth, Henry Kieser, and William and P. W. McAdow of Bozeman settled there.

P. W. McAdow started a store and hotel which also became a stage stop the following year when a stage line connecting with Bozeman was started in the Yellowstone valley. A post office was established, located next to Chicago Jane's Boudoir. Because of rapids and islands in the river, the boats did not attempt to go much beyond the mouth of the Big Horn River, where Junction City was located. Goods were freighted overland from that point.

McAdow set up a sawmill, and the logs were rafted down the river. Soon two men, Ash and Boots, built a brewery. Coulson took on stature and had an estimated population of 1000 when the Northern Pacific railroad arrived on August 22, 1882.

Billings was started two miles to the west and was called "The Magic City." A count on October 22, 1882, showed 155 business houses, 99 residences, one church, six railroad buildings, and 25 tents, and the town was estimated to contain 1500 to 2000 people.

The county commissioners of newly organized Fremont County, in their meeting of May 6, 1884, declared the following route a county road, the first in the Basin to be defined: "Commencing at the present wagon crossing on South Fork of Owl Creek, thence to the North Fork of Owl Creek, thence down Grass Creek to Baxter's Ranch, thence over to Sage Creek, thence to Stinking Water at Wagon Crossing."

The Stinking Water was crossed on a bridge built in 1883 and paid for by subscriptions from the cattlemen, the Northern Pacific railroad and the merchants of Billings, cost $5000. Just north of Corbett, as this point became known, the road forked, the early mail route going up Cottonwood Creek to Pat O'Hara Creek and Clark's Fork, which stream it followed down to Billings; and the freight road ascending Pole Cat Bench on the southwestern corner, crossing the Bench to the east side at the head of Pole Cat Creek, then up Sage Creek and through Pryor Gap, down Pryor Creek and across by Blue Creek to the Yellowstone River, which was crossed on a ferry to Billings.

The trek busses retraced the route to Meeteetse, where they stopped at the city park and heard two papers relating to the history of the town.

THE STORY BEHIND THE NAMING OF MEETEETSE

By David J. Wasden

Originally published in Cody Enterprise Stampede Edition, 1976

There is much speculation as to how the name of "Meeteetse" originated. To find an answer it is necessary to review a number of historical incidents.

In the summer of 1873, Captain William A. Jones was commissioned by the Army to investigate the possibility of establishing a wagon road to Fort Ellis in Montana. At Fort Brown he acquired a number of Shoshone Indians to act as guides on the expedition.

Proceeding north from the Greybull river, he crossed a divide and came to the headwaters of a small stream that flowed north into the Stinking Water. His Shoshone guides called this stream

"Mee-tee-tse" Creek.   This name thus appeared on a map, sheet number 3, of Western Territories prepared by Major G. L. Gillespie of the Corps of Engineers under date of January 1876.

On a map dated 1879 of the Territory of Wyoming, issued by the General Land Office of the Department of the Interior, what is now known as Sage Creek was still designated as "Mee-tee-tse Creek", its drainage course being northerly into the Stinking Water.

The Andrew B. Wilson family moved westward from their home at Lawrence, Kansas, settling for a time near Pueblo, Colorado. In the summer of 1880 the family started for the Yellowstone valley in Montana, their route taking them through the Big Horn Basin.

In the late fall, as they came to Mee-tee-tse Creek, they were caught in a severe storm and decided to spend the winter near what was later known as the Frost Ranch.   The Wilsons liked the site and decided to stay, naming their new location "Mee-tee-tse", after the creek.

The first post office in the Basin was established as "Franc" at the Pitchfork Ranch on September 15, 1882, with Otto Franc as postmaster.   Nine months later, June 14, 1883, the post office was moved to the Wilson ranch and took the name of "Meeteetse", with Mrs. Margaret B. Wilson as postmaster.   After Mr. Wilson's death March 2, 1886, his wife and sons continued the ranching operation.   The Wilson ranch location, as well as the post office, were known as "Meeteetse".

By the early 1890's, a new community was forming on the north bank of the Greybull River some four miles south of Meeteetse post office.   This was on a popular travel route and was replacing Arland as a trade and social center.   A saloon or two came into operation along with a bawdy house and a small assortment of miscellaneous buildings appeared.

The bright lights proved too much of a temptation for Mrs. Wilson, who left the ranch and moved "to town", taking the Meeteetse post office with her.   Just when she made the move has not been verified but it was some time before 1896, possibly in 1893.

Atwood C. Thomas owned a store and took care of the post office at Sunshine on Wood River.   Perceiving the possibility of establishing a permanent town where the community was developing on the Greybull River, he and his wife had W. S. Collins survey a townsite in January, 1896.   A plot of ground was obtained from William McMally who had filed on a homestead in 1887, where he had operated a blacksmith shop.

The area surveyed and platted contained 36.6 acres.   When it came to selecting a name for the new town, it was only natural to select Meeteetse, the name of the post office already in operation on the north side of the river.   The instrument of dedication was signed in the presence of M. F. Clark and J. M. Frost, and the map drawn by Collins was duly filed in the office of John Gillis, County Clerk and Registrar of Deeds for Fremont County in Lander on February 25, 1896. Thus the town acquired the name originally given to a creek draining into the Stinking Water.

The Shoshone Indian word has been variously interpreted to mean the "meeting place", "a long way to water", and "near by". The late L. G. Phelps was told by the Indians the word indicated the meeting place, and the distance to it was determined by the pronunciation of Meeteetse. If the syllables were long and drawn out, the place was far away, but if the word was said in short, clipped syllables the place was close by.

By 1904, Meeteetse had a population of 400. At one time it had two banks and two newspapers. The Meeteetse Mercantile boasted of having the largest and most complete stock of merchandise of any store in the Basin.

HISTORY OF THE MEETEETSE MERCANTILE

By J. Randle Moody

In Wyoming is Meeteetse, and in Meeteetse is the Mercantile. This store is worth traveling to Wyoming to inspect . . . . Mail order houses find it hard sledding to Meeteetse because the people who came in for miles around to buy supplies have confidence in the store and its management. High quality goods are featured, and there is system and snap to the business in every department.
—*Ginger,* Duluth, Minnesota, 1917.

In the spring of 1899, A. J. McDonald purchased Sylvia Mikkelson's millinery store on the corner of Park and State Streets in Meeteetse. Here he opened his general merchandise store with a small stock consisting of groceries, hardware, shoes, dry goods, and ladies' and gentlemen's furnishings. The success of this small store encouraged McDonald to expand the building to a total area of forty-two by fifty feet. His capital investment then totalled some $30,000.

On September 1, 1902, McDonald sold the store to Fred C. Nagel & Co., which was formed by Nagel, R. B. West, and E. E. Lonabaugh. Because of financial difficulties they turned the business back to McDonald in 1903, when the Meeteetse Mercantile Company was incorporated with Angus J. McDonald, E. E. Lonabaugh, W. S. Metz, Alex A. Linton, and C. L. Tewksbury as stockholders. In 1904 they were joined by W. O. Steele, Robert Steele, and W. T. Hogg. Alex A. Linton became manager when the company was formed and remained so until the store was sold to L. G. Phelps in 1917.

Soon after the incorporation of the Mercantile, an annex was built and was used as the company's entire store. The original building was used as a warehouse and occasionally housed the post office.

The original Mikkelson building and the addition built by Mc-Donald were razed in September of 1917. Work began on construction of an addition, which, when completed, would make the Mercantile one of the largest general merchandise stores in the Big Horn Basin. In early September, 1918, Mercantile Manager C. H. Davidson announced that the building was nearly complete, and on Saturday, September 21, 1918, the addition was dedicated by a free dance on its new forty-two by forty-four foot floor, the largest room offered to that date for a Meeteetse dance. Throughout the ensuing fifty-nine years the Meeteetse Mercantile has changed little in outward appearance, and has remained a viable institution.

The next stop was near the old Mahlon Frost ranch on Sage Creek. Dick Frost, grandson of Mahlon Frost, gave an informal talk that included humorous anecdotes of his grandfather's early ranching experiences.

Returning to Cody, the trekkers enjoyed a delicious lunch at the Cody Auditorium then disbanded for the afternoon. Many people visited the Buffalo Bill Historical Center and the Whitney Gallery of Western Art, and others visited Bob Edgar's Trail Town, the Homesteader's Museum at Powell and the Edward T. Grigware mural at the L.D.S. Church.

The group gathered again in the Auditorium for dinner and a delightful program of music directed by Anita Hindman of Cody.

The trek was resumed at 8 a.m. Sunday morning and the busses headed north. Again, a paper prepared by Mr. Wasden was read on each bus.

TRAVEL LOG FOR SUNDAY, JULY 17

This morning we will travel north forty miles to Chance, Montana, to see portions of the old mail route from Billings to Lander and a later road, the so-called Red Lodge to Meeteetse Trail, which continued south.) We will cross the Shoshone River on the third bridge to span the stream at this point. (The first was promoted by George T. Beck, and was in use by April 20, 1898. It eliminated a half day of travel via Corbett on the way to Red Lodge.) The second was a Burlington Railroad bridge. The present concrete bridge was built by the Wyoming Highway Department in 1949.

The fire-scarred mountain to the west is Rattlesnake Mountain. The fire started on Monday, July 29, 1960, shortly after noon on a clear sunshiny day. A thunderhead came across the mountain and a bolt of lightning struck dry down-timber in a steep canyon about midway on the mountain. The fire quickly worked up out of the canyon, and, spread by mountain winds, was soon out of control. Some natural reseeding is taking place along with a small number of planted seedlings. Perhaps in a hundred years the mountain will be green again.

Trail Creek, which runs through a narrow valley at the base of the mountain, was named for the old Indian Trace which traversed its length. It was on this creek, ten miles from Cody, that Victor Arland and John F. Corbett set up the first mercantile establishment in the Basin upon their arrival, September 10, 1880. It was here that the first potatoes and vegetables of record were raised in the Big Horn Basin.

Arland and Corbett moved their trading post to Cottonwood Creek in the summer of 1883. The finished lumber, windows, and other materials would have been hauled from Billings, for by that time the railroad was hauling supplies in from the east. The two partners used this location for only a short time, moving their business south to Meeteetse Creek the next year. The property on Cottonwood Creek was sold to a Frenchman, Count De Mailly, who had bought 1500 head of cattle in 1883. Wishing to return to France, he left the operation in care of a countryman, Reue Vion. The number of cattle assessed for taxes in 1886 was 800. It dropped to 500 in 1889.

The early mail route passed this way, going down the creek a mile and a half before swinging northeast to the wagon crossing on the Stinking Water. Dave McFall had the ranch for a time after Vion left the country. Near the turn of the century Reuben C. Hargraves, a sheepman from Lusk, acquired the property. In addition to sheep, Hargraves had a string of harness race horses and a practice track down the creek. The small stream we will follow for a distance now is called Cottonwood Creek. On the early Colter map published in 1814, it was designated Valley River. The present highway parallels the original mail route.

At the second bridge a later cut-off road left the old mail road, going over to Corbett to cross the river. Today this is called Three Crossings, although the location is a mile north of where the early road crossed the creek three times in a short distance. This is just below the buildings to the right of us, the location of an early fish hatchery.

To the west of us is Monument Hill, so named because of stone monuments built by sheepherders. Possibly some were a legacy of the Indians, who were accustomed to mark their way with stone cairns.

Heart Mountain is on our right. The name comes from an Indian word meaning "heart", because to them the highest pinnacle resembled the point of a human heart. Looking at it from the Cody side, it could well be called "Face Mountain," for it has the appearance of a giant face with a wart on the chin.

Argument still persists as to the correct spelling of this mountain. On the first map Captain William Clark made of the area in 1808 when he descended the Missouri River with Manuel Lisa, the "e" was deleted, resulting in "Hart" Mountain. This type of spelling was characteristic of Clark, as any one will discover in reading his journals. On the map published in 1814 giving Colter's route of 1807-1808, the placement is wrong but the spelling is correct, and thus it continued to appear on early maps. There have been many tales about it being named for a horse thief or some non-existent army officer. But it was definitely not named for any individual, saint or sinner.

Skull Creek Divide was named, according to legend, because of the number of human skulls found lying in the vicinity, evidently the result of an Indian battle. This is a divide between the watersheds of the Shoshone and Clark's Fork rivers. This ridge, because of its gumbo soil, as well as its steep grade, was very difficult to negotiate when wet. As one old-timer explained the situation, the mud would build up in the wheels and against the wagon box to where the wheels "would turn backwards". This was one of the reasons for locating a road around the east side of Heart Mountain after the railroad came to Red Lodge.

We are now following Skull Creek down into Pat O'Hara Creek. The old road was on the west side of the creek. Remnants of an improved roadway can be seen. We are still following quite closely the early mail route.

The mountain peak to the west was originally labeled "Blue Bead Mountain," and the stream that drains from it, "Blue Bead River." The names were changed from Blue Bead to Pat O'Hara, a legacy of an Irish mountain man.

Ahead and to the right is Pryor Mountain. The notch to the west is Pryor Gap, through which the freight wagon passed on its way south from Billings. The eastern part of the Basin was served by this route for mail as well as freight. This was the favored freight road for the western part of the Basin, as it was shorter than the mail route. The stream that heads in the mountain area and drains into the Yellowstone River was named for Sergeant Nathaniel Pryor of the Corps of Discovery. The mountain did not take the name of Pryor until the late 1800s.

To the west is Bald Ridge. This is pointed out as being the logical escape route of the Nez Perce Indians under the leadership of Chief Joseph in early September, 1877. Chief Joseph was a great military strategist and had infuriated the officers of the United States army by outwitting and out-maneuvering them all the way from Oregon. After the encounter with the army in the Park during the last days of August, where the Nez Perce again outsmarted General O. O. Howard, the Indians left the Park and went down the Clark's Fork drainage. Colonel Samuel D. Sturgis was detailed to stop them as they emerged from the mountains. While much of the Indian movement can be determined from army records, there is a period of a few days when they were separated from the army and their movements are unclear.

Colonel Sturgis broke camp on Red Lodge Creek September 1, 1877, and marched up the Clark's Fork, arriving at the Canyon on September 4, and remained there until September 8. He waited for the Indians to fall into the trap the army had set, but no Indians appeared. A reconnaissance was made, which found the Indian camp back in the mountains. They appeared to be headed for Stinking Water Pass, but this actually was a ruse to draw the army away from the escape route. A few Indians made it appear the entire camp was moving by dragging small trees and brush, stirring up the dust. The army fell for this and made a hurried march toward the Stinking Water Pass. They camped for the night on upper Pat O'Hara Creek. There were no signs of Indians, and the troops proceeded to Stinking River the next day, marched up to a basin and camped for the night. When they realized that they had again been outwitted, they retraced their steps and, on September 11, picked up the Indian trail twelve miles from the Canyon. They met Chief Joseph's party at Canyon Creek west of present day Billings the morning of September 12. A skirmish was fought and the Indians were again victorious.

Some writers have claimed that the Indians came down through Clark's Fork Canyon, but others consider this impossible, contending that, with the army out of the way as a result of their ruse, a fast march was made over Bald Ridge.

The army was composed of 295 enlisted men, fourteen officers and an unknown number of Crow scouts. Major Jeremy B. Wright, U.S. Army, Retired, supplied information from army records, the source of much of the above.

TWO DOT RANCH

By David J. Wasden

Among the first three cattle ranches in the Big Horn Basin a century ago was the notable one started by John W. Chapman which later became known as the "Two Dot". Chapman was born June 15, 1850, at Springfield, Illinois, and died at Red Lodge, Montana, December 18, 1933. Chapman settled in western Oregon as a child. The range land in western Oregon had become overstocked, and during the summer of 1878 Chapman helped move some cattle eastward to Harney County. Upon completing the job, he took a pack outfit and started on an exploratory trip to find a new ranch location. He passed through Idaho, over Monida Pass to Virginia City, Montana; then over Bozeman Pass and down the Yellowstone valley as far as Miles City. On his return west, he went up the Clark's Fork. He followed one of its tributaries, Pat O'Hara Creek, for a distance. From the brow of a hill, he had a view of a small valley that abounded in luxuriant ripened grass.

Chapman returned to Oregon and began making preparations to move to that site in Wyoming. As he retraced his way down the Clark's Fork, he encountered the soldiers under General Miles who had participated in a battle with the Bannock Indians. Chapman accompanied General Miles and his troops through Yellowstone Park as they followed some of the Bannocks who had escaped from the battle.

In the summer of 1879, Chapman brought a herd of 1200 Oregon cows and 80 head of good quality horses to the Basin, coming via Virginia City and Bozeman. Upon his arrival he began putting up buildings for a ranch headquarters. Later he returned to Oregon for a bride, Miss Alphia Chapman (no previous relationship). He married her in April, 1881 and returned with her to Wyoming, bringing along a band of 600 horses, which he divided with John Weaver.

Chapman used Percheron stallions and produced good quality work horses, for which there was a ready market. Horse thieves also found these horses desirable. In the late fall of 1891, when riding the range, Chapman found himself short some 200 head. With some extra men, he picked up the trail of the thieves on the north side of Heart Mountain and followed it south to the Frost Ranch on Sage Creek, over the Meeteetse Rim and to Jackson Hole, where the horses were found on the Cunningham Ranch on Spread Creek. Four men were implicated in the theft. The ring leaders were shot and killed, while the others were allowed to go.

The next spring brought more horse thievery when horses belonging to several ranchers were moved east. In March a group of men met at the Dilworth Ranch to go in pursuit, and Otto Franc sent a rider from the Pitchfork to join in the hunt. It is noted that about this time work horses sold for a cent a pound.

Chapman's cattle, also, were of good quality, and his bulls were in demand by other stockmen in the Basin. He ranged his stock from the Stinking Water north into Montana. Figures differ as to the size of his operation. The assessment roll of Fremont County for 1886 showed him assessed with sixty cattle and one stud horse. Three years later he was assessed on 300 cattle and 68 horses. On the other hand, individuals acquainted with his operation estimated his horse herd to number between 700 and 800 head, and the cattle to run about 3000 head.

Much of the story of the Two Dot ranch is sketchy and incomplete. Some of it can only be guessed at. In 1903 Chapman sold the ranch to John P. Allison, a banker from Sioux City, Iowa, and his partner, E. M. Bent. Allison visited the ranch in the summer, but never made it his home. There is a question as to the scope of the operation under their ownership. In addition to 1000 cattle bought from Chapman for $38 a head, they expanded into the

sheep business. Apparently Chapman also had been interested in
sheep, as he had been assessed for 2250 sheep valued at $2812 in
1886 on the Fremont County taxrolls, the first band of sheep on
record in the Basin.

Martin and John Jobe, in addition to managing the ranch for
Chapman before he sold it, had a partnership agreement with him
in regard to livestock. This relationship continued while Allison
owned the property, for when his estate was settled, only real estate
was considered. The Jobe brothers continued their association
with the ranch while Barth and Ganguet owned it, after Allison's
death.

Allison died in Woodbury County, Iowa, July 19, 1910. On
November 18, 1910, the court appointed C. S. Parks, Jr., Martin
A. Jobe, and A. J. Martin as appraisers. They found the ranch
included 3510.79 acres, valued at $46,000. The real estate passed
to Allison's living heirs. Joseph Ganguet, a Frenchman, after
being in the country for some time, formed a partnership with
August H. Barth, a sheepman living in Billings who ran sheep
along the Clark's Fork and near Big Timber. Ganguet had a one-
fourth interest in the Two Dot Ranch, and Barth the remaining
three-fourths, having bought out the interests of the Allison heirs
in late 1915 or early 1916. Ganguet brought his wife and three
daughters from France and took over active management of the
ranch. There are some interesting stories told of the difficulties
the family had with the English language and in adjusting to
western customs of living, and of Mrs. Ganguet's physical strength
and size.

Ganguet was a great trader and the number of sheep belonging
to the ranch at any one time varied considerably. According to
stories, he would buy bands of sheep if he felt the price to be right.
The sheep would be started for the home range, but if a buyer
came along and offered a price that would show a profit on the
transaction, the sheep would be sold. The public domain was
still open and the forage was there for one forceful enough to take
it. It has been estimated that the Barth and Ganguet operation
at times would run as high as 20,000 head, occasionally probably
more. It was necessary to have a sizeable crew of men, in addition
to the Jobe brothers, who continued to stay on with the ranch. As
several of the men had families, a school was established. A census taken in 1922 showed ten children between the ages of six and
eighteen. In 1918 the county set up a polling district for the
benefit of the voters under the name of Ganguet and the name
remained in use until the election in 1964.

During Prohibition, some of the ranch help engaged in the
profitable activity of moonshining. With large amounts of supplies
on hand for the ranch and sheep camp needs, it was easly to
syphon off ingredients to make distilled spirits without arousing too
much suspicion. The law officers suspected the activity was going

on but had little luck apprehending the violators. According to stories, Charley Kraus and Leon Vandierendonk, who had a homestead on the creek and worked for the ranch, would have a stock of several fifty-gallon barrels of booze hidden in various places at any one time. Jack Spicer was another known moonshiner in the area. Those in the know say there were at least a half dozen known distillery locations adjacent to the ranch proper.

The question arises as to when the name "Two Dot" was applied to the ranch. When Chapman owned it, it was referred to as the Chapman ranch. During the time Allison and Bent owned the property it was called the Allison ranch. The legacy came about from a sheep brand that Ganguet used, that of two dots. Thus the name came into use, identifying the ranch with the brand, and has so remained.

On January 3, 1919, Barth sold the ranch to Frank L. Hudson of Lander on contract. The principal sum was $83,000, $11,000 being paid on signing the agreement and a note given for the remaining $72,000 to be paid before January 3, 1922, bearing eight percent interest. This included the deeded land which by now had increased to 4481 acres, and interest in a number of land leases. The transaction included "all farm machinery, ranch horses, swine, farm implements, cattle, wagons, harness and household furniture now on said ranch."

August H. Barth died at Rochester, Minnesota, March 25, 1920. On August 25, 1920, Joseph Ganguet was granted ancillary letters of administration in regard to the estate by the district court. The court records note that under date of December 15, 1921, Hudson had defaulted on his note for the "Two Dot" ranch. The estate was closed on May 14, 1923, with an appraised value of $78,925.28. Ganguet's share was one-fourth, or $19,731.32 and Barth's heirs' share was $59,193.96.

When Hudson defaulted on the purchase agreement in 1921, it appears that Ganguet again took over the management of the ranch. In 1924, Annie Barth sold the ranch to James N. McKnight of Texas who continued with a sheep operation. But evil days came upon the sheep industry and McKnight went bankrupt. On January 31, 1931, McKnight gave a warranty deed to Ernest J. Goppert as trustee in bankruptcy for the ranch land. McKnight remained on the place for a time, leasing the holdings in 1933 to Frank L. Clark and George M. Heald.

Charles W. and Lloyd Taggart, who had a general contracting business in Cody, became interested in the Two Dot property and bought it in 1934. They did not take possession until the following year because of the Clark and Heald lease. The ranch once again became a cattle operation, the Taggarts running a fine herd of Hereford cattle. At the time of this transaction there was about 7000 acres of deeded land. Aware that with changing times and conditions free grazing on public lands was drawing to a close, the

Taggarts began buying up homesteads and deeded land that previously had been leased. When they disposed of their holdings in 1963 to the Nolaco Growth Fund, there was about 60,000 deeded acres under consideration. The Taggart interests owned and operated the Two Dot for 29 years, longer than any other owner.

The next owners continued running cattle, bringing in a trainload of rather common stock from Browning, Montana. This operation continued until 1975 when the Ken Rogge Lumber Company of Oregon was interested briefly before a transfer was made to the present ownership only in 1977.

PAT O'HARA CREEK

By David J. Wasden

Information about the first white resident of this area, for whom Pat O'Hara Creek is named, is sketchy and incomplete. According to stories, Pat O'Hara first came to the Basin in 1854 and worked for the American Fur Company. He lived in a dug-out in a hillside downstream from the Two Dot ranch.

Early in the winter of 1879 after John W. Chapman had started the Two Dot, O'Hara left the country to visit Fort C. F. Smith on the Big Horn River. His visit was an extended one—O'Hara felt the Basin country was getting altogether too settled and civilized.

But he did come back for a final visit before moving on. According to Mrs. Manuelle Hoffman, who lived on a homestead on Blaine Creek:

"He appeared one day in the fall of 1914 at our ranch on Blaine Creek, a tributary of Pat O'Hara Creek. He was tall, thin and straight, soft spoken and shy. He was loath to speak much of his past, but reminisced a little. He recalled that he had lived in a cave on Pat O'Hara Creek about the George Heald ranch buildings. I had seen this cave in a cut bank and had wondered as to its occupant. Sagebrush six feet high had concealed the entrance. He had accumulated an assortment of pelts and was preparing to take them out one morning. As he moved the buffalo hide which served as a door for his cave, several arrows penetrated the hide. He remained in the cave until dark, then crept away, leaving the pelts behind. Another time he and two other trappers stopped to camp. He advised the other two men to leave their saddles cinched because he had noticed that the 'deer were running' (an indication that the Indians were on the move) but they failed to heed the advice. They were just ready to eat when the Indians appeared and they had to mount their horses hurriedly and flee. One man's saddle came loose and as he tried to mount he was killed. As Pat looked back, the second man's saddle turned because of the loose cinch, and he was killed. Pat alone escaped.

"One time he became very ill and it was evident that he was

unable to continue with his partner while they were escaping from the Indians, so he lay down to die alone. His partner shot a deer and left it beside Pat as the last kindness he could show him. The weather was hot and the meat soured. He ate some of the tainted meat, which had a purgative effect and this, he felt, saved his life.

"The second morning he prepared to leave our ranch on his trek to Oregon. His equipment consisted of a frying pan, a coffee pot, a blanket and a slicker. As we reluctantly said good-bye he rode slowly down the creek toward his final camp."

What happened to Pat after leaving the Hoffman's, or the location of his final resting place is unknown. In later years Mrs. Hoffman made a determined effort to find out what may have happened to Pat O'Hara. A search in the vital statistics records of Wyoming, Montana, Washington and Oregon failed to give evidence of his demise. It is certain, that despite some claims, he was never buried on the creek that bears his name.

At the site of the Bennett Battlefield, Blanche House read a paper prepared by May N. Ballinger. She related the encounter in the Clark's Fork area of General O. O. Howard and the Nez Perce and General Nelson Miles' later attack on a Bannock camp. One of the casualties of the fight was Captain Andrew S. Bennett, a Civil War veteran, for whom Bennett Creek, Bennett Buttes and a Montana military post were named.

Here another paper was read on a more contemporary episode, when Mr. Wasden related the Earl Durand story. In March, 1939, the young Powell man, after killing two law officers in Powell, hid out in the mountains in this area for several days. After slipping out of his hiding place he caught a ride to Denver where he had a cache of ammunition. He then returned to Powell, staged a hold-up in the bank, was severely wounded by gunfire and ended his life by a shot from his own gun.

The next two stops were at the Eagles Nest Stage Station and the site of the Arland and Corbett Trading Post.

EAGLES NEST STAGE STATION

In 1880 Thomas Lanchbury packed up his possessions and along with Emma, his wife, and their small daughter, Polly, left Dudley, England, to settle in the Americas. After living in Canada, Pennsylvania, Oklahoma Indian Territory and Colorado they finally came to Red Lodge, Montana, where Thomas worked for a while as a miner. In 1891 he was hired by the Bell stage and Freight line to build a way station near Eagles Nest Springs in Wyoming. When he arrived at Eagles Nest he found three log buildings, a combination cabin and barn on the hill above the springs and two cabins below the hill. A Mr. Moore who had been living here for approximately fifteen years said that they had been here when he arrived and he had no idea who had built them. Thomas and his eldest son John lined up the two cabins below the hill and built the main house between them. When the house was nearly completed he brought Emma and the other five children to the way station. In the following years the barn, corrals and various other outbuildings were built.

This was the midway point between Red Lodge and Meeteetse and the stages met at Eagles Nest at midnight. In the summer they stopped over only for meals and drove on to avoid the heat of Big Sand Coulee, but in the winter they stayed over for a nights lodging as well. Besides the stages there was a large number of freighters, travelers and cowboys who made Eagles Nest their stopover too, and from the tales of the old timers it was not only to give their horses a rest! Emma Lanchburys' skill in the culinary arts was widely known, and for a quarter you not only got a delicious meal but one served on a properly set table—and always on a white linen tablecloth.

Those were the days when there was no Powell or Cody and Meeteetse was the "Big Town" in the territory. Due to the subdividing of Wyoming counties, Eagles Nest was situated, at different times, in three different counties, Fremont, Big Horn and Park. Eagles Nest became the focal point for much of the activity in what was to become known as the Powell Valley. These were busy times—there were always stage passengers and freighters to feed and house for the night, and on Saturday nights the cowboys and settlers would often gather for a dance. In the fall and spring there were roundups and sheep shearings. Eagles Nest built the first dipping facilities in the area and sheep were brought from all over Wyoming and southern Montana to use them. Twice a year there was a wagon trip to Red Lodge for supplies.

After the buildings were completed some of the land was broken up for farming. Emma filed a desert claim on the adjoining land and part of it was farmed. A dam across Eagles Nest Creek provided water for irrigating and on Emma's claim a large water wheel in the Shoshone river furnished water for hay.

As if farming, caring for his own herds of cattle, sheep and horses, as well as catering to travelers and their livestock, plus raising a large family was not enough work for Thomas, he built and operated a saloon in the early 1900s. Thomas had been a brewmaster in England, and the specialty of the house was his fine homebrewed English ale.

With the coming of the railroads the freight and stage business ceased, but Eagles Nest was still headquarters for a lot of the cattle and sheep men in the area. When the valley was opened for homesteading the survey parties also headquartered there.

Emma Lanchbury died in July of 1915, and Thomas in March of 1916, following an auto accident. Following their deaths, Eagles Nest was taken over by their second son, Samuel Moore

Lanchbury. The oldest son, John, had already homesteaded on Cottonwood Creek out of Cody, and the youngest boy, Walter, had been killed in an accident hauling hay. Sam had filed a homestead on the land adjoining that of his parents, and, following their deaths combined the property into the Eagles Nest Ranch. Sam died in 1960 and John in 1967. Of the four Lanchbury girls all are now dead—Sarah, who died before the family came to Wyoming from Red Lodge; Lizzie, (Mrs. Joe Howell) died in Portland, Oregon, in 1966; the youngest, Mrs. Florence Hansen Sumpter, died at her farm home adjoining Eagles Nest; Polly, (Mrs. Frak MaCumber) the eldest, died in Seattle in 1976.

Eagles Nest is now owned by John Lanchbury, Jr., a grandson of Thomas and Emma.

THE OLD ARLAND AND CORBETT TRADING POST ON COTTONWOOD CREEK

To the west of us is a narrow valley at the base of Rattlesnake Mountain through which Trail Creek runs, so named because of the old Indian Trace which traversed its length. It was on this Creek, ten miles from Cody, that Victor Arland and John F. Corbett set up the first mercantile establishment in the Basin upon their arrival on September 10, 1880. Here they carried on trading with the Indians as they moved back and forth on the travel route. It was at this location on Trail Creek that the first potatoes and vegetables of record were raised in the Big Horn Basin, during the growing season of 1882.

During the summer of 1881 the two men put up a set of ranch buildings five miles below their trading post for a cattleman who did not come to take possession of them. This location later on became known as the Newton Ranch. A year later the buildings, which had cost them $200 in labor, were sold to a Frenchman, the Count Ivan du Doré for $600 and the ranch became known as the "Crown Ranch" because of the cattle brand used. This was a gathering place for a number of French noblemen who came west for big game hunting. According to legends handed down they indulged in wild and lavish parties.

Looking to expanding their trade to include the cattle interests, Arland and Corbett put up a set of buildings here on Cottonwood Creek and moved their business to the new location in the summer of 1883. The finished lumber and windows would have been hauled from Billings, for by that time the railroad was hauling supplies in from the east. The building you see in the valley is all that is left of the original set-up. One log building you see in the valley was taken down and moved west of Cody in 1938 by Hans Reiss and is now owned by Bob Edgar.

The early mail route came past the trading post, went down the creek a mile and a half or so when it ascended the bench to the north and circled around some deep gullies, going north of east to the wagon crossing on Stinking Water at what later was called Corbett.

At the site of the Heart Mountain Relocation Center, where several thousand West Coast Japanese Americans were relocated during World War II, Mary Blackburn read a paper on the history of the Center and outlined plans to place a historical marker at the site.

The trekkers returned to Cody shortly after noon and disbanded, after a most enjoyable and informative two days. This trek concluded the three-part one over the Rawlins to Red Lodge stage and freight road.

An account of the trek over the first segment of the road, from Rawlins to Lander, was published in the Fall, 1975, issue of *Annals of Wyoming*. The second segment of the route was traveled in the summer of 1976, but no account of it appeared in *Annals of Wyoming* because historical papers were not available for publication.

Book Reviews

Wyoming. A History. By T. A. Larson. (New York: W. W. Norton & Co.; Nashville: The American Association for State and Local History, 1977). Index. Illus. 198 pp. $8.95.

This book is part of a series on The States and the Nation published for the National Bicentennial of the American Revolution.

Wyoming. A History, is written in an easy, readable, narrative style with emphasis on the individuals who left their footprints in Wyoming and those who came and stayed to assist in building an empire.

Coming to Wyoming in 1936, the author, as Professor of History at the University of Wyoming, has accumulated a wealth of information about the state and territory. He is able to look back down the years without bias.

"Wyoming," he. says, "in 1976 is as it was in 1776, too high, dry and cold for the needs and tastes of most people."

Through research at the Huntington and other libraries the author has made a study of the diaries and journals kept by men and women along the trails which crossed central and southern Wyoming. Most of the travelers wrote that the area was isolated, lonely and "a place no one wanted." Few of them realized that there were fertile valleys and beautiful mountain parks in many parts of the territory.

The author documents his statements with references to the early diaries and journals, to government documents, to session laws, to early and late newspapers and to reports of state officials.

The names of the chapters speak for themselves: The Fur Territory, The Trails Territory, The Equality State, The Cowboy State, and the Energy State.

I enjoyed the book especially because I knew personally so many of the individuals mentioned: Mrs. Campbell, wife of Governor Campbell; Robert Morris, son of Esther Morris; Mrs. Theresa Jenkins, who told me how she trained her speaking voice; Governor Joseph M. Carey; Mrs. Nellie Tayloe Ross, and many, many others.

In the chapter on The Cowboy State mention is made of John B. Kendrick, a millionaire. He did become one, but he enjoyed telling of his life as a cowboy on the Texas Trail.

The chapter on the Equality State is outstanding and is undoubtedly the most complete report ever printed of woman suffrage as related to Wyoming.

Wyomingites who have been away from the state for some years should find the last chapter, The Equality State, quite informative.

The author discusses in detail the development of the oil and coal industries from the beginning to 1976, including data on the Missouri Basin Power Project near Wheatland.

Bob Peterson contributes "The Photographer's Essay," a group of well-selected, unique and artistic, modern photographs showing glimpses of various parts of Wyoming.

Suggestions for Further Reading, which brings the book to a close, contains the titles of many books and articles which portray the advantages still extant in "the land no one wanted," but which "now is coveted by hosts of outsiders."

Wyoming. A History is of handy size, just right to take along for vacation reading.

We agree with the author that: "Wyoming still has enough of the old magic to stir the blood of visitor and native alike."

Fort Collins, Colorado   AGNES WRIGHT SPRING

The Bonanza Kings: The Social Origins and Business Behavior of Western Mining Entrepreneurs, 1870-1900. By Richard H. Peterson. (Lincoln: University of Nebraska Press, 1977). Index. 191 pp. $9.95.

The discovery of precious metals in the American West during the late nineteenth century opened this vast region to permanent settlement, and in most cases the earliest leader of these new immigrants was the ubiquitous prospector and his faithful mule. This romanticised picture of the mining frontier is effectively displaced by Richard H. Peterson's *The Bonanza Kings*. Just as giant eastern industrialists dominated the fields of oil, steel, and railroads, these western moguls assumed absolute business leadership. During the period from 1870 to 1900 western mining matured into an increasingly technical and highly sophisticated industry. The causes for this economic success can be determined by examining how the mining magnates secured property, employed labor, enticed capital, and applied technology.

The social backgrounds and business activities of fifty of the leading mining entrepreneurs contributed to the over-all achievement of western economic development. Behavioral determinants which influenced the bonanza kings, such as family origin, father's occupation, birth place, and educational level, are illustrated, and give an understanding of social mobility on the frontier as contrasted with procedures in the East. These men moved westward for a variety of reasons, not only to avoid boredom, crowding, and economic distress, but also to enjoy adventure, freedom, and unspoiled nature. Nevertheless, the most influential motive for migration was the lure of great and instant wealth.

However, success required an extensive knowledge of mining technology. Many of the fifty magnates served long apprenticeships in the various operations of mining. Practical, on-the-job experience was supplemented with independent study and formal scientific education. Additional experience as merchants and bankers offered new avenues for the application of technology and capital. Mining was big business—complex, complicated, and frequently callous.

The best strategy for success was the acquisition of mining properties. The inherent instability of the industry demonstrated the perpetual risks and encouraged consolidation. During times of economic depression, the bonanza kings realized their opportunities to purchase depreciated property. Thus they were able to mine on a larger scale and thereby achieve lower production cost and increased efficiency and profit. Moreover, depressed times spurred buying and consolidation and prosperity provided periods for profit maximizing and selling. Thus the shrewd businessman would buy when property taxes were low and sell when they were high.

An additional element which influenced success was the manner in which organized labor was confronted. A number of mine owners adopted hard-line attitudes toward the emerging unions, and used every weapon available to them, such as injunctions, private armies, lockouts, and blacklists, to resist union demands. A common response to this uncompromising position was labor unrest and violence. However, this was not uniformly common to all mining areas. Many mining moguls realized that uninterrupted production was preferable to explosive confrontations with union members. These leaders attempted to create a consensus with their workers, and opened various avenues to redress grievances.

The Bonanza Kings is an excellent introduction to the personalities of the men who dominated the mining frontier of the trans-Mississippi West. Although it included the attitudes and behavior of fifty individuals, it was not a tedious listing of their chronological actions and character traits, but rather a view of specific and collective response to various challenges and developments. An extensive section of notes and bibliography is given for additional study and investigation. Peterson illustrates a high degree of objectivity as he vividly demonstrates how these opportunistic and ambitious mining magnates were able to produce great success and huge wealth.

Oklahoma State University   W. EDWIN DERRICK

Wyoming. A Guide to Historic Sites. Wyoming Recreation Commission. (Basin: Big Horn Book Company, 1976). Illus. 327 pp. $10.95 hardback. $8.95 softback.

While most history books will spend their time on library bookshelves, *Wyoming. A Guide to Historic Sites* should more properly find its place on the front seat of an automobile. This is a book that begs to be used daily by the residents and visitors who travel this state. It is a "guide" in the truest sense.

In three hundred and three pages, the Guide details two hundred and thirty-two Wyoming historic and archeological places. The concise and well-written copy answers all the questions relating to each—who, what, where, why, when and how. In addition, the documentation of many of the sites is augmented by quotations from diaries, journals and reports written on location at the time of its major historical significance. This excellent technique results in a book that goes beyond the reporting of pertinent historical data, giving the user a personal contact and human involvement with each place.

Some may argue with the sites selected but such arguments will find little support. The editors have done a thoughtful job of striking both a geographical and historical balance throughout Wyoming and have included sites that touch on all phases of the state's development. The sites are organized in chapters by county and each county division page includes a key map. The text for each site opens with a detailed description of its location and access. In the case of sites that are remote or not generally accessible to the public, the user is advised to "inquire locally for directions and road conditions."

The text for most historic sites is supported by excellent photography. Here, the editors have selected both modern and historic photographs to help tell the story. Each picture is identified by a cutline that includes the date, or approximate date, it was taken and each is further identified as to photographer or source in a list of illustrations at the back of the book. In some cases, art work and sketches are used to illustrate sites and events of which no photographs exist.

Museums are not included in the text of the book, but a complete listing of all Wyoming museums, by county, is printed in the back. An index identifies each historic site by page number.

The Guide is printed in both a soft cover and a hard cover edition in a convenient 5 3/4" x 8 3/4" size. The paper stock chosen as cover material on the soft version appears to be most durable. The binding is also high quality, giving this edition of the Guide the potential for a long life of hard use (even on the front seat of an automobile). The printing throughout is sharp, clean and most readable. About the only criticism of the printing is that many of the illustrations have lost the good black and white contrast of the original prints and appear somewhat dull and grey.

The original idea for the Guide was carried to the Wyoming Consulting Committee on Nominations to the National Register of Historic Places by J. Reuel Armstrong of Rawlins as a project for the Bicentennial. The project was undertaken by the Historical Division of the Wyoming Recreation Commission with the assistance of a grant-in-aid from the Department of the Interior, National Park Service under the provisions of the National Historic Preservation Act of 1966. The bulk of the work in editing and compiling the Guide was accomplished by Mark Junge of the Recreation Commission staff who worked with the aid of numerous Wyoming historians all listed by name in the Guide's introduction. The Guide is introduced by the late Paul H. Westedt, Director of the Wyoming Recreation Commission, and is dedicated to Ned Frost, ". . . citizen, historian and the architect of Wyoming's Historic preservation program."

Printing difficulties delayed the publication of the Guide beyond the Bicentennial year, but the final result more than makes up for the delay. Simply put, *Wyoming. A Guide to Historic Sites* was well worth the wait. Its careful research, content, style, presentation and subject make it a valued addition to any collection of historic books and to the permanent traveling kit of any resident and visitor with even a casual interest in Wyoming's past.

Wyoming Travel Commission   RANDALL A. WAGNER

Cow Country Legacies. By Agnes Wright Spring. (Kansas City: The Lowell Press, 1976). Illus. 123 pp. $8.95.

Agnes Wright Spring needs no introduction to anyone familiar with Wyoming history. Her previous books have set a standard of historical accuracy, presented in a lively style, that are models for all writers on the west. Her positions as Wyoming state librarian and as state historian of both Wyoming and Colorado have given her an unequaled intimacy with the region about which she writes.

Mrs. Spring's latest book is a collection of vignettes of people and places in and around Wyoming. Some of these are only a few lines long; others extend several pages. Each is drawn from her extensive, and sometimes personal, knowledge of her subject.

The overall theme of *Cow Country Legacies* is the culture of frontier Wyoming. Many of the early settlers came from distinguished families in the east, and some from titled families in England or Scotland. These were not content to abandon the social and cultural fineries to which they were accustomed. As a result a group of wealthy young cattlemen, several of whom were graduates of prestigious eastern universities, founded the Cheyenne Club in 1880. The Cheyenne Club offered to its select members a taste of fine living that would have been difficult to match anywhere. To increase cultural opportunities for the public at large an Opera House had been completed in Cheyenne by 1882. Visitors to the "Magic City of the Plains" could also view a number of Cheyenne homes that boasted of elaborate furnishings, fine silver services, and well-stocked libraries. Ornate iron fences frequently surrounded these homes, and trees, bushes, flowers, and carefully kept lawns soon replaced the prairie grasses.

Throughout this book we catch intimate glimpses of many of the people who were responsible for this cultural transplant in the west. We read of some of the first Wyoming and Montana cattlemen—Granville Stuart, E. W. Whitcomb, John W. Prowers, Hiram (Hi) B. Kelly, John Hunton—and their Indian wives. We encounter Edward Creighton, who built the first transcontinental telegraph line, and his brother John, who amassed a fortune in the cattle he ran in eastern Wyoming and western Nebraska. Their fortunes went toward endowing the university in Omaha which bears their name, and which celebrates its centennial in 1978.

In addition there are two sections of pictures of early settlers, churches, schools, homes, and a reproduction of the famous Paul Potter painting of a bull. This painting originally hung in the Cheyenne Club. One evening John Coble shot several holes into it because, Coble said, "the painting is a travesty on purebred stock." The painting—along with the bullet holes—is now among the holdings of the Wyoming State Museum.

The book is a tribute to the printer's art. The layout is neat and uncrowded. The pages are printed in large clear type with the chapter title at the top of each right hand page and each new section clearly set off by an appropriate topic heading.

It is impossible to present a full summary of this book in the brief space of a review or to do it full justice. This is a book to be sampled and savored. The reader is presented a series of snapshots of the cultural life of the new territory and state. When finished, he might wish for more, but he will not be disappointed with what he has.

Southwest Missouri State University   ROBERT J. WHITAKER

Flaming Gorge Country. The Story of Daggett County, Utah. By
Dick and Vivian Dunham. (Denver: Eastwood Printing and
Publishing Company, 1977.) Index. Illus. 384 pp. $7.00.

Brown's Park, in the minds of many is almost mythical—steeped
in both mythology and legend of the "old West." For many,
many persons Brown's Park is something out of a story book, but
Brown's Park and Daggett County, Utah, which encompasses part
of the Park, are real country that has seen the history of the West
unfold.

The unfolding is well told in Dick Dunham's *Flaming Gorge
Country,* written as a history of Daggett County. However, the
unfolding also includes much about Sweetwater and Uinta Counties in Wyoming, and Routt County, Colorado, because the history
of eastern Utah, southwestern Wyoming and a bit of northwestern
Colorado that lap into the Park all intertwine.

Brown's Park and Henry's Fork Valley to the westward have
supplied writers many stories, very fanciful at times, and published
mostly in western adventure pulps. A few novels have been written with the area as background.

Dunham has none of the imaginary Brown's Park. Reaching
back to the times when Indians and fur traders wintered in the
Park and along the Henry's Fork river following the first Rendezvous in 1825, Dunham has drawn real people and documented
stories through his pages in a book that brings the history of
Daggett County down to today's Flaming Gorge and Dam recreation area.

Many of the people in his work he has known personally, so
that he has been able to draw well upon the memories of old
timers who also knew those who had gone on before. Too, he
has well researched records and old printed accounts and diaries.

Here, one learns to understand why Brown's Park has remained
in the minds of many persons as the storied haven of the outlaw
as well as of the fur traders and ranchers of more than a century
ago—to many persons it remains the picture of the old wild and
wooly west.

Queen Ann Bassett and her family, the Davenports, Sparks,
Crouses, Taylors, Hoy brothers and Warrens, are among the more
solid folks over in the fabled Hole, or Park—and then, the less
favorably known Tom Horn, Lant, Tracy, Pete Johnson, Bennett,
Cassidy and his Wild Bunch, plus members of other gangs hiding
out—the in between figures such as Isom Dart and Matt Rash all
become persons as Dunham puts them on display.

Here the reader meets the squawman and other earliest settlers
of the Daggett-Henry's Fork area—and those old timers who had
moved eastward from Fort Bridger into the Henry's Valley, to
Lucerne Valley and down along the Green.

Shade Large, the Finches, the Sons, John and Jim Baker, Phil Mass, the Widdops, the Stolls, the Lambs, the easterner Keith Smith who led business, ranching and education for decades, the Larsons and dozens upon dozens of others who came into the area during the 150 years after Bridger, who had first seen the Valley during the 1825 Rendezvous and began running livestock there in the 1840s—these are a few of the scores of persons Dunham brings to the reader today.

Flaming Gorge Country is not the usual book of dates and places and events. It is the history of an area told in terms of people and their activities, good or bad, the story of a region little known, told in a manner most will enjoy.

Dick (Richard) Dunham, with pianist wife Vivian and their small daughter, in the 1940s left a professorship at Detroit (Wayne University) and came west for adventure and a new home. After an unguided pack trip the length of the Wind River, with the intended destination of Taos, circumstances saw the trio spend a winter in a log cabin in the Uinta Mountains, followed by an abortive attempt at raising hay in a lonely mountain valley.

At the time of the Mormon Centennial in 1947 he wrote, with his wife, *Our Strip of Land,* a commemorative history of the area, at the request of the L.D.S. Ward at Manila, Utah.

Soon afterwards, he found himself at the University of Wyoming, heading up a new speech department. He has since retired from this post. *Flaming Gorge Country* began as a revision of *Our Strip of Land,* developed into a definitive story of the lives and ways of living of the area's Indians, trappers, explorers, ranchers and outlaws over a period of 150 years. In his opening pages he delves into the geologic past but soon moved forward into the period of modern man.

Green River, Wyoming   ADRIAN REYNOLDS

Land of Tall Skies. "A Pageant of the Colorado High Plains." By Dabney Otis Collins. (Colorado Springs: Century One Press, 1977.) Index. Map. 159 pp. $7.00 hardback. $5.00 softback.

Dabney Otis Collins came west for his health many years ago and fell in love with the High Plains area of Colorado, that area stretching eastward from the Rocky Mountains to the borders of Nebraska, Kansas, and Oklahoma, a "comparatively level, treeless, semiarid region [which] forms almost half of the area of the state." Collins believes that the spectacular mountains and mountain parks have precluded writings about the plains and that they represent only one-half of the story of Colorado. This booklet is the result of his love affair with the region and his attempt to set the record straight through this analysis and presentation.

After an introduction by Marshall Sprague, Collins begins at the beginning and details the formation of the High Plains through millennia of geologic time. He views the development of the area as high drama, dividing the story into Prologue, nine Acts, and a Curtain Call broken by an Intermission. Each Act is an interpretation in broad perspective of the High Plains in each major period of their history.

From the formation of the current earth's crust of the High Plains, Collins traces the migrations of people to the area from Siberia and the flowering of native grasses able to sustain millions of animals. He tells how the descendants of those early people acquired the horse from the Spaniards to the south and became an efficient light cavalry and able to exploit the tremendous number of buffalos. Each interpretative essay contains a great deal of insight into how each period fits into the broader context.

The author is at his best describing the land, the native grasses and routes of travel for one can certainly carp at his interpretation of "Picuries Pueblos" (p. 27), what he says was America's policy of extermination of Indians (p. 80), the "Wild Indians of the Plains" (p. 29), and their use of poisoned arrows (p. 45). Other mistakes and carelessness mar somewhat an otherwise delightful and readable booklet. For example, it was Joseph who had a coat of many colors, not Jacob (pp. 23 and 146).

One can feel the harshness of life on the High Plains—the sod houses, the dust storms and, the sadness and frustration of the Great Depression for the inhabitants. But one can also feel a faster heartbeat reading about the fur trappers, the military posts, the shameful Sand Creek Massacre, the sea of buffalo, and the replanting of native grasses after breaking the sod to partake of some of the money brought about by war.

On balance, the author accomplishes what he sets out to do because one does see emerge and unfold the pageant of the Colorado High Plains. It is a useful synthesis. Professional and buff alike will find it a welcome addition to the bookshelf and a book to look to when concerned about the grass, the buffalo, the geology, or travel routes across the High Plains of Colorado.

Fort Lewis College   ROBERT W. DELANEY

I Married Wyatt Earp. The Recollections of Josephine Sarah Marcus Earp. Ed., Glenn G. Boyer. (Tucson: The University of Arizona Press, 1976.) Index. Illus. 277 pp. $10.50 hardback. $4.95 softback.

Josephine Sarah Marcus Earp was the third and last wife of Wyatt Earp, frontier marshal, gunfighter, folk hero, outlaw, lawman, boomer, as one chooses to identify him. Josephine's marriage might not have been by legal ceremony, but she and Earp lived together from the time their relationship began about 1881 in Tombstone, Arizona Territory, until he died in California in 1929.

Josie Earp's purpose in writing was "if not an attempt to vindicate, at least an attempt to explain" her husband. She hopes, she writes, to give a "firsthand going-over" to the "malarky" about Tombstone and to finish the Earp story with an account of his later and less controversial years.

As a young girl, Josie toured the West with a theatrical company, became enamored of Earp, who was married, and was living with him at the time of the misnamed Gunfight at the OK Corral. Josie exonerates Wyatt and characterizes this fight as part of a struggle over economic and political power. She does believe that he participated in a vendetta resulting in the killing of several gunfighters probably responsible for his brother's murder. But, according to Josie, after these frays, she and Wyatt left Arizona for a peaceful, normal life.

And therein lies the disappointment. She does metamorphose Earp into a different personality from the cool, steely-eyed, triggerhappy, gunman of film and faction. He becomes instead an ordinary, not very interesting opportunist, drifting through the West and Alaska, searching for a lucky mining strike while earning some money here and there as gambler, saloon keeper, and race horse owner. Although the western gunfighter-marshal-outlaw types are not true subjects for myths, they have been the most interesting myth-like subjects that we have. Josie removes Earp from this category and makes him an average man who loves his wife and hopes to get rich some day. Since Josie obviously has not written an accurate, objective account of Earp, better almost that she had enhanced the lies.

The narrative is simple, almost childlike. This prose has a certain appeal in its naiveté. In fact, the prose might be the most appealing thing about the book, had not the editor thrown a shadow of doubt on its authenticity. He says that in combining two manuscripts written by Josie Earp which were "presented in widely varying styles," he arrived at a "vocabulary and syntax that closely approximated the speech of the living Earps. Thus while Wyatt is stripped of his villainy, Josie is deprived of her naturalness and spontaneity.

Readers never agree on just the right amount of footnotes; I suggest that this book is over noted for the general reader, but a source of minutia for the scholar of western outlawry. The illustrations are superb. Unfortunately there is only one picture of Josie. It portrays her as a young woman, head lifted dramatically, with long flowing black hair. She would have been a great gunfighter's moll.

Wyoming Council for the Humanities   BETSY PETERS

Keep the Last Bullet for Yourself. The True Story of Custer's Last Stand. By Thomas B. Marquis. (New York: Two Continents Publishing Group, 1976). Index. Illus. 203 pp. $8.95.

To be a Custer buff is almost to be a Thomas Marquis buff. His list of publications, all based on direct, personal interviews. have added significantly to our library of source materials on the Plains Indian and especially toward an explanation of the Custer controversy. His *Wooden Leg, A Warrior Who Fought Custer,* published in 1931, has become a minor classic portraying the Indian attitude and perspective in the Custer fight. *Keep The Last Bullet For Yourself* was to have been his final assessment of the battle. The manuscript was ready for publication in 1934 (he died in 1935), but it was rejected then, undoubtedly because the publishers feared a repugnance toward the author's thesis. It has only now been published.

Quite simply, Marquis' thesis is that the troops under Custer committed mass suicide, or, in his rather quaint phrasing, "general self-extinction." As the surviving Indians he interviewed eloquently said, the "Everywhere Spirit" intervened and the soldiers "threw themselves away."

Marquis gives a rather pedestrian analysis of Custer's own character. He is, in fact, an apologist for Custer, and it is against this backdrop of Custer apology that the "pitiable fiasco," as Marquis sees it, is such a sad story.

Marquis makes the argument, which military historian S. L. A. Marshall was to reaffirm much later, that Custer's troops were unprepared to fight and undeserving of the reputation of premier Indian fighters. At least 30 per cent of his men were raw recruits and 75 per cent of the men including veterans had very little actual experience fighting Indians.

Concentrating on the soldiers' mental state, Marquis attempts to recapture the psychology of the battle scene with the young, untried, frightened soldiers who popularly had been led to expect "fiendish" savages, and to anticipate "excruciating tortures" if they were captured. They were fully conscious of the western slogan, "when fighting Indians, keep the last bullet for yourself." His rather stolid style aside, we come to feel and hear wounded men aching for water amid a din of war cries, death songs, and stampeding horses. And as Marquis says, "on a critical day and at a critical moment, they became victims of this indoctrination." Marquis' close observation and extensive primary research makes the book's conclusion that the battle turned on a temporary wave of insanity altogether plausible.

While Marquis' style is neither majestic nor poetic it has the ring of truth. The results of his research among the Indians reveals moments, values, and characteristics that neither culture should allow itself to forget.

Northwest Wyoming Community College   ROY JORDAN

Fort Stanwix. History, Historic Furnishing and Historic Structure Reports. By John F. Luzader, Louis Torres and Orville W. Carroll. (Washington, D.C.: Office of Park Historic Preservation National Park Service, 1976). Illus. 200 pp. $3.50.

Mountain Home. The Walker Family Farmstead. Great Smoky Mountains National Park. By Robert R. Madden and T. Russell Jones. Washington, D.C., U. S. Department of the Interior, National Park Service, 1977.) Illus. 55 pp.

These titles are recent additions to the Park Service's growing list of publications dealing with the cultural history, archeology and preservation of historic sites. The reconstruction of Fort Stanwix, at Rome, New York, was one of the Park Service's major Bicentennial projects. The Walker family homesite, located in the Great Smoky Mountains National Park, is one of few remaining original mid-19th century farmsteads in the Park. The preservation of the farm's structures is aimed at generating a finer appreciation for the quality of life once experienced within the natural resources of the Park.

Fort Stanwix is divided into three parts: "Construction and Military History," by John F. Luzader, Park Service historian; "Historic Furnishings Study," by Louis Torres; "Historic Structure Report" by Park Service architect Orville W. Carroll. Luzader's essay is a history of the building of the fort, in all of its stages— fur trading center in the Mohawk Valley, military outpost in the wars with the French and Indian tribes, and Continental Army post during the Revolutionary War. Because of its location, the so-called Oneida Carrying Place, Fort Stanwix played a pivotal role in all of these historical developments. In 1757 the British built the fort to improve their access to the fur territories and to try to limit French activity in the same areas. Beyond its participation in the Seven Years War and other Indian battles, the fort's place in our history centers upon its experience in the Revolutionary War. In August, 1777, it withstood a siege by the British for twenty-two days, which helped to defeat the forces of Barry St. Leger and contributed to the defeat of General Burgoyne.

Louis Torres' "furnishings" study lists and describes all of the items that were used to outfit the activities and spaces of the fort. Since there was little archeological evidence to substantiate the actual presence of many things, Torres researched the use of similar items in the region and in military life. His treatment includes provisions, arms and accoutrements, clothing, Indian supplies (Stanwix was always a trading center), livestock, hardware, utensils, furniture and accessories, and objects in the furnished areas (all the barracks and special use locations).

The final section, "Historic Structure Report," describes in full detail the structural elements in every unit of the fort. Carroll's report is really a handbook for the reconstruction of the fort, and it includes a thorough and unusual military glossary. As a guidebook this article prescribes the materials, forms, and techniques the restoration team will need to reconstruct the fort authentically.

Fort Stanwix is noteworthy because of its careful research and it will provide much data for studies in the cultural history of the region and the period. The text is also a handbook on the process of undertaking the reconstruction of a military site. If the book has any shortcomings they are in its style, which often reads like an archeology field report, and in its lack of an analysis of the stylistic significance of the fort's architecture. Are such arrangements of members, with their strict adherence to Renaissance geometry, ordinary? What is the cultural derivation of the plan? Were there many other forts like this one in the original colonies? A short discussion of these considerations would have enlarged the scope of the reports.

Mountain Home is a less ambitious volume and concentrates on narrating the development and daily activities of the Walker family farm. The Walkers were resilient Tennessee mountain people who established a truly self-sufficient farm through a lifetime of hard work, adaptation and accommodation. John and Margaret Walker moved to the farmstead's current location in the late 1860s or early 1870s. They raised eleven children, all of whom participated in the labor intensive style of family life. John Walker was a skilled craftsman, and it was said of him that he could make practically anything from wood, leather or metal. He was first a successful farmer, but he was also a competent blacksmith, carpenter, grist miller, herder and builder. Walker laid down life patterns his surviving children would emulate long after his death, and the real story of *Mountain Home* is the story of the seven daughters' success at continuing their parent's lifestyle. Only one daughter married; the rest remained attached to the rigors of mountain life. Not until their very late years did the Walker women come to trade for manufactured goods, and from all accounts rarely did they avail themselves of available services.

The last section of the book deals with the architecture of the farm. Russell Jones describes the character of the structures and the nature of the building methods. While these are helpful, his report would benefit from an assessment of Smoky Mountain vernacular building and the place of the Walker buildings in the local vernacular tradition. Of special interest to the reviewer is the spatial layout of the farm. The ultimate shape that the living, working, and growing areas take is an impressive bit of planning and orientation to site. Additional information and analysis of such land use could prove valuable to the student of American environmental design.

Oklahoma State University   HERBERT GOTTFRIED

Hour of Trial: The Conservation Conflict in Colorado and the West, 1891-1907. By G. Michael McCarthy. (Norman: University of Oklahoma Press, 1977). Index. Illus. 327 pp. $12.50.

During the last half of the nineteenth century the prevailing American sentiment toward the environment reflected an unsophisticated national belief that land existed to be exploited. These attitudes carried into the twentieth century. G. Michael McCarthy examines these attitudes and analyzes the clash between those for and against conservation of Colorado's natural resources between 1891 and 1907. Using numerous primary sources, McCarthy makes Colorado a case study to illustrate the conservation conflict which was developing on a national scale. Examining both sides of the argument, he concludes that the conservationists and anti-conservationists were both right and wrong in their battle for the land.

McCarthy traces the history of the American conservation movement which had its roots in the mid-1870s. The ultimate goal of the movement was to establish a federal land policy, and this was accomplished on March 3, 1891, when President Benjamin Harrison signed the General Revision Act which gave the chief executive power to remove timber land from the public domain. When the first Colorado timber reserve was created in

October of 1891, the conservation conflict ignited. Opposition to the reserves and consequent legislation dealing with grazing permits, leasing, and coal land withdrawals quickly arose from such diverse factions as timber cutters, cattlemen, and farmers who feared a loss of personal investments.

Between 1891 and 1907 presidents Benjamin Harrison, Grover Cleveland, William McKinley, and Theodore Roosevelt carried the governmental banner for conservation, as they set aside millions of acres of public lands for federal reserves. Gifford Pinchot, architect of Roosevelt's conservation policy, joined this fight for the preservation of the nation's resources. However, the opposition to governmental policy had such able leaders as Colorado's Senator Henry M. Teller who advocated the maximum use of public lands. Moreover, with the anti-conservationists holding political power in Colorado, exploitation on reserves went unheeded. This activity in Colorado typified the general western experience, and it reflected the western fear that easterners would confiscate their natural resources for esthetic purposes. In 1907 the "watershed" of the conservation conflict occurred at the Denver Public Lands Convention. This meeting illustrated the ineffectiveness of the anti-conservationists and marked the decline of their power in Colorado and the West.

McCarthy points out that today Colorado faces such similar ecological problems as the development of oil shale, strip mining, and recreational areas. He claims that this is a classic case of history repeating itself but with an ironic reverse. At the turn of the century the government supported conservation, but federal officials now advocate development of Colorado's natural resources for national use.

Although admitting some environmentalist bias, McCarthy presents a balanced book on the conservation struggle in Colorado. This readable work deftly shows how Colorado's experience was a lucid example of the ongoing national debate over conservation in the West. McCarthy has done a commendable job with this study, and it will be of interest to students of the period, region, and American conservation movement. Perhaps this book, as did the pioneer and the preserver, will leave a legacy to Colorado and the West.

Oklahoma State University   TIMOTHY A. ZWINK

Contributors

GORDON O. HENDRICKSON is a research associate at the Immigration History Research Center at the University of Minnesota. He holds degrees from Wisconsin State University-River Falls, Colorado State University and a Ph.D from the University of Wyoming. He has served as consultant historian at the Wyoming State Archives and Historical Department and was project director of the research project, "Wyoming's European Heritage" a joint undertaking of the University of Wyoming's Department of History and College of Education and the Historical Research and Publications Division of the Wyoming State Archives and Historical Department.

THOMAS R. NINNEMAN is associate professor of history and chairman of the Social Science Department at the University of Wisconsin-Stout, Menomonie. He earned the doctorate at the University of Wyoming where he studied under T. A. Larson.

GREGORY J. SCHEURMAN is associated with the University of Wyoming as Field Coordinator for the Humanities Teaching Project, an in-service training program for teachers. He received his B.A. degree in Social Studies and his M.A. in history from the University of Wyoming. He is a member of the Wyoming Education Association.

DOUGLAS C. McCHRISTIAN is supervisory historian at Fort Laramie National Historic Site. He previously served with the National Park Service as seasonal historian at Fort Larned National Historic Site and as a park technician at Fort Larned. He is a graduate of Fort Hays State University with a degree in history.

Index

WYOMING STATE ARCHIVES AND HISTORICAL DEPARTMENT

The Wyoming State Archives and Historical Department has as its function the collection and preservation of the record of the people of Wyoming. It maintains the state's historical library and research center, the Wyoming State Museum and branch museums, the Wyoming State Art Gallery and the State archives.

The aid of the citizens of Wyoming is solicited in the carrying out of its function. The Department is anxious to secure and preserve records and materials now in private hands where they cannot be long preserved. Such records and materials include:

Biographical materials of pioneers: diaries, letters, account books, autobiographical accounts.

Business records of industries of the state: livestock, mining, agriculture, railroads, manufacturers, merchants, small business establishments and of professional men such as bankers, lawyers, physicians, dentists, ministers and educators.

Private records of individual citizens, such as correspondence, manuscript materials and scrapbooks.

Records of organizations active in the religious, educational, social, economic and political life of the state, including their publications such as yearbooks and reports.

Manuscript and printed articles on towns, counties and any significant topic dealing with the history of the state.

Early newspapers, maps, pictures, pamphlets, and books on western subjects.

Current publications by individuals or organizations throughout the state.

Museum materials with historic significance: early equipment, Indian artifacts, relics dealing with the activities of persons in Wyoming and with special events in the state's history.

Original art works of a western flavor including, but not limited to, etchings, paintings in all media, sculpture and other art forms.

CPSIA information can be obtained
at www.ICGtesting.com
Printed in the USA
BVHW04*1139210818
525177BV00005B/167/P